FUNDAMENTALS OF ENGINEERING
SUPPLIED-REFERENCE HANDBOOK
SIXTH EDITION

Published by the

National Council of Examiners for Engineering and Surveying®

280 Seneca Creek Road, Clemson, SC 29631   800-250-3196   www.ncees.org

ISBN 1-932613-00-5

Printed in the United States of America
November 2003

FOREWORD

During its August 1991 Annual Business Meeting, the National Council of Examiners for Engineering and Surveying (NCEES) voted to make the Fundamentals of Engineering (FE) examination an NCEES supplied-reference examination. Then during its August 1994 Annual Business Meeting, the NCEES voted to make the FE examination a discipline-specific examination. As a result of the 1994 vote, the FE examination was developed to test the lower-division subjects of a typical bachelor engineering degree program during the morning portion of the examination, and to test the upper-division subjects of a typical bachelor engineering degree program during the afternoon. The lower-division subjects refer to the first 90 semester credit hours (five semesters at 18 credit hours per semester) of engineering coursework. The upper-division subjects refer to the remainder of the engineering coursework.

Since engineers rely heavily on reference materials, the *FE Supplied-Reference Handbook* will be made available prior to the examination. The examinee may use this handbook while preparing for the examination. The handbook contains only reference formulas and tables; no example questions are included. Many commercially available books contain worked examples and sample questions. An examinee can also perform a self-test using one of the NCEES *FE Sample Questions and Solutions* books, CD-ROMs, or an Internet diagnostic (all partial examinations), which may be purchased by calling (800) 250-3196 or visiting our Web site at www.ncees.org.

The examinee is not allowed to bring reference material into the examination room. Another copy of the *FE Supplied-Reference Handbook* will be made available to each examinee in the room. When the examinee departs the examination room, the *FE Supplied-Reference Handbook* supplied in the room must be returned to the examination proctors.

The *FE Supplied-Reference Handbook* has been prepared to support the FE examination process. The *FE Supplied-Reference Handbook* is not designed to assist in all parts of the FE examination. For example, some of the basic theories, conversions, formulas, and definitions that examinees are expected to know have not been included. The *FE Supplied-Reference Handbook* may not include some special material required for the solution of a particular question. In such a situation, the required special information will be included in the question statement.

DISCLAIMER: *The NCEES in no event shall be liable for not providing reference material to support all the questions in the FE examination. In the interest of constant improvement, the NCEES reserves the right to revise and update the* FE Supplied-Reference Handbook *as it deems appropriate without informing interested parties. Each NCEES FE examination will be administered using the latest version of the* FE Supplied-Reference Handbook.

PLEASE DO NOT WRITE IN THIS HANDBOOK
so that it may be reused at the examination site.

CONTENTS

UNITS

This handbook uses the metric system of units. Ultimately, the FE examination will be entirely metric. However, currently some of the problems use both metric and U.S. Customary System (USCS). In the USCS system of units, both force and mass are called pounds. Therefore, one must distinguish the pound-force (lbf) from the pound-mass (lbm).

The pound-force is that force which accelerates one pound-mass at 32.174 ft/s². Thus, 1 lbf = 32.174 lbm-ft/s². The expression 32.174 lbm-ft/(lbf-s²) is designated as g_c and is used to resolve expressions involving both mass and force expressed as pounds. For instance, in writing Newton's second law, the equation would be written as $F = ma/g_c$, where F is in lbf, m in lbm, and a is in ft/s².

Similar expressions exist for other quantities. Kinetic Energy: $KE = mv^2/2g_c$, with KE in (ft-lbf); Potential Energy: $PE = mgh/g_c$, with PE in (ft-lbf); Fluid Pressure: $p = \rho gh/g_c$, with p in (lbf/ft²); Specific Weight: $SW = \rho g/g_c$, in (lbf/ft³); Shear Stress: $\tau = (\mu/g_c)(dv/dy)$, with shear stress in (lbf/ft²). In all these examples, g_c should be regarded as a unit conversion factor. It is frequently not written explicitly in engineering equations. However, its use is required to produce a consistent set of units.

Note that the conversion factor g_c [lbm-ft/(lbf-s²)] should not be confused with the local acceleration of gravity g, which has different units (m/s²) and may be either its standard value (9.807 m/s²) or some other local value.

If the problem is presented in USCS units, it may be necessary to use the constant g_c in the equation to have a consistent set of units.

METRIC PREFIXES		
Multiple	Prefix	Symbol
10^{-18}	atto	a
10^{-15}	femto	f
10^{-12}	pico	p
10^{-9}	nano	n
10^{-6}	**micro**	**μ**
10^{-3}	milli	m
10^{-2}	centi	c
10^{-1}	deci	d
10^{1}	deka	da
10^{2}	**hecto**	**h**
10^{3}	kilo	k
10^{6}	mega	M
10^{9}	giga	G
10^{12}	tera	T
10^{15}	**peta**	**P**
10^{18}	exa	E

COMMONLY USED EQUIVALENTS

1 gallon of water weighs	8.34 lbf
1 cubic foot of water weighs	62.4 lbf
1 cubic inch of mercury weighs	0.491 lbf
The mass of one cubic meter of water is 1,000 kilograms	

TEMPERATURE CONVERSIONS

$^\circ$F = 1.8 ($^\circ$C) + 32

$^\circ$C = ($^\circ$F − 32)/1.8

$^\circ$R = $^\circ$F + 459.69

K = $^\circ$C + 273.15

FUNDAMENTAL CONSTANTS

Quantity		Symbol	Value	Units
electron charge		e	1.6022×10^{-19}	C (coulombs)
Faraday constant		$\mathcal{F}$	96,485	coulombs/(mol)
gas constant	metric	$\bar{R}$	8,314	J/(kmol·K)
gas constant	metric	$\bar{R}$	8.314	kPa·m³/(kmol·K)
gas constant	USCS	$\bar{R}$	1,545	ft-lbf/(lb mole-$^\circ$R)
		$\bar{R}$	0.08206	L-atm/mole-K
gravitation - newtonian constant		G	6.673×10^{-11}	m³/(kg·s²)
gravitation - newtonian constant		G	6.673×10^{-11}	N·m²/kg²
gravity acceleration (standard)	metric	g	9.807	m/s²
gravity acceleration (standard)	USCS	g	32.174	ft/s²
molar volume (ideal gas), $T = 273.15$K, $p = 101.3$ kPa		V_m	22,414	L/kmol
speed of light in vacuum		c	299,792,000	m/s

CONVERSION FACTORS

Multiply	By	To Obtain	Multiply	By	To Obtain
acre	43,560	square feet (ft²)	joule (J)	9.478×10^{-4}	Btu
ampere-hr (A-hr)	3,600	coulomb (C)	J	0.7376	ft-lbf
ångström (Å)	1×10^{-10}	meter (m)	J	1	newton·m (N·m)
atmosphere (atm)	76.0	cm, mercury (Hg)	J/s	1	watt (W)
atm, std	29.92	in, mercury (Hg)			
atm, std	14.70	lbf/in² abs (psia)	kilogram (kg)	2.205	pound (lbm)
atm, std	33.90	ft, water	kgf	9.8066	newton (N)
atm, std	1.013×10^{5}	pascal (Pa)	kilometer (km)	3,281	feet (ft)
			km/hr	0.621	mph
bar	1×10^{5}	Pa	kilopascal (kPa)	0.145	lbf/in² (psi)
barrels–oil	42	gallons–oil	kilowatt (kW)	1.341	horsepower (hp)
Btu	1,055	joule (J)	kW	3,413	Btu/hr
Btu	2.928×10^{-4}	kilowatt-hr (kWh)	kW	737.6	(ft-lbf)/sec
Btu	778	ft-lbf	kW-hour (kWh)	3,413	Btu
Btu/hr	3.930×10^{-4}	horsepower (hp)	kWh	1.341	hp-hr
Btu/hr	0.293	watt (W)	kWh	3.6×10^{6}	joule (J)
Btu/hr	0.216	ft-lbf/sec	kip (K)	1,000	lbf
			K	4,448	newton (N)
calorie (g-cal)	3.968×10^{-3}	Btu			
cal	1.560×10^{-6}	hp-hr	liter (L)	61.02	in³
cal	4.186	joule (J)	L	0.264	gal (US Liq)
cal/sec	4.186	watt (W)	L	10^{-3}	m³
centimeter (cm)	3.281×10^{-2}	foot (ft)	L/second (L/s)	2.119	ft³/min (cfm)
cm	0.394	inch (in)	L/s	15.85	gal (US)/min (gpm)
centipoise (cP)	0.001	pascal·sec (Pa·s)			
centistokes (cSt)	1×10^{-6}	m²/sec (m²/s)	meter (m)	3.281	feet (ft)
cubic feet/second (cfs)	0.646317	million gallons/day (mgd)	m	1.094	yard
cubic foot (ft³)	7.481	gallon	m/second (m/s)	196.8	feet/min (ft/min)
cubic meters (m³)	1,000	Liters	mile (statute)	5,280	feet (ft)
electronvolt (eV)	1.602×10^{-19}	joule (J)	mile (statute)	1.609	kilometer (km)
			mile/hour (mph)	88.0	ft/min (fpm)
foot (ft)	30.48	cm	mph	1.609	km/h
ft	0.3048	meter (m)	mm of Hg	1.316×10^{-3}	atm
ft-pound (ft-lbf)	1.285×10^{-3}	Btu	mm of H₂O	9.678×10^{-5}	atm
ft-lbf	3.766×10^{-7}	kilowatt-hr (kWh)			
ft-lbf	0.324	calorie (g-cal)	newton (N)	0.225	lbf
ft-lbf	1.356	joule (J)	N·m	0.7376	ft-lbf
ft-lbf/sec	1.818×10^{-3}	horsepower (hp)	N·m	1	joule (J)
gallon (US Liq)	3.785	liter (L)	pascal (Pa)	9.869×10^{-6}	atmosphere (atm)
gallon (US Liq)	0.134	ft³	Pa	1	newton/m² (N/m²)
gallons of water	8.3453	pounds of water	Pa·sec (Pa·s)	10	poise (P)
gamma (γ, Γ)	1×10^{-9}	tesla (T)	pound (lbm,avdp)	0.454	kilogram (kg)
gauss	1×10^{-4}	T	lbf	4.448	N
gram (g)	2.205×10^{-3}	pound (lbm)	lbf-ft	1.356	N·m
			lbf/in² (psi)	0.068	atm
hectare	1×10^{4}	square meters (m²)	psi	2.307	ft of H₂O
hectare	2.47104	acres	psi	2.036	in of Hg
horsepower (hp)	42.4	Btu/min	psi	6,895	Pa
hp	745.7	watt (W)			
hp	33,000	(ft-lbf)/min	radian	180/π	degree
hp	550	(ft-lbf)/sec			
hp-hr	2,544	Btu	stokes	1×10^{-4}	m²/s
hp-hr	1.98×10^{6}	ft-lbf			
hp-hr	2.68×10^{6}	joule (J)	therm	1×10^{5}	Btu
hp-hr	0.746	kWh			
			watt (W)	3.413	Btu/hr
inch (in)	2.540	centimeter (cm)	W	1.341×10^{-3}	horsepower (hp)
in of Hg	0.0334	atm	W	1	joule/sec (J/s)
in of Hg	13.60	in of H₂O	weber/m² (Wb/m²)	10,000	gauss
in of H₂O	0.0361	lbf/in² (psi)			
in of H₂O	0.002458	atm			

MATHEMATICS

STRAIGHT LINE

The general form of the equation is

$$Ax + By + C = 0$$

The standard form of the equation is

$$y = mx + b,$$

which is also known as the *slope-intercept* form.

The *point-slope* form is $\quad y - y_1 = m(x - x_1)$

Given two points: slope, $\quad m = (y_2 - y_1)/(x_2 - x_1)$

The angle between lines with slopes m_1 and m_2 is

$$\alpha = \arctan\left[(m_2 - m_1)/(1 + m_2 \cdot m_1)\right]$$

Two lines are perpendicular if $\quad m_1 = -1/m_2$

The distance between two points is

$$d = \sqrt{(y_2 - y_1)^2 + (x_2 - x_1)^2}$$

QUADRATIC EQUATION

$$ax^2 + bx + c = 0$$

$$Roots = \frac{-b \pm \sqrt{b^2 - 4ac}}{2a}$$

CONIC SECTIONS

$$e = \text{eccentricity} = \cos\theta/(\cos\phi)$$

[Note: X' and Y', in the following cases, are translated axes.]

Case 1. Parabola $\quad e = 1$:

$(y - k)^2 = 2p(x - h)$; Center at (h, k)

is the standard form of the equation. When $h = k = 0$,
Focus: $(p/2, 0)$;   Directrix: $x = -p/2$

Case 2. Ellipse $\quad e < 1$:

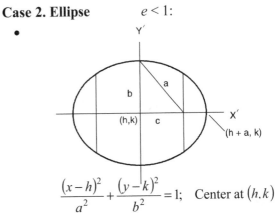

$$\frac{(x-h)^2}{a^2} + \frac{(y-k)^2}{b^2} = 1; \quad \text{Center at } (h, k)$$

is the standard form of the equation. When $h = k = 0$,

Eccentricity: $\quad e = \sqrt{1 - (b^2/a^2)} = c/a$

$b = a\sqrt{1 - e^2}$;

Focus: $(\pm ae, 0)$;   Directrix: $x = \pm a/e$

Case 3. Hyperbola $\quad e > 1$:

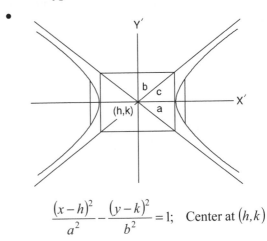

$$\frac{(x-h)^2}{a^2} - \frac{(y-k)^2}{b^2} = 1; \quad \text{Center at } (h, k)$$

is the standard form of the equation. When $h = k = 0$,

Eccentricity: $\quad e = \sqrt{1 + (b^2/a^2)} = c/a$

$b = a\sqrt{e^2 - 1}$;

Focus: $(\pm ae, 0)$;   Directrix: $x = \pm a/e$

Case 4. Circle $e = 0$:

$$(x - h)^2 + (y - k)^2 = r^2; \quad \text{Center at } (h, k)$$

is the general form of the equation with radius

$$r = \sqrt{(x - h)^2 + (y - k)^2}$$

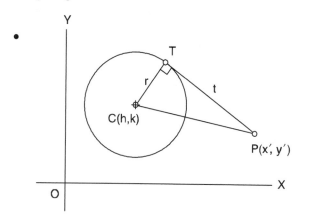

Length of the tangent from a point. Using the general form of the equation of a circle, the length of the tangent is found from

$$t^2 = (x' - h)^2 + (y' - k)^2 - r^2$$

by substituting the coordinates of a point $P(x', y')$ and the coordinates of the center of the circle into the equation and computing.

Conic Section Equation

The general form of the conic section equation is

$$Ax^2 + 2Bxy + Cy^2 + 2Dx + 2Ey + F = 0$$

where not both A and C are zero.

If $B^2 - AC < 0$, an *ellipse* is defined.

If $B^2 - AC > 0$, a *hyperbola* is defined.

If $B^2 - AC = 0$, the conic is a *parabola*.

If $A = C$ and $B = 0$, a *circle* is defined.

If $A = B = C = 0$, a *straight line* is defined.

$$x^2 + y^2 + 2ax + 2by + c = 0$$

is the normal form of the conic section equation, if that conic section has a principal axis parallel to a coordinate axis.

$$h = -a; \quad k = -b$$

$$r = \sqrt{a^2 + b^2 - c}$$

If $a^2 + b^2 - c$ is positive, a *circle*, center $(-a, -b)$.

If $a^2 + b^2 - c$ equals zero, a *point* at $(-a, -b)$.

If $a^2 + b^2 - c$ is negative, locus is *imaginary*.

QUADRIC SURFACE (SPHERE)

The general form of the equation is

$$(x - h)^2 + (y - k)^2 + (z - m)^2 = r^2$$

with center at (h, k, m).

In a three-dimensional space, the distance between two points is

$$d = \sqrt{(x_2 - x_1)^2 + (y_2 - y_1)^2 + (z_2 - z_1)^2}$$

LOGARITHMS

The logarithm of x to the Base b is defined by

$$\log_b (x) = c, \text{ where } \qquad b^c = x$$

Special definitions for $b = e$ or $b = 10$ are:

$$\ln x, \text{ Base } = e$$

$$\log x, \text{ Base } = 10$$

To change from one Base to another:

$$\log_b x = (\log_a x)/(\log_a b)$$

e.g., $\ln x = (\log_{10} x)/(\log_{10} e) = 2.302585 \, (\log_{10} x)$

Identities

$$\log_b b^n = n$$

$$\log x^c = c \log x; \quad x^c = \text{antilog} \, (c \log x)$$

$$\log xy = \log x + \log y$$

$$\log_b b = 1; \log 1 = 0$$

$$\log x/y = \log x - \log y$$

Brink, R.W., *A First Year of College Mathematics*, Copyright © 1937 by D. Appleton-Century Co., Inc. Reprinted by permission of Prentice-Hall, Inc., Englewood Cliffs, NJ.

TRIGONOMETRY

Trigonometric functions are defined using a right triangle.

$\sin \theta = y/r,\ \cos \theta = x/r$

$\tan \theta = y/x,\ \cot \theta = x/y$

$\csc \theta = r/y,\ \sec \theta = r/x$

Law of Sines $\dfrac{a}{\sin A} = \dfrac{b}{\sin B} = \dfrac{c}{\sin C}$

Law of Cosines

$a^2 = b^2 + c^2 - 2bc \cos A$

$b^2 = a^2 + c^2 - 2ac \cos B$

$c^2 = a^2 + b^2 - 2ab \cos C$

Identities

$\csc \theta = 1/\sin \theta$

$\sec \theta = 1/\cos \theta$

$\tan \theta = \sin \theta/\cos \theta$

$\cot \theta = 1/\tan \theta$

$\sin^2\theta + \cos^2\theta = 1$

$\tan^2\theta + 1 = \sec^2\theta$

$\cot^2\theta + 1 = \csc^2\theta$

$\sin (\alpha + \beta) = \sin \alpha \cos \beta + \cos \alpha \sin \beta$

$\cos (\alpha + \beta) = \cos \alpha \cos \beta - \sin \alpha \sin \beta$

$\sin 2\alpha = 2 \sin \alpha \cos \alpha$

$\cos 2\alpha = \cos^2\alpha - \sin^2\alpha = 1 - 2 \sin^2\alpha = 2 \cos^2\alpha - 1$

$\tan 2\alpha = (2 \tan \alpha)/(1 - \tan^2\alpha)$

$\cot 2\alpha = (\cot^2\alpha - 1)/(2 \cot \alpha)$

$\tan (\alpha + \beta) = (\tan \alpha + \tan \beta)/(1 - \tan \alpha \tan \beta)$

$\cot (\alpha + \beta) = (\cot \alpha \cot \beta - 1)/(\cot \alpha + \cot \beta)$

$\sin (\alpha - \beta) = \sin \alpha \cos \beta - \cos \alpha \sin \beta$

$\cos (\alpha - \beta) = \cos \alpha \cos \beta + \sin \alpha \sin \beta$

$\tan (\alpha - \beta) = (\tan \alpha - \tan \beta)/(1 + \tan \alpha \tan \beta)$

$\cot (\alpha - \beta) = (\cot \alpha \cot \beta + 1)/(\cot \beta - \cot \alpha)$

$\sin (\alpha/2) = \pm \sqrt{(1 - \cos \alpha)/2}$

$\cos (\alpha/2) = \pm \sqrt{(1 + \cos \alpha)/2}$

$\tan (\alpha/2) = \pm \sqrt{(1 - \cos \alpha)/(1 + \cos \alpha)}$

$\cot (\alpha/2) = \pm \sqrt{(1 + \cos \alpha)/(1 - \cos \alpha)}$

$\sin \alpha \sin \beta = (1/2)[\cos (\alpha - \beta) - \cos (\alpha + \beta)]$

$\cos \alpha \cos \beta = (1/2)[\cos (\alpha - \beta) + \cos (\alpha + \beta)]$

$\sin \alpha \cos \beta = (1/2)[\sin (\alpha + \beta) + \sin (\alpha - \beta)]$

$\sin \alpha + \sin \beta = 2 \sin (1/2)(\alpha + \beta) \cos (1/2)(\alpha - \beta)$

$\sin \alpha - \sin \beta = 2 \cos (1/2)(\alpha + \beta) \sin (1/2)(\alpha - \beta)$

$\cos \alpha + \cos \beta = 2 \cos (1/2)(\alpha + \beta) \cos (1/2)(\alpha - \beta)$

$\cos \alpha - \cos \beta = -2 \sin (1/2)(\alpha + \beta) \sin (1/2)(\alpha - \beta)$

COMPLEX NUMBERS

Definition $i = \sqrt{-1}$

$(a + ib) + (c + id) = (a + c) + i (b + d)$

$(a + ib) - (c + id) = (a - c) + i (b - d)$

$(a + ib)(c + id) = (ac - bd) + i (ad + bc)$

$\dfrac{a + ib}{c + id} = \dfrac{(a + ib)(c - id)}{(c + id)(c - id)} = \dfrac{(ac + bd) + i(bc - ad)}{c^2 + d^2}$

$(a + ib) + (a - ib) = 2a$

$(a + ib) - (a - ib) = 2ib$

$(a + ib)(a - ib) = a^2 + b^2$

Polar Coordinates

$x = r \cos \theta;\ y = r \sin \theta;\ \theta = \arctan (y/x)$

$r = |x + iy| = \sqrt{x^2 + y^2}$

$x + iy = r (\cos \theta + i \sin \theta) = re^{i\theta}$

$[r_1(\cos \theta_1 + i \sin \theta_1)][r_2(\cos \theta_2 + i \sin \theta_2)] =$
$$r_1r_2[\cos (\theta_1 + \theta_2) + i \sin (\theta_1 + \theta_2)]$$

$(x + iy)^n = [r (\cos \theta + i \sin \theta)]^n$
$$= r^n(\cos n\theta + i \sin n\theta)$$

$\dfrac{r_1(\cos \theta + i \sin \theta_1)}{r_2(\cos \theta_2 + i \sin \theta_2)} = \dfrac{r_1}{r_2}[\cos(\theta_1 - \theta_2) + i \sin(\theta_1 - \theta_2)]$

Euler's Identity

$e^{i\theta} = \cos \theta + i \sin \theta$

$e^{-i\theta} = \cos \theta - i \sin \theta$

$\cos\theta = \dfrac{e^{i\theta} + e^{-i\theta}}{2}, \quad \sin\theta = \dfrac{e^{i\theta} - e^{-i\theta}}{2i}$

Roots

If k is any positive integer, any complex number (other than zero) has k distinct roots. The k roots of $r (\cos \theta + i \sin \theta)$ can be found by substituting successively $n = 0, 1, 2, \ldots,$ $(k - 1)$ in the formula

$$w = \sqrt[k]{r}\left[\cos\left(\frac{\theta}{k} + n\frac{360°}{k}\right) + i \sin\left(\frac{\theta}{k} + n\frac{360°}{k}\right)\right]$$

MATRICES

A matrix is an ordered rectangular array of numbers with m rows and n columns. The element a_{ij} refers to row i and column j.

Multiplication

If $A = (a_{ik})$ is an $m \times n$ matrix and $B = (b_{kj})$ is an $n \times s$ matrix, the matrix product AB is an $m \times s$ matrix

$$C = \left(c_{ij}\right) = \left(\sum_{l=1}^{n} a_{il} b_{lj}\right)$$

where n is the common integer representing the number of columns of A and the number of rows of B (l and $k = 1, 2, \ldots, n$).

Addition

If $A = (a_{ij})$ and $B = (b_{ij})$ are two matrices of the same size $m \times n$, the sum $A + B$ is the $m \times n$ matrix $C = (c_{ij})$ where $c_{ij} = a_{ij} + b_{ij}$.

Identity

The matrix $I = (a_{ij})$ is a square $n \times n$ identity matrix where $a_{ii} = 1$ for $i = 1, 2, \ldots, n$ and $a_{ij} = 0$ for $i \neq j$.

Transpose

The matrix B is the transpose of the matrix A if each entry b_{ji} in B is the same as the entry a_{ij} in A and conversely. In equation form, the transpose is $B = A^{T}$.

Inverse

The inverse B of a square $n \times n$ matrix A is

$$B = A^{-1} = \frac{adj(A)}{|A|}, \text{ where}$$

$adj(A)$ = adjoint of A (obtained by replacing A^{T} elements with their cofactors, see **DETERMINANTS**) and

$|A|$ = determinant of A.

DETERMINANTS

A *determinant of order n* consists of n^2 numbers, called the *elements* of the determinant, arranged in n rows and n columns and enclosed by two vertical lines. In any determinant, the *minor* of a given element is the determinant that remains after all of the elements are struck out that lie in the same row and in the same column as the given element. Consider an element which lies in the hth column and the kth row. The *cofactor* of this element is the value of the minor of the element (if $h + k$ is *even*), and it is the negative of the value of the minor of the element (if $h + k$ is *odd*).

If n is greater than 1, the *value* of a determinant of order n is the sum of the n products formed by multiplying each element of some specified row (or column) by its cofactor. This sum is called the *expansion of the determinant* [according to the elements of the specified row (or column)]. For a second-order determinant:

$$\begin{vmatrix} a_1 & a_2 \\ b_1 & b_2 \end{vmatrix} = a_1 b_2 - a_2 b_1$$

For a third-order determinant:

$$\begin{vmatrix} a_1 & a_2 & a_3 \\ b_1 & b_2 & b_3 \\ c_1 & c_2 & c_3 \end{vmatrix} = a_1 b_2 c_3 + a_2 b_3 c_1 + a_3 b_1 c_2 - a_3 b_2 c_1 - a_2 b_1 c_3 - a_1 b_3 c_2$$

VECTORS

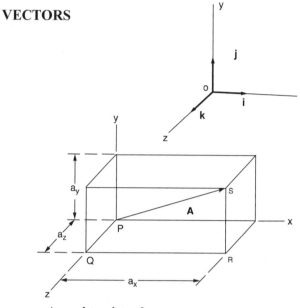

$$A = a_x \mathbf{i} + a_y \mathbf{j} + a_z \mathbf{k}$$

Addition and *subtraction:*

$$A + B = (a_x + b_x)\mathbf{i} + (a_y + b_y)\mathbf{j} + (a_z + b_z)\mathbf{k}$$
$$A - B = (a_x - b_x)\mathbf{i} + (a_y - b_y)\mathbf{j} + (a_z - b_z)\mathbf{k}$$

The *dot product* is a *scalar product* and represents the projection of B onto A times $|A|$. It is given by

$$A \cdot B = a_x b_x + a_y b_y + a_z b_z$$
$$= |A||B| \cos \theta = B \cdot A$$

The *cross product* is a *vector product* of magnitude $|B||A| \sin \theta$ which is perpendicular to the plane containing A and B. The product is

$$A \times B = \begin{vmatrix} \mathbf{i} & \mathbf{j} & \mathbf{k} \\ a_x & a_y & a_z \\ b_x & b_y & b_z \end{vmatrix} = -B \times A$$

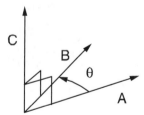

The sense of $\mathbf{A} \times \mathbf{B}$ is determined by the right-hand rule.

$$\mathbf{A} \times \mathbf{B} = |\mathbf{A}| \, |\mathbf{B}| \, \mathbf{n} \sin \theta, \text{ where}$$

$\mathbf{n}$ = unit vector perpendicular to the plane of $\mathbf{A}$ and $\mathbf{B}$.

Gradient, Divergence, and Curl

$$\nabla \phi = \left(\frac{\partial}{\partial x} \mathbf{i} + \frac{\partial}{\partial y} \mathbf{j} + \frac{\partial}{\partial z} \mathbf{k} \right) \phi$$

$$\nabla \cdot \mathbf{V} = \left(\frac{\partial}{\partial x} \mathbf{i} + \frac{\partial}{\partial y} \mathbf{j} + \frac{\partial}{\partial z} \mathbf{k} \right) \cdot \left(V_1 \mathbf{i} + V_2 \mathbf{j} + V_3 \mathbf{k} \right)$$

$$\nabla \times \mathbf{V} = \left(\frac{\partial}{\partial x} \mathbf{i} + \frac{\partial}{\partial y} \mathbf{j} + \frac{\partial}{\partial z} \mathbf{k} \right) \times \left(V_1 \mathbf{i} + V_2 \mathbf{j} + V_3 \mathbf{k} \right)$$

The Laplacian of a scalar function ϕ is

$$\nabla^2 \phi = \frac{\partial^2 \phi}{\partial x^2} + \frac{\partial^2 \phi}{\partial y^2} + \frac{\partial^2 \phi}{\partial z^2}$$

Identities

$\mathbf{A} \cdot \mathbf{B} = \mathbf{B} \cdot \mathbf{A}; \ \mathbf{A} \cdot (\mathbf{B} + \mathbf{C}) = \mathbf{A} \cdot \mathbf{B} + \mathbf{A} \cdot \mathbf{C}$

$\mathbf{A} \cdot \mathbf{A} = |\mathbf{A}|^2$

$\mathbf{i} \cdot \mathbf{i} = \mathbf{j} \cdot \mathbf{j} = \mathbf{k} \cdot \mathbf{k} = 1$

$\mathbf{i} \cdot \mathbf{j} = \mathbf{j} \cdot \mathbf{k} = \mathbf{k} \cdot \mathbf{i} = 0$

If $\mathbf{A} \cdot \mathbf{B} = 0$, then either $\mathbf{A} = 0$, $\mathbf{B} = 0$, or $\mathbf{A}$ is perpendicular to $\mathbf{B}$.

$\mathbf{A} \times \mathbf{B} = -\mathbf{B} \times \mathbf{A}$

$\mathbf{A} \times (\mathbf{B} + \mathbf{C}) = (\mathbf{A} \times \mathbf{B}) + (\mathbf{A} \times \mathbf{C})$

$(\mathbf{B} + \mathbf{C}) \times \mathbf{A} = (\mathbf{B} \times \mathbf{A}) + (\mathbf{C} \times \mathbf{A})$

$\mathbf{i} \times \mathbf{i} = \mathbf{j} \times \mathbf{j} = \mathbf{k} \times \mathbf{k} = 0$

$\mathbf{i} \times \mathbf{j} = \mathbf{k} = -\mathbf{j} \times \mathbf{i}; \ \mathbf{j} \times \mathbf{k} = \mathbf{i} = -\mathbf{k} \times \mathbf{j}$

$\mathbf{k} \times \mathbf{i} = \mathbf{j} = -\mathbf{i} \times \mathbf{k}$

If $\mathbf{A} \times \mathbf{B} = 0$, then either $\mathbf{A} = 0$, $\mathbf{B} = 0$, or $\mathbf{A}$ is parallel to $\mathbf{B}$.

$\nabla^2 \phi = \nabla \cdot (\nabla \phi) = (\nabla \cdot \nabla) \phi$

$\nabla \times \nabla \phi = 0$

$\nabla \cdot (\nabla \times A) = 0$

$\nabla \times (\nabla \times A) = \nabla (\nabla \cdot A) - \nabla^2 A$

PROGRESSIONS AND SERIES

Arithmetic Progression

To determine whether a given finite sequence of numbers is an arithmetic progression, subtract each number from the following number. If the differences are equal, the series is arithmetic.

1. The first term is a.
2. The common difference is d.
3. The number of terms is n.
4. The last or nth term is l.
5. The sum of n terms is S.

$$l = a + (n-1)d$$
$$S = n(a+l)/2 = n\,[2a + (n-1)\,d]/2$$

Geometric Progression

To determine whether a given finite sequence is a geometric progression (G.P.), divide each number after the first by the preceding number. If the quotients are equal, the series is geometric.

1. The first term is a.
2. The common ratio is r.
3. The number of terms is n.
4. The last or nth term is l.
5. The sum of n terms is S.

$$l = ar^{n-1}$$
$$S = a\,(1 - r^n)/(1 - r); \ r \neq 1$$
$$S = (a - rl)/(1 - r); \ r \neq 1$$
$$\lim_{n \to \infty} S_n = a/(1 - r); \quad r < 1$$

A G.P. converges if $|r| < 1$ and it diverges if $|r| \geq 1$.

Properties of Series

$$\sum_{i=1}^{n} c = nc; \quad c = \text{constant}$$

$$\sum_{i=1}^{n} c x_i = c \sum_{i=1}^{n} x_i$$

$$\sum_{i=1}^{n} (x_i + y_i - z_i) = \sum_{i=1}^{n} x_i + \sum_{i=1}^{n} y_i - \sum_{i=1}^{n} z_i$$

$$\sum_{x=1}^{n} x = (n + n^2)/2$$

1. A power series in x, or in $x - a$, which is convergent in the interval $-1 < x < 1$ (or $-1 < x - a < 1$), defines a function of x which is continuous for all values of x within the interval and is said to represent the function in that interval.

2. A power series may be differentiated term by term, and the resulting series has the same interval of convergence as the original series (except possibly at the end points of the interval).

3. A power series may be integrated term by term provided the limits of integration are within the interval of convergence of the series.

4. Two power series may be added, subtracted, or multiplied, and the resulting series in each case is convergent, at least, in the interval common to the two series.

5. Using the process of long division (as for polynomials), two power series may be divided one by the other.

Taylor's Series

$$f(x) = f(a) + \frac{f'(a)}{1!}(x-a) + \frac{f''(a)}{2!}(x-a)^2$$

$$+ \ldots + \frac{f^{(n)}(a)}{n!}(x-a)^n + \ldots$$

is called *Taylor's series*, and the function $f(x)$ is said to be expanded about the point a in a Taylor's series.

If $a = 0$, the Taylor's series equation becomes a *Maclaurin's series*.

PROBABILITY AND STATISTICS

Permutations and Combinations

A *permutation* is a particular sequence of a given set of objects. A *combination* is the set itself without reference to order.

1. The number of different *permutations* of n distinct objects *taken r at a time* is

$$P(n,r) = \frac{n!}{(n-r)!}$$

2. The number of different *combinations* of n distinct objects *taken r at a time* is

$$C(n,r) = \frac{P(n,r)}{r!} = \frac{n!}{[r!(n-r)!]}$$

3. The number of different *permutations* of n objects *taken n at a time*, given that n_i are of type i, where $i = 1, 2, \ldots, k$ and $\Sigma n_i = n$, is

$$P(n; n_1, n_2, \ldots n_k) = \frac{n!}{n_1! n_2! \ldots n_k!}$$

Laws of Probability

Property 1. General Character of Probability

The probability $P(E)$ of an event E is a real number in the range of 0 to 1. The probability of an impossible event is 0 and that of an event certain to occur is 1.

Property 2. Law of Total Probability

$P(A + B) = P(A) + P(B) - P(A, B)$, where

$P(A + B)$ = the probability that either A or B occur alone or that both occur together,

$P(A)$ = the probability that A occurs,

$P(B)$ = the probability that B occurs, and

$P(A, B)$ = the probability that both A and B occur simultaneously.

Property 3. Law of Compound or Joint Probability

If neither $P(A)$ nor $P(B)$ is zero,

$P(A, B) = P(A)P(B \mid A) = P(B)P(A \mid B)$, where

$P(B \mid A)$ = the probability that B occurs given the fact that A has occurred, and

$P(A \mid B)$ = the probability that A occurs given the fact that B has occurred.

If either $P(A)$ or $P(B)$ is zero, then $P(A, B) = 0$.

Probability Functions

A random variable X has a probability associated with each of its possible values. The probability is termed a discrete probability if X can assume only discrete values or

$$X = x_1, x_2, x_3, \ldots, x_n$$

The *discrete probability* of any single event, $X = x_i$, occurring is defined as $P(x_i)$ while the *probability mass function* of the random variable X is defined by

$$f(x_k) = P(X = x_k), k = 1, 2, \ldots, n$$

Probability Density Function

If X is continuous, the *probability density function, f,* is defined such that

$$P(a \le X \le b) = \int_a^b f(x)\, dx$$

The probability is determined by defining the equation for $f(x)$ and then integrating between the values of a and b.

Cumulative Distribution Functions

The *cumulative distribution function, F,* of a discrete random variable X having a discrete probability function $P(x_i)$ is defined as

$$F(x_m) = \sum_{k=1}^{m} P(x_k) = P(X \le x_m), m = 1, 2, \ldots, n$$

If X is continuous, the *cumulative distribution function, F,* is defined by

$$F(x) = \int_{-\infty}^{x} f(t)\, dt$$

which implies that $F(a)$ is the probability that $X \le a$.

Expected Values

Let X be a continuous random variable having a density function $f(X)$ and let $Y = g(X)$ be some general function that is to be averaged over the values of the random variable. The expected value of Y may be written as

$$E[Y] = E[g(X)] = \int_{-\infty}^{\infty} g(x) f(x)\, dx$$

The mean or expected value of the random variable X is now defined as

$$\mu = E[X] = \int_{-\infty}^{\infty} x f(x)\, dx$$

while the variance is given by

$$\sigma^2 = V[X] = E[(X-\mu)^2] = \int_{-\infty}^{\infty} (x-\mu)^2 f(x)\, dx$$

The standard deviation is given by

$$\sigma = \sqrt{V[X]}$$

Sums of Random Variables

$$Y = a_1 X_1 + a_2 X_2 + \ldots + a_n X_n$$

The expected value of Y is:

$$\mu_y = E(Y) = a_1 E(X_1) + a_2 E(X_2) + \ldots + a_n E(X_n)$$

If the random variables are statistically *independent*, then the variance of Y is:

$$\sigma_y^2 = V(Y) = a_1^2 V(X_1) + a_2^2 V(X_2) + \ldots + a_n^2 V(X_n)$$

$$= a_1^2 \sigma_1^2 + a_2^2 \sigma_2^2 + \ldots + a_n^2 \sigma_n^2$$

Also, the standard deviation of Y is:

$$\sigma_y = \sqrt{\sigma_y^2}$$

Binomial Distribution

$P(x)$ is the probability that X will occur in n trials. If p = probability of success and q = probability of failure = $1 - p$, then

$$P(x) = C(n,x) p^x q^{n-x} = \frac{n!}{x!(n-x)!} p^x q^{n-x}, \text{ where}$$

$x \qquad = 0, 1, 2, \ldots, n,$

$C(n, x) \;$ = the number of combinations, and

$n, p \qquad$ = parameters.

Normal Distribution (Gaussian Distribution)

This is a unimodal distribution, the mode being $x = \mu$, with two points of inflection (each located at a distance σ to either side of the mode). The averages of n observations tend to become normally distributed as n increases. The variate x is said to be normally distributed if its density function $f(x)$ is given by an expression of the form

$$f(x) = \frac{1}{\sigma\sqrt{2\pi}} e^{-\frac{1}{2}\left(\frac{x-m}{\sigma}\right)^2}, \text{ where}$$

μ = the population mean,

σ = the standard deviation of the population, and

$-\infty \leq x \leq \infty$

When $\mu = 0$ and $\sigma^2 = \sigma = 1$, the distribution is called a *standardized* or *unit normal* distribution. Then

$$f(x) = \frac{1}{\sqrt{2\pi}} e^{-x^2/2}, \quad \text{where} -\infty \leq x \leq \infty.$$

A unit normal distribution table is included at the end of this section. In the table, the following notations are utilized:

$F(x)$ = the area under the curve from $-\infty$ to x,

$R(x)$ = the area under the curve from x to ∞, and

$W(x)$ = the area under the curve between $-x$ and x.

Dispersion, Mean, Median, and Mode Values

If X_1, X_2, …, X_n represent the values of n items or observations, the *arithmetic mean* of these items or observations, denoted $\overline{X}$, is defined as

$$\overline{X} = (1/n)(X_1 + X_2 + \ldots + X_n) = (1/n)\sum_{i=1}^{n} X_i$$

$\overline{X} \to \mu$ for sufficiently large values of n.

The *weighted arithmetic mean* is

$$\overline{X}_w = \frac{\sum w_i X_i}{\sum w_i}, \text{ where}$$

$\overline{X}_w \;$ = the weighted arithmetic mean,

$X_i \quad$ = the values of the observations to be averaged, and

$w_i \quad$ = the weight applied to the X_i value.

The *variance* of the observations is the *arithmetic mean* of the *squared deviations from the population mean*. In symbols, X_1, X_2, …, X_n represent the values of the *n sample* observations of a *population of size N*. If μ is the arithmetic mean of the population, the *population variance* is defined by

$$\sigma^2 = (1/N)[(X_1 - \mu)^2 + (X_2 - \mu)^2 + \ldots + (X_N - \mu)^2]$$

$$= (1/N)\sum_{i=1}^{N}(X_i - \mu)^2$$

The *standard deviation* of a population is

$$\sigma = \sqrt{(1/N)\sum(X_i - \mu)^2}$$

The *sample variance* is

$$s^2 = [1/(n-1)]\sum_{i=1}^{n}(X_i - \overline{X})^2$$

The *sample standard deviation* is

$$s = \sqrt{[1/(n-1)]\sum_{i=1}^{n}(X_i - \overline{X})^2}$$

The *coefficient of variation* $= CV = s/\overline{X}$

The *geometric mean* $= \sqrt[n]{X_1 X_2 X_3 \ldots X_n}$

The *root-mean-square value* $= \sqrt{(1/n)\sum X_i^2}$

The *median* is defined as the *value of the middle item* when the data are *rank-ordered* and the number of items is *odd*. The *median* is the *average of the middle two items* when the rank-ordered data consists of an *even* number of items.

The *mode* of a set of data is the *value that occurs with greatest frequency*.

t-Distribution

The variate t is defined as the quotient of two independent variates x and r where x is unit normal and r is the root mean square of n other independent unit normal variates; that is, $t = x/r$. The following is the *t*-distribution with n degrees of freedom:

$$f(t) = \frac{\Gamma[(n+1)]/2}{\Gamma(n/2)\sqrt{n\pi}} \frac{1}{\left(1 + t^2/n\right)^{(n+1)/2}}$$

where $-\infty \leq t \leq \infty$.

A table at the end of this section gives the values of $t_{\alpha, n}$ for values of α and n. Note that in view of the symmetry of the t-distribution, $t_{1-\alpha,n} = -t_{\alpha,n}$.

The function for α follows:

$$\alpha = \int_{t_{\alpha,n}}^{\infty} f(t)dt$$

A table showing probability and density functions is included in the **INDUSTRIAL ENGINEERING SECTION** of this handbook.

GAMMA FUNCTION

$$\Gamma(n) = \int_{o}^{\infty} t^{n-1}e^{-t}dt, \quad n > 0$$

CONFIDENCE INTERVALS

Confidence Interval for the Mean μ of a Normal Distribution

(a) Standard deviation σ is known

$$\overline{X} - Z_{\alpha/2}\frac{\sigma}{\sqrt{n}} \leq \mu \leq \overline{X} + Z_{\alpha/2}\frac{\sigma}{\sqrt{n}}$$

(b) Standard deviation σ is not known

$$\overline{X} - t_{\alpha/2}\frac{s}{\sqrt{n}} \leq \mu \leq \overline{X} + t_{\alpha/2}\frac{s}{\sqrt{n}}$$

where $t_{\alpha/2}$ corresponds to $n - 1$ degrees of freedom.

Confidence Interval for the Difference Between Two Means μ_1 and μ_2

(a) Standard deviations σ_1 and σ_2 known

$$\overline{X}_1 - \overline{X}_2 - Z_{\alpha/2}\sqrt{\frac{\sigma_1^2}{n_1} + \frac{\sigma_2^2}{n_2}} \leq \mu_1 - \mu_2 \leq \overline{X}_1 - \overline{X}_2 + Z_{\alpha/2}\sqrt{\frac{\sigma_1^2}{n_1} + \frac{\sigma_2^2}{n_2}}$$

(b) Standard deviations σ_1 and σ_2 are not known

$$\overline{X}_1 - \overline{X}_2 - t_{\alpha/2}\sqrt{\frac{\left(\frac{1}{n_1} + \frac{1}{n_2}\right)\left[(n-1)S_1^2 + (n_2-1)S_2^2\right]}{n_1 + n_2 - 2}} \leq \mu_1 - \mu_2 \leq \overline{X}_1 - \overline{X}_2 - t_{\alpha/2}\sqrt{\frac{\left(\frac{1}{n_1} + \frac{1}{n_2}\right)\left[(n-1)S_1^2 + (n_2-1)S_2^2\right]}{n_1 + n_2 - 2}}$$

where $t_{\alpha/2}$ corresponds to $n_1 + n_2 - 2$ degrees of freedom.

UNIT NORMAL DISTRIBUTION TABLE

x	$f(x)$	$F(x)$	$R(x)$	$2R(x)$	$W(x)$
0.0	0.3989	0.5000	0.5000	1.0000	0.0000
0.1	0.3970	0.5398	0.4602	0.9203	0.0797
0.2	0.3910	0.5793	0.4207	0.8415	0.1585
0.3	0.3814	0.6179	0.3821	0.7642	0.2358
0.4	0.3683	0.6554	0.3446	0.6892	0.3108
0.5	0.3521	0.6915	0.3085	0.6171	0.3829
0.6	0.3332	0.7257	0.2743	0.5485	0.4515
0.7	0.3123	0.7580	0.2420	0.4839	0.5161
0.8	0.2897	0.7881	0.2119	0.4237	0.5763
0.9	0.2661	0.8159	0.1841	0.3681	0.6319
1.0	0.2420	0.8413	0.1587	0.3173	0.6827
1.1	0.2179	0.8643	0.1357	0.2713	0.7287
1.2	0.1942	0.8849	0.1151	0.2301	0.7699
1.3	0.1714	0.9032	0.0968	0.1936	0.8064
1.4	0.1497	0.9192	0.0808	0.1615	0.8385
1.5	0.1295	0.9332	0.0668	0.1336	0.8664
1.6	0.1109	0.9452	0.0548	0.1096	0.8904
1.7	0.0940	0.9554	0.0446	0.0891	0.9109
1.8	0.0790	0.9641	0.0359	0.0719	0.9281
1.9	0.0656	0.9713	0.0287	0.0574	0.9426
2.0	0.0540	0.9772	0.0228	0.0455	0.9545
2.1	0.0440	0.9821	0.0179	0.0357	0.9643
2.2	0.0355	0.9861	0.0139	0.0278	0.9722
2.3	0.0283	0.9893	0.0107	0.0214	0.9786
2.4	0.0224	0.9918	0.0082	0.0164	0.9836
2.5	0.0175	0.9938	0.0062	0.0124	0.9876
2.6	0.0136	0.9953	0.0047	0.0093	0.9907
2.7	0.0104	0.9965	0.0035	0.0069	0.9931
2.8	0.0079	0.9974	0.0026	1.0051	0.9949
2.9	0.0060	0.9981	0.0019	0.0037	0.9963
3.0	0.0044	0.9987	0.0013	0.0027	0.9973
Fractiles					
1.2816	0.1755	0.9000	0.1000	0.2000	0.8000
1.6449	0.1031	0.9500	0.0500	0.1000	0.9000
1.9600	0.0584	0.9750	0.0250	0.0500	0.9500
2.0537	0.0484	0.9800	0.0200	0.0400	0.9600
2.3263	0.0267	0.9900	0.0100	0.0200	0.9800
2.5758	0.0145	0.9950	0.0050	0.0100	0.9900

t-DISTRIBUTION TABLE

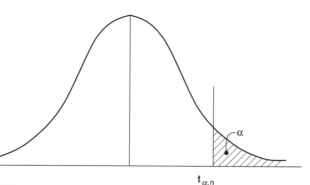

VALUES OF $t_{\alpha,n}$

n	$\alpha = 0.10$	$\alpha = 0.05$	$\alpha = 0.025$	$\alpha = 0.01$	$\alpha = 0.005$	*n*
1	3.078	6.314	12.706	31.821	63.657	1
2	1.886	2.920	4.303	6.965	9.925	2
3	1.638	2.353	3.182	4.541	5.841	3
4	1.533	2.132	2.776	3.747	4.604	4
5	1.476	2.015	2.571	3.365	4.032	5
6	1.440	1.943	2.447	3.143	3.707	6
7	1.415	1.895	2.365	2.998	3.499	7
8	1.397	1.860	2.306	2.896	3.355	8
9	1.383	1.833	2.262	2.821	3.250	9
10	1.372	1.812	2.228	2.764	3.169	10
11	1.363	1.796	2.201	2.718	3.106	11
12	1.356	1.782	2.179	2.681	3.055	12
13	1.350	1.771	2.160	2.650	3.012	13
14	1.345	1.761	2.145	2.624	2.977	14
15	1.341	1.753	2.131	2.602	2.947	15
16	1.337	1.746	2.120	2.583	2.921	16
17	1.333	1.740	2.110	2.567	2.898	17
18	1.330	1.734	2.101	2.552	2.878	18
19	1.328	1.729	2.093	2.539	2.861	19
20	1.325	1.725	2.086	2.528	2.845	20
21	1.323	1.721	2.080	2.518	2.831	21
22	1.321	1.717	2.074	2.508	2.819	22
23	1.319	1.714	2.069	2.500	2.807	23
24	1.318	1.711	2.064	2.492	2.797	24
25	1.316	1.708	2.060	2.485	2.787	25
26	1.315	1.706	2.056	2.479	2.779	26
27	1.314	1.703	2.052	2.473	2.771	27
28	1.313	1.701	2.048	2.467	2.763	28
29	1.311	1.699	2.045	2.462	2.756	29
∞	1.282	1.645	1.960	2.326	2.576	∞

CRITICAL VALUES OF THE F DISTRIBUTION – TABLE

For a particular combination of numerator and denominator degrees of freedom, entry represents the critical values of F corresponding to a specified upper tail area (α).

$\alpha = 0.05$

$F(\alpha, df_1, df_2)$

Denominator df_2	Numerator df_1																		
	1	2	3	4	5	6	7	8	9	10	12	15	20	24	30	40	60	120	∞
1	161.4	199.5	215.7	224.6	230.2	234.0	236.8	238.9	240.5	241.9	243.9	245.9	248.0	249.1	250.1	251.1	252.2	253.3	254.3
2	18.51	19.00	19.16	19.25	19.30	19.33	19.35	19.37	19.38	19.40	19.41	19.43	19.45	19.45	19.46	19.47	19.48	19.49	19.50
3	10.13	9.55	9.28	9.12	9.01	8.94	8.89	8.85	8.81	8.79	8.74	8.70	8.66	8.64	8.62	8.59	8.57	8.55	8.53
4	7.71	6.94	6.59	6.39	6.26	6.16	6.09	6.04	6.00	5.96	5.91	5.86	5.80	5.77	5.75	5.72	5.69	5.66	5.63
5	6.61	5.79	5.41	5.19	5.05	4.95	4.88	4.82	4.77	4.74	4.68	4.62	4.56	4.53	4.50	4.46	4.43	4.40	4.36
6	5.99	5.14	4.76	4.53	4.39	4.28	4.21	4.15	4.10	4.06	4.00	3.94	3.87	3.84	3.81	3.77	3.74	3.70	3.67
7	5.59	4.74	4.35	4.12	3.97	3.87	3.79	3.73	3.68	3.64	3.57	3.51	3.44	3.41	3.38	3.34	3.30	3.27	3.23
8	5.32	4.46	4.07	3.84	3.69	3.58	3.50	3.44	3.39	3.35	3.28	3.22	3.15	3.12	3.08	3.04	3.01	2.97	2.93
9	5.12	4.26	3.86	3.63	3.48	3.37	3.29	3.23	3.18	3.14	3.07	3.01	2.94	2.90	2.86	2.83	2.79	2.75	2.71
10	4.96	4.10	3.71	3.48	3.33	3.22	3.14	3.07	3.02	2.98	2.91	2.85	2.77	2.74	2.70	2.66	2.62	2.58	2.54
11	4.84	3.98	3.59	3.36	3.20	3.09	3.01	2.95	2.90	2.85	2.79	2.72	2.65	2.61	2.57	2.53	2.49	2.45	2.40
12	4.75	3.89	3.49	3.26	3.11	3.00	2.91	2.85	2.80	2.75	2.69	2.62	2.54	2.51	2.47	2.43	2.38	2.34	2.30
13	4.67	3.81	3.41	3.18	3.03	2.92	2.83	2.77	2.71	2.67	2.60	2.53	2.46	2.42	2.38	2.34	2.30	2.25	2.21
14	4.60	3.74	3.34	3.11	2.96	2.85	2.76	2.70	2.65	2.60	2.53	2.46	2.39	2.35	2.31	2.27	2.22	2.18	2.13
15	4.54	3.68	3.29	3.06	2.90	2.79	2.71	2.64	2.59	2.54	2.48	2.40	2.33	2.29	2.25	2.20	2.16	2.11	2.07
16	4.49	3.63	3.24	3.01	2.85	2.74	2.66	2.59	2.54	2.49	2.42	2.35	2.28	2.24	2.19	2.15	2.11	2.06	2.01
17	4.45	3.59	3.20	2.96	2.81	2.70	2.61	2.55	2.49	2.45	2.38	2.31	2.23	2.19	2.15	2.10	2.06	2.01	1.96
18	4.41	3.55	3.16	2.93	2.77	2.66	2.58	2.51	2.46	2.41	2.34	2.27	2.19	2.15	2.11	2.06	2.02	1.97	1.92
19	4.38	3.52	3.13	2.90	2.74	2.63	2.54	2.48	2.42	2.38	2.31	2.23	2.16	2.11	2.07	2.03	1.98	1.93	1.88
20	4.35	3.49	3.10	2.87	2.71	2.60	2.51	2.45	2.39	2.35	2.28	2.20	2.12	2.08	2.04	1.99	1.95	1.90	1.84
21	4.32	3.47	3.07	2.84	2.68	2.57	2.49	2.42	2.37	2.32	2.25	2.18	2.10	2.05	2.01	1.96	1.92	1.87	1.81
22	4.30	3.44	3.05	2.82	2.66	2.55	2.46	2.40	2.34	2.30	2.23	2.15	2.07	2.03	1.98	1.94	1.89	1.84	1.78
23	4.28	3.42	3.03	2.80	2.64	2.53	2.44	2.37	2.32	2.27	2.20	2.13	2.05	2.01	1.96	1.91	1.86	1.81	1.76
24	4.26	3.40	3.01	2.78	2.62	2.51	2.42	2.36	2.30	2.25	2.18	2.11	2.03	1.98	1.94	1.89	1.84	1.79	1.73
25	4.24	3.39	2.99	2.76	2.60	2.49	2.40	2.34	2.28	2.24	2.16	2.09	2.01	1.96	1.92	1.87	1.82	1.77	1.71
26	4.23	3.37	2.98	2.74	2.59	2.47	2.39	2.32	2.27	2.22	2.15	2.07	1.99	1.95	1.90	1.85	1.80	1.75	1.69
27	4.21	3.35	2.96	2.73	2.57	2.46	2.37	2.31	2.25	2.20	2.13	2.06	1.97	1.93	1.88	1.84	1.79	1.73	1.67
28	4.20	3.34	2.95	2.71	2.56	2.45	2.36	2.29	2.24	2.19	2.12	2.04	1.96	1.91	1.87	1.82	1.77	1.71	1.65
29	4.18	3.33	2.93	2.70	2.55	2.43	2.35	2.28	2.22	2.18	2.10	2.03	1.94	1.90	1.85	1.81	1.75	1.70	1.64
30	4.17	3.32	2.92	2.69	2.53	2.42	2.33	2.27	2.21	2.16	2.09	2.01	1.93	1.89	1.84	1.79	1.74	1.68	1.62
40	4.08	3.23	2.84	2.61	2.45	2.34	2.25	2.18	2.12	2.08	2.00	1.92	1.84	1.79	1.74	1.69	1.64	1.58	1.51
60	4.00	3.15	2.76	2.53	2.37	2.25	2.17	2.10	2.04	1.99	1.92	1.84	1.75	1.70	1.65	1.59	1.53	1.47	1.39
120	3.92	3.07	2.68	2.45	2.29	2.17	2.09	2.02	1.96	1.91	1.83	1.75	1.66	1.61	1.55	1.50	1.43	1.35	1.25
∞	3.84	3.00	2.60	2.37	2.21	2.10	2.01	1.94	1.88	1.83	1.75	1.67	1.57	1.52	1.46	1.39	1.32	1.22	1.00

DIFFERENTIAL CALCULUS

The Derivative

For any function $y = f(x)$,

the derivative $= D_x y = dy/dx = y'$

$$y' = \lim_{\Delta x \to 0} [(\Delta y)/(\Delta x)]$$

$$= \lim_{\Delta x \to 0} \{[f(x + \Delta x) - f(x)]/(\Delta x)\}$$

$y' = $ the slope of the curve $f(x)$.

Test for a Maximum

$y = f(x)$ is a maximum for

$x = a$, if $f'(a) = 0$ and $f''(a) < 0$.

Test for a Minimum

$y = f(x)$ is a minimum for

$x = a$, if $f'(a) = 0$ and $f''(a) > 0$.

Test for a Point of Inflection

$y = f(x)$ has a point of inflection at $x = a$,

if $f''(a) = 0$, and

if $f''(x)$ changes sign as x increases through

$x = a$.

The Partial Derivative

In a function of two independent variables x and y, a derivative with respect to one of the variables may be found if the other variable is *assumed* to remain constant. If y *is kept fixed*, the function

$$z = f(x, y)$$

becomes a function of the *single variable* x, and its derivative (if it exists) can be found. This derivative is called the *partial derivative of z with respect to x*. The partial derivative with respect to x is denoted as follows:

$$\frac{\partial z}{\partial x} = \frac{\partial f(x, y)}{\partial x}$$

The Curvature of Any Curve

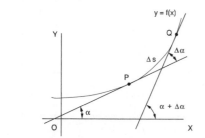

The curvature K of a curve at P is the limit of its average curvature for the arc PQ as Q approaches P. This is also expressed as: the curvature of a curve at a given point is the rate-of-change of its inclination with respect to its arc length.

$$K = \lim_{\Delta s \to 0} \frac{\Delta \alpha}{\Delta s} = \frac{d\alpha}{ds}$$

Curvature in Rectangular Coordinates

$$K = \frac{y''}{\left[1 + (y')^2\right]^{3/2}}$$

When it may be easier to differentiate the function with respect to y rather than x, the notation x' will be used for the derivative.

$$x' = dx/dy$$

$$K = \frac{-x''}{\left[1 + (x')^2\right]^{3/2}}$$

The Radius of Curvature

The *radius of curvature R* at any point on a curve is defined as the absolute value of the reciprocal of the curvature K at that point.

$$R = \frac{1}{|K|} \qquad (K \neq 0)$$

$$R = \left| \frac{\left[1 + (y')^2\right]^{3/2}}{|y''|} \right| \qquad (y'' \neq 0)$$

L'Hospital's Rule (L'Hôpital's Rule)

If the fractional function $f(x)/g(x)$ assumes one of the indeterminate forms $0/0$ or ∞/∞ (where α is finite or infinite), then

$$\lim_{x \to \alpha} f(x)/g(x)$$

is equal to the first of the expressions

$$\lim_{x \to \alpha} \frac{f'(x)}{g'(x)}, \lim_{x \to \alpha} \frac{f''(x)}{g''(x)}, \lim_{x \to \alpha} \frac{f'''(x)}{g'''(x)}$$

which is not indeterminate, provided such first indicated limit exists.

INTEGRAL CALCULUS

The definite integral is defined as:

$$\lim_{n \to \infty} \sum_{i=1}^{n} f(x_i)\Delta x_i = \int_a^b f(x)dx$$

Also, $\Delta x_i \to 0$ for all i.

A table of derivatives and integrals is available on page 15. The integral equations can be used along with the following methods of integration:

A. Integration by Parts (integral equation #6),

B. Integration by Substitution, and

C. Separation of Rational Fractions into Partial Fractions.

DERIVATIVES AND INDEFINITE INTEGRALS

In these formulas, u, v, and w represent functions of x. Also, a, c, and n represent constants. All arguments of the trigonometric functions are in radians. A constant of integration should be added to the integrals. To avoid terminology difficulty, the following definitions are followed: $\arcsin u = \sin^{-1} u$, $(\sin u)^{-1} = 1/\sin u$.

1. $dc/dx = 0$
2. $dx/dx = 1$
3. $d(cu)/dx = c\, du/dx$
4. $d(u + v - w)/dx = du/dx + dv/dx - dw/dx$
5. $d(uv)/dx = u\, dv/dx + v\, du/dx$
6. $d(uvw)/dx = uv\, dw/dx + uw\, dv/dx + vw\, du/dx$
7. $\dfrac{d(u/v)}{dx} = \dfrac{v\, du/dx - u\, dv/dx}{v^2}$
8. $d(u^n)/dx = nu^{n-1}\, du/dx$
9. $d[f(u)]/dx = \{d[f(u)]/du\}\, du/dx$
10. $du/dx = 1/(dx/du)$
11. $\dfrac{d(\log_a u)}{dx} = (\log_a e)\dfrac{1}{u}\dfrac{du}{dx}$
12. $\dfrac{d(\ln u)}{dx} = \dfrac{1}{u}\dfrac{du}{dx}$
13. $\dfrac{d(a^u)}{dx} = (\ln a)a^u \dfrac{du}{dx}$
14. $d(e^u)/dx = e^u\, du/dx$
15. $d(u^v)/dx = vu^{v-1}\, du/dx + (\ln u)\, u^v\, dv/dx$
16. $d(\sin u)/dx = \cos u\, du/dx$
17. $d(\cos u)/dx = -\sin u\, du/dx$
18. $d(\tan u)/dx = \sec^2 u\, du/dx$
19. $d(\cot u)/dx = -\csc^2 u\, du/dx$
20. $d(\sec u)/dx = \sec u \tan u\, du/dx$
21. $d(\csc u)/dx = -\csc u \cot u\, du/dx$
22. $\dfrac{d(\sin^{-1}u)}{dx} = \dfrac{1}{\sqrt{1-u^2}}\dfrac{du}{dx}$ $\left(-\pi/2 \le \sin^{-1}u \le \pi/2\right)$
23. $\dfrac{d(\cos^{-1}u)}{dx} = -\dfrac{1}{\sqrt{1-u^2}}\dfrac{du}{dx}$ $\left(0 \le \cos^{-1}u \le \pi\right)$
24. $\dfrac{d(\tan^{-1}u)}{dx} = \dfrac{1}{1+u^2}\dfrac{du}{dx}$ $\left(-\pi/2 < \tan^{-1}u < \pi/2\right)$
25. $\dfrac{d(\cot^{-1}u)}{dx} = -\dfrac{1}{1+u^2}\dfrac{du}{dx}$ $\left(0 < \cot^{-1}u < \pi\right)$
26. $\dfrac{d(\sec^{-1}u)}{dx} = \dfrac{1}{u\sqrt{u^2-1}}\dfrac{du}{dx}$

$\left(0 \le \sec^{-1}u < \pi/2\right)\left(-\pi \le \sec^{-1}u < -\pi/2\right)$

27. $\dfrac{d(\csc^{-1}u)}{dx} = -\dfrac{1}{u\sqrt{u^2-1}}\dfrac{du}{dx}$

$\left(0 < \csc^{-1}u \le \pi/2\right)\left(-\pi < \csc^{-1}u \le -\pi/2\right)$

1. $\int df(x) = f(x)$
2. $\int dx = x$
3. $\int a f(x)\, dx = a \int f(x)\, dx$
4. $\int [u(x) \pm v(x)]\, dx = \int u(x)\, dx \pm \int v(x)\, dx$
5. $\int x^m dx = \dfrac{x^{m+1}}{m+1}$ $(m \ne -1)$
6. $\int u(x)\, dv(x) = u(x)\, v(x) - \int v(x)\, du(x)$
7. $\int \dfrac{dx}{ax+b} = \dfrac{1}{a}\ln|ax+b|$
8. $\int \dfrac{dx}{\sqrt{x}} = 2\sqrt{x}$
9. $\int a^x dx = \dfrac{a^x}{\ln a}$
10. $\int \sin x\, dx = -\cos x$
11. $\int \cos x\, dx = \sin x$
12. $\int \sin^2 x\, dx = \dfrac{x}{2} - \dfrac{\sin 2x}{4}$
13. $\int \cos^2 x\, dx = \dfrac{x}{2} + \dfrac{\sin 2x}{4}$
14. $\int x \sin x\, dx = \sin x - x \cos x$
15. $\int x \cos x\, dx = \cos x + x \sin x$
16. $\int \sin x \cos x\, dx = (\sin^2 x)/2$
17. $\int \sin ax \cos bx\, dx = -\dfrac{\cos(a-b)x}{2(a-b)} - \dfrac{\cos(a+b)x}{2(a+b)}$ $\left(a^2 \ne b^2\right)$
18. $\int \tan x\, dx = -\ln|\cos x| = \ln|\sec x|$
19. $\int \cot x\, dx = -\ln|\csc x| = \ln|\sin x|$
20. $\int \tan^2 x\, dx = \tan x - x$
21. $\int \cot^2 x\, dx = -\cot x - x$
22. $\int e^{ax}\, dx = (1/a)\, e^{ax}$
23. $\int xe^{ax}\, dx = (e^{ax}/a^2)(ax-1)$
24. $\int \ln x\, dx = x[\ln(x) - 1]$ $(x > 0)$
25. $\int \dfrac{dx}{a^2+x^2} = \dfrac{1}{a}\tan^{-1}\dfrac{x}{a}$ $(a \ne 0)$
26. $\int \dfrac{dx}{ax^2+c} = \dfrac{1}{\sqrt{ac}}\tan^{-1}\left(x\sqrt{\dfrac{a}{c}}\right),$ $(a > 0, c > 0)$

27a. $\int \dfrac{dx}{ax^2+bx+c} = \dfrac{2}{\sqrt{4ac-b^2}}\tan^{-1}\dfrac{2ax+b}{\sqrt{4ac-b^2}}$

$\left(4ac-b^2 > 0\right)$

27b. $\int \dfrac{dx}{ax^2+bx+c} = \dfrac{1}{\sqrt{b^2-4ac}}\ln\left|\dfrac{2ax+b-\sqrt{b^2-4ac}}{2ax+b+\sqrt{b^2-4ac}}\right|$

$\left(b^2-4ac > 0\right)$

27c. $\int \dfrac{dx}{ax^2+bx+c} = -\dfrac{2}{2ax+b},$ $\left(b^2-4ac = 0\right)$

MENSURATION OF AREAS AND VOLUMES

Nomenclature

A = total surface area

P = perimeter

V = volume

Parabola

A = 2bh/3

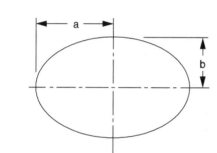

A = bh/3

Ellipse

♦

A = πab

$$P_{approx} = 2\pi\sqrt{(a^2 + b^2)/2}$$

$$P = \pi(a+b)\left[\begin{array}{l} 1 + (\tfrac{1}{2})^2\lambda^2 + (\tfrac{1}{2}\times\tfrac{1}{4})^2\lambda^4 \\ + (\tfrac{1}{2}\times\tfrac{1}{4}\times\tfrac{3}{6})^2\lambda^6 + (\tfrac{1}{2}\times\tfrac{1}{4}\times\tfrac{3}{6}\times\tfrac{5}{8})^2\lambda^8 \\ + (\tfrac{1}{2}\times\tfrac{1}{4}\times\tfrac{3}{6}\times\tfrac{5}{8}\times\tfrac{7}{10})^2\lambda^{10} + \ldots \end{array}\right],$$

where

$$\lambda = (a-b)/(a+b)$$

Circular Segment

♦

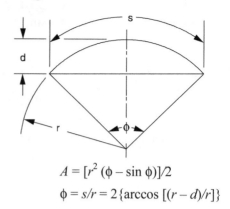

$$A = [r^2(\phi - \sin\phi)]/2$$

$$\phi = s/r = 2\{\arccos[(r-d)/r]\}$$

Circular Sector

♦

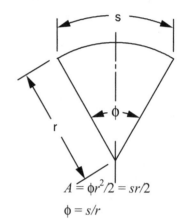

$$A = \phi r^2/2 = sr/2$$

$$\phi = s/r$$

Sphere

♦

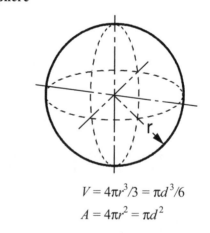

$$V = 4\pi r^3/3 = \pi d^3/6$$

$$A = 4\pi r^2 = \pi d^2$$

♦ Gieck, K. & Gieck R., *Engineering Formulas*, 6th Ed., Copyright © 1967 by Gieck Publishing. Diagrams reprinted by permission of Kurt Gieck.

MENSURATION OF AREAS AND VOLUMES

Parallelogram

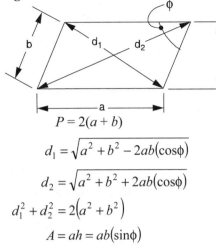

$$P = 2(a + b)$$

$$d_1 = \sqrt{a^2 + b^2 - 2ab(\cos\phi)}$$

$$d_2 = \sqrt{a^2 + b^2 + 2ab(\cos\phi)}$$

$$d_1^2 + d_2^2 = 2(a^2 + b^2)$$

$$A = ah = ab(\sin\phi)$$

If $a = b$, the parallelogram is a rhombus.

Regular Polygon (*n* equal sides)

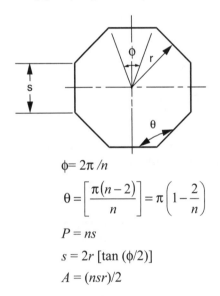

$$\phi = 2\pi / n$$

$$\theta = \left[\frac{\pi(n-2)}{n}\right] = \pi\left(1 - \frac{2}{n}\right)$$

$$P = ns$$

$$s = 2r\,[\tan(\phi/2)]$$

$$A = (nsr)/2$$

Prismoid

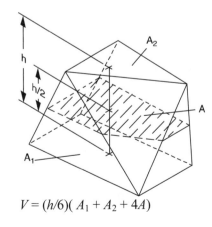

$$V = (h/6)(A_1 + A_2 + 4A)$$

Right Circular Cone

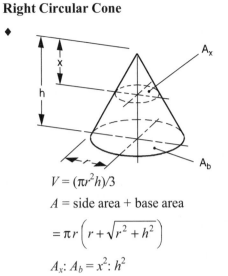

$$V = (\pi r^2 h)/3$$

$$A = \text{side area} + \text{base area}$$

$$= \pi r\left(r + \sqrt{r^2 + h^2}\right)$$

$$A_x : A_b = x^2 : h^2$$

Right Circular Cylinder

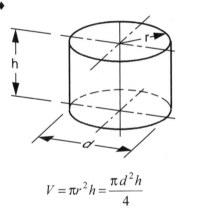

$$V = \pi r^2 h = \frac{\pi d^2 h}{4}$$

$$A = \text{side area} + \text{end areas} = 2\pi r(h + r)$$

Paraboloid of Revolution

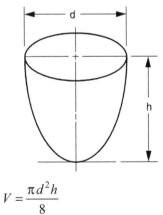

$$V = \frac{\pi d^2 h}{8}$$

♦ Gieck, K. & R. Gieck, *Engineering Formulas*, 6th Ed., Copyright 8 1967 by Gieck Publishing. Diagrams reprinted by permission of Kurt Gieck.

CENTROIDS AND MOMENTS OF INERTIA

The *location of the centroid of an area*, bounded by the axes and the function $y = f(x)$, can be found by integration.

$$x_c = \frac{\int x\,dA}{A}$$

$$y_c = \frac{\int y\,dA}{A}$$

$$A = \int f(x)\,dx$$

$$dA = f(x)\,dx = g(y)\,dy$$

The *first moment of area* with respect to the y-axis and the x-axis, respectively, are:

$$M_y = \int x\,dA = x_c\,A$$

$$M_x = \int y\,dA = y_c\,A$$

when either $\bar{x}$ or $\bar{y}$ is of finite dimensions then $\int x\,dA$ or $\int y\,dA$ refer to the centroid x or y of dA in these integrals. The *moment of inertia* (*second moment of area*) with respect to the y-axis and the x-axis, respectively, are:

$$I_y = \int x^2\,dA$$

$$I_x = \int y^2\,dA$$

The moment of inertia taken with respect to an axis passing through the area's centroid is the *centroidal moment of inertia*. The *parallel axis theorem* for the moment of inertia with respect to another axis parallel with and located d units from the centroidal axis is expressed by

$$I_{\text{parallel axis}} = I_c + Ad^2$$

In a plane, $J = \int r^2\,dA = I_x + I_y$

Values for standard shapes are presented in a table in the **DYNAMICS** section.

DIFFERENTIAL EQUATIONS

A common class of ordinary linear differential equations is

$$b_n \frac{d^n y(x)}{dx^n} + \ldots + b_1 \frac{dy(x)}{dx} + b_0 y(x) = f(x)$$

where $b_n, \ldots, b_i, \ldots, b_1, b_0$ are constants.

When the equation is a homogeneous differential equation, $f(x) = 0$, the solution is

$$y_h(x) = C_1 e^{r_1 x} + C_2 e^{r_2 x} + \ldots + C_i e^{r_i x} + \ldots + C_n e^{r_n x}$$

where r_n is the nth distinct root of the characteristic polynomial $P(x)$ with

$$P(r) = b_n r^n + b_{n-1} r^{n-1} + \ldots + b_1 r + b_0$$

If the root $r_1 = r_2$, then $C_2 e^{r_2 x}$ is replaced with $C_2 x e^{r_1 x}$.

Higher orders of multiplicity imply higher powers of x. The complete solution for the differential equation is

$$y(x) = y_h(x) + y_p(x),$$

where $y_p(x)$ is any solution with $f(x)$ present. If $f(x)$ has $e^{r_n x}$ terms, then resonance is manifested. Furthermore, specific $f(x)$ forms result in specific $y_p(x)$ forms, some of which are:

$f(x)$	$y_p^{(x)}$
A	B
$Ae^{\alpha x}$	$Be^{\alpha x}, \ \alpha \neq r_n$
$A_1 \sin \omega x + A_2 \cos \omega x$	$B_1 \sin \omega x + B_2 \cos \omega x$

If the independent variable is time t, then transient dynamic solutions are implied.

First-Order Linear Homogeneous Differential Equations With Constant Coefficients

$y' + ay = 0$, where a is a real constant:

Solution, $y = Ce^{-at}$

where C = a constant that satisfies the initial conditions.

First-Order Linear Nonhomogeneous Differential Equations

$$\tau \frac{dy}{dt} + y = Kx(t) \qquad x(t) = \begin{cases} A & t < 0 \\ B & t > 0 \end{cases}$$

$$y(0) = KA$$

τ is the time constant

K is the gain

The solution is

$$y(t) = KA + (KB - KA)\left(1 - \exp\left(\frac{-t}{\tau}\right)\right) \quad \text{or}$$

$$\frac{t}{\tau} = \ln\left[\frac{KB - KA}{KB - y}\right]$$

Second-Order Linear Homogeneous Differential Equations with Constant Coefficients

An equation of the form

$$y'' + 2ay' + by = 0$$

can be solved by the method of undetermined coefficients where a solution of the form $y = Ce^{rx}$ is sought. Substitution of this solution gives

$$(r^2 + 2ar + b)\,Ce^{rx} = 0$$

and since Ce^{rx} cannot be zero, the characteristic equation must vanish or

$$r^2 + 2ar + b = 0$$

The roots of the characteristic equation are

$$r_{1,2} = -a \pm \sqrt{a^2 - b}$$

and can be real and distinct for $a^2 > b$, real and equal for $a^2 = b$, and complex for $a^2 < b$.

If $a^2 > b$, the solution is of the form (overdamped)

$$y = C_1 e^{r_1 x} + C_2 e^{r_2 x}$$

If $a^2 = b$, the solution is of the form (critically damped)

$$y = (C_1 + C_2 x)e^{r_1 x}$$

If $a^2 < b$, the solution is of the form (underdamped)

$$y = e^{\alpha x}(C_1 \cos \beta x + C_2 \sin \beta x), \text{ where}$$

$$\alpha = -a$$

$$\beta = \sqrt{b - a^2}$$

FOURIER SERIES

Every periodic function $f(t)$ which has the period $T = 2\pi / \omega_0$ and has certain continuity conditions can be represented by a series plus a constant

$$f(t) = a_0 / 2 + \sum_{n=1}^{\infty} \left[a_n \cos(n\omega_0 t) + b_n \sin(n\omega_0 t) \right]$$

The above holds if $f(t)$ has a continuous derivative $f'(t)$ for all t. It should be noted that the various sinusoids present in the series are orthogonal on the interval 0 to T and as a result the coefficients are given by

$$a_n = (2/T) \int_0^T f(t) \cos(n\omega_0 T) dt \quad n = 0, 1, 2, \ldots$$

$$b_n = (2/T) \int_0^T f(t) \sin(n\omega_0 T) dt \quad n = 1, 2, \ldots$$

The constants a_n and b_n are the *Fourier coefficients* of $f(t)$ for the interval 0 to T and the corresponding series is called the *Fourier series of $f(t)$* over the same interval. The integrals have the same value when evaluated over any interval of length T.

If a Fourier series representing a periodic function is truncated after term $n = N$ the mean square value F_N^2 of the truncated series is given by the Parseval relation. This relation says that the mean-square value is the sum of the mean-square values of the Fourier components, or

$$F_N^2 = (a_0 / 2)^2 + (1/2) \sum_{n=1}^{N} \left(a_n^2 + b_n^2 \right)$$

and the RMS value is then defined to be the square root of this quantity or F_N.

FOURIER TRANSFORM

The Fourier transform pair, one form of which is

$$F(\omega) = \int_{-\infty}^{\infty} f(t) e^{-j\omega t} dt$$

$$f(t) = [1/(2\pi)] \int_{-\infty}^{\infty} F(\omega) e^{j\omega t} d\omega$$

can be used to characterize a broad class of signal models in terms of their frequency or spectral content. Some useful transform pairs are:

$f(t)$	$F(\omega)$
$\delta(t)$	1
$u(t)$	$\pi \delta(\omega) + 1/j\omega$
$u\left(t + \dfrac{\tau}{2}\right) - u\left(t - \dfrac{\tau}{2}\right) = r_{rect} \dfrac{t}{\tau}$	$\tau \dfrac{\sin(\omega\tau/2)}{\omega\tau/2}$
$e^{j\omega_0 t}$	$2\pi\delta(\omega - \omega_o)$

Some mathematical liberties are required to obtain the second and fourth form. Other Fourier transforms are derivable from the Laplace transform by replacing s with $j\omega$ provided

$$f(t) = 0, t < 0$$

$$\int_0^{\infty} |f(t)| \, dt < \infty$$

LAPLACE TRANSFORMS

The unilateral Laplace transform pair

$$F(s) = \int_0^{\infty} f(t) e^{-st} dt$$

$$f(t) = \frac{1}{2\pi i} \int_{\sigma - i\infty}^{\sigma + i\infty} F(s) e^{st} dt$$

represents a powerful tool for the transient and frequency response of linear time invariant systems. Some useful Laplace transform pairs are [Note: The last two transforms represent the Final Value Theorem (F.V.T.) and Initial Value Theorem (I.V.T.) respectively. It is assumed that the limits exist.]:

$f(t)$	$F(s)$
$\delta(t)$, Impulse at $t = 0$	1
$u(t)$, Step at $t = 0$	$1/s$
$t[u(t)]$, Ramp at $t = 0$	$1/s^2$
$e^{-\alpha t}$	$1/(s + \alpha)$
$te^{-\alpha t}$	$1/(s + \alpha)^2$
$e^{-\alpha t} \sin \beta t$	$\beta/[(s + \alpha)^2 + \beta^2]$
$e^{-\alpha t} \cos \beta t$	$(s + \alpha)/[(s + \alpha)^2 + \beta^2]$
$\dfrac{d^n f(t)}{dt^n}$	$s^n F(s) - \displaystyle\sum_{m=0}^{n-1} s^{n-m-1} \dfrac{d^m f(0)}{d^m t}$
$\int_0^t f(\tau) d\tau$	$(1/s)F(s)$
$\int_0^t x(t - \tau)h(t) d\tau$	$H(s)X(s)$
$f(t - \tau)$	$e^{-\tau s}F(s)$
$\displaystyle\lim_{t \to \infty} f(t)$	$\displaystyle\lim_{s \to 0} sF(s)$
$\displaystyle\lim_{t \to 0} f(t)$	$\displaystyle\lim_{s \to \infty} sF(s)$

DIFFERENCE EQUATIONS

Difference equations are used to model discrete systems. Systems which can be described by difference equations include computer program variables iteratively evaluated in a loop, sequential circuits, cash flows, recursive processes, systems with time-delay components, etc. Any system whose input $v(t)$ and output $y(t)$ are defined only at the equally spaced intervals $t = kT$ can be described by a difference equation.

First-Order Linear Difference Equation

The difference equation

$$P_k = P_{k-1}(1 + i) - A$$

represents the balance P of a loan after the kth payment A. If P_k is defined as $y(k)$, the model becomes

$$y(k) - (1 + i)\,y(k - 1) = -A$$

Second-Order Linear Difference Equation

The Fibonacci number sequence can be generated by

$$y(k) = y(k - 1) + y(k - 2)$$

where $y(-1) = 1$ and $y(-2) = 1$. An alternate form for this model is $f(k + 2) = f(k + 1) + f(k)$

with $f(0) = 1$ and $f(1) = 1$.

z-Transforms

The transform definition is

$$F(z) = \sum_{k=0}^{\infty} f(k) z^{-k}$$

The inverse transform is given by the contour integral

$$f(k) = \frac{1}{2\pi i} \oint_{\Gamma} F(z) z^{k-1} dz$$

and it represents a powerful tool for solving linear shift invariant difference equations. A limited unilateral list of z-transform pairs follows [Note: The last two transform pairs represent the Initial Value Theorem (I.V.T.) and the Final Value Theorem (F.V.T.) respectively.]:

$f(k)$	$F(z)$
$\delta(k)$, Impulse at $k = 0$	1
$u(k)$, Step at $k = 0$	$1/(1 - z^{-1})$
β^k	$1/(1 - \beta z^{-1})$
$y(k - 1)$	$z^{-1} Y(z) + y(-1)$
$y(k - 2)$	$z^{-2} Y(z) + y(-2) + y(-1) z^{-1}$
$y(k + 1)$	$z Y(z) - z y(0)$
$y(k + 2)$	$z^2 Y(z) - z^2 y(0) - z y(1)$
$\sum_{m=0}^{\infty} X(k - m) h(m)$	$H(z) X(z)$
$\underset{k \to 0}{\text{limit}}\, f(k)$	$\underset{z \to \infty}{\text{limit}}\, F(z)$
$\underset{k \to \infty}{\text{limit}}\, f(k)$	$\underset{z \to 1}{\text{limit}}(1 - z^{-1}) F(z)$

NUMERICAL METHODS

Newton's Method for Root Extraction

Given a function $f(x)$ which has a simple root of $f(x) = 0$ at $x = a$ an important computational task would be to find that root. If $f(x)$ has a continuous first derivative then the $(j + 1)$st estimate of the root is

$$a^{j+1} = a^j - \left. \frac{f(x)}{\dfrac{df(x)}{dx}} \right|_{x=a^j}$$

The initial estimate of the root a^0 must be near enough to the actual root to cause the algorithm to converge to the root.

Newton's Method of Minimization

Given a scalar value function

$$h(\boldsymbol{x}) = h(x_1, x_2, \ldots, x_n)$$

find a vector $\boldsymbol{x}^* \in R_n$ such that

$$h(\boldsymbol{x}^*) \leq h(\boldsymbol{x}) \text{ for all } \boldsymbol{x}$$

Newton's algorithm is

$$\boldsymbol{x}_{K+1} = \boldsymbol{x}_K - \left(\left. \frac{\partial^2 h}{\partial x^2} \right|_{\boldsymbol{x} = \boldsymbol{x}_K} \right)^{-1} \left. \frac{\partial h}{\partial x} \right|_{\boldsymbol{x} = \boldsymbol{x}_K} , \text{ where}$$

$$\frac{\partial h}{\partial x} = \begin{bmatrix} \dfrac{\partial h}{\partial x_1} \\ \dfrac{\partial h}{\partial x_2} \\ \ldots \\ \ldots \\ \dfrac{\partial h}{\partial x_n} \end{bmatrix}$$

and

$$\frac{\partial^2 h}{\partial x^2} = \begin{bmatrix} \dfrac{\partial^2 h}{\partial x_1^2} & \dfrac{\partial^2 h}{\partial x_1 \partial x_2} & \cdots & \cdots & \dfrac{\partial^2 h}{\partial x_1 \partial x_n} \\ \dfrac{\partial^2 h}{\partial x_1 \partial x_2} & \dfrac{\partial^2 h}{\partial x_2^2} & \cdots & \cdots & \dfrac{\partial^2 h}{\partial x_2 \partial x_n} \\ \ldots & \ldots & \ldots & \ldots & \ldots \\ \ldots & \ldots & \ldots & \ldots & \ldots \\ \dfrac{\partial^2 h}{\partial x_1 \partial x_n} & \dfrac{\partial^2 h}{\partial x_2 \partial x_n} & \cdots & \cdots & \dfrac{\partial^2 h}{\partial x_n^2} \end{bmatrix}$$

Numerical Integration

Three of the more common numerical integration algorithms used to evaluate the integral

$$\int_a^b f(x)dx$$

are:

Euler's or Forward Rectangular Rule

$$\int_a^b f(x)dx \approx \Delta x \sum_{k=0}^{n-1} f(a + k\Delta x)$$

Trapezoidal Rule

for $n = 1$

$$\int_a^b f(x)dx \approx \Delta x \left[\frac{f(a) + f(b)}{2} \right]$$

for $n > 1$

$$\int_a^b f(x)dx \approx \frac{\Delta x}{2} \left[f(a) + 2 \sum_{k=1}^{n-1} f(a + k\Delta x) + f(b) \right]$$

Simpson's Rule/Parabolic Rule (*n* must be an even integer)

for $n = 2$

$$\int_a^b f(x)dx \approx \left(\frac{b-a}{6} \right) \left[f(a) + 4f\left(\frac{a+b}{2} \right) + f(b) \right]$$

for n ≥ 4

$$\int_a^b f(x)dx \approx \frac{\Delta x}{3} \left[\begin{array}{c} f(a) + 2 \sum_{k=2,4,6,\ldots}^{n-2} f(a + k\Delta x) \\ + 4 \sum_{k=1,3,5,\ldots}^{n-1} f(a + k\Delta x) + f(b) \end{array} \right]$$

with $\Delta x = (b - a)/n$

n = number of intervals between data points

Numerical Solution of Ordinary Differential Equations

Euler's Approximation

Given a differential equation

$$dx/dt = f(x, t) \text{ with } x(0) = x_o$$

At some general time $k\Delta t$

$$x[(k + 1)\Delta t] \cong x(k\Delta t) + \Delta t \, f[x(k\Delta t), k\Delta t]$$

which can be used with starting condition x_o to solve recursively for $x(\Delta t)$, $x(2\Delta t)$, …, $x(n\Delta t)$.

The method can be extended to *n*th order differential equations by recasting them as *n* first-order equations.

In particular, when $dx/dt = f(x)$

$$x[(k + 1)\Delta t] \cong x(k\Delta t) + \Delta t f[x(k\Delta t)]$$

which can be expressed as the recursive equation

$$x_{k+1} = x_k + \Delta t \, (dx_k / dt)$$

STATICS

FORCE

A *force* is a *vector* quantity. It is defined when its **(1)** magnitude, **(2)** point of application, and **(3)** direction are known.

RESULTANT (TWO DIMENSIONS)

The *resultant*, F, of n forces with components $F_{x,i}$ and $F_{y,i}$ has the magnitude of

$$F = \left[\left(\sum_{i=1}^{n} F_{x,i} \right)^2 + \left(\sum_{i=1}^{n} F_{y,i} \right)^2 \right]^{1/2}$$

The resultant direction with respect to the x-axis using four-quadrant angle functions is

$$\theta = \arctan\left(\sum_{i=1}^{n} F_{y,i} \middle/ \sum_{i=1}^{n} F_{x,i} \right)$$

The vector form of the force is
$$\boldsymbol{F} = F_x \mathbf{i} + F_y \mathbf{j}$$

RESOLUTION OF A FORCE

$F_x = F \cos \theta_x$; $F_y = F \cos \theta_y$; $F_z = F \cos \theta_z$

$\cos \theta_x = F_x/F$; $\cos \theta_y = F_y/F$; $\cos \theta_z = F_z/F$

Separating a force into components (geometry of force is known $R = \sqrt{x^2 + y^2 + z^2}$)

$F_x = (x/R)F$; $\qquad F_y = (y/R)F$; $\qquad F_z = (z/R)F$

MOMENTS (COUPLES)

A system of two forces that are equal in magnitude, opposite in direction, and parallel to each other is called a *couple*.

A *moment* $\boldsymbol{M}$ is defined as the cross product of the *radius vector* distance $\boldsymbol{r}$ and the *force* $\boldsymbol{F}$ from a point to the line of action of the force.

$\boldsymbol{M} = \boldsymbol{r} \times \boldsymbol{F}$; $\qquad M_x = yF_z - zF_y$,

$\qquad\qquad\qquad M_y = zF_x - xF_z$, and

$\qquad\qquad\qquad M_z = xF_y - yF_x$.

SYSTEMS OF FORCES

$\boldsymbol{F} = \Sigma \, \boldsymbol{F}_n$

$\boldsymbol{M} = \Sigma \, (\boldsymbol{r}_n \times \boldsymbol{F}_n)$

Equilibrium Requirements

$\Sigma \, \boldsymbol{F}_n = 0$

$\Sigma \, \boldsymbol{M}_n = 0$

CENTROIDS OF MASSES, AREAS, LENGTHS, AND VOLUMES

Formulas for centroids, moments of inertia, and first moment of areas are presented in the **MATHEMATICS** section for continuous functions. The following discrete formulas are for defined regular masses, areas, lengths, and volumes:

$$\boldsymbol{r}_c = \Sigma \, m_n \boldsymbol{r}_n / \Sigma \, m_n, \text{ where}$$

$m_n = $ the *mass of each particle* making up the system,

$\boldsymbol{r}_n = $ the *radius vector* to each particle from a selected reference point, and

$\boldsymbol{r}_c = $ the *radius vector* to the *center of the total mass* from the selected reference point.

The *moment of area* (M_a) is defined as

$$M_{ay} = \Sigma \, x_n a_n$$
$$M_{ax} = \Sigma \, y_n a_n$$
$$M_{az} = \Sigma \, z_n a_n$$

The *centroid of area* is defined as

$x_{ac} = M_{ay}/A$ $\left.\right]$ with respect to center

$y_{ac} = M_{ax}/A$ $\left.\right\}$ of the coordinate system

$z_{ac} = M_{az}/A$ $\left.\right]$

where $\quad A = \Sigma \, a_n$

The *centroid of a line* is defined as

$x_{lc} = (\Sigma \, x_n l_n)/L$, where $L = \Sigma \, l_n$

$y_{lc} = (\Sigma \, y_n l_n)/L$

$z_{lc} = (\Sigma \, z_n l_n)/L$

The *centroid of volume* is defined as

$x_{vc} = (\Sigma \, x_n v_n)/V$, where $V = \Sigma \, v_n$

$y_{vc} = (\Sigma \, y_n v_n)/V$

$z_{vc} = (\Sigma \, z_n v_n)/V$

MOMENT OF INERTIA

The *moment of inertia*, or the second moment of area, is defined as

$$I_y = \int x^2 \, dA$$
$$I_x = \int y^2 \, dA$$

The *polar moment of inertia* J of an area about a point is equal to the sum of the moments of inertia of the area about any two perpendicular axes in the area and passing through the same point.

$$I_z = J = I_y + I_x = \int (x^2 + y^2) \, dA$$
$$= r_p^2 A, \text{ where}$$

$r_p = $ the *radius of gyration* (see page 23).

Moment of Inertia Transfer Theorem

The moment of inertia of an area about any axis is defined as the moment of inertia of the area about a parallel centroidal axis plus a term equal to the area multiplied by the square of the perpendicular distance d from the centroidal axis to the axis in question.

$$I'_x = I_{x_c} + d_x^2 A$$

$$I'_y = I_{y_c} + d_y^2 A \text{, where}$$

d_x, d_y = distance between the two axes in question,

I_{x_c}, I_{y_c} = the moment of inertia about the centroidal axis, and

I'_x, I'_y = the moment of inertia about the new axis.

Radius of Gyration

The *radius of gyration* r_p, r_x, r_y is the distance from a reference axis at which all of the area can be considered to be concentrated to produce the moment of inertia.

$$r_x = \sqrt{I_x/A}; \quad r_y = \sqrt{I_y/A}; \quad r_p = \sqrt{J/A}$$

Product of Inertia

The *product of inertia* (I_{xy}, etc.) is defined as:

$I_{xy} = \int xy\,dA$, with respect to the *xy*-coordinate system,

$I_{xz} = \int xz\,dA$, with respect to the *xz*-coordinate system, and

$I_{yz} = \int yz\,dA$, with respect to the *yz*-coordinate system.

The *transfer theorem* also applies:

$$I'_{xy} = I_{x_c y_c} + d_x d_y A \text{ for the } xy\text{-coordinate system, etc.}$$

where

d_x = *x*-axis distance between the two axes in question, and

d_y = *y*-axis distance between the two axes in question.

FRICTION

The largest frictional force is called the *limiting friction*. Any further increase in applied forces will cause motion.

$$F = \mu\,N \text{, where}$$

F = friction force,

μ = *coefficient of static friction*, and

N = normal force between surfaces in contact.

SCREW THREAD

For a *screw-jack, square thread*,

$$M = Pr \tan\left(\alpha \pm \phi\right) \text{, where}$$

+ is for screw tightening,

− is for screw loosening,

M = external moment applied to axis of screw,

P = load on jack applied along and on the line of the axis,

r = the mean thread radius,

α = the *pitch angle* of the thread, and

μ = $\tan\phi$ = the appropriate coefficient of friction.

BRAKE-BAND OR BELT FRICTION

$$F_1 = F_2\,e^{\mu\theta} \text{, where}$$

F_1 = force being applied in the direction of impending motion,

F_2 = force applied to resist impending motion,

μ = coefficient of static friction, and

θ = the total *angle of contact* between the surfaces expressed in radians.

STATICALLY DETERMINATE TRUSS

Plane Truss

A plane truss is a rigid framework satisfying the following conditions:

1. The members of the truss lie in the same plane.
2. The members are connected at their ends by frictionless pins.
3. All of the external loads lie in the plane of the truss and are applied at the joints only.
4. The truss reactions and member forces can be determined using the equations of equilibrium.

   $$\Sigma\,F = 0; \Sigma\,M = 0$$

5. A truss is statically indeterminate if the reactions and member forces cannot be solved with the equations of equilibrium.

Plane Truss: Method of Joints

The method consists of solving for the forces in the members by writing the two equilibrium equations for each joint of the truss.

$$\Sigma\,F_V = 0 \text{ and } \Sigma\,F_H = 0 \text{, where}$$

F_H = horizontal forces and member components and

F_V = vertical forces and member components.

Plane Truss: Method of Sections

The method consists of drawing a free-body diagram of a portion of the truss in such a way that the unknown truss member force is exposed as an external force.

CONCURRENT FORCES

A system of forces wherein their lines of action all meet at one point.

Two Dimensions

$$\Sigma\,F_x = 0; \Sigma\,F_y = 0$$

Three Dimensions

$$\Sigma\,F_x = 0; \Sigma\,F_y = 0; \Sigma\,F_z = 0$$

DYNAMICS

KINEMATICS

Vector representation of motion in space: Let $r(t)$ be the position vector of a particle. Then the velocity is

$$v = dr/dt, \text{ where}$$

v = the instantaneous velocity of the particle, (length/time), and

t = time.

The acceleration is

$$a = dv/dt = d^2r/dt^2, \text{ where}$$

a = the instantaneous acceleration of the particle, (length/time/time).

Rectangular Coordinates

$$r = xi + yj + zk$$

$$v = dr/dt = \dot{x}i + \dot{y}j + \dot{z}k$$

$$a = d^2r/dt^2 = \ddot{x}i + \ddot{y}j + \ddot{z}k, \text{ where}$$

$$\dot{x} = dx/dt = v_x, \text{ etc.}$$

$$\ddot{x} = d^2x/dt^2 = a_x, \text{ etc.}$$

Transverse and Radial Components for Planar Problems

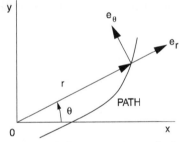

Unit vectors e_r and e_θ are, respectively, colinear with and normal to the position vector.

$$r = re_r$$

$$v = \dot{r}e_r + r\dot{\theta}e_\theta$$

$$a = \left(\ddot{r} - r\dot{\theta}^2\right)e_r + \left(r\ddot{\theta} + 2\dot{r}\dot{\theta}\right)e_\theta, \text{ where}$$

r = the radius,

θ = the angle between the x-axis and r,

$\dot{r} = dr/dt$, etc., and

$\ddot{r} = d^2r/dt^2$, etc.

Normal and Tangential Components

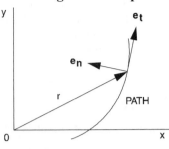

Unit vectors e_n and e_t are, respectively, normal and tangent to the path.

$$v = v_t e_t$$

$$a = (dv_t/dt)\, e_t + (v_t^2/\rho)\, e_n, \text{ where}$$

ρ = instantaneous radius of curvature, and

v_t = tangential velocity.

Plane Circular Motion

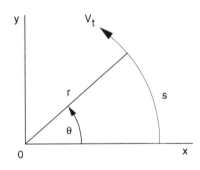

Rotation about the origin with constant radius: The unit vectors are $e_t = e_\theta$ and $e_r = -e_n$.

Angular velocity

$$\omega = \dot{\theta} = v_t/r$$

Angular acceleration

$$\alpha = \dot{\omega} = \ddot{\theta} = a_t/r$$

$$s = r\theta$$

$$v_t = r\omega$$

Tangential acceleration

$$a_t = r\alpha = dv_t/dt$$

Normal acceleration

$$a_n = v_t^2/r = r\omega^2$$

Straight Line Motion

Constant acceleration equations:

$$s = s_0 + v_0 t + (a_0 t^2)/2$$

$$v = v_0 + a_0 t$$

$$v^2 = v_0^2 + 2a_0(s - s_0), \text{ where}$$

s = distance along the line traveled,

s_0 = an initial distance from origin (constant),

v_0 = an initial velocity (constant),

a_0 = a constant acceleration,

t = time, and

v = velocity at time t.

For a free-falling body, $a_0 = g$ (downward)

Using variable velocity, $v(t)$

$$s = s_o + \int_0^t v(t)\, dt$$

Using variable acceleration, $a(t)$

$$v = v_o + \int_0^t a(t)\, dt$$

INSTANTANEOUS CENTER OF ROTATION (INSTANT CENTERS)

An instantaneous center of rotation (instant center) is a point, common to two bodies, at which each has the same velocity (magnitude and direction) at a given instant.

It is also a point on one body about which another body rotates, instantaneously.

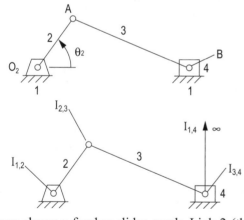

The figure shows a fourbar slider-crank. Link 2 (the crank) rotates about the fixed center, O_2. Link 3 couples the crank to the slider (link 4), which slides against ground (link 1). Using the definition of an instant center (IC), we see that the pins at O_2, A, and B are ICs that are designated $I_{1,2}$, $I_{2,3}$, and $I_{3,4}$. The easily observable IC is $I_{1,4}$, which is located at infinity with its direction perpendicular to the interface between links 1 and 4 (the direction of sliding). To locate the remaining two ICs (for a 4-bar) we must make use of Kennedy's rule.

Kennedy's Rule: When three bodies move relative to one another they have three instantaneous centers, all of which lie on the same straight line.

To apply this rule to the slider-crank mechanism, consider links 1, 2, and 3 whose ICs are $I_{1,2}$, $I_{2,3}$, and $I_{1,3}$, all of which lie on a straight line. Consider also links 1, 3, and 4 whose ICs are $I_{1,3}$, $I_{3,4}$, and $I_{1,4}$, all of which lie on a straight line. Extending the line through $I_{1,2}$ and $I_{2,3}$, and the line through $I_{3,4}$ and $I_{1,4}$ to their intersection locates $I_{1,3}$, which is common to the two groups of links that were considered.

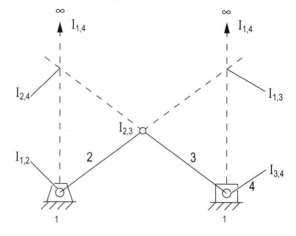

Similarly, if we consider the two groups of three bodies 1, 2, 4 and 2, 3, 4, we extend a line through known ICs $I_{1,2}$ and $I_{1,4}$ to the intersection of a line through known ICs $I_{2,3}$ and $I_{3,4}$, which locates $I_{2,4}$.

The number of ICs, c, for a given mechanism is related to the number of links, n, by

$$c = \frac{n(n-1)}{2}$$

PROJECTILE MOTION

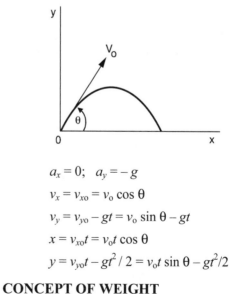

$$a_x = 0; \quad a_y = -g$$

$$v_x = v_{xo} = v_0 \cos\theta$$

$$v_y = v_{yo} - gt = v_0 \sin\theta - gt$$

$$x = v_{xo}t = v_0 t \cos\theta$$

$$y = v_{yo}t - gt^2/2 = v_0 t \sin\theta - gt^2/2$$

CONCEPT OF WEIGHT

$W = mg$, where

W = weight, N (lbf),

m = mass, kg (lbf-sec^2/ft), and

g = local acceleration of gravity, m/sec^2 (ft/sec^2).

KINETICS

Newton's second law for a particle

$\Sigma F = d(mv)/dt$, where

$\Sigma F =$ the sum of the applied forces acting on the particle, N (lbf).

For a constant mass,

$\Sigma F = mdv/dt = ma$

One-Dimensional Motion of Particle

When referring to motion in the x-direction,

$a_x = F_x/m$, where

$F_x =$ the resultant of the applied forces in the x-direction. F_x can depend on t, x and v_x in general.

If F_x depends only on t, then

$$v_x(t) = v_{xo} + \int_0^t [F_x(t')/m] dt'$$

$$x(t) = x_o + v_{xo}t + \int_0^t v_x(t') dt'$$

If the force is constant (independent of time, displacement, or velocity),

$$a_x = F_x/m$$

$$v_x = v_{x0} + (F_x/m)\, t = v_{x0} + a_x t$$

$$x = x_0 + v_{x0}t + F_x t^2/(2m)$$

$$= x_0 + v_{x0}t + a_x t^2/2$$

Normal and Tangential Kinetics for Planar Problems

Working with the normal and tangential directions,

$\Sigma F_t = ma_t = mdv_t/dt$ and

$\Sigma F_n = ma_n = m\,(v_t^2/\rho)$

Impulse and Momentum

Assuming the mass is constant, the equation of motion is

$$mdv_x/dt = F_x$$

$$mdv_x = F_x dt$$

$$m[v_x(t) - v_x(0)] = \int_0^t F_x(t') dt'$$

The left side of the equation represents the change in linear momentum of a body or particle. The right side is termed the impulse of the force $F_x(t')$ between $t' = 0$ and $t' = t$.

Work and Energy

Work W is defined as

$$W = \int \boldsymbol{F} \cdot d\boldsymbol{r}$$

(For particle flow, see **FLUID MECHANICS** section.)

Kinetic Energy

The kinetic energy of a particle is the work done by an external agent in accelerating the particle from rest to a velocity v.

$$T = mv^2/2$$

In changing the velocity from v_1 to v_2, the change in kinetic energy is

$$T_2 - T_1 = mv_2^2/2 - mv_1^2/2$$

Potential Energy

The work done by an external agent in the presence of a conservative field is termed the change in potential energy.

Potential Energy in Gravity Field

$U = mgh$, where

$h =$ the elevation above a specified datum.

Elastic Potential Energy

For a linear elastic spring with modulus, stiffness, or spring constant k, the force is

$F_s = k\,x$, where

$x =$ the change in length of the spring from the undeformed length of the spring.

The potential energy stored in the spring when compressed or extended by an amount x is

$$U = k\,x^2/2$$

The change of potential energy in deforming a spring from position x_1 to position x_2 is

$$U_2 - U_1 = k\,x_2^2/2 - k\,x_1^2/2$$

Principle of Work and Energy

If T_i and U_i are kinetic energy and potential energy at state i, then for conservative systems (no energy dissipation), the law of conservation of energy is

$$U_1 + T_1 = U_2 + T_2.$$

If nonconservative forces are present, then the work done by these forces must be accounted for.

$$U_1 + T_1 + W_{1 \to 2} = U_2 + T_2$$

(Care must be exercised during computations to correctly compute the algebraic sign of the work term).

Impact

Momentum is conserved while energy may or may not be conserved. For direct central impact with no external forces

$$m_1 v_1 + m_2 v_2 = m_1 v_1' + m_2 v_2', \text{ where}$$

$m_1, m_2 =$ the masses of the two bodies,

$v_1, v_2 =$ their velocities before impact, and

$v_1', v_2' =$ their velocities after impact.

For impact with dissipation of energy, the relative velocity expression is

$$e = \frac{v_{2_n}' - v_{1_n}'}{v_{1_n} - v_{2_n}} \text{, where}$$

e = the coefficient of restitution for the materials, and the subscript n denotes the components normal to the plane of impact.

Knowing e, the velocities after rebound are

$$v_{1_n}' = \frac{m_2 v_{2_n}(1+e) + (m_1 - em_2)v_{1_n}}{m_1 + m_2}$$

$$v_{2_n}' = \frac{m_1 v_{1_n}(1+e) - (em_1 - m_2)v_{2_n}}{m_1 + m_2}$$

where $0 \le e \le 1$,

$e = 1$, perfectly elastic, and

$e = 0$, perfectly plastic (no rebound).

FRICTION

The Laws of Friction are

1. The total friction force F that can be developed is independent of the magnitude of the area of contact.

2. The total friction force F that can be developed is proportional to the normal force N.

3. For low velocities of sliding, the total friction force that can be developed is practically independent of the velocity, although experiments show that the force F necessary to start sliding is greater than that necessary to maintain sliding.

The formula expressing the laws of friction is

$$F = \mu N \text{, where}$$

μ = the coefficient of friction.

Static friction will be less than or equal to $\mu_s N$, where μ_s is the coefficient of static friction. At the point of impending motion,

$$F = \mu_s N$$

When motion is present

$$F = \mu_k N \text{, where}$$

μ_k = the coefficient of kinetic friction. The value of μ_k is often taken to be 75% of μ_s.

Belt friction is discussed in the **STATICS** section.

MASS MOMENT OF INERTIA

$$I_z = \int (x^2 + y^2)\, dm$$

A table listing moment of inertia formulas is available at the end of this section for some standard shapes.

Parallel Axis Theorem

$$I_z = I_{zc} + md^2 \text{, where}$$

I_z = the mass moment of inertia about a specific axis (in this case, the z-axis),

I_{zc} = the mass moment of inertia about the body's mass center (in this case, parallel to the z-axis),

m = the mass of the body, and

d = the normal distance from the mass center to the specific desired axis (in this case, the z-axis).

Also,

$$I_z = mr_z^2 \text{, where}$$

m = the total mass of the body, and

r_z = the radius of gyration (in this case, about the z-axis).

PLANE MOTION OF A RIGID BODY

For a rigid body in plane motion in the x-y plane

$$\begin{aligned}
\Sigma F_x &= ma_{xc} \\
\Sigma F_y &= ma_{yc} \\
\Sigma M_{zc} &= I_{zc}\alpha \text{, where}
\end{aligned}$$

c = the center of gravity, and

α = angular acceleration of the body.

Rotation About a Fixed Axis

$$\Sigma M_O = I_O \alpha \text{, where}$$

O denotes the axis about which rotation occurs.

For rotation about a fixed axis caused by a constant applied moment M

$$\begin{aligned}
\alpha &= M/I \\
\omega &= \omega_O + (M/I)\, t \\
\theta &= \theta_O + \omega_O t + (M/2I)\, t^2
\end{aligned}$$

The change in kinetic energy of rotation is the work done in accelerating the rigid body from ω_O to ω.

$$I_O \omega^2/2 - I_O \omega_O^2/2 = \int_{\theta_o}^{\theta} M d\theta$$

Kinetic Energy

The kinetic energy of a body in plane motion is

$$T = m\left(v_{xc}^2 + v_{yc}^2\right)/2 + I_c \omega^2/2$$

CENTRIFUGAL FORCE

For a rigid body (of mass m) rotating about a fixed axis, the centrifugal force of the body at the point of rotation is

$$F_c = mr\omega^2 = mv^2/r \text{, where}$$

r = the distance from the center of rotation to the center of the mass of the body.

BANKING OF CURVES (WITHOUT FRICTION)

$\tan\theta = v^2/(gr)$, where

θ = the angle between the roadway surface and the horizontal,

v = the velocity of the vehicle, and

r = the radius of the curve.

FREE VIBRATION

POSITION OF STATIC EQUILIBRIUM

The equation of motion is

$$m\ddot{x} = mg - k\left(x + \delta_{st}\right)$$

From static equilibrium

$$mg = k\delta_{st},$$

where

k = the spring constant, and

δ_{st} = the static deflection of the spring supporting the weight (mg).

The above equation of motion may now be rewritten as

$$m\ddot{x} + kx = 0, \quad \text{or}$$
$$\ddot{x} + \left(k/m\right)x = 0.$$

The solution to this differential equation is

$$x(t) = C_1 \cos\sqrt{(k/m)}\,t + C_2 \sin\sqrt{(k/m)}\,t, \text{ where}$$

$x(t)$ = the displacement in the x-direction, and

C_1, C_2 = constants of integration whose values depend on the initial conditions of the problem.

The quantity $\sqrt{k/m}$ is called the undamped natural frequency ω_n or $\omega_n = \sqrt{k/m}$

From the static deflection relation

$$\omega_n = \sqrt{g/\delta_{st}}$$

The period of vibration is

$$\tau = 2\pi/\omega_n = 2\pi\sqrt{m/k} = 2\pi\sqrt{\delta_{st}/g}$$

If the initial conditions are $x(0) = x_0$ and $\dot{x}(0) = v_0$, then

$$x(t) = x_0 \cos\omega_n t + (v_0/\omega_n)\sin\omega_n t$$

If the initial conditions are $x(0) = x_0$ and $\dot{x}(0) = 0$, then

$$x(t) = x_0 \cos\omega_n t,$$

which is the equation for simple harmonic motion where the amplitude of vibration is x_0.

Torsional Free Vibration

$$\ddot{\theta} + \omega_n^2\theta = 0, \text{ where}$$

$\omega_n = \sqrt{k_t/I} = \sqrt{GJ/IL}$,

k_t = the torsional spring constant = GJ/L,

I = the mass moment of inertia of the body,

G = the shear modulus,

J = the area polar moment of inertia of the round shaft cross section, and

L = the length of the round shaft.

The solution to the equation of motion is

$$\theta = \theta_0\cos\omega_n t + \left(\dot{\theta}_0/\omega_n\right)\sin\omega_n t, \text{ where}$$

θ_0 = the initial angle of rotation and

$\dot{\theta}_0$ = the initial angular velocity.

The undamped circular natural frequency of torsional vibration is

$$\omega_n = \sqrt{GJ/IL}$$

The period of torsional vibration is

$$\tau = 2\pi/\omega_n = 2\pi\sqrt{IL/GJ}$$

• Timoshenko, S. and D.H. Young, *Engineering Mechanics*, Copyright © 1951 by McGraw-Hill Company, Inc. Diagrams reproduction permission pending.

Figure	Area & Centroid	Area Moment of Inertia	(Radius of Gyration)²	Product of Inertia
	$A = bh/2$ $x_c = 2b/3$ $y_c = h/3$	$I_{x_c} = bh^3/36$ $I_{y_c} = b^3h/36$ $I_x = bh^3/12$ $I_y = b^3h/4$	$r^2_{x_c} = h^2/18$ $r^2_{y_c} = b^2/18$ $r^2_x = h^2/6$ $r^2_y = b^2/2$	$I_{x_c y_c} = Abh/36 = b^2h^2/72$ $I_{xy} = Abh/4 = b^2h^2/8$
	$A = bh/2$ $x_c = b/3$ $y_c = h/3$	$I_{x_c} = bh^3/36$ $I_{y_c} = b^3h/36$ $I_x = bh^3/12$ $I_y = b^3h/12$	$r^2_{x_c} = h^2/18$ $r^2_{y_c} = b^2/18$ $r^2_x = h^2/6$ $r^2_y = b^2/6$	$I_{x_c y_c} = -Abh/36 = -b^2h^2/72$ $I_{xy} = Abh/12 = b^2h^2/24$
	$A = bh/2$ $x_c = (a+b)/3$ $y_c = h/3$	$I_{x_c} = bh^3/36$ $I_{y_c} = \left[bh(b^2 - ab + a^2)\right]/36$ $I_x = bh^3/12$ $I_y = \left[bh(b^2 + ab + a^2)\right]/12$	$r^2_{x_c} = h^2/18$ $r^2_{y_c} = (b^2 - ab + a^2)/18$ $r^2_x = h^2/6$ $r^2_y = (b^2 + ab + a^2)/6$	$I_{x_c y_c} = \left[Ah(2a - b)\right]/36 = \left[bh^2(2a - b)\right]/72$ $I_{xy} = \left[Ah(2a + b)\right]/12 = \left[bh^2(2a + b)\right]/24$
	$A = bh$ $x_c = b/2$ $y_c = h/2$	$I_{x_c} = bh^3/12$ $I_{y_c} = b^3h/12$ $I_x = bh^3/3$ $I_y = b^3h/3$ $J = \left[bh(b^2 + h^2)\right]/12$	$r^2_{x_c} = h^2/12$ $r^2_{y_c} = b^2/12$ $r^2_x = h^2/3$ $r^2_y = b^2/3$ $r^2_p = (b^2 + h^2)/12$	$I_{x_c y_c} = 0$ $I_{xy} = Abh/4 = b^2h^2/4$
	$A = h(a+b)/2$ $y_c = \dfrac{h(2a+b)}{3(a+b)}$	$I_{x_c} = \dfrac{h^3(a^2 + 4ab + b^2)}{36(a+b)}$ $I_x = \dfrac{h^3(3a+b)}{12}$	$r^2_{x_c} = \dfrac{h^2(a^2 + 4ab + b^2)}{18(a+b)}$ $r^2_x = \dfrac{h^2(3a+b)}{6(a+b)}$	
	$A = ab\sin\theta$ $x_c = (b + a\cos\theta)/2$ $y_c = (a\sin\theta)/2$	$I_{x_c} = (a^3 b\sin^3\theta)/12$ $I_{y_c} = \left[ab\sin\theta(b^2 + a^2\cos^2\theta)\right]/12$ $I_x = (a^3 b\sin^3\theta)/3$ $I_y = \left[ab\sin\theta(b + a\cos\theta)^2\right]/3$ $\quad - (a^2 b^2 \sin\theta\cos\theta)/6$	$r^2_{x_c} = (a\sin\theta)^2/12$ $r^2_{y_c} = (b^2 + a^2\cos^2\theta)/12$ $r^2_x = (a\sin\theta)^2/3$ $r^2_y = (b + a\cos\theta)^2/3$ $\quad - (ab\cos\theta)/6$	$I_{x_c y_c} = (a^3 b\sin^2\theta\cos\theta)/12$

Housner, George W. & Donald E. Hudson, *Applied Mechanics Dynamics*, Copyright © 1959 by D. Van Nostrand Company, Inc., Princeton, NJ. Table reprinted by permission of G.W. Housner & D.E. Hudson.

Figure	Area & Centroid	Area Moment of Inertia	(Radius of Gyration)^2	Product of Inertia
	$A = \pi a^2$ $x_c = a$ $y_c = a$	$I_{x_c} = I_{y_c} = \pi a^4/4$ $I_x = I_y = 5\pi a^4/4$ $J = \pi a^4/2$	$r_{x_c}^2 = r_{y_c}^2 = a^2/4$ $r_x^2 = r_y^2 = 5a^2/4$ $r_p^2 = a^2/2$	$I_{x_c y_c} = 0$ $I_{xy} = Aa^2$
	$A = \pi(a^2 - b^2)$ $x_c = a$ $y_c = a$	$I_{x_c} = I_{y_c} = \pi(a^4 - b^4)/4$ $I_x = I_y = \dfrac{5\pi a^4}{4} - \pi a^2 b^2 - \dfrac{\pi b^4}{4}$ $J = \pi(a^4 - b^4)/2$	$r_{x_c}^2 = r_{y_c}^2 = (a^2 + b^2)/4$ $r_x^2 = r_y^2 = (5a^2 + b^2)/4$ $r_p^2 = (a^2 + b^2)/2$	$I_{x_c y_c} = 0$ $I_{xy} = Aa^2$ $\quad = \pi a^2(a^2 - b^2)$
	$A = \pi a^2/2$ $x_c = a$ $y_c = 4a/(3\pi)$	$I_{x_c} = \dfrac{a^4(9\pi^2 - 64)}{72\pi}$ $I_{y_c} = \pi a^4/8$ $I_x = \pi a^4/8$ $I_y = 5\pi a^4/8$	$r_{x_c}^2 = \dfrac{a^2(9\pi^2 - 64)}{36\pi^2}$ $r_{y_c}^2 = a^2/4$ $r_x^2 = a^2/4$ $r_y^2 = 5a^2/4$	$I_{x_c y_c} = 0$ $I_{xy} = 2a^2/3$
 CIRCULAR SECTOR	$A = a^2\theta$ $x_c = \dfrac{2a}{3}\dfrac{\sin\theta}{\theta}$ $y_c = 0$	$I_x = a^4(\theta - \sin\theta\cos\theta)/4$ $I_y = a^4(\theta + \sin\theta\cos\theta)/4$	$r_x^2 = \dfrac{a^2}{4}\dfrac{(\theta - \sin\theta\cos\theta)}{\theta}$ $r_y^2 = \dfrac{a^2}{4}\dfrac{(\theta + \sin\theta\cos\theta)}{\theta}$	$I_{x_c y_c} = 0$ $I_{xy} = 0$
 CIRCULAR SEGMENT	$A = a^2\left(\theta - \dfrac{\sin 2\theta}{2}\right)$ $x_c = \dfrac{2a}{3}\dfrac{\sin^3\theta}{\theta - \sin\theta\cos\theta}$ $y_c = 0$	$I_x = \dfrac{Aa^2}{4}\left[1 - \dfrac{2\sin^3\theta\cos\theta}{3\theta - 3\sin\theta\cos\theta}\right]$ $I_y = \dfrac{Aa^2}{4}\left[1 + \dfrac{2\sin^3\theta\cos\theta}{\theta - \sin\theta\cos\theta}\right]$	$r_x^2 = \dfrac{a^2}{4}\left[1 - \dfrac{2\sin^3\theta\cos\theta}{3\theta - 3\sin\theta\cos\theta}\right]$ $r_y^2 = \dfrac{a^2}{4}\left[1 + \dfrac{2\sin^3\theta\cos\theta}{\theta - \sin\theta\cos\theta}\right]$	$I_{x_c y_c} = 0$ $I_{xy} = 0$

Housner, George W. & Donald E. Hudson, *Applied Mechanics Dynamics*, Copyright © 1959 by D. Van Nostrand Company, Inc., Princeton, NJ. Table reprinted by permission of G.W. Housner & D.E. Hudson.

Figure	Area & Centroid	Area Moment of Inertia	(Radius of Gyration)²	Product of Inertia
PARABOLA	$A = 4ab/3$ $x_c = 3a/5$ $y_c = 0$	$I_{x_c} = I_x = 4ab^3/15$ $I_{y_c} = 16a^3b/175$ $I_y = 4a^3b/7$	$r_{x_c}^2 = r_x^2 = b^2/5$ $r_{y_c}^2 = 12a^2/175$ $r_y^2 = 3a^2/7$	$I_{x_c y_c} = 0$ $I_{xy} = 0$
HALF A PARABOLA	$A = 2ab/3$ $x_c = 3a/5$ $y_c = 3b/8$	$I_x = 2ab^3/15$ $I_y = 2a^3b/7$	$r_x^2 = b^2/5$ $r_y^2 = 3a^2/7$	$I_{xy} = Aab/4 = \ a^2b^2$
$y = (h/b^n)x^n$ n^{th} DEGREE PARABOLA	$A = bh/(n+1)$ $x_c = \dfrac{n+1}{n+2}b$ $y_c = \dfrac{h}{2}\dfrac{n+1}{2n+1}$	$I_x = \dfrac{bh^3}{3(3n+1)}$ $I_y = \dfrac{hb^3}{n+3}$	$r_x^2 = \dfrac{h^2(n+1)}{3(3n+1)}$ $r_y^2 = \dfrac{n+1}{n+3}b^2$	
$y = (h/b^{1/n})x^{1/n}$ n^{th} DEGREE PARABOLA	$A = \dfrac{n}{n+1}bh$ $x_c = \dfrac{n+1}{2n+1}b$ $y_c = \dfrac{n+1}{2(n+2)}h$	$I_x = \dfrac{n}{3(n+3)}bh^3$ $I_y = \dfrac{n}{3n+1}b^3h$	$r_x^2 = \dfrac{n+1}{3(n+3)}h^2$ $r_y^2 = \dfrac{n+1}{3n+1}b^2$	

Housner, George W. & Donald E. Hudson, *Applied Mechanics Dynamics*, Copyright © 1959 by D. Van Nostrand Company, Inc., Princeton, NJ. Table reprinted by permission of G.W. Housner & D.E. Hudson.

Figure	Mass & Centroid	Mass Moment of Inertia	(Radius of Gyration)²	Product of Inertia
	$M = \rho L A$ $x_c = L/2$ $y_c = 0$ $z_c = 0$ A = cross-sectional area of rod ρ = mass/vol.	$I_x = I_{x_c} = 0$ $I_{y_c} = I_{z_c} = ML^2/12$ $I_y = I_z = ML^2/3$	$r_x^2 = r_{x_c}^2 = 0$ $r_{y_c}^2 = r_{z_c}^2 = L^2/12$ $r_y^2 = r_z^2 = L^2/3$	$I_{x_c y_c}$, etc. $= 0$ I_{xy}, etc. $= 0$
	$M = 2\pi R \rho A$ $x_c = R$ = mean radius $y_c = R$ = mean radius $z_c = 0$ A = cross-sectional area of ring ρ = mass/vol.	$I_{x_c} = I_{y_c} = MR^2/2$ $I_{z_c} = MR^2$ $I_x = I_y = 3MR^2/2$ $I_z = 3MR^2$	$r_{x_c}^2 = r_{y_c}^2 = R^2/2$ $r_{z_c}^2 = R^2$ $r_x^2 = r_y^2 = 3R^2/2$ $r_z^2 = 3R^2$	$I_{x_c y_c}$, etc. $= 0$ $I_{z_c z_c} = MR^2$ $I_{xz} = I_{yz} = 0$
	$M = \pi R^2 \rho h$ $x_c = 0$ $y_c = h/2$ $z_c = 0$ ρ = mass/vol.	$I_{x_c} = I_{z_c}$ $= M(3R^2 + h^2)/12$ $I_{y_c} = I_y = MR^2/2$ $I_x = I_z = M(3R^2 + 4h^2)/12$	$r_{x_c}^2 = r_{z_c}^2 = (3R^2 + h^2)/12$ $r_{y_c}^2 = r_y^2 = R^2/2$ $r_x^2 = r_z^2 = (3R^2 + 4h^2)/12$	$I_{x_c y_c}$, etc. $= 0$ I_{xy}, etc. $= 0$
	$M = \pi\left(R_1^2 - R_2^2\right)\rho h$ $x_c = 0$ $y_c = h/2$ $z_c = 0$ ρ = mass/vol.	$I_{x_c} = I_{z_c}$ $= M\left(3R_1^2 + 3R_2^2 + h^2\right)/12$ $I_{y_c} = I_y = M\left(R_1^2 + R_2^2\right)/2$ $I_x = I_z$ $= M\left(3R_1^2 + 3R_2^2 + 4h^2\right)/12$	$r_{x_c}^2 = r_{z_c}^2 = \left(3R_1^2 + 3R_2^2 + h^2\right)/12$ $r_{y_c}^2 = r_y^2 = \left(R_1^2 + R_2^2\right)/2$ $r_x^2 = r_z^2$ $= \left(3R_1^2 + 3R_2^2 + 4h^2\right)/12$	$I_{x_c y_c}$, etc. $= 0$ I_{xy}, etc. $= 0$
	$M = \dfrac{4}{3}\pi R^3 \rho$ $x_c = 0$ $y_c = 0$ $z_c = 0$ ρ = mass/vol.	$I_{x_c} = I_x = 2MR^2/5$ $I_{y_c} = I_y = 2MR^2/5$ $I_{z_c} = I_z = 2MR^2/5$	$r_{x_c}^2 = r_x^2 = 2R^2/5$ $r_{y_c}^2 = r_y^2 = 2R^2/5$ $r_{z_c}^2 = r_z^2 = 2R^2/5$	$I_{x_c y_c}$, etc. $= 0$

Housner, George W. & Donald E. Hudson. *Applied Mechanics Dynamics*, Copyright © 1959 by D. Van Nostrand Company, Inc., Princeton, NJ. Table reprinted by permission of G.W. Housner & D.E. Hudson.

MECHANICS OF MATERIALS

UNIAXIAL STRESS-STRAIN

Stress-Strain Curve for Mild Steel

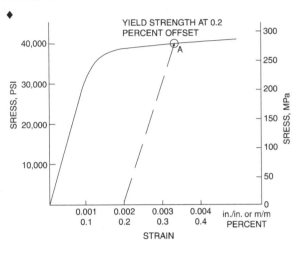

The slope of the linear portion of the curve equals the modulus of elasticity.

Engineering Strain

$$\varepsilon = \Delta L / L_0, \text{ where}$$

ε = engineering strain (units per unit),

ΔL = change in length (units) of member,

L_0 = original length (units) of member,

ε_{pl} = plastic deformation (permanent), and

ε_{el} = elastic deformation (recoverable).

Equilibrium requirements: $\Sigma F = 0$; $\Sigma M = 0$

Determine geometric compatibility with the restraints. Use a linear force-deformation relationship;

$$F = k\delta.$$

DEFINITIONS

Shear Stress-Strain

$$\gamma = \tau/G, \text{ where}$$

γ = shear strain,

τ = shear stress, and

G = *shear modulus* (constant in linear force-deformation relationship).

$$G = \frac{E}{2(1+\nu)}, \text{ where}$$

E = modulus of elasticity

ν = *Poisson's ratio*, and

  = – (lateral strain)/(longitudinal strain).

Uniaxial Loading and Deformation

$$\sigma = P/A, \text{ where}$$

σ = stress on the cross section,

P = loading, and

A = cross-sectional area.

$$\varepsilon = \delta/L, \text{ where}$$

δ = longitudinal deformation and

L = length of member.

$$E = \sigma/\varepsilon = \frac{P/A}{\delta/L}$$

$$\delta = \frac{PL}{AE}$$

THERMAL DEFORMATIONS

$$\delta_t = \alpha L (T - T_o), \text{ where}$$

δ_t = deformation caused by a change in temperature,

α = temperature coefficient of expansion,

L = length of member,

T = final temperature, and

T_o = initial temperature.

CYLINDRICAL PRESSURE VESSEL

Cylindrical Pressure Vessel

For internal pressure only, the stresses at the inside wall are:

$$\sigma_t = P_i \frac{r_o^2 + r_i^2}{r_o^2 - r_i^2} \quad \text{and} \quad 0 > \sigma_r > -P_i$$

For external pressure only, the stresses at the outside wall are:

$$\sigma_t = -P_o \frac{r_o^2 + r_i^2}{r_o^2 - r_i^2} \quad \text{and} \quad 0 > \sigma_r > -P_o, \text{ where}$$

σ_t = tangential (hoop) stress,

σ_r = radial stress,

P_i = internal pressure,

P_o = external pressure,

r_i = inside radius, and

r_o = outside radius.

For vessels with end caps, the axial stress is:

$$\sigma_a = P_i \frac{r_i^2}{r_o^2 - r_i^2}$$

These are principal stresses.

When the thickness of the cylinder wall is about one-tenth or less, of inside radius, the cylinder can be considered as thin-walled. In which case, the internal pressure is resisted by the hoop stress and the axial stress.

$$\sigma_t = \frac{P_i r}{t} \quad \text{and} \quad \sigma_a = \frac{P_i r}{2t}$$

where t = wall thickness.

♦Flinn, Richard A. & Paul K. Trojan, *Engineering Materials & Their Applications*, 4th Ed. Copyright © 1990 by Houghton Mifflin Co. Figure used with permission.

STRESS AND STRAIN

Principal Stresses

For the special case of a *two-dimensional* stress state, the equations for principal stress reduce to

$$\sigma_a, \sigma_b = \frac{\sigma_x + \sigma_y}{2} \pm \sqrt{\left(\frac{\sigma_x - \sigma_y}{2}\right)^2 + \tau_{xy}^2}$$

$$\sigma_c = 0$$

The two nonzero values calculated from this equation are temporarily labeled σ_a and σ_b and the third value σ_c is always zero in this case. Depending on their values, the three roots are then labeled according to the convention: *algebraically largest* = σ_1, *algebraically smallest* = σ_3, *other* = σ_2. A typical 2D stress element is shown below with all indicated components shown in their positive sense.

Mohr's Circle – Stress, 2D

To construct a Mohr's circle, the following sign conventions are used.

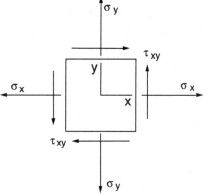

1. Tensile normal stress components are plotted on the horizontal axis and are considered positive. Compressive normal stress components are negative.

2. For constructing Mohr's circle only, shearing stresses are plotted above the normal stress axis when the pair of shearing stresses, acting on opposite and parallel faces of an element, forms a clockwise couple. Shearing stresses are plotted below the normal axis when the shear stresses form a counterclockwise couple.

   The circle drawn with the center on the normal stress (horizontal) axis with center, C, and radius, *R,* where

$$C = \frac{\sigma_x + \sigma_y}{2}, \quad R = \sqrt{\left(\frac{\sigma_x - \sigma_y}{2}\right)^2 + \tau_{xy}^2}$$

The two nonzero principal stresses are then:

$$\sigma_a = C + R$$
$$\sigma_b = C - R$$

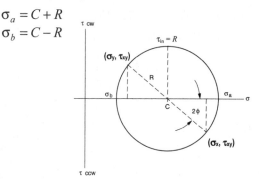

The maximum *inplane* shear stress is $\tau_{in} = R$. However, the maximum shear stress considering three dimensions is always

$$\tau_{max} = \frac{\sigma_1 - \sigma_3}{2}.$$

Hooke's Law

Three-dimensional case:

$$\varepsilon_x = (1/E)[\sigma_x - v(\sigma_y + \sigma_z)] \qquad \gamma_{xy} = \tau_{xy}/G$$
$$\varepsilon_y = (1/E)[\sigma_y - v(\sigma_z + \sigma_x)] \qquad \gamma_{yz} = \tau_{yz}/G$$
$$\varepsilon_z = (1/E)[\sigma_z - v(\sigma_x + \sigma_y)] \qquad \gamma_{zx} = \tau_{zx}/G$$

Plane stress case ($\sigma_z = 0$):

$$\varepsilon_x = (1/E)(\sigma_x - v\sigma_y)$$
$$\varepsilon_y = (1/E)(\sigma_y - v\sigma_x)$$
$$\varepsilon_z = -(1/E)(v\sigma_x + v\sigma_y)$$

$$\begin{Bmatrix} \sigma_x \\ \sigma_y \\ \tau_{xy} \end{Bmatrix} = \frac{E}{1-v^2} \begin{bmatrix} 1 & v & 0 \\ v & 1 & 0 \\ 0 & 0 & \frac{1-v}{2} \end{bmatrix} \begin{Bmatrix} \varepsilon_x \\ \varepsilon_y \\ \gamma_{xy} \end{Bmatrix}$$

Uniaxial case ($\sigma_y = \sigma_z = 0$): $\qquad \sigma_x = E\varepsilon_x$ or $\sigma = E\varepsilon$, where

$\varepsilon_x, \varepsilon_y, \varepsilon_z$ = normal strain,

$\sigma_x, \sigma_y, \sigma_z$ = normal stress,

$\gamma_{xy}, \gamma_{yz}, \gamma_{zx}$ = shear strain,

$\tau_{xy}, \tau_{yz}, \tau_{zx}$ = shear stress,

E = modulus of elasticity,

G = shear modulus, and

v = Poisson's ratio.

STATIC LOADING FAILURE THEORIES

Maximum-Normal-Stress Theory

The maximum-normal-stress theory states that failure occurs when one of the three principal stresses equals the strength of the material. If $\sigma_1 > \sigma_2 > \sigma_3$, then the theory predicts that failure occurs whenever $\sigma_1 \geq S_t$ or $\sigma_3 \leq -S_c$ where S_t and S_c are the tensile and compressive strengths, respectively.

Maximum-Shear-Stress Theory

The maximum-shear-stress theory states that yielding begins when the maximum shear stress equals the maximum shear stress in a tension-test specimen of the same material when that specimen begins to yield. If $\sigma_1 \geq \sigma_2 \geq \sigma_3$, then the theory predicts that yielding will occur whenever $\tau_{max} \geq S_y/2$ where S_y is the yield strength.

Distortion-Energy Theory

The distortion-energy theory states that yielding begins whenever the distortion energy in a unit volume equals the distortion energy in the same volume when uniaxially stressed to the yield strength. The theory predicts that yielding will occur whenever

$$\left[\frac{(\sigma_1-\sigma_2)^2+(\sigma_2-\sigma_3)^2+(\sigma_1-\sigma_3)^2}{2}\right]^{1/2} \geq S_y$$

TORSION

Torsion stress in circular solid or thick-walled (t > 0.1 r) shafts:

$$T=\frac{Tr}{J}$$

*where: J = polar moment of inertia (see table at end of **DYNAMICS** section).*

TORSIONAL STRAIN

$$\gamma_{\phi z} = \lim_{\Delta z \to 0} r(\Delta\phi/\Delta z) = r(d\phi/dz)$$

The shear strain varies in direct proportion to the radius, from zero strain at the center to the greatest strain at the outside of the shaft. $d\phi/dz$ is the twist per unit length or the rate of twist.

$$\tau_{\phi z} = G\,\gamma_{\phi z} = Gr\,(d\phi/dz)$$

$$T = G\,(d\phi/dz)\int_A r^2 dA = GJ(d\phi/dz)$$

$$\phi = \int_o^L \frac{T}{GJ}\,dz = \frac{TL}{GJ}, \text{ where}$$

ϕ = total angle (radians) of twist,

T = torque, and

L = length of shaft.

T/ϕ gives the *twisting moment per radian of twist*. This is called the *torsional stiffness* and is often denoted by the symbol k or c.

For Hollow, Thin-Walled Shafts

$$\tau = \frac{T}{2A_m t}, \text{ where}$$

t = thickness of shaft wall and

A_m = the total mean area enclosed by the shaft measured to the midpoint of the wall.

BEAMS

Shearing Force and Bending Moment Sign Conventions

1. The bending moment is *positive* if it produces bending of the beam *concave upward* (compression in top fibers and tension in bottom fibers).

2. The shearing force is *positive* if the *right portion of the beam tends to shear downward with respect to the left.*

POSITIVE BENDING   NEGATIVE BENDING

POSITIVE SHEAR   NEGATIVE SHEAR

The relationship between the load (q), shear (V), and moment (M) equations are:

$$q(x)=-\frac{dV(x)}{dx}$$

$$V=\frac{dM(x)}{dx}$$

$$V_2-V_1=\int_{x_1}^{x_2}\left[-q(x)\right]dx$$

$$M_2-M_1=\int_{x_1}^{x_2}V(x)\,dx$$

Stresses in Beams

$$\varepsilon_x = -y/\rho, \text{ where}$$

ρ = the radius of curvature of the deflected axis of the beam, and

y = the distance from the neutral axis to the longitudinal fiber in question.

Using the stress-strain relationship $\sigma = E\varepsilon$,

Axial Stress: $\sigma_x = -Ey/\rho$, where

σ_x = the normal stress of the fiber located y-distance from the neutral axis.

$$1/\rho = M/(EI), \text{ where}$$

M = the moment at the section and

I = the *moment of inertia* of the cross-section.

$$\sigma_x = -My/I, \text{ where}$$

y = the distance from the neutral axis to the fiber location above or below the axis. Let $y = c$, where c = distance from the neutral axis to the outermost fiber of a symmetrical beam section.

$$\sigma_x = \pm Mc/I$$

Let $S = I/c$: then, $\sigma_x = \pm M/S$, where

S = the *elastic section modulus* of the beam member.

Transverse shear flow: $q = VQ/I$ and

Transverse shear stress: $\tau_{xy} = VQ/(Ib)$, where

q = shear flow,

τ_{xy} = shear stress on the surface,

V = shear force at the section,

• Timoshenko, S. & Gleason H. MacCullough, *Elements of Strength of Materials*, ©1949 by K. Van Nostrand Co. Used with permission from Wadsworth Publishing Co.

b = width or thickness of the cross-section, and

Q = $A'\bar{y}'$, where

A' = area above the layer (or plane) upon which the desired transverse shear stress acts and

$\bar{y}'$ = distance from neutral axis to area centroid.

Deflection of Beams

Using $1/\rho = M/(EI)$,

$$EI\frac{d^2y}{dx^2} = M, \text{ differential equation of deflection curve}$$

$$EI\frac{d^3y}{dx^3} = dM(x)/dx = V$$

$$EI\frac{d^4y}{dx^4} = dV(x)/dx = -q$$

Determine the deflection curve equation by double integration (apply boundary conditions applicable to the deflection and/or slope).

$$EI\,(dy/dx) = \int M(x)\,dx$$

$$EIy = \int [\int M(x)\,dx]\,dx$$

The constants of integration can be determined from the physical geometry of the beam.

COLUMNS

For long columns with pinned ends:

Euler's Formula

$$P_{cr} = \frac{\pi^2 EI}{\ell^2}, \text{ where}$$

P_{cr} = critical axial loading,

ℓ = unbraced column length.

substitute $I = r^2 A$:

$$\frac{P_{cr}}{A} = \frac{\pi^2 E}{(\ell/r)^2}, \text{ where}$$

r = *radius of gyration* and

ℓ/r = *slenderness ratio* for the column.

For further column design theory, see the **CIVIL ENGINEERING** and **MECHANICAL ENGINEERING** sections.

ELASTIC STRAIN ENERGY

If the strain remains within the elastic limit, the work done during deflection (extension) of a member will be transformed into potential energy and can be recovered.

If the final load is P and the corresponding elongation of a tension member is δ, then the total energy U stored is equal to the work W done during loading.

$$U = W = P\delta/2$$

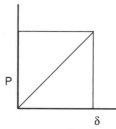

The strain energy per unit volume is

$$u = U/AL = \sigma^2/2E \qquad \text{(for tension)}$$

MATERIAL PROPERTIES

Material	Units	Steel	Aluminum	Cast Iron	Wood (Fir)
Modulus of Elasticity, E	Mpsi	30.0	10.0	14.5	1.6
	GPa	207.0	69.0	100.0	11.0
Modulus of Rigidity, G	Mpsi	11.5	3.8	6.0	0.6
	GPa	80.0	26.0	41.4	4.1
Poisson's Ratio, v		0.30	0.33	0.21	0.33

Beam Deflection Formulas – Special Cases (δ is positive downward)

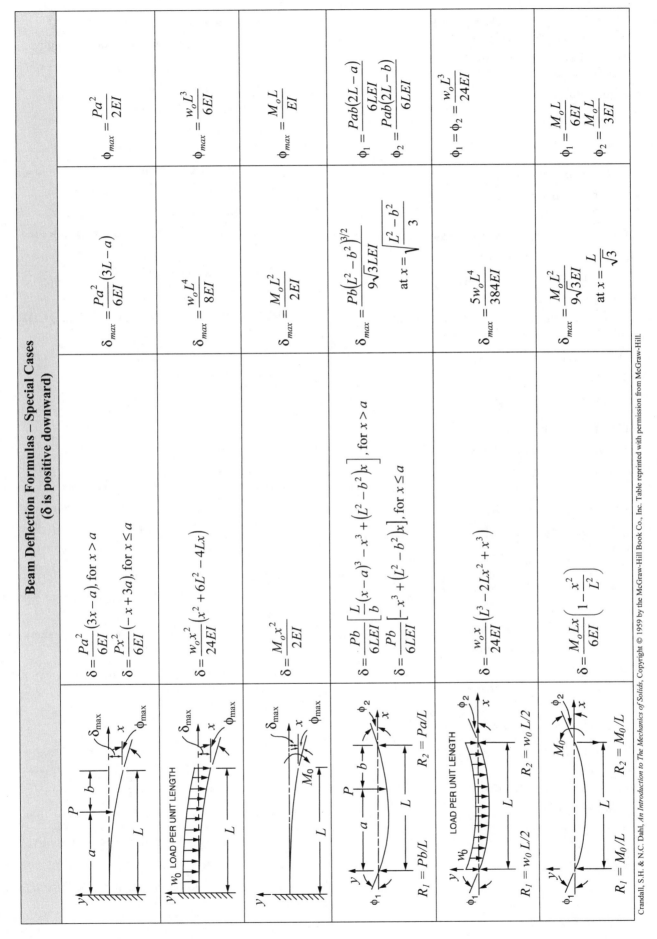

Figure	δ	δ_{max}	ϕ
Cantilever, point load P at a; L	$\delta = \dfrac{Pa^2}{6EI}(3x-a)$, for $x>a$ $\qquad \delta = \dfrac{Px^2}{6EI}(-x+3a)$, for $x\le a$	$\delta_{max} = \dfrac{Pa^2}{6EI}(3L-a)$	$\phi_{max} = \dfrac{Pa^2}{2EI}$
Cantilever, w_0 LOAD PER UNIT LENGTH; L	$\delta = \dfrac{w_o x^2}{24EI}\left(x^2+6L^2-4Lx\right)$	$\delta_{max} = \dfrac{w_o L^4}{8EI}$	$\phi_{max} = \dfrac{w_o L^3}{6EI}$
Cantilever, moment M_0; L	$\delta = \dfrac{M_o x^2}{2EI}$	$\delta_{max} = \dfrac{M_o L^2}{2EI}$	$\phi_{max} = \dfrac{M_o L}{EI}$
Simply supported, point load P; a, b, L; $R_1 = Pb/L$, $R_2 = Pa/L$	$\delta = \dfrac{Pb}{6LEI}\left[\dfrac{L}{b}(x-a)^3 - x^3 + (L^2-b^2)x\right]$, for $x>a$ $\qquad \delta = \dfrac{Pb}{6LEI}\left[-x^3+(L^2-b^2)x\right]$, for $x\le a$	$\delta_{max} = \dfrac{Pb\left(L^2-b^2\right)^{3/2}}{9\sqrt{3}LEI}$ at $x=\sqrt{\dfrac{L^2-b^2}{3}}$	$\phi_1 = \dfrac{Pab(2L-a)}{6LEI}$ $\phi_2 = \dfrac{Pab(2L-b)}{6LEI}$
Simply supported, w_0 LOAD PER UNIT LENGTH; L; $R_1 = w_0 L/2$, $R_2 = w_0 L/2$	$\delta = \dfrac{w_o x}{24EI}\left(L^3 - 2Lx^2 + x^3\right)$	$\delta_{max} = \dfrac{5w_o L^4}{384EI}$	$\phi_1 = \phi_2 = \dfrac{w_o L^3}{24EI}$
Simply supported, moment M_0; L; $R_1 = M_0/L$, $R_2 = M_0/L$	$\delta = \dfrac{M_o Lx}{6EI}\left(1-\dfrac{x^2}{L^2}\right)$	$\delta_{max} = \dfrac{M_o L^2}{9\sqrt{3}EI}$ at $x=\dfrac{L}{\sqrt{3}}$	$\phi_1 = \dfrac{M_o L}{6EI}$ $\phi_2 = \dfrac{M_o L}{3EI}$

Crandall, S.H. & N.C. Dahl, *An Introduction to The Mechanics of Solids*, Copyright © 1959 by the McGraw-Hill Book Co., Inc. Table reprinted with permission from McGraw-Hill.

FLUID MECHANICS

DENSITY, SPECIFIC VOLUME, SPECIFIC WEIGHT, AND SPECIFIC GRAVITY

The definitions of density, specific volume, specific weight, and specific gravity follow:

$$\rho = \lim_{\Delta V \to 0} \Delta m / \Delta V$$

$$\gamma = \lim_{\Delta V \to 0} \Delta W / \Delta V$$

$$\gamma = \lim_{\Delta V \to 0} g \cdot \Delta m / \Delta V = \rho g$$

also $SG = \gamma / \gamma_w = \rho / \rho_w$, where

ρ = *density* (also *mass density*),

Δm = mass of infinitesimal volume,

ΔV = volume of infinitesimal object considered,

γ = *specific weight,*

ΔW = weight of an infinitesimal volume,

SG = *specific gravity*, and

ρ_w = mass density of water at standard conditions = 1,000 kg/m^3 (62.43 lbm/ft^3).

STRESS, PRESSURE, AND VISCOSITY

Stress is defined as

$$\tau(P) = \lim_{\Delta A \to 0} \Delta F / \Delta A, \text{ where}$$

$\tau(P)$ = surface stress vector at point P,

ΔF = force acting on infinitesimal area ΔA, and

ΔA = infinitesimal area at point P.

$$\tau_n = -p$$

$$\tau_t = \mu \, (dv/dy) \quad \text{(one-dimensional; i.e., } y\text{), where}$$

τ_n and τ_t = the normal and tangential stress components at point P,

p = the pressure at point P,

μ = *absolute dynamic viscosity* of the fluid N·s/m^2 [lbm/(ft-sec)],

dv = velocity at boundary condition, and

dy = normal distance, measured from boundary.

$$v = \mu/\rho, \text{ where}$$

v = *kinematic viscosity*; m^2/s (ft^2/sec).

For a thin Newtonian fluid film and a linear velocity profile,

$$v(y) = Vy/\delta; \, dv/dy = V/\delta, \text{ where}$$

V = velocity of plate on film and

δ = thickness of fluid film.

For a power law (non-Newtonian) fluid

$$\tau_t = K \, (dv/dy)^n, \text{ where}$$

K = consistency index, and

n = power law index.

$n < 1 \equiv$ pseudo plastic

$n > 1 \equiv$ dilatant

SURFACE TENSION AND CAPILLARITY

Surface tension σ is the force per unit contact length

$$\sigma = F/L, \text{ where}$$

σ = surface tension, force/length,

F = surface force at the interface, and

L = length of interface.

The *capillary rise h* is approximated by

$$h = 4\sigma \cos \beta / (\gamma d), \text{ where}$$

h = the height of the liquid in the vertical tube,

σ = the surface tension,

β = the angle made by the liquid with the wetted tube wall,

γ = specific weight of the liquid, and

d = the diameter of the capillary tube.

THE PRESSURE FIELD IN A STATIC LIQUID

◆

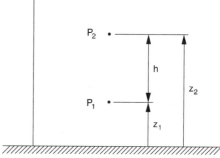

The difference in pressure between two different points is

$$p_2 - p_1 = -\gamma \, (z_2 - z_1) = -\gamma h$$

For a simple manometer,

$$p_o = p_2 + \gamma_2 h_2 - \gamma_1 h_1$$

Absolute pressure = atmospheric pressure + gage pressure reading

Absolute pressure = atmospheric pressure − vacuum gage pressure reading

FORCES ON SUBMERGED SURFACES AND THE CENTER OF PRESSURE

◆

Forces on a submerged plane wall. (a) Submerged plane surface. (b) Pressure distribution.

The pressure on a point at a distance Z' below the surface is

$$p = p_o + \gamma Z', \text{ for } Z' \geq 0$$

If the tank were open to the atmosphere, the effects of p_o could be ignored.

The coordinates of the *center of pressure CP* are

$$y^* = \left(\gamma I_{y_c z_c} \sin\alpha\right)/\left(p_c A\right) \quad \text{and}$$

$$z^* = \left(\gamma I_{y_c} \sin\alpha\right)/\left(p_c A\right), \text{ where}$$

y^* = the y-distance from the centroid (C) of area (A) to the center of pressure,

z^* = the z-distance from the centroid (C) of area (A) to the center of pressure,

I_{y_c} and $I_{y_c z_c}$ = the moment and product of inertia of the area,

p_c = the pressure at the centroid of area (A), and

Z_c = the slant distance from the water surface to the centroid (C) of area (A).

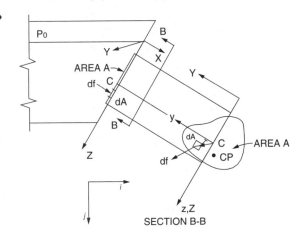

SECTION B-B

If the free surface is open to the atmosphere, then

$p_o = 0$ and $p_c = \gamma Z_c \sin\alpha$.

$$y^* = I_{y_c z_c}/\left(A Z_c\right) \quad \text{and} \quad z^* = I_{y_c}/\left(A Z_c\right)$$

The force on a rectangular plate can be computed as

$$\boldsymbol{F} = [p_1 A_v + (p_2 - p_1) A_v/2]\mathbf{i} + V_f \gamma_f \mathbf{j}, \text{ where}$$

F = force on the plate,

p_1 = pressure at the top edge of the plate area,

p_2 = pressure at the bottom edge of the plate area,

A_v = vertical projection of the plate area,

V_f = volume of column of fluid above plate, and

γ_f = specific weight of the fluid.

ARCHIMEDES PRINCIPLE AND BUOYANCY

1. The buoyant force exerted on a submerged or floating body is equal to the weight of the fluid displaced by the body.

2. A floating body displaces a weight of fluid equal to its own weight; i.e., a floating body is in equilibrium.

The *center of buoyancy* is located at the centroid of the displaced fluid volume.

In the case of a body lying at the *interface of two immiscible fluids*, the buoyant force equals the sum of the weights of the fluids displaced by the body.

ONE-DIMENSIONAL FLOWS

The Continuity Equation So long as the flow Q is continuous, the *continuity equation*, as applied to one-dimensional flows, states that the flow passing two points (1 and 2) in a stream is equal at each point, $A_1 V_1 = A_2 V_2$.

$$Q = AV$$

$$\dot{m} = \rho Q = \rho A V, \text{ where}$$

Q = volumetric flow rate,

$\dot{m}$ = mass flow rate,

A = cross section of area of flow,

V = average flow velocity, and

ρ = the fluid density.

For steady, one-dimensional flow, $\dot{m}$ is a constant. If, in addition, the density is constant, then Q is constant.

The Field Equation is derived when the energy equation is applied to one-dimensional flows.

Assuming no friction losses and that no pump or turbine exists between sections 1 and 2 in the system,

$$\frac{p_2}{\gamma} + \frac{V_2^2}{2g} + z_2 = \frac{p_1}{\gamma} + \frac{V_1^2}{2g} + z_1, \text{ where}$$

p_1, p_2 = pressure at sections 1 and 2,

V_1, V_2 = average velocity of the fluid at the sections,

z_1, z_2 = the vertical distance from a datum to the sections (the potential energy),

γ = the specific weight of the fluid, and

g = the acceleration of gravity.

FLOW OF A REAL FLUID

$$\frac{p_1}{\gamma} + z_1 + \frac{V_1^2}{2g} = \frac{p_2}{\gamma} + z_2 + \frac{V_2^2}{2g} + h_f$$

The pressure drop as fluid flows through a pipe of constant cross-section and which is held at a fixed elevation is

$$h_f = (p_1 - p_2)/\gamma, \text{ where}$$

h_f = the head loss, considered a friction effect, and all remaining terms are defined above.

♦ Bober, W. & R.A. Kenyon, *Fluid Mechanics*, Copyright © 1980 by John Wiley & Sons, Inc. Diagrams reprinted by permission of William Bober & Richard A. Kenyon.

FLUID FLOW

The velocity distribution for *laminar flow* in circular tubes or between planes is

$$v = v_{max}\left[1-\left(\frac{r}{R}\right)^2\right], \text{ where}$$

r = the distance (m) from the centerline,

R = the radius (m) of the tube or half the distance between the parallel planes,

v = the local velocity (m/s) at r, and

v_{max} = the velocity (m/s) at the centerline of the duct.

v_{max} = 1.18V, for fully turbulent flow (Re > 10,000)

v_{max} = 2V, for circular tubes in laminar flow and

v_{max} = 1.5V, for parallel planes in laminar flow, where

V = the average velocity (m/s) in the duct.

The shear stress distribution is

$$\frac{\tau}{\tau_w} = \frac{r}{R}, \text{ where}$$

τ and τ_w are the shear stresses at radii r and R respectively.

The *drag force* F_D on **objects immersed in a large body of flowing fluid or objects moving through a stagnant fluid** is

$$F_D = \frac{C_D \rho V^2 A}{2}, \text{ where}$$

C_D = the *drag coefficient* (see page 47),

V = the velocity (m/s) of the undisturbed fluid, and

A = the *projected area* (m^2) of bluff objects such as spheres, ellipsoids, and disks and plates, cylinders, ellipses, and air foils with axes perpendicular to the flow.

For **flat plates placed parallel with the flow**

$$C_D = 1.33/\text{Re}^{0.5} \ (10^4 < \text{Re} < 5 \times 10^5)$$

$$C_D = 0.031/\text{Re}^{1/7} \ (10^6 < \text{Re} < 10^9)$$

The characteristic length in the Reynolds Number (Re) is the length of the plate parallel with the flow. For bluff objects, the characteristic length is the largest linear dimension (diameter of cylinder, sphere, disk, etc.) which is perpendicular to the flow.

Reynolds Number

$$\text{Re} = VD\rho/\mu = VD/v$$

$$\text{Re}' = \frac{V^{(2-n)}D^n\rho}{K\left(\dfrac{3n+1}{4n}\right)^n 8^{(n-1)}}, \text{ where}$$

ρ = the mass density,

D = the diameter of the pipe or dimension of the fluid streamline,

μ = the dynamic viscosity,

v = the kinematic viscosity,

Re = the Reynolds number (Newtonian fluid),

Re' = the Reynolds number (Power law fluid), and

K and n are defined on page 38.

The critical Reynolds number $(\text{Re})_c$ is defined to be the minimum Reynolds number at which a flow will turn turbulent.

Hydraulic Gradient (Grade Line)

The hydraulic gradient (grade line) is defined as an imaginary line above a pipe so that the vertical distance from the pipe axis to the line represents the *pressure head* at that point. If a row of piezometers were placed at intervals along the pipe, the grade line would join the water levels in the piezometer water columns.

Energy Line (Bernoulli Equation)

The Bernoulli equation states that the sum of the pressure, velocity, and elevation heads is constant. The energy line is this sum or the "total head line" above a horizontal datum.

The difference between the hydraulic grade line and the energy line is the $V^2/2g$ term.

STEADY, INCOMPRESSIBLE FLOW IN CONDUITS AND PIPES

The energy equation for incompressible flow is

$$\frac{p_1}{\gamma} + z_1 + \frac{V_1^2}{2g} = \frac{p_2}{\gamma} + z_2 + \frac{V_2^2}{2g} + h_f$$

If the cross-sectional area and the elevation of the pipe are the same at both sections (1 and 2), then $z_1 = z_2$ and $V_1 = V_2$. The pressure drop $p_1 - p_2$ is given by the following:

$$p_1 - p_2 = \gamma h_f$$

The *Darcy equation* is

$$h_f = f\frac{L}{D}\frac{V^2}{2g}, \text{ where}$$

f = f(Re, e/D), the friction factor,

D = diameter of the pipe,

L = length over which the pressure drop occurs,

e = roughness factor for the pipe, and all other symbols are defined as before.

A chart that gives f versus Re for various values of e/D, known as a *Moody* or *Stanton diagram*, is available at the end of this section on page 46.

Friction Factor for Laminar Flow

The equation for Q in terms of the pressure drop Δp_f is the Hagen-Poiseuille equation. This relation is valid only for flow in the laminar region.

$$Q = \frac{\pi R^4 \Delta p_f}{8\mu L} = \frac{\pi D^4 \Delta p_f}{128\mu L}$$

Flow in Noncircular Conduits

Analysis of flow in conduits having a noncircular cross section uses the *hydraulic diameter* D_H, or the *hydraulic radius* R_H, as follows

40

$$R_H = \frac{\text{cross - sectional area}}{\text{wetted perimeter}} = \frac{D_H}{4}$$

Minor Losses in Pipe Fittings, Contractions, and Expansions

Head losses also occur as the fluid flows through pipe fittings (i.e., elbows, valves, couplings, etc.) and sudden pipe contractions and expansions.

$$\frac{p_1}{\gamma} + z_1 + \frac{V_1^2}{2g} = \frac{p_2}{\gamma} + z_2 + \frac{V_2^2}{2g} + h_f + h_{f,\text{ fitting}}, \text{ where}$$

$$h_{f,\text{ fitting}} = C\frac{V^2}{2g}$$

Specific fittings have characteristic values of C, which will be provided in the problem statement. A generally accepted *nominal value* for head loss in *well-streamlined gradual contractions* is

$$h_{f,\text{ fitting}} = 0.04 \, V^2/ \, 2g$$

The *head loss* at either an *entrance* or *exit* of a pipe from or to a reservoir is also given by the $h_{f,\text{ fitting}}$ equation. Values for C for various cases are shown as follows.

| SHARP EXIT $C = 1.0$ | PROTRUDING PIPE ENTRANCE $C = 0.8$ | SHARP ENTRANCE $C = 0.5$ | ROUND ENTRANCE $C = 0.1$ |

PUMP POWER EQUATION

$$\dot{W} = \, Q\gamma h/\eta, \text{ where}$$

Q = quantity of flow (m³/s or cfs),

h = head (m or ft) the fluid has to be lifted,

η = efficiency, and

$\dot{W}$ = power (watts or ft-lbf/sec).

THE IMPULSE-MOMENTUM PRINCIPLE

The resultant force in a given direction acting on the fluid equals the rate of change of momentum of the fluid.

$$\Sigma F = Q_2\rho_2 V_2 - Q_1\rho_1 V_1, \text{ where}$$

ΣF = the resultant of all external forces acting on the control volume,

$Q_1\rho_1 V_1$ = the rate of momentum of the fluid flow entering the control volume in the same direction of the force, and

$Q_2\rho_2 V_2$ = the rate of momentum of the fluid flow leaving the control volume in the same direction of the force.

Pipe Bends, Enlargements, and Contractions

The force exerted by a flowing fluid on a bend, enlargement, or contraction in a pipe line may be computed using the impulse-momentum principle.

$$p_1A_1 - p_2A_2\cos \alpha - F_x = Q\rho \, (V_2\cos \alpha - V_1)$$

$$F_y - W - p_2A_2\sin \alpha = Q\rho \, (V_2\sin \alpha - 0), \text{ where}$$

F = the force exerted by the bend on the fluid (the force exerted by the fluid on the bend is equal in magnitude and opposite in sign), F_x and F_y are the x-component and y-component of the force,

p = the internal pressure in the pipe line,

A = the cross-sectional area of the pipe line,

W = the weight of the fluid,

V = the velocity of the fluid flow,

α = the angle the pipe bend makes with the horizontal,

ρ = the density of the fluid, and

Q = the quantity of fluid flow.

Jet Propulsion

$$F = Q\rho(V_2 - 0)$$

$$F = 2\gamma hA_2, \text{ where}$$

F = the propulsive force,

γ = the specific weight of the fluid,

h = the height of the fluid above the outlet,

A_2 = the area of the nozzle tip,

Q = $A_2\sqrt{2gh}$, and

V_2 = $\sqrt{2gh}$.

Deflectors and Blades

Fixed Blade

$$-F_x = \, Q\rho(V_2\cos \alpha - V_1)$$

$$F_y = \, Q\rho(V_2\sin \alpha - 0)$$

♦ Bober, W. & R.A. Kenyon, *Fluid Mechanics*, Copyright © 1980 by John Wiley & sons, Inc. Diagram reprinted by permission of William Bober & Richard A. Kenyon.

• Vennard, J.K., *Elementary Fluid Mechanics*, Copyright © 1954 by J.K. Vennard. Diagrams reprinted by permission of John Wiley & Sons, Inc.

Moving Blade

$$-F_x = Q\rho(V_{2x} - V_{1x})$$
$$= -Q\rho(V_1 - v)(1 - \cos\alpha)$$
$$F_y = Q\rho(V_{2y} - V_{1y})$$
$$= +Q\rho(V_1 - v)\sin\alpha, \text{ where}$$

v = the velocity of the blade.

Impulse Turbine

$$\dot{W} = Q\rho(V_1 - v)(1 - \cos\alpha)\,v, \text{ where}$$

$\dot{W}$ = power of the turbine.

$$\dot{W}_{max} = Q\rho(V_1^2/4)(1 - \cos\alpha)$$

When $\alpha = 180°$,

$$\dot{W}_{max} = (Q\rho V_1^2)/2 = (Q\gamma V_1^2)/2g$$

MULTIPATH PIPELINE PROBLEMS

The same head loss occurs in each branch as in the combination of the two. The following equations may be solved simultaneously for V_A and V_B:

$$h_L = f_A \frac{l_A}{D_A}\frac{V_A^2}{2g} = f_B \frac{l_B}{D_B}\frac{V_B^2}{2g}$$
$$\left(\pi D^2/4\right)V = \left(\pi D_A^2/4\right)V_A + \left(\pi D_B^2/4\right)V_B$$

The flow Q can be divided into Q_A and Q_B when the pipe characteristics are known.

OPEN-CHANNEL FLOW AND/OR PIPE FLOW

Manning's Equation
$$V = (k/n)R^{2/3}S^{1/2}, \text{ where}$$

k = 1 for SI units,

k = 1.486 for USCS units,

V = velocity (m/s, ft/sec),

n = roughness coefficient,

R = hydraulic radius (m, ft), and

S = slope of energy grade line (m/m, ft/ft).

Hazen-Williams Equation
$$V = k_1 CR^{0.63}S^{0.54}, \text{ where}$$

C = roughness coefficient,

k_1 = 0.849 for SI units, and

k_1 = 1.318 for USCS units.

Other terms defined as above.

MACH NUMBER

The *speed of sound c* in an ideal gas is given by

$$c = \sqrt{kRT}, \text{ where}$$

$k = c_P/c_v$.

This shows that the acoustic velocity in an ideal gas depends only on its temperature.

The *Mach number* Ma is a ratio of the fluid velocity V to the speed of sound:

$$\text{Ma} = V/c$$

FLUID MEASUREMENTS

The Pitot Tube – From the stagnation pressure equation for an *incompressible fluid*,

$$V = \sqrt{(2/\rho)(p_o - p_s)} = \sqrt{2g(p_o - p_s)/\gamma}, \text{ where}$$

V = the velocity of the fluid,

p_o = the stagnation pressure, and

p_s = the static pressure of the fluid at the elevation where the measurement is taken.

For a *compressible fluid*, use the above incompressible fluid equation if the mach number ≤ 0.3.

MANOMETERS

♦

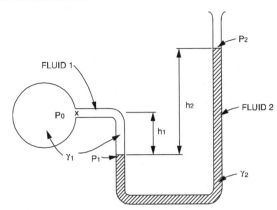

For a simple manometer,

$$p_0 = p_2 + \gamma_2 h_2 - \gamma_1 h_1$$

If $h_1 = h_2 = h$

$$p_0 = p_2 + (\gamma_2 - \gamma_1)h = p_2 + (\rho_2 - \rho_1)gh$$

Note that the difference between the two densities is used.

Another device that works on the same principle as the manometer is the simple barometer.

$$p_{atm} = p_A = p_v + \gamma h = p_B + \gamma h$$

♦

p_v = vapor pressure of the barometer fluid

Venturi Meters

$$Q = \frac{C_v A_2}{\sqrt{1 - (A_2/A_1)^2}} \sqrt{2g\left(\frac{p_1}{\gamma} + z_1 - \frac{p_2}{\gamma} - z_2\right)}, \text{ where}$$

C_v = the coefficient of velocity.

The above equation is for *incompressible fluids*.

♦

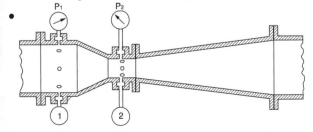

Orifices The cross-sectional area at the vena contracta A_2 is characterized by a *coefficient of contraction C_c* and given by $C_c A$.

•

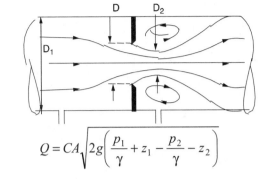

$$Q = CA\sqrt{2g\left(\frac{p_1}{\gamma} + z_1 - \frac{p_2}{\gamma} - z_2\right)}$$

where C, the *coefficient of the meter*, is given by

$$C = \frac{C_v C_c}{\sqrt{1 - C_c^2 (A/A_1)^2}}$$

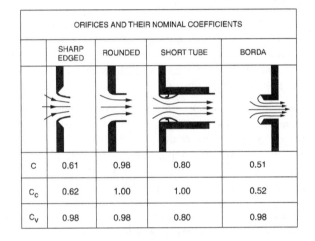

ORIFICES AND THEIR NOMINAL COEFFICIENTS			
SHARP EDGED	ROUNDED	SHORT TUBE	BORDA
C	0.61	0.98	0.80	0.51
C_c	0.62	1.00	1.00	0.52
C_v	0.98	0.98	0.80	0.98

Submerged Orifice operating under steady-flow conditions:

•

$$Q = A_2 V_2 = C_c C_v A\sqrt{2g(h_1 - h_2)}$$
$$= CA\sqrt{2g(h_1 - h_2)}$$

in which the product of C_c and C_v is defined as the *coefficient of discharge* of the orifice.

Orifice Discharging Freely Into Atmosphere

$$Q = CA\sqrt{2gh}$$

in which h is measured from the liquid surface to the centroid of the orifice opening.

DIMENSIONAL HOMOGENEITY AND DIMENSIONAL ANALYSIS

Equations that are in a form that do not depend on the fundamental units of measurement are called *dimensionally homogeneous* equations. A special form of the dimensionally homogeneous equation is one that involves only *dimensionless groups* of terms.

Buckingham's Theorem: The *number of independent dimensionless groups* that may be employed to describe a phenomenon known to involve n variables is equal to the number $(n - \bar{r})$, where $\bar{r}$ is the number of basic dimensions (i.e., M, L, T) needed to express the variables dimensionally.

SIMILITUDE

In order to use a model to simulate the conditions of the prototype, the model must be *geometrically*, *kinematically*, and *dynamically similar* to the prototype system.

To obtain dynamic similarity between two flow pictures, all independent force ratios that can be written must be the same in both the model and the prototype. Thus, dynamic similarity between two flow pictures (when all possible forces are acting) is expressed in the five simultaneous equations below.

$$\left[\frac{F_I}{F_P}\right]_p = \left[\frac{F_I}{F_P}\right]_m = \left[\frac{\rho V^2}{p}\right]_p = \left[\frac{\rho V^2}{p}\right]_m$$

$$\left[\frac{F_I}{F_V}\right]_p = \left[\frac{F_I}{F_V}\right]_m = \left[\frac{Vl\rho}{\mu}\right]_p = \left[\frac{Vl\rho}{\mu}\right]_m = [Re]_p = [Re]_m$$

$$\left[\frac{F_I}{F_G}\right]_p = \left[\frac{F_I}{F_G}\right]_m = \left[\frac{V^2}{lg}\right]_p = \left[\frac{V^2}{lg}\right]_m = [Fr]_p = [Fr]_m$$

$$\left[\frac{F_I}{F_E}\right]_p = \left[\frac{F_I}{F_E}\right]_m = \left[\frac{\rho V^2}{E_v}\right]_p = \left[\frac{\rho V^2}{E_v}\right]_m = [Ca]_p = [Ca]_m$$

$$\left[\frac{F_I}{F_T}\right]_p = \left[\frac{F_I}{F_T}\right]_m = \left[\frac{\rho l V^2}{\sigma}\right]_p = \left[\frac{\rho l V^2}{\sigma}\right]_m = [We]_p = [We]_m$$

where

the subscripts p and m stand for *prototype* and *model* respectively, and

F_I = inertia force,

F_P = pressure force,

F_V = viscous force,

F_G = gravity force,

F_E = elastic force,

F_T = surface tension force,

Re = Reynolds number,

We = Weber number,

Ca = Cauchy number,

Fr = Froude number,

l = characteristic length,

V = velocity,

ρ = density,

σ = surface tension,

E_v = bulk modulus,

μ = dynamic viscosity,

v = kinematic viscosity,

p = pressure, and

g = acceleration of gravity.

$$Re = \frac{VD\rho}{\mu} = \frac{VD}{v}$$

PROPERTIES OF WATER[f]

Temperature °C	Specific Weight[a], γ, kN/m³	Density[a], ρ, kg/m³	Viscosity[a],[2], $\mu \times 10^3$, Pa·s	Kinematic Viscosity[a],[2], $\nu \times 10^6$, m²/s	Vapor Pressure[e], p_v, kPa
0	9.805	999.8	1.781	1.785	0.61
5	9.807	1000.0	1.518	1.518	0.87
10	9.804	999.7	1.307	1.306	1.23
15	9.798	999.1	1.139	1.139	1.70
20	9.789	998.2	1.002	1.003	2.34
25	9.777	997.0	0.890	0.893	3.17
30	9.764	995.7	0.798	0.800	4.24
40	9.730	992.2	0.653	0.658	7.38
50	9.689	988.0	0.547	0.553	12.33
60	9.642	983.2	0.466	0.474	19.92
70	9.589	977.8	0.404	0.413	31.16
80	9.530	971.8	0.354	0.364	47.34
90	9.466	965.3	0.315	0.326	70.10
100	9.399	958.4	0.282	0.294	101.33

[a]From "Hydraulic Models," *A.S.C.E. Manual of Engineering Practice*, No. 25, A.S.C.E., 1942. See footnote 2.

[e]From J.H. Keenan and F.G. Keyes, *Thermodynamic Properties of Steam*, John Wiley & Sons, 1936.

[f]Compiled from many sources including those indicated, *Handbook of Chemistry and Physics*, 54th Ed., The CRC Press, 1973, and *Handbook of Tables for Applied Engineering Science*, The Chemical Rubber Co., 1970.

[2]Here, if $E/10^6 = 1.98$ then $E = 1.98 \times 10^6$ kPa, while if $\mu \times 10^3 = 1.781$, then $\mu = 1.781 \times 10^{-3}$ Pa's, and so on.

Vennard, J.K. and Robert L. Street, *Elementary Fluid Mechanics*, Copyright 1954, John Wiley & Sons, Inc.

MOODY (STANTON) DIAGRAM

	e, (ft)	e, (mm)
Riveted steel	l0.003-0.03	0.9-9.0
Concrete	0.001-0.01	0.3-3.0
Cast iron	0.00085	0.25
Galvanized iron	0.0005	0.15
Commercial steel or wrought iron	0.00015	0.046
Drawn tubing	0.000005	0.0015

Reprinted by permission of ASHRAE.

DRAG COEFFICIENTS FOR SPHERES, DISKS, AND CYLINDERS

$$C_D = \frac{24}{Re}, \ Re < 10$$

REYNOLDS NUMBER $\ Re = \dfrac{DV\rho}{\mu}$

DRAG COEFFICIENT $\ C_D = \dfrac{2F_D}{\rho V^2 A}$

SPHERES

DISKS

CYLINDERS

Note: Intermediate divisions are 2, 4, 6, and 8.

47

THERMODYNAMICS

PROPERTIES OF SINGLE-COMPONENT SYSTEMS

Nomenclature

1. Intensive properties are independent of mass.
2. Extensive properties are proportional to mass.
3. Specific properties are lower case (extensive/mass).

State Functions (properties)

Absolute Pressure, p (lbf/in^2 or Pa)

Absolute Temperature, T (°R or K)

Specific Volume, v (ft^3/lbm or m^3/kg)

Internal Energy, u (usually in Btu/lbm or kJ/kg)

Enthalpy, $h = u + Pv$ (same units as u)

Entropy, s [in Btu/(lbm-°R) or kJ/(kg·K)]

Gibbs Free Energy, $g = h - Ts$ (same units as u)

Helmholz Free Energy, $a = u - Ts$ (same units as u)

Heat Capacity at Constant Pressure, $c_p = \left(\dfrac{\partial h}{\partial T} \right)_P$

Heat Capacity at Constant Volume, $c_v = \left(\dfrac{\partial u}{\partial T} \right)_v$

Quality x (applies to liquid-vapor systems at saturation) is defined as the mass fraction of the vapor phase:

$x = m_g/(m_g + m_f)$, where

m_g = mass of vapor, and

m_f = mass of liquid.

Specific volume of a two-phase system can be written:

$v = xv_g + (1-x)v_f$ or $v = xv_{fg} + v_f$, where

v_f = specific volume of saturated liquid,

v_g = specific volume of saturated vapor, and

v_{fg} = specific volume change upon vaporization.

     $= v_g - v_f$.

Similar expressions exist for u, h, and s:

$u = xu_g + (1-x)u_f$

$h = xh_g + (1-x)h_f$

$s = xs_g + (1-x)s_f$

For a simple substance, *specification of any two intensive, independent properties is sufficient* to fix all the rest.

For an ideal gas, $Pv = RT$ or $PV = mRT$, and

     $P_1v_1/T_1 = P_2v_2/T_2$, where

p = pressure,

v = specific volume,

m = mass of gas,

R = gas constant, and

T = temperature.

R is *specific to each gas* but can be found from

$$R = \frac{\overline{R}}{(mol.\ wt.)}, \text{ where}$$

$\overline{R}$ = the universal gas constant

     = 1,545 ft-lbf/(lbmol-°R) = 8,314 J/(kmol·K).

For *Ideal Gases*, $c_P - c_v = R$

Also, for *Ideal Gases*:

$$\left(\frac{\partial h}{\partial v} \right)_T = 0 \qquad\qquad \left(\frac{\partial u}{\partial v} \right)_T = 0$$

For cold air standard, *heat capacities are assumed to be constant* at their room temperature values. In that case, the following are true:

$\Delta u = c_v \Delta T;$ $\Delta h = c_P \Delta T$

$\Delta s = c_P \ln (T_2/T_1) - R \ln (P_2/P_1);$ and

$\Delta s = c_v \ln (T_2/T_1) + R \ln (v_2/v_1).$

For heat capacities that are temperature dependent, the value to be used in the above equations for Δh is known as the mean heat capacity ($\overline{c}_p$) and is given by

$$\overline{c}_p = \frac{\int_{T_1}^{T_2} c_p \, dT}{T_2 - T_1}$$

Also, for *constant entropy* processes:

$P_1v_1^k = P_2v_2^k;$ $T_1P_1^{(1-k)/k} = T_2P_2^{(1-k)/k}$

$T_1v_1^{(k-1)} = T_2v_2^{(k-1)}$, where $k = c_p/c_v$

FIRST LAW OF THERMODYNAMICS

The *First Law of Thermodynamics* is a statement of conservation of energy in a thermodynamic system. The net energy crossing the system boundary is equal to the change in energy inside the system.

Heat Q is *energy transferred* due to temperature difference and is considered positive if it is inward or added to the system.

Closed Thermodynamic System

(no mass crosses boundary)

$$Q - w = \Delta U + \Delta KE + \Delta PE$$

where

ΔKE = change in kinetic energy, and

ΔPE = change in potential energy.

Energy can cross the boundary only in the form of heat or work. Work can be boundary work, w_b, or other work forms (electrical work, etc.)

Work w is considered *positive if it is outward* or *work done by the system.*

Reversible boundary work is given by $w_b = \int P \, dv$.

Special Cases of Closed Systems

Constant Pressure (***Charles' Law***): $w_b = P\Delta v$

     (ideal gas) T/v = constant

Constant Volume: $w_b = 0$

     (ideal gas) T/P = constant

Isentropic (ideal gas), $Pv^k = $ constant:

$$w = (P_2v_2 - P_1v_1)/(1 - k)$$
$$= R(T_2 - T_1)/(1 - k)$$

Constant Temperature (**Boyle's Law**):

$$\text{(ideal gas) } Pv = \text{constant}$$
$$w_b = RT\ln(v_2/v_1) = RT\ln(P_1/P_2)$$

Polytropic (ideal gas), $Pv^n = $ constant:

$$w = (P_2v_2 - P_1v_1)/(1 - n)$$

Open Thermodynamic System

(allowing mass to cross the boundary)

There is flow work (PV) done by mass entering the system. The reversible flow work is given by:

$$w_{rev} = -\int v\, dP + \Delta KE + \Delta PE$$

First Law applies whether or not processes are reversible.

FIRST LAW (energy balance)

$$\Sigma \dot{m}[h_i + V_i^2/2 + gZ_i] - \Sigma \dot{m}[h_e + V_e^2/2 + gZ_e]$$
$$+ \dot{Q}_{in} - \dot{W}_{net} = d(m_s u_s)/dt \text{, where}$$

$\dot{W}_{net}$ = rate of net or shaft work transfer,

m_s = mass of fluid within the system,

u_s = specific internal energy of system, and

$\dot{Q}$ = rate of heat transfer (neglecting kinetic and potential energy).

Special Cases of Open Systems

Constant Volume: $\qquad w_{rev} = -v(P_2 - P_1)$

Constant Pressure: $\qquad w_{rev} = 0$

Constant Temperature: (ideal gas) $Pv = $ constant:

$$w_{rev} = RT\ln(v_2/v_1) = RT\ln(P_1/P_2)$$

Isentropic (ideal gas): $\qquad Pv^k = $ constant:

$$w_{rev} = k(P_2v_2 - P_1v_1)/(1 - k)$$
$$= kR(T_2 - T_1)/(1 - k)$$
$$w_{rev} = \frac{k}{k-1}RT_1\left[1 - \left(\frac{P_2}{P_1}\right)^{(k-1)/k}\right]$$

Polytropic: $\qquad Pv^n = $ constant

$$w_{rev} = n(P_2v_2 - P_1v_1)/(1 - n)$$

Steady-State Systems

The system does not change state with time. This assumption is valid for steady operation of turbines, pumps, compressors, throttling valves, nozzles, and heat exchangers, including boilers and condensers.

$$\Sigma \dot{m}_i\left(h_i + V_i^2/2 + gZ_i\right) - \Sigma \dot{m}_e\left(h_e + V_e^2/2 + gZ_e\right)$$
$$+ \dot{Q}_{in} - \dot{W}_{out} = 0 \quad \text{and}$$
$$\Sigma \dot{m}_i = \Sigma \dot{m}_e$$

where

$\dot{m}$ = mass flow rate (subscripts i and e refer to inlet and exit states of system),

g = acceleration of gravity,

Z = elevation,

V = velocity, and

$\dot{w}$ = rate of work.

Special Cases of Steady-Flow Energy Equation

Nozzles, Diffusers: Velocity terms are significant. No elevation change, no heat transfer, and no work. Single mass stream.

$$h_i + V_i^2/2 = h_e + V_e^2/2$$

Efficiency (nozzle) $= \dfrac{V_e^2 - V_i^2}{2(h_i - h_{es})}$, where

h_{es} = enthalpy at isentropic exit state.

Turbines, Pumps, Compressors: Often considered adiabatic (no heat transfer). Velocity terms usually can be ignored. There are significant work terms and a single mass stream.

$$h_i = h_e + w$$

Efficiency (turbine) $= \dfrac{h_i - h_e}{h_i - h_{es}}$

Efficiency (compressor, pump) $= \dfrac{h_{es} - h_i}{h_e - h_i}$

Throttling Valves and Throttling Processes: No work, no heat transfer, and single-mass stream. Velocity terms often insignificant.

$$h_i = h_e$$

Boilers, Condensers, Evaporators, One Side in a Heat Exchanger: Heat transfer terms are significant. For a single-mass stream, the following applies:

$$h_i + q = h_e$$

Heat Exchangers: No heat or work. Two separate flow rates $\dot{m}_1$ and m_2:

$$\dot{m}_1\left(h_{1i} - h_{1e}\right) = \dot{m}_2\left(h_{2e} - h_{2i}\right)$$

Mixers, Separators, Open or Closed Feedwater Heaters:

$$\Sigma \dot{m}_i h_i = \Sigma \dot{m}_e h_e \quad \text{and}$$
$$\Sigma \dot{m}_i = \Sigma \dot{m}_e$$

BASIC CYCLES

Heat engines take in heat Q_H at a high temperature T_H, produce a net amount of work w, and reject heat Q_L at a low temperature T_L. The efficiency η of a heat engine is given by:

$$\eta = w/Q_H = (Q_H - Q_L)/Q_H$$

The most efficient engine possible is the *Carnot Cycle*. Its efficiency is given by:

$$\eta_c = (T_H - T_L)/T_H \text{, where}$$

T_H and T_L = absolute temperatures (Kelvin or Rankine).

The following heat-engine cycles are plotted on *P-v* and *T-s* diagrams (see page 52):

> Carnot, Otto, Rankine

Refrigeration Cycles are the reverse of heat-engine cycles. Heat is moved from low to high temperature requiring work *W*. Cycles can be used either for refrigeration or as heat pumps.

Coefficient of Performance (COP) is defined as:

> COP = Q_H/W for heat pumps, and as

> COP = Q_L/W for refrigerators and air conditioners.

Upper limit of COP is based on reversed Carnot Cycle:

> $COP_c = T_H/(T_H - T_L)$ for heat pumps and

> $COP_c = T_L/(T_H - T_L)$ for refrigeration.

1 ton refrigeration = 12,000 Btu/hr = 3,516 W

IDEAL GAS MIXTURES

$i = 1, 2, ..., n$ constituents. Each constituent is an ideal gas.

Mole Fraction: N_i = number of moles of component *i*.

$$x_i = N_i/N; N = \Sigma N_i; \Sigma x_i = 1$$

Mass Fraction: $y_i = m_i/m; m = \Sigma m_i; \Sigma y_i = 1$

Molecular Weight: $M = m/N = \Sigma x_i M_i$

Gas Constant: $R = \overline{R}/M$

To convert *mole fractions to mass fractions*:

$$y_i = \frac{x_i M_i}{\Sigma(x_i M_i)}$$

To convert *mass fractions to mole fractions*:

$$x_i = \frac{y_i/M_i}{\Sigma(y_i/M_i)}$$

Partial Pressures $p = \Sigma p_i; p_i = \dfrac{m_i R_i T}{V}$

Partial Volumes $V = \Sigma V_i; V_i = \dfrac{m_i R_i T}{p}$, where

p, V, T = the pressure, volume, and temperature of the mixture.

$$x_i = p_i/p = V_i/V$$

Other Properties

$u = \Sigma(y_i u_i); h = \Sigma(y_i h_i); s = \Sigma(y_i s_i)$

u_i and h_i are evaluated at *T*, and

s_i is evaluated at *T* and p_i.

PSYCHROMETRICS

We deal here with a mixture of dry air (subscript *a*) and water vapor (subscript *v*):

$$p = p_a + p_v$$

Specific Humidity (absolute humidity) ω:

> $\omega = m_v/m_a$, where

m_v = mass of water vapor and

m_a = mass of dry air.

$$\omega = 0.622 p_v/p_a = 0.622 p_v/(p - p_v)$$

Relative Humidity ϕ:

> $\phi = m_v/m_g = p_v/p_g$, where

m_g = mass of vapor at saturation, and

p_g = saturation pressure at *T*.

Enthalpy *h*: $h = h_a + \omega h_v$

Dew-Point Temperature T_{dp}:

> $T_{dp} = T_{sat}$ at $p_g = p_v$

Wet-bulb temperature T_{wb} is the temperature indicated by a thermometer covered by a wick saturated with liquid water and in contact with moving air.

Humidity Volume: Volume of moist air/mass of dry air.

Psychrometric Chart

A plot of specific humidity as a function of dry-bulb temperature plotted for a value of atmospheric pressure. (See chart at end of section.)

PHASE RELATIONS

Clapeyron Equation for Phase Transitions:

$$\left(\frac{dp}{dT}\right)_{sat} = \frac{h_{fg}}{Tv_{fg}} = \frac{s_{fg}}{v_{fg}}, \text{ where}$$

h_{fg} = enthalpy change for phase transitions,

v_{fg} = volume change,

s_{fg} = entropy change,

T = absolute temperature, and

$(dP/dT)_{sat}$ = slope of vapor-liquid saturation line.

Gibbs Phase Rule

> $P + F = C + 2$, where

P = number of phases making up a system,

F = degrees of freedom, and

C = number of components in a system.

Gibbs Free Energy

Energy released or absorbed in a reaction occurring reversibly at constant pressure and temperature ΔG.

Helmholtz Free Energy

Energy released or absorbed in a reaction occurring reversibly at constant volume and temperature ΔA.

COMBUSTION PROCESSES

First, the combustion equation should be written and balanced. For example, for the stoichiometric combustion of methane in oxygen:

$$CH_4 + 2 O_2 \rightarrow CO_2 + 2 H_2O$$

Combustion in Air

For each mole of oxygen, there will be 3.76 moles of nitrogen. For stoichiometric combustion of methane in air:

$$CH_4 + 2 O_2 + 2(3.76) N_2 \rightarrow CO_2 + 2 H_2O + 7.52 N_2$$

Combustion in Excess Air

The excess oxygen appears as oxygen on the right side of the combustion equation.

Incomplete Combustion

Some carbon is burned to create carbon monoxide (CO).

Air-Fuel Ratio (A/F): $A/F = \dfrac{\text{mass of air}}{\text{mass of fuel}}$

Stoichiometric (theoretical) air-fuel ratio is the air-fuel ratio calculated from the stoichiometric combustion equation.

$$\text{Percent Theoretical Air} = \frac{(A/F)_{\text{actual}}}{(A/F)_{\text{stoichiometric}}} \times 100$$

$$\text{Percent Excess Air} = \frac{(A/F)_{\text{actual}} - (A/F)_{\text{stoichiometric}}}{(A/F)_{\text{stoichiometric}}} \times 100$$

SECOND LAW OF THERMODYNAMICS

Thermal Energy Reservoirs

$$\Delta S_{\text{reservoir}} = Q/T_{\text{reservoir}} \text{, where}$$

Q is measured with respect to the reservoir.

Kelvin-Planck Statement of Second Law

No heat engine can operate in a cycle while transferring heat with a single heat reservoir.

COROLLARY to Kelvin-Planck: No heat engine can have a higher efficiency than a Carnot cycle operating between the same reservoirs.

Clausius' Statement of Second Law

No refrigeration or heat pump cycle can operate without a net work input.

COROLLARY: No refrigerator or heat pump can have a higher COP than a Carnot cycle refrigerator or heat pump.

VAPOR-LIQUID MIXTURES

Henry's Law at Constant Temperature

At equilibrium, the partial pressure of a gas is proportional to its concentration in a liquid. Henry's Law is valid for low concentrations; i.e., $x \approx 0$.

$$p_i = py_i = hx_i, \text{ where}$$

h = Henry's Law constant,

p_i = partial pressure of a gas in contact with a liquid,

x_i = mol fraction of the gas in the liquid,

y_i = mol fraction of the gas in the vapor, and

p = total pressure.

Raoult's Law for Vapor-Liquid Equilibrium

Valid for concentrations near 1; i.e., $x_i \approx 1$.

$$p_i = x_i p_i^{*}, \text{ where}$$

p_i = partial pressure of component i,

x_i = mol fraction of component i in the liquid, and

p_i^{*} = vapor pressure of pure component i at the temperature of the mixture.

ENTROPY

$$ds = (1/T)\,\delta Q_{\text{rev}}$$

$$s_2 - s_1 = \int_1^2 (1/T)\delta Q_{rev}$$

Inequality of Clausius

$$\oint (1/T)\,\delta Q_{rev} \leq 0$$

$$\int_1^2 (1/T)\delta Q \leq s_2 - s_1$$

Isothermal, Reversible Process

$$\Delta s = s_2 - s_1 = Q/T$$

Isentropic Process

$$\Delta s = 0; \; ds = 0$$

A reversible adiabatic process is isentropic.

Adiabatic Process

$$\delta Q = 0; \; \Delta s \geq 0$$

Increase of Entropy Principle

$$\Delta s_{\text{total}} = \Delta s_{\text{system}} + \Delta s_{\text{surroundings}} \geq 0$$

$$\Delta \dot{s}_{\text{total}} = \sum \dot{m}_{\text{out}} s_{\text{out}} - \sum \dot{m}_{\text{in}} s_{\text{in}}$$
$$- \sum \left(\dot{Q}_{\text{external}} / T_{\text{external}} \right) \geq 0$$

Temperature-Entropy (*T-s*) Diagram

$$Q_{rev} = \int_1^2 T\,ds$$

AREA = HEAT

Entropy Change for Solids and Liquids

$$ds = c\,(dT/T)$$

$$s_2 - s_1 = \int c\,(dT/T) = c_{\text{mean}} \ln (T_2/T_1),$$

where c equals the heat capacity of the solid or liquid.

Irreversibility

$$I = w_{\text{rev}} - w_{\text{actual}}$$

Closed-System Availability

(no chemical reactions)

$$\phi = (u - u_o) - T_o(s - s_o) + p_o(v - v_o)$$

$$w_{\text{reversible}} = \phi_1 - \phi_2$$

Open-System Availability

$$\psi = (h - h_o) - T_o(s - s_o) + V^2/2 + gz$$

$$w_{\text{reversible}} = \psi_1 - \psi_2$$

COMMON THERMODYNAMIC CYCLES

Carnot

$$\eta = 1 - \frac{T_L}{T_H}$$

Reversed Carnot

Otto

(*gasoline engine*)

$$\eta = 1 - r^{1-k}$$

$$r = v_1/v_2$$

Rankine

$$\eta = \frac{(h_3 - h_4) - (h_2 - h_1)}{h_3 - h_2}$$

Refrigeration

(Reversed Rankine Cycle)

$$\text{COP}_{\text{ref}} = \frac{h_1 - h_4}{h_2 - h_1} \qquad \text{COP}_{\text{HP}} = \frac{h_2 - h_3}{h_2 - h_1}$$

Temp. °C T	Sat. Press. kPa p_{sat}	Specific Volume m³/kg		Internal Energy kJ/kg			Enthalpy kJ/kg			Entropy kJ/(kg·K)		
		Sat. liquid v_f	Sat. vapor v_g	Sat. liquid u_f	Evap. u_{fg}	Sat. vapor u_g	Sat. liquid h_f	Evap. h_{fg}	Sat. vapor h_g	Sat. liquid s_f	Evap. s_{fg}	Sat. vapor s_g
0.01	0.6113	0.001 000	206.14	0.00	2375.3	2375.3	0.01	2501.3	2501.4	0.0000	9.1562	9.1562
5	0.8721	0.001 000	147.12	20.97	2361.3	2382.3	20.98	2489.6	2510.6	0.0761	8.9496	9.0257
10	1.2276	0.001 000	106.38	42.00	2347.2	2389.2	42.01	2477.7	2519.8	0.1510	8.7498	8.9008
15	1.7051	0.001 001	77.93	62.99	2333.1	2396.1	62.99	2465.9	2528.9	0.2245	8.5569	8.7814
20	2.339	0.001 002	57.79	83.95	2319.0	2402.9	83.96	2454.1	2538.1	0.2966	8.3706	8.6672
25	3.169	0.001 003	43.36	104.88	2304.9	2409.8	104.89	2442.3	2547.2	0.3674	8.1905	8.5580
30	4.246	0.001 004	32.89	125.78	2290.8	2416.6	125.79	2430.5	2556.3	0.4369	8.0164	8.4533
35	5.628	0.001 006	25.22	146.67	2276.7	2423.4	146.68	2418.6	2565.3	0.5053	7.8478	8.3531
40	7.384	0.001 008	19.52	167.56	2262.6	2430.1	167.57	2406.7	2574.3	0.5725	7.6845	8.2570
45	9.593	0.001 010	15.26	188.44	2248.4	2436.8	188.45	2394.8	2583.2	0.6387	7.5261	8.1648
50	12.349	0.001 012	12.03	209.32	2234.2	2443.5	209.33	2382.7	2592.1	0.7038	7.3725	8.0763
55	15.758	0.001 015	9.568	230.21	2219.9	2450.1	230.23	2370.7	2600.9	0.7679	7.2234	7.9913
60	19.940	0.001 017	7.671	251.11	2205.5	2456.6	251.13	2358.5	2609.6	0.8312	7.0784	7.9096
65	25.03	0.001 020	6.197	272.02	2191.1	2463.1	272.06	2346.2	2618.3	0.8935	6.9375	7.8310
70	31.19	0.001 023	5.042	292.95	2176.6	2569.6	292.98	2333.8	2626.8	0.9549	6.8004	7.7553
75	38.58	0.001 026	4.131	313.90	2162.0	2475.9	313.93	2321.4	2635.3	1.0155	6.6669	7.6824
80	47.39	0.001 029	3.407	334.86	2147.4	2482.2	334.91	2308.8	2643.7	1.0753	6.5369	7.6122
85	57.83	0.001 033	2.828	355.84	2132.6	2488.4	355.90	2296.0	2651.9	1.1343	6.4102	7.5445
90	70.14	0.001 036	2.361	376.85	2117.7	2494.5	376.92	2283.2	2660.1	1.1925	6.2866	7.4791
95	84.55	0.001 040	1.982	397.88	2102.7	2500.6	397.96	2270.2	2668.1	1.2500	6.1659	7.4159
	MPa											
100	0.101 35	0.001 044	1.6729	418.94	2087.6	2506.5	419.04	2257.0	2676.1	1.3069	6.0480	7.3549
105	0.120 82	0.001 048	1.4194	440.02	2072.3	2512.4	440.15	2243.7	2683.8	1.3630	5.9328	7.2958
110	0.143 27	0.001 052	1.2102	461.14	2057.0	2518.1	461.30	2230.2	2691.5	1.4185	5.8202	7.2387
115	0.169 06	0.001 056	1.0366	482.30	2041.4	2523.7	482.48	2216.5	2699.0	1.4734	5.7100	7.1833
120	0.198 53	0.001 060	0.8919	503.50	2025.8	2529.3	503.71	2202.6	2706.3	1.5276	5.6020	7.1296
125	0.2321	0.001 065	0.7706	524.74	2009.9	2534.6	524.99	2188.5	2713.5	1.5813	5.4962	7.0775
130	0.2701	0.001 070	0.6685	546.02	1993.9	2539.9	546.31	2174.2	2720.5	1.6344	5.3925	7.0269
135	0.3130	0.001 075	0.5822	567.35	1977.7	2545.0	567.69	2159.6	2727.3	1.6870	5.2907	6.9777
140	0.3613	0.001 080	0.5089	588.74	1961.3	2550.0	589.13	2144.7	2733.9	1.7391	5.1908	6.9299
145	0.4154	0.001 085	0.4463	610.18	1944.7	2554.9	610.63	2129.6	2740.3	1.7907	5.0926	6.8833
150	0.4758	0.001 091	0.3928	631.68	1927.9	2559.5	632.20	2114.3	2746.5	1.8418	4.9960	6.8379
155	0.5431	0.001 096	0.3468	653.24	1910.8	2564.1	653.84	2098.6	2752.4	1.8925	4.9010	6.7935
160	0.6178	0.001 102	0.3071	674.87	1893.5	2568.4	675.55	2082.6	2758.1	1.9427	4.8075	6.7502
165	0.7005	0.001 108	0.2727	696.56	1876.0	2572.5	697.34	2066.2	2763.5	1.9925	4.7153	6.7078
170	0.7917	0.001 114	0.2428	718.33	1858.1	2576.5	719.21	2049.5	2768.7	2.0419	4.6244	6.6663
175	0.8920	0.001 121	0.2168	740.17	1840.0	2580.2	741.17	2032.4	2773.6	2.0909	4.5347	6.6256
180	1.0021	0.001 127	0.194 05	762.09	1821.6	2583.7	763.22	2015.0	2778.2	2.1396	4.4461	6.5857
185	1.1227	0.001 134	0.174 09	784.10	1802.9	2587.0	785.37	1997.1	2782.4	2.1879	4.3586	6.5465
190	1.2544	0.001 141	0.156 54	806.19	1783.8	2590.0	807.62	1978.8	2786.4	2.2359	4.2720	6.5079
195	1.3978	0.001 149	0.141 05	828.37	1764.4	2592.8	829.98	1960.0	2790.0	2.2835	4.1863	6.4698
200	1.5538	0.001 157	0.127 36	850.65	1744.7	2595.3	852.45	1940.7	2793.2	2.3309	4.1014	6.4323
205	1.7230	0.001 164	0.115 21	873.04	1724.5	2597.5	875.04	1921.0	2796.0	2.3780	4.0172	6.3952
210	1.9062	0.001 173	0.104 41	895.53	1703.9	2599.5	897.76	1900.7	2798.5	2.4248	3.9337	6.3585
215	2.104	0.001 181	0.094 79	918.14	1682.9	2601.1	920.62	1879.9	2800.5	2.4714	3.8507	6.3221
220	2.318	0.001 190	0.086 19	940.87	1661.5	2602.4	943.62	1858.5	2802.1	2.5178	3.7683	6.2861
225	2.548	0.001 199	0.078 49	963.73	1639.6	2603.3	966.78	1836.5	2803.3	2.5639	3.6863	6.2503
230	2.795	0.001 209	0.071 58	986.74	1617.2	2603.9	990.12	1813.8	2804.0	2.6099	3.6047	6.2146
235	3.060	0.001 219	0.065 37	1009.89	1594.2	2604.1	1013.62	1790.5	2804.2	2.6558	3.5233	6.1791
240	3.344	0.001 229	0.059 76	1033.21	1570.8	2604.0	1037.32	1766.5	2803.8	2.7015	3.4422	6.1437
245	3.648	0.001 240	0.054 71	1056.71	1546.7	2603.4	1061.23	1741.7	2803.0	2.7472	3.3612	6.1083
250	3.973	0.001 251	0.050 13	1080.39	1522.0	2602.4	1085.36	1716.2	2801.5	2.7927	3.2802	6.0730
255	4.319	0.001 263	0.045 98	1104.28	1596.7	2600.9	1109.73	1689.8	2799.5	2.8383	3.1992	6.0375
260	4.688	0.001 276	0.042 21	1128.39	1470.6	2599.0	1134.37	1662.5	2796.6	2.8838	3.1181	6.0019
265	5.081	0.001 289	0.038 77	1152.74	1443.9	2596.6	1159.28	1634.4	2793.6	2.9294	3.0368	5.9662
270	5.499	0.001 302	0.035 64	1177.36	1416.3	2593.7	1184.51	1605.2	2789.7	2.9751	2.9551	5.9301
275	5.942	0.001 317	0.032 79	1202.25	1387.9	2590.2	1210.07	1574.9	2785.0	3.0208	2.8730	5.8938
280	6.412	0.001 332	0.030 17	1227.46	1358.7	2586.1	1235.99	1543.6	2779.6	3.0668	2.7903	5.8571
285	6.909	0.001 348	0.027 77	1253.00	1328.4	2581.4	1262.31	1511.0	2773.3	3.1130	2.7070	5.8199
290	7.436	0.001 366	0.025 57	1278.92	1297.1	2576.0	1289.07	1477.1	2766.2	3.1594	2.6227	5.7821
295	7.993	0.001 384	0.023 54	1305.2	1264.7	2569.9	1316.3	1441.8	2758.1	3.2062	2.5375	5.7437
300	8.581	0.001 404	0.021 67	1332.0	1231.0	2563.0	1344.0	1404.9	2749.0	3.2534	2.4511	5.7045
305	9.202	0.001 425	0.019 948	1359.3	1195.9	2555.2	1372.4	1366.4	2738.7	3.3010	2.3633	5.6643
310	9.856	0.001 447	0.018 350	1387.1	1159.4	2546.4	1401.3	1326.0	2727.3	3.3493	2.2737	5.6230
315	10.547	0.001 472	0.016 867	1415.5	1121.1	2536.6	1431.0	1283.5	2714.5	3.3982	2.1821	5.5804
320	11.274	0.001 499	0.015 488	1444.6	1080.9	2525.5	1461.5	1238.6	2700.1	3.4480	2.0882	5.5362
330	12.845	0.001 561	0.012 996	1505.3	993.7	2498.9	1525.3	1140.6	2665.9	3.5507	1.8909	5.4417
340	14.586	0.001 638	0.010 797	1570.3	894.3	2464.6	1594.2	1027.9	2622.0	3.6594	1.6763	5.3357
350	16.513	0.001 740	0.008 813	1641.9	776.6	2418.4	1670.6	893.4	2563.9	3.7777	1.4335	5.2112
360	18.651	0.001 893	0.006 945	1725.2	626.3	2351.5	1760.5	720.3	2481.0	3.9147	1.1379	5.0526
370	21.03	0.002 213	0.004 925	1844.0	384.5	2228.5	1890.5	441.6	2332.1	4.1106	0.6865	4.7971
374.14	22.09	0.003 155	0.003 155	2029.6	0	2029.6	2099.3	0	2099.3	4.4298	0	4.4298

53

Superheated Water Tables

T Temp. ^oC	v m³/kg	u kJ/kg	h kJ/kg	s kJ/(kg·K)	v m³/kg	u kJ/kg	h kJ/kg	s kJ/(kg·K)
		$p = 0.01$ MPa (45.81^oC)				$p = 0.05$ MPa (81.33^oC)		
Sat.	14.674	2437.9	2584.7	8.1502	3.240	2483.9	2645.9	7.5939
50	14.869	2443.9	2592.6	8.1749				
100	17.196	2515.5	2687.5	8.4479	3.418	2511.6	2682.5	7.6947
150	19.512	2587.9	2783.0	8.6882	3.889	2585.6	2780.1	7.9401
200	21.825	2661.3	2879.5	8.9038	4.356	2659.9	2877.7	8.1580
250	24.136	2736.0	2977.3	9.1002	4.820	2735.0	2976.0	8.3556
300	26.445	2812.1	3076.5	9.2813	5.284	2811.3	3075.5	8.5373
400	31.063	2968.9	3279.6	9.6077	6.209	2968.5	3278.9	8.8642
500	35.679	3132.3	3489.1	9.8978	7.134	3132.0	3488.7	9.1546
600	40.295	3302.5	3705.4	10.1608	8.057	3302.2	3705.1	9.4178
700	44.911	3479.6	3928.7	10.4028	8.981	3479.4	3928.5	9.6599
800	49.526	3663.8	4159.0	10.6281	9.904	3663.6	4158.9	9.8852
900	54.141	3855.0	4396.4	10.8396	10.828	3854.9	4396.3	10.0967
1000	58.757	4053.0	4640.6	11.0393	11.751	4052.9	4640.5	10.2964
1100	63.372	4257.5	4891.2	11.2287	12.674	4257.4	4891.1	10.4859
1200	67.987	4467.9	5147.8	11.4091	13.597	4467.8	5147.7	10.6662
1300	72.602	4683.7	5409.7	11.5811	14.521	4683.6	5409.6	10.8382
		$p = 0.10$ MPa (99.63^oC)				$p = 0.20$ MPa (120.23^oC)		
Sat.	1.6940	2506.1	2675.5	7.3594	0.8857	2529.5	2706.7	7.1272
100	1.6958	2506.7	2676.2	7.3614				
150	1.9364	2582.8	2776.4	7.6134	0.9596	2576.9	2768.8	7.2795
200	2.172	2658.1	2875.3	7.8343	1.0803	2654.4	2870.5	7.5066
250	2.406	2733.7	2974.3	8.0333	1.1988	2731.2	2971.0	7.7086
300	2.639	2810.4	3074.3	8.2158	1.3162	2808.6	3071.8	7.8926
400	3.103	2967.9	3278.2	8.5435	1.5493	2966.7	3276.6	8.2218
500	3.565	3131.6	3488.1	8.8342	1.7814	3130.8	3487.1	8.5133
600	4.028	3301.9	3704.4	9.0976	2.013	3301.4	3704.0	8.7770
700	4.490	3479.2	3928.2	9.3398	2.244	3478.8	3927.6	9.0194
800	4.952	3663.5	4158.6	9.5652	2.475	3663.1	4158.2	9.2449
900	5.414	3854.8	4396.1	9.7767	2.705	3854.5	4395.8	9.4566
1000	5.875	4052.8	4640.3	9.9764	2.937	4052.5	4640.0	9.6563
1100	6.337	4257.3	4891.0	10.1659	3.168	4257.0	4890.7	9.8458
1200	6.799	4467.7	5147.6	10.3463	3.399	4467.5	5147.5	10.0262
1300	7.260	4683.5	5409.5	10.5183	3.630	4683.2	5409.3	10.1982
		$p = 0.40$ MPa (143.63^oC)				$p = 0.60$ MPa (158.85^oC)		
Sat.	0.4625	2553.6	2738.6	6.8959	0.3157	2567.4	2756.8	6.7600
150	0.4708	2564.5	2752.8	6.9299				
200	0.5342	2646.8	2860.5	7.1706	0.3520	2638.9	2850.1	6.9665
250	0.5951	2726.1	2964.2	7.3789	0.3938	2720.9	2957.2	7.1816
300	0.6548	2804.8	3066.8	7.5662	0.4344	2801.0	3061.6	7.3724
350					0.4742	2881.2	3165.7	7.5464
400	0.7726	2964.4	3273.4	7.8985	0.5137	2962.1	3270.3	7.7079
500	0.8893	3129.2	3484.9	8.1913	0.5920	3127.6	3482.8	8.0021
600	1.0055	3300.2	3702.4	8.4558	0.6697	3299.1	3700.9	8.2674
700	1.1215	3477.9	3926.5	8.6987	0.7472	3477.0	3925.3	8.5107
800	1.2372	3662.4	4157.3	8.9244	0.8245	3661.8	4156.5	8.7367
900	1.3529	3853.9	4395.1	9.1362	0.9017	3853.4	4394.4	8.9486
1000	1.4685	4052.0	4639.4	9.3360	0.9788	4051.5	4638.8	9.1485
1100	1.5840	4256.5	4890.2	9.5256	1.0559	4256.1	4889.6	9.3381
1200	1.6996	4467.0	5146.8	9.7060	1.1330	4466.5	5146.3	9.5185
1300	1.8151	4682.8	5408.8	9.8780	1.2101	4682.3	5408.3	9.6906
		$p = 0.80$ MPa (170.43^oC)				$p = 1.00$ MPa (179.91^oC)		
Sat.	0.2404	2576.8	2769.1	6.6628	0.194 44	2583.6	2778.1	6.5865
200	0.2608	2630.6	2839.3	6.8158	0.2060	2621.9	2827.9	6.6940
250	0.2931	2715.5	2950.0	7.0384	0.2327	2709.9	2942.6	6.9247
300	0.3241	2797.2	3056.5	7.2328	0.2579	2793.2	3051.2	7.1229
350	0.3544	2878.2	3161.7	7.4089	0.2825	2875.2	3157.7	7.3011
400	0.3843	2959.7	3267.1	7.5716	0.3066	2957.3	3263.9	7.4651
500	0.4433	3126.0	3480.6	7.8673	0.3541	3124.4	3478.5	7.7622
600	0.5018	3297.9	3699.4	8.1333	0.4011	3296.8	3697.9	8.0290
700	0.5601	3476.2	3924.2	8.3770	0.4478	3475.3	3923.1	8.2731
800	0.6181	3661.1	4155.6	8.6033	0.4943	3660.4	4154.7	8.4996
900	0.6761	3852.8	4393.7	8.8153	0.5407	3852.2	4392.9	8.7118
1000	0.7340	4051.0	4638.2	9.0153	0.5871	4050.5	4637.6	8.9119
1100	0.7919	4255.6	4889.1	9.2050	0.6335	4255.1	4888.6	9.1017
1200	0.8497	4466.1	5145.9	9.3855	0.6798	4465.6	5145.4	9.2822
1300	0.9076	4681.8	5407.9	9.5575	0.7261	4681.3	5407.4	9.4543

P-h DIAGRAM FOR REFRIGERANT HFC-134a

(metric units)

(Reproduced by permission of the DuPont Company)

ASHRAE PSYCHROMETRIC CHART NO. 1

(metric units)

Reproduced by permission of ASHRAE

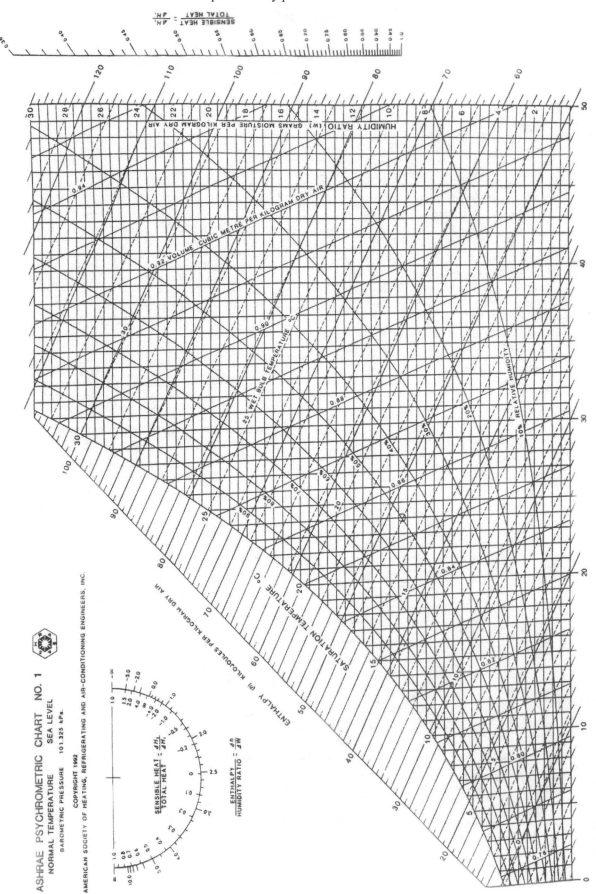

HEAT CAPACITY

(at Room Temperature)

Substance	Mol wt	c_p		c_v		k
		kJ/(kg·K)	Btu/(lbm-°R)	kJ/(kg·K)	Btu/(lbm-°R)	
Gases						
Air	29	1.00	0.240	0.718	0.171	1.40
Argon	40	0.520	0.125	0.312	0.0756	1.67
Butane	58	1.72	0.415	1.57	0.381	1.09
Carbon dioxide	44	0.846	0.203	0.657	0.158	1.29
Carbon monoxide	28	1.04	0.249	0.744	0.178	1.40
Ethane	30	1.77	0.427	1.49	0.361	1.18
Helium	4	5.19	1.25	3.12	0.753	1.67
Hydrogen	2	14.3	3.43	10.2	2.44	1.40
Methane	16	2.25	0.532	1.74	0.403	1.30
Neon	20	1.03	0.246	0.618	0.148	1.67
Nitrogen	28	1.04	0.248	0.743	0.177	1.40
Octane vapor	114	1.71	0.409	1.64	0.392	1.04
Oxygen	32	0.918	0.219	0.658	0.157	1.40
Propane	44	1.68	0.407	1.49	0.362	1.12
Steam	18	1.87	0.445	1.41	0.335	1.33

Substance	c_P		Density	
	kJ/(kg·K)	Btu/(lbm-°R)	kg/m³	lbm/ft³
Liquids				
Ammonia	4.80	1.146	602	38
Mercury	0.139	0.033	13,560	847
Water	4.18	1.000	997	62.4
Solids				
Aluminum	0.900	0.215	2,700	170
Copper	0.386	0.092	8,900	555
Ice (0°C; 32°F)	2.11	0.502	917	57.2
Iron	0.450	0.107	7,840	490
Lead	0.128	0.030	11,310	705

HEAT TRANSFER

There are three modes of heat transfer: conduction, convection, and radiation. Boiling and condensation are classified as convection.

Conduction

Fourier's Law of Conduction

$$\dot{Q} = -kA(dT/dx), \text{ where}$$

$\dot{Q}$ = rate of heat transfer.

Conduction Through a Plane Wall:

$$\dot{Q} = -kA(T_2 - T_1)/L, \text{ where}$$

k = the thermal conductivity of the wall,

A = the wall surface area,

L = the wall thickness, and

T_1, T_2 = the temperature on the near side and far side of the wall respectively.

Thermal resistance of the wall is given by

$$R = L/(kA)$$

Resistances in series are added.

Composite Walls:

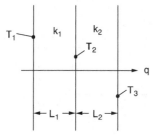

$$R_{\text{total}} = R_1 + R_2, \text{ where}$$

R_1 = $L_1/(k_1 A)$, and

R_2 = $L_2/(k_2 A)$.

To Evaluate Surface or Intermediate Temperatures:

$$T_2 = T_1 - \dot{Q}R_1; T_3 = T_2 - \dot{Q}R_2$$

Conduction through a cylindrical wall is given by

CYLINDER (LENGTH = L)

$$\dot{Q} = \frac{2\pi k L (T_1 - T_2)}{\ln(r_2/r_1)}$$

$$R = \frac{\ln(r_2/r_1)}{2\pi k L}$$

Convection

Convection is determined using a convection coefficient (heat transfer coefficient) h.

$$\dot{Q} = hA(T_w - T_\infty), \text{ where}$$

A = the heat transfer area,

T_w = work temperature, and

T_∞ = bulk fluid temperature.

Resistance due to convection is given by

$$R = 1/(hA)$$

FINS: For a straight fin,

$$\dot{Q} = \sqrt{hpkA_c}\,(T_b - T_\infty)\tanh mL_c, \text{ where}$$

h = heat transfer coefficient,

p = exposed perimeter,

k = thermal conductivity,

A_c = cross-sectional area,

T_b = temperature at base of fin,

T_∞ = fluid temperature,

m = $\sqrt{hp/(kA_c)}$, and

L_c = $L + A_c/p$, corrected length.

Radiation

The radiation emitted by a body is given by

$$\dot{Q} = \varepsilon\sigma A T^4, \text{ where}$$

T = the absolute temperature (K or °R),

σ = 5.67×10^{-8} W/(m²·K⁴)
$\qquad [0.173 \times 10^{-8}$ Btu/(hr-ft²–°R⁴)],

ε = the emissivity of the body, and

A = the body surface area.

For a body (1) which is small compared to its surroundings (2)

$$\dot{Q}_{12} = \varepsilon\sigma A(T_1^4 - T_2^4), \text{ where}$$

$\dot{Q}_{12}$ = the net heat transfer rate from the body.

A *black body* is defined as one which absorbs all energy incident upon it. It also emits radiation at the maximum rate for a body of a particular size at a particular temperature. For such a body

$$\alpha = \varepsilon = 1, \text{ where}$$

α = the absorptivity (energy absorbed/incident energy).

A *gray body* is one for which $\alpha = \varepsilon$, where

$$0 < \alpha < 1; \ 0 < \varepsilon < 1$$

Real bodies are frequently approximated as gray bodies.

The net energy exchange by radiation between two black bodies, which see each other, is given by

$$\dot{Q}_{12} = A_1 F_{12} \sigma \left(T_1^4 - T_2^4 \right), \text{ where}$$

F_{12} = the shape factor (view factor, configuration factor); $0 \leq F_{12} \leq 1$.

For any body, $\alpha + \rho + \tau = 1$, where

α = absorptivity,

ρ = reflectivity (ratio of energy reflected to incident energy), and

τ = transmissivity (ratio of energy transmitted to incident energy).

For an opaque body, $\alpha + \rho = 1$

For a gray body, $\varepsilon + \rho = 1$

The following is applicable to the PM examination for mechanical and chemical engineers.

The overall *heat-transfer coefficient* for a shell-and-tube heat exchanger is

$$\frac{1}{UA} = \frac{1}{h_i A_i} + \frac{R_{fi}}{A_i} + \frac{t}{k A_{avg}} + \frac{R_{fo}}{A_o} + \frac{1}{h_o A_o}, \text{ where}$$

A = any convenient reference area (m²),

A_{avg} = average of inside and outside area (for thin-walled tubes) (m²),

A_i = inside area of tubes (m²),

A_o = outside area of tubes (m²),

h_i = *heat-transfer coefficient* for inside of tubes [W/(m²·K)],

h_o = *heat-transfer coefficient* for outside of tubes [W/(m²·K)],

k = *thermal conductivity* of tube material [W/(m·K)],

R_{fi} = *fouling factor* for inside of tube (m²·K/W),

R_{fo} = *fouling factor* for outside of tube (m²·K/W),

t = tube-wall thickness (m), and

U = *overall heat-transfer coefficient* based on area A and the log mean temperature difference [W/(m²·K)].

The *log mean temperature difference (LMTD) for countercurrent flow in tubular heat exchangers* is

$$\Delta T_{lm} = \frac{(T_{Ho} - T_{Ci}) - (T_{Hi} - T_{Co})}{\ln\left(\dfrac{T_{Ho} - T_{Ci}}{T_{Hi} - T_{Co}}\right)}$$

The *log mean temperature difference for concurrent (parallel) flow in tubular heat exchangers* is

$$\Delta T_{lm} = \frac{(T_{Ho} - T_{Co}) - (T_{Hi} - T_{Ci})}{\ln\left(\dfrac{T_{Ho} - T_{Co}}{T_{Hi} - T_{Ci}}\right)}, \text{ where}$$

ΔT_{lm} = log mean temperature difference (K),

T_{Hi} = inlet temperature of the hot fluid (K),

T_{Ho} = outlet temperature of the hot fluid (K),

T_{Ci} = inlet temperature of the cold fluid (K), and

T_{Co} = outlet temperature of the cold fluid (K).

For individual heat-transfer coefficients of a fluid being heated or cooled in a tube, one pair of temperatures (either the hot or the cold) are the surface temperatures at the inlet and outlet of the tube.

Heat exchanger effectiveness =

$$\frac{\text{actual heat transfer}}{\text{max possible heat transfer}} = \frac{q}{q_{max}}$$

$$\varepsilon = \frac{C_H (T_{Hi} - T_{Ho})}{C_{min}(T_{Hi} - T_{Ci})}$$

or

$$\varepsilon = \frac{C_C (T_{Co} - T_{Ci})}{C_{min}(T_{Hi} - T_{Ci})}$$

Where C_{min} = smaller of C_c or C_H and $C = \dot{m}c_p$

Number of transfer units, $\text{NTU} = \dfrac{UA}{C_{min}}$

At a cross-section in a tube where heat is being transferred

$$\frac{\dot{Q}}{A} = h(T_w - T_b) = \left[k_f \left(\frac{dt}{dr} \right)_w \right]_{fluid}$$

$$= \left[k_m \left(\frac{dt}{dr} \right)_w \right]_{metal}, \text{ where}$$

$\dot{Q}/A$ = local inward radial heat flux (W/m²),

h = local heat-transfer coefficient [W/(m²·K)],

k_f = thermal conductivity of the fluid [W/(m·K)],

k_m = thermal conductivity of the tube metal [W/(m·K)],

$(dt/dr)_w$ = radial temperature gradient at the tube surface (K/m),

T_b = local bulk temperature of the fluid (K), and

T_w = local inside surface temperature of the tube (K).

Rate of Heat Transfer in a Tubular Heat Exchanger

For the equations below, the following definitions along with definitions previously supplied are required.

D = inside diameter

Gz = Graetz number [$RePr\,(D/L)$],

Nu = Nusselt number (hD/k),

Pr = Prandtl number ($c_P\mu/k$),

A = area upon which U is based (m^2),

F = configuration correction factor,

g = acceleration of gravity (9.81 m/s^2),

L = heated (or cooled) length of conduit or surface (m),

$\dot{Q}$ = inward rate of heat transfer (W),

T_s = temperature of the surface (K),

T_{sv} = temperature of saturated vapor (K), and

λ = heat of vaporization (J/kg).

$$\dot{Q} = UAF\Delta T_{lm}$$

Heat-transfer for laminar flow (Re < 2,000) in a closed conduit.

$$Nu = 3.66 + \frac{0.19Gz^{0.8}}{1 + 0.117Gz^{0.467}}$$

Heat-transfer for turbulent flow (Re > 10^4, Pr > 0.7) in a closed conduit (Sieder-Tate equation).

$$Nu = \frac{h_i D}{k_f} = 0.023Re^{0.8}Pr^{1/3}\left(\mu_b/\mu_w\right)^{0.14}, \text{ where}$$

μ_b = $\mu\,(T_b)$, and

μ_w = $\mu\,(T_w)$, and Re and Pr are evaluated at T_b.

For non-circular ducts, use the equivalent diameter.

The equivalent diameter is defined as

$$D_H = \frac{4\,(\text{cross - sectional area})}{\text{wetted perimeter}}$$

For a circular annulus (D$_o$ > D$_i$) the equivalent diameter is

$$D_H = D_o - D_i$$

For liquid metals (0.003 < Pr < 0.05) flowing in closed conduits.

$Nu = 6.3 + 0.0167Re^{0.85}Pr^{0.93}$ (constant heat flux)

$Nu = 7.0 + 0.025Re^{0.8}Pr^{0.8}$ (constant wall temperature)

Heat-transfer coefficient for condensation of a pure vapor on a vertical surface.

$$\frac{hL}{k} = 0.943\left(\frac{L^3\rho^2 g\lambda}{k\mu\left(T_{sv} - T_s\right)}\right)^{0.25}$$

Properties other than λ are for the liquid and are evaluated at the average between T_{sv} and T_s.

For condensation outside horizontal tubes, change 0.943 to 0.73 and replace L with the tube outside diameter.

Heat Transfer to/from Bodies Immersed in a Large Body of Flowing Fluid

In all cases, evaluate fluid properties at average temperature between that of the body and that of the flowing fluid.

For flow parallel to a constant-temperature flat plate of length L (m)

$Nu = 0.648Re^{0.5}Pr^{1/3}$ (Re < 10^5)

$Nu = 0.0366Re^{0.8}Pr^{1/3}$ (Re > 10^5)

Use the plate length in the evaluation of the Nusselt and Reynolds numbers.

For flow perpendicular to the axis of a constant-temperature circular cylinder

$Nu = cRe^nPr^{1/3}$ (values of c and n follow)

Use the cylinder diameter in the evaluation of the Nusselt and Reynolds numbers.

Re	n	c
1 – 4	0.330	0.989
4 – 40	0.385	0.911
40 – 4,000	0.466	0.683
4,000 – 40,000	0.618	0.193
40,000 – 250,000	0.805	0.0266

For flow past a constant-temperature sphere. $Nu = 2.0 + 0.60Re^{0.5}Pr^{1/3}$

(1 < Re < 70,000, 0.6 < Pr < 400)

Use the sphere diameter in the evaluation of the Nusselt and Reynolds numbers.

Conductive Heat Transfer

Steady Conduction with Internal Energy Generation

For one-dimensional steady conduction, the equation is

$$d^2T/dx^2 + \dot{Q}_{gen}/k = 0, \text{ where}$$

$\dot{Q}_{gen}$ = the heat generation rate per unit volume, and

k = the thermal conductivity.

For a plane wall:

$$T(x) = \frac{\dot{Q}_{gen}L^2}{2k}\left(1 - \frac{x^2}{L^2}\right) + \left(\frac{T_{s2} - T_{s1}}{2}\right)\left(\frac{x}{L}\right) + \left(\frac{T_{s1} + T_{s2}}{2}\right)$$

$$\dot{Q}_1'' + \dot{Q}_2'' = 2\dot{Q}_{gen}L, \text{ where}$$

$$\dot{Q}_1'' = k(dT/dx)_{-L}$$
$$\dot{Q}_2'' = -k(dT/dx)_L$$

For a long circular cylinder:

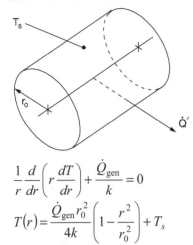

$$\frac{1}{r}\frac{d}{dr}\left(r\frac{dT}{dr}\right)+\frac{\dot{Q}_{gen}}{k}=0$$

$$T(r)=\frac{\dot{Q}_{gen}r_0^2}{4k}\left(1-\frac{r^2}{r_0^2}\right)+T_s$$

$$\dot{Q}'=\pi r_0^2\dot{Q}_{gen}\text{, where}$$

$\dot{Q}'$ = the heat-transfer rate from the cylinder per unit length.

Transient Conduction Using the Lumped Capacitance Method

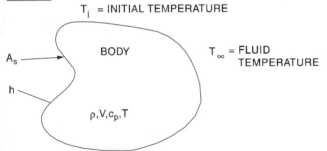

If the temperature may be considered uniform within the body at any time, the change of body temperature is given by

$$\dot{Q}=hA_s(T-T_\infty)=-\rho c_p V(dT/dt)$$

The temperature variation with time is

$$T-T_\infty=(T_i-T_\infty)e^{-(hA_s/\rho c_p V)t}$$

The total heat transferred up to time t is

$$Q_{total}=\rho c_P V(T_i-T)\text{, where}$$

ρ = density,

V = volume,

c_P = heat capacity,

t = time,

A_s = surface area of the body,

T = temperature, and

h = the heat-transfer coefficient.

The lumped capacitance method is valid if

$$\text{Biot number}=\text{Bi}=hV/kA_s\ll 1$$

Natural (Free) Convection

For free convection between a vertical flat plate (or a vertical cylinder of sufficiently large diameter) and a large body of stationary fluid,

$$h=C(k/L)\text{Ra}_L^n\text{, where}$$

L = the length of the plate in the vertical direction,

Ra_L = Rayleigh Number = $\dfrac{g\beta(T_s-T_\infty)L^3}{v^2}\text{Pr}$,

T_s = surface temperature,

T_∞ = fluid temperature,

β = coefficient of thermal expansion ($\dfrac{2}{T_s+T_\infty}$ for an ideal gas where T is absolute temperature), and

v = kinematic viscosity.

Range of Ra$_L$	C	n
10^4-10^9	0.59	1/4
10^9-10^{13}	0.10	1/3

For free convection between a long horizontal cylinder and a large body of stationary fluid

$$h=C(k/D)\text{Ra}_D^n\text{, where}$$

$$\text{Ra}_D=\frac{g\beta(T_s-T_\infty)D^3}{v^2}\text{Pr}$$

Range of Ra$_D$	C	n
$10^{-3}-10^2$	1.02	0.148
10^2-10^4	0.850	0.188
10^4-10^7	0.480	0.250
10^7-10^{12}	0.125	0.333

Radiation

Two-Body Problem

Applicable to any two diffuse-gray surfaces that form an enclosure.

$$\dot{Q}_{12}=\frac{\sigma(T_1^4-T_2^4)}{\dfrac{1-\varepsilon_1}{\varepsilon_1 A_1}+\dfrac{1}{A_1 F_{12}}+\dfrac{1-\varepsilon_2}{\varepsilon_2 A_2}}$$

Generalized Cases

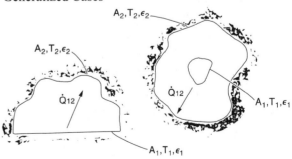

Radiation Shields

One-dimensional geometry with low-emissivity shield inserted between two parallel plates.

Reradiating Surface

Reradiating surfaces are considered to be insulated, or adiabatic ($\dot{Q}_R = 0$).

$$\dot{Q}_{12} = \frac{\sigma\left(T_1^4 - T_2^4\right)}{\dfrac{1-\varepsilon_1}{\varepsilon_1 A_1} + \dfrac{1}{A_1 F_{13}} + \dfrac{1-\varepsilon_{3,1}}{\varepsilon_{3,1} A_3} + \dfrac{1-\varepsilon_{3,2}}{\varepsilon_{3,2} A_3} + \dfrac{1}{A_3 F_{32}} + \dfrac{1-\varepsilon_2}{\varepsilon_2 A_2}}$$

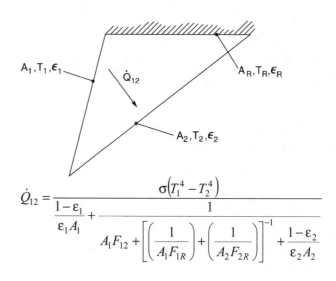

$$\dot{Q}_{12} = \frac{\sigma\left(T_1^4 - T_2^4\right)}{\dfrac{1-\varepsilon_1}{\varepsilon_1 A_1} + \dfrac{1}{A_1 F_{12} + \left[\left(\dfrac{1}{A_1 F_{1R}}\right) + \left(\dfrac{1}{A_2 F_{2R}}\right)\right]^{-1}} + \dfrac{1-\varepsilon_2}{\varepsilon_2 A_2}}$$

Shape Factor Relations

Reciprocity relations:

$$A_i F_{ij} = A_j F_{ji}$$

Summation rule:

$$\sum_{j=1}^{N} F_{ij} = 1$$

TRANSPORT PHENOMENA

MOMENTUM, HEAT, AND MASS TRANSFER ANALOGY

For the equations which apply to **turbulent flow in circular tubes**, the following definitions apply:

Nu = Nusselt Number $\left[\dfrac{hD}{k}\right]$

Pr = Prandtl Number $(c_P\mu/k)$,

Re = Reynolds Number $(DV\rho/\mu)$,

Sc = Schmidt Number $[\mu/(\rho D_m)]$,

Sh = Sherwood Number $(k_m D/D_m)$,

St = Stanton Number $[h/(c_p G)]$,

c_m = concentration (mol/m^3),

c_P = heat capacity of fluid $[J/(kg\cdot K)]$,

D = tube inside diameter (m),

D_m = diffusion coefficient (m^2/s),

$(dc_m/dy)_w$ = concentration gradient at the wall (mol/m^4),

$(dT/dy)_w$ = temperature gradient at the wall (K/m),

$(dv/dy)_w$ = velocity gradient at the wall (s^{-1}),

f = Moody friction factor,

G = mass velocity $[kg/(m^2\cdot s)]$,

h = heat-transfer coefficient at the wall $[W/(m^2\cdot K)]$,

k = thermal conductivity of fluid $[W/(m\cdot K)]$,

k_m = mass-transfer coefficient (m/s),

L = length over which pressure drop occurs (m),

$(N/A)_w$ = inward mass-transfer flux at the wall $[mol/(m^2\cdot s)]$,

$\left(\dot{Q}/A\right)_w$ = inward heat-transfer flux at the wall (W/m^2),

y = distance measured from inner wall toward centerline (m),

Δc_m = concentration difference between wall and bulk fluid (mol/m^3),

ΔT = temperature difference between wall and bulk fluid (K),

μ = absolute dynamic viscosity $(N\cdot s/m^2)$, and

τ_w = shear stress (momentum flux) at the tube wall (N/m^2).

Definitions already introduced also apply.

Rate of transfer as a function of gradients at the wall

Momentum Transfer:

$$\tau_w = -\mu\left(\frac{dv}{dy}\right)_w = -\frac{f\rho V^2}{8} = \left(\frac{D}{4}\right)\left(-\frac{\Delta p}{L}\right)_f$$

Heat Transfer:

$$\left(\frac{\dot{Q}}{A}\right)_w = -k\left(\frac{dT}{dy}\right)_w$$

Mass Transfer in Dilute Solutions:

$$\left(\frac{N}{A}\right)_w = -D_m\left(\frac{dc_m}{dy}\right)_w$$

Rate of transfer in terms of coefficients

Momentum Transfer:

$$\tau_w = \frac{f\rho V^2}{8}$$

Heat Transfer:

$$\left(\frac{\dot{Q}}{A}\right)_w = h\Delta T$$

Mass Transfer:

$$\left(\frac{N}{A}\right)_w = k_m\Delta c_m$$

Use of friction factor (f) to predict heat-transfer and mass-transfer coefficients (turbulent flow)

Heat Transfer:

$$j_H = \left(\frac{Nu}{Re\,Pr}\right)Pr^{2/3} = \frac{f}{8}$$

Mass Transfer:

$$j_M = \left(\frac{Sh}{Re\,Sc}\right)Sc^{2/3} = \frac{f}{8}$$

CHEMISTRY

Avogadro's Number: The number of elementary particles in a mol of a substance.

$$1 \text{ mol} = 1 \text{ gram-mole}$$
$$1 \text{ mol} = 6.02 \times 10^{23} \text{ particles}$$

A *mol* is defined as an amount of a substance that contains as many particles as 12 grams of ^{12}C (carbon 12). The elementary particles may be atoms, molecules, ions, or electrons.

ACIDS AND BASES (aqueous solutions)

$$pH = \log_{10}\left(\frac{1}{[H^+]}\right), \text{ where}$$

$[H^+]$ = molar concentration of hydrogen ion,

Acids have pH < 7.

Bases have pH > 7.

ELECTROCHEMISTRY

Cathode – The electrode at which reduction occurs.

Anode – The electrode at which oxidation occurs.

Oxidation – The loss of electrons.

Reduction – The gaining of electrons.

Oxidizing Agent – A species that causes others to become oxidized.

Reducing Agent – A species that causes others to be reduced.

Cation – Positive ion

Anion – Negative ion

DEFINITIONS

Molarity of Solutions – The number of gram moles of a substance dissolved in a liter of solution.

Molality of Solutions – The number of gram moles of a substance per 1,000 grams of solvent.

Normality of Solutions – The product of the molarity of a solution and the number of valences taking place in a reaction.

Equivalent Mass – The number of parts by mass of an element or compound which will combine with or replace directly or indirectly 1.008 parts by mass of hydrogen, 8.000 parts of oxygen, or the equivalent mass of any other element or compound. For all elements, the atomic mass is the product of the equivalent mass and the valence.

Molar Volume of an Ideal Gas [at 0°C (32°F) and 1 atm (14.7 psia)]; 22.4 L/(g mole) [359 ft^3/(lb mole)].

Mole Fraction of a Substance – The ratio of the number of moles of a substance to the total moles present in a mixture of substances. Mixture may be a solid, a liquid solution, or a gas.

Equilibrium Constant of a Chemical Reaction

$$aA + bB \rightleftarrows cC + dD$$

$$K_{eq} = \frac{[C]^c [D]^d}{[A]^a [B]^b}$$

Le Chatelier's Principle for Chemical Equilibrium – When a stress (such as a change in concentration, pressure, or temperature) is applied to a system in equilibrium, the equilibrium shifts in such a way that tends to relieve the stress.

Heats of Reaction, Solution, Formation, and Combustion – Chemical processes generally involve the absorption or evolution of heat. In an endothermic process, heat is absorbed (enthalpy change is positive). In an exothermic process, heat is evolved (enthalpy change is negative).

Solubility Product of a slightly soluble substance *AB*:

$$A_mB_n \rightarrow mA^{n+} + nB^{m-}$$

Solubility Product Constant = $K_{SP} = [A^+]^m [B^-]^n$

Metallic Elements – In general, metallic elements are distinguished from non-metallic elements by their luster, malleability, conductivity, and usual ability to form positive ions.

Non-Metallic Elements – In general, non-metallic elements are not malleable, have low electrical conductivity, and rarely form positive ions.

Faraday's Law – In the process of electrolytic changes, equal quantities of electricity charge or discharge equivalent quantities of ions at each electrode. One gram equivalent weight of matter is chemically altered at each electrode for 96,485 coulombs, or one Faraday, of electricity passed through the electrolyte.

A *catalyst* is a substance that alters the rate of a chemical reaction and may be recovered unaltered in nature and amount at the end of the reaction. The catalyst does not affect the position of equilibrium of a reversible reaction.

The *atomic number* is the number of protons in the atomic nucleus. The atomic number is the essential feature which distinguishes one element from another and determines the position of the element in the periodic table.

Boiling Point Elevation – The presence of a non-volatile solute in a solvent raises the boiling point of the resulting solution compared to the pure solvent; i.e., to achieve a given vapor pressure, the temperature of the solution must be higher than that of the pure substance.

Freezing Point Depression – The presence of a solute lowers the freezing point of the resulting solution compared to that of the pure solvent.

PERIODIC TABLE OF ELEMENTS

Legend:
Atomic Number
Symbol
Atomic Weight

Group 1	2	3	4	5	6	7	8	9	10	11	12	13	14	15	16	17	18
1 **H** 1.0079																	2 **He** 4.0026
3 **Li** 6.941	4 **Be** 9.0122											5 **B** 10.811	6 **C** 12.011	7 **N** 14.007	8 **O** 15.999	9 **F** 18.998	10 **Ne** 20.179
11 **Na** 22.990	12 **Mg** 24.305											13 **Al** 26.981	14 **Si** 28.086	15 **P** 30.974	16 **S** 32.066	17 **Cl** 35.453	18 **Ar** 39.948
19 **K** 39.098	20 **Ca** 40.078	21 **Sc** 44.956	22 **Ti** 47.88	23 **V** 50.941	24 **Cr** 51.996	25 **Mn** 54.938	26 **Fe** 55.847	27 **Co** 58.933	28 **Ni** 58.69	29 **Cu** 63.546	30 **Zn** 65.39	31 **Ga** 69.723	32 **Ge** 72.61	33 **As** 74.921	34 **Se** 78.96	35 **Br** 79.904	36 **Kr** 83.80
37 **Rb** 85.468	38 **Sr** 87.62	39 **Y** 88.906	40 **Zr** 91.224	41 **Nb** 92.906	42 **Mo** 95.94	43 **Tc** (98)	44 **Ru** 101.07	45 **Rh** 102.91	46 **Pd** 106.42	47 **Ag** 107.87	48 **Cd** 112.41	49 **In** 114.82	50 **Sn** 118.71	51 **Sb** 121.75	52 **Te** 127.60	53 **I** 126.90	54 **Xe** 131.29
55 **Cs** 132.91	56 **Ba** 137.33	57* **La** 138.91	72 **Hf** 178.49	73 **Ta** 180.95	74 **W** 183.85	75 **Re** 186.21	76 **Os** 190.2	77 **Ir** 192.22	78 **Pt** 195.08	79 **Au** 196.97	80 **Hg** 200.59	81 **Tl** 204.38	82 **Pb** 207.2	83 **Bi** 208.98	84 **Po** (209)	85 **At** (210)	86 **Rn** (222)
87 **Fr** (223)	88 **Ra** 226.02	89** **Ac** 227.03	104 **Rf** (261)	105 **Ha** (262)													

*Lanthanide Series

58 **Ce** 140.12	59 **Pr** 140.91	60 **Nd** 144.24	61 **Pm** (145)	62 **Sm** 150.36	63 **Eu** 151.96	64 **Gd** 157.25	65 **Tb** 158.92	66 **Dy** 162.50	67 **Ho** 164.93	68 **Er** 167.26	69 **Tm** 168.93	70 **Yb** 173.04	71 **Lu** 174.97

**Actinide Series

90 **Th** 232.04	91 **Pa** 231.04	92 **U** 238.03	93 **Np** 237.05	94 **Pu** (244)	95 **Am** (243)	96 **Cm** (247)	97 **Bk** (247)	98 **Cf** (251)	99 **Es** (252)	100 **Fm** (257)	101 **Md** (258)	102 **No** (259)	103 **Lr** (260)

IMPORTANT FAMILIES OF ORGANIC COMPOUNDS

	FAMILY										
	Alkane	Alkene	Alkyne	Arene	Haloalkane	Alcohol	Ether	Amine	Aldehyde	Carboxylic Acid	Ester
Specific Example	CH_3CH_3	$H_2C = CH_2$	$HC \equiv CH$		CH_3CH_2Cl	CH_3CH_2OH	CH_3OCH_3	CH_3NH_2	$CH_3CH{=}O$	$CH_3COH{=}O$	$CH_3COCH{=}O$
IUPAC Name	Ethane	Ethene or Ethylene	Ethyne or Acetylene	Benzene	Chloroethane	Ethanol	Methoxy-methane	Methan-amine	Ethanal	Ethanoic Acid	Methyl ethanoate
Common Name	Ethane	Ethylene	Acetylene	Benzene	Ethyl chloride	Ethyl alcohol	Dimethyl ether	Methyl-amine	Acetal-dehyde	Acetic Acid	Methyl acetate
General Formula	RH	$RCH = CH_2$ $RCH = CHR$ $R_2C = CHR$ $R_2C = CR_2$	$RC \equiv CH$ $RC \equiv CR$	ArH	RX	ROH	ROR	RNH_2 R_2NH R_3N	$RCH{=}O$	$RCOH{=}O$	$RCOR{=}O$
Functional Group	C–H and C–C bonds	$\mathrm{C = C}$	$-C \equiv C-$	Aromatic Ring	$-C-X$	$-C-OH$	$-C-O-C-$	$-C-N-$	$-C-H{=}O$	$-C-OH{=}O$	$-C-O-C-{=}O$

Standard Oxidation Potentials for Corrosion Reactions*	
Corrosion Reaction	**Potential, E_o, Volts vs. Normal Hydrogen Electrode**
$Au \rightarrow Au^{3+} + 3e$	-1.498
$2H_2O \rightarrow O_2 + 4H^+ + 4e$	-1.229
$Pt \rightarrow Pt^{2+} + 2e$	-1.200
$Pd \rightarrow Pd^{2+} + 2e$	-0.987
$Ag \rightarrow Ag^+ + e$	-0.799
$2Hg \rightarrow Hg_2^{2+} + 2e$	-0.788
$Fe^{2+} \rightarrow Fe^{3+} + e$	-0.771
$4(OH)^- \rightarrow O_2 + 2H_2O + 4e$	-0.401
$Cu \rightarrow Cu^{2+} + 2e$	-0.337
$Sn^{2+} \rightarrow n^{4+} + 2e$	-0.150
$H_2 \rightarrow 2H^+ + 2e$	0.000
$Pb \rightarrow Pb^{2+} + 2e$	$+0.126$
$Sn \rightarrow Sn^{2+} + 2e$	$+0.136$
$Ni \rightarrow Ni^{2+} + 2e$	$+0.250$
$Co \rightarrow Co^{2+} + 2e$	$+0.277$
$Cd \rightarrow Cd^{2+} + 2e$	$+0.403$
$Fe \rightarrow Fe^{2+} + 2e$	$+0.440$
$Cr \rightarrow Cr^{3+} + 3e$	$+0.744$
$Zn \rightarrow Zn^{2+} + 2e$	$+0.763$
$Al \rightarrow Al^{3+} + 3e$	$+1.662$
$Mg \rightarrow Mg^{2+} + 2e$	$+2.363$
$Na \rightarrow Na^+ + e$	$+2.714$
$K \rightarrow K^+ + e$	$+2.925$

* Measured at 25°C. Reactions are written as anode half-cells. Arrows are reversed for cathode half-cells.

Flinn, Richard A. and Paul K. Trojan, *Engineering Materials and Their Applications*, 4th Edition. Copyright © 1990 by Houghton Mifflin Company. Table used with permission.

NOTE: In some chemistry texts, the reactions and the signs of the values (in this table) are reversed; for example, the half-cell potential of zinc is given as -0.763 volt for the reaction $Zn^{2+} + 2e \rightarrow Zn$. When the potential E_o is positive, the reaction proceeds spontaneously as written.

MATERIALS SCIENCE/STRUCTURE OF MATTER

CRYSTALLOGRAPHY

Common Metallic Crystal Structures

body-centered cubic, face-centered cubic, and hexagonal close-packed.

♦

Body-
Centered
Cubic
(BCC)

Face-
Centered
Cubic
(FCC)

Hexagonal
Close-Packed
(HCP)

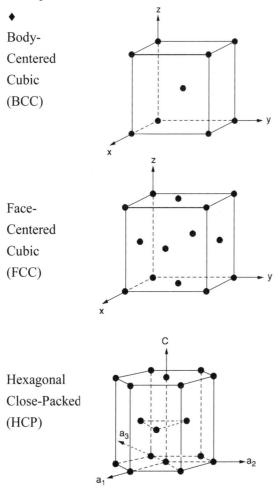

Number of Atoms in a Cell

BCC: 2

FCC: 4

HCP: 6

Packing Factor

The packing factor is the volume of the atoms in a cell (assuming touching, hard spheres) divided by the total cell volume.

BCC: 0.68

FCC: 0.74

HCP: 0.74

Coordination Number

The coordination number is the number of closest neighboring (touching) atoms in a given lattice.

Miller Indices

The rationalized reciprocal intercepts of the intersections of the plane with the crystallographic axes:

●

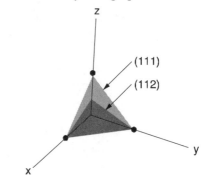

(111) plane. (axis intercepts at $x = y = z$)

(112) plane. (axis intercepts at $x = 1, y = 1, z = 1/2$)

●

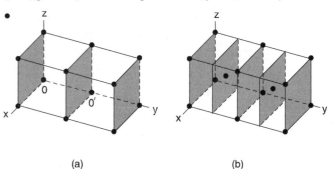

(a)　　　　　　　　　(b)

(010) planes in cubic structures. (*a*) Simple cubic. (*b*) BCC. (axis intercepts at $x = \infty, y = 1, z = \infty$)

●

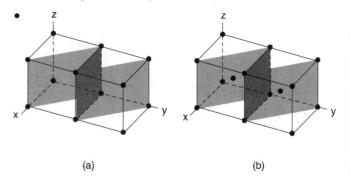

(a)　　　　　　　　　(b)

(110) planes in cubic structures. (*a*) Simple cubic. (*b*) BCC. (axis intercepts at $x = 1, y = 1, z = \infty$)

ATOMIC BONDING

Primary Bonds

Ionic (e.g., salts, metal oxides)

Covalent (e.g., within polymer molecules)

Metallic (e.g., metals)

♦Flinn, Richard A. & Paul K. Trojan, *Engineering Materials & Their Application*, 4th Ed. Copyright © 1990 by Houghton Mifflin Co. Figure used with permission.

●Van Vlack, L., *Elements of Materials Science & Engineering*, Copyright © 1989 by Addison-Wesley Publishing Co., Inc. Diagram reprinted with permission of the publisher.

CORROSION

A table listing the standard electromotive potentials of metals is shown on page 67.

For corrosion to occur, there must be an anode and a cathode in electrical contact in the presence of an electrolyte.

Anode Reaction (oxidation)

$M^o \rightarrow M^{n+} + ne^-$

Possible Cathode Reactions (reduction)

$\frac{1}{2} O_2 + 2 e^- + H_2O \rightarrow 2 OH^-$

$\frac{1}{2} O_2 + 2 e^- + 2 H_3O^+ \rightarrow 3 H_2O$

$2 e^- + 2 H_3O^+ \rightarrow 2 H_2O + H_2$

When dissimilar metals are in contact, the more electropositive one becomes the anode in a corrosion cell. Different regions of carbon steel can also result in a corrosion reaction: e.g., cold-worked regions are anodic to non-cold-worked; different oxygen concentrations can cause oxygen-deficient region to become cathodic to oxygen-rich regions; grain boundary regions are anodic to bulk grain; in multiphase alloys, various phases may not have the same galvanic potential.

DIFFUSION

Diffusion coefficient

$D = D_o\, e^{-Q/(RT)}$, where

D = the diffusion coefficient,

D_o = the proportionality constant,

Q = the activation energy,

R = the gas constant [1.987 cal/(g mol·K)], and

T = the absolute temperature.

BINARY PHASE DIAGRAMS

Allows determination of (1) what phases are present at equilibrium at any temperature and average composition, (2) the compositions of those phases, and (3) the fractions of those phases.

Eutectic reaction (liquid → two solid phases)

Eutectoid reaction (solid → two solid phases)

Peritectic reaction (liquid + solid → solid)

Pertectoid reaction (two solid phases → solid)

Lever Rule

The following phase diagram and equations illustrate how the weight of each phase in a two-phase system can be determined:

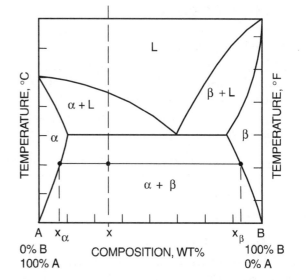

(In diagram, L = liquid) If x = the average composition at temperature T, then

$$\text{wt \%}\ \alpha = \frac{x_\beta - x}{x_\beta - x_\alpha} \times 100$$

$$\text{wt \%}\ \beta = \frac{x - x_\alpha}{x_\beta - x_\alpha} \times 100$$

Iron-Iron Carbide Phase Diagram

Gibbs Phase Rule

$P + F = C + 2$, where

P = the number of phases that can coexist in equilibrium,

F = the number of degrees of freedom, and

C = the number of components involved.

•Van Vlack, L., *Elements of Materials Science & Engineering*, Copyright © 1989 by Addison-Wesley Publishing Co., Inc. Diagram reprinted with permission of the publisher.

THERMAL PROCESSING

Cold working (plastically deforming) a metal increases strength and lowers ductility.

Raising temperature causes (1) recovery (stress relief), (2) recrystallization, and (3) grain growth. *Hot working* allows these processes to occur simultaneously with deformation.

Quenching is rapid cooling from elevated temperature, preventing the formation of equilibrium phases.

In steels, quenching austenite [FCC (γ) iron] can result in martensite instead of equilibrium phases—ferrite [BCC (α) iron] and cementite (iron carbide).

TESTING METHODS

Standard Tensile Test

Using the standard tensile test, one can determine elastic modulus, yield strength, ultimate tensile strength, and ductility (% elongation).

Endurance Test

Endurance tests (fatigue tests to find endurance limit) apply a cyclical loading of constant maximum amplitude. The plot (usually semi-log or log-log) of the maximum stress (σ) and the number (N) of cycles to failure is known as an *S-N* plot. (Typical of steel, may not be true for other metals; i.e., aluminum alloys, etc.)

The *endurance stress* (*endurance limit* or *fatigue limit*) is the maximum stress which can be repeated indefinitely without causing failure. The *fatigue life* is the number of cycles required to cause failure for a given stress level.

Impact Test

The *Charpy Impact Test* is used to find energy required to fracture and to identify ductile to brittle transition.

Impact tests determine the amount of energy required to cause failure in standardized test samples. The tests are repeated over a range of temperatures to determine the *transition temperature*.

HARDENABILITY

Hardenability is the "ease" with which hardness may be attained. *Hardness* is a measure of resistance to plastic deformation.

(#2) and (#8) indicated ASTM grain size

Hardenability Curves for Six Steels

Cooling Rates for Bars Quenched in
(a) Agitated Water and (b) Agitated Oil.

• Van Vlack, L., *Elements of Materials Science & Engineering*, Copyright © 1989 by Addison-Wesley Pub. Co., Inc. Diagrams reprinted with permission of the publisher.

ASTM GRAIN SIZE

$$S_V = 2P_L$$

$$N_{(0.0645\,\text{mm}^2)} = 2^{(n-1)}$$

$$\frac{N_{\text{actual}}}{\text{Actual Area}} = \frac{N}{(0.0645\,\text{mm}^2)}, \text{ where}$$

S_V = grain-boundary surface per unit volume,

P_L = number of points of intersection per unit length between the line and the boundaries,

N = number of grains observed in a area of 0.0645 mm^2, and

n = grain size (nearest integer > 1).

COMPOSITE MATERIALS

$$\rho_c = \Sigma f_i \rho_i$$
$$C_c = \Sigma f_i c_i$$
$$E_c = \Sigma f_i E_i, \text{ where}$$

ρ_c = density of composite,

C_c = heat capacity of composite per unit volume,

E_c = Young's modulus of composite,

f_i = volume fraction of individual material,

c_i = heat capacity of individual material per unit volume, and

E_i = Young's modulus of individual material.

Also

$$(\Delta L/L)_1 = (\Delta L/L)_2$$

$$(\alpha \Delta T + e)_1 = (\alpha \Delta T + e)_2$$

$$[\alpha \Delta T + (F/A)/E]_1 = [\alpha \Delta T + (F/A)/E]_2, \text{ where}$$

ΔL = change in length of a material,

L = original length of the material,

α = coefficient of expansion for a material,

ΔT = change in temperature for the material,

e = elongation of the material,

F = force in a material,

A = cross-sectional area of the material, and

E = Young's modulus for the material.

HALF-LIFE

$$N = N_o e^{-0.693t/\tau}, \text{ where}$$

N_o = original number of atoms,

N = final number of atoms,

t = time, and

τ = half-life.

Material	Density ρ Mg/m^3	Young's Modulus E GPa	E/ρ N·m/g
Aluminum	2.7	70	26,000
Steel	7.8	205	26,000
Magnesium	1.7	45	26,000
Glass	2.5	70	28,000
Polystyrene	1.05	2	2,700
Polyvinyl Chloride	1.3	< 4	< 3,500
Alumina fiber	3.9	400	100,000
Aramide fiber	1.3	125	100,000
Boron fiber	2.3	400	170,000
Beryllium fiber	1.9	300	160,000
BeO fiber	3.0	400	130,000
Carbon fiber	2.3	700	300,000
Silicon Carbide fiber	3.2	400	120,000

ELECTRIC CIRCUITS

UNITS

The basic electrical units are coulombs for charge, volts for voltage, amperes for current, and ohms for resistance and impedance.

ELECTROSTATICS

$$\mathbf{F}_2 = \frac{Q_1 Q_2}{4\pi\varepsilon r^2}\mathbf{a}_{r12}, \text{ where}$$

$\mathbf{F}_2$ = the force on charge 2 due to charge 1,

Q_i = the ith point charge,

r = the distance between charges 1 and 2,

$\mathbf{a}_{r12}$ = a unit vector directed from 1 to 2, and

ε = the permittivity of the medium.

For free space or air:

$$\varepsilon = \varepsilon_o = 8.85 \times 10^{-12} \text{ Farads/meter}$$

Electrostatic Fields

Electric field intensity $\mathbf{E}$ (volts/meter) at point 2 due to a point charge Q_1 at point 1 is

$$\mathbf{E} = \frac{Q_1}{4\pi\varepsilon r^2}\mathbf{a}_{r12}$$

For a line charge of density ρ_L C/m on the z-axis, the radial electric field is

$$\mathbf{E}_L = \frac{\rho_L}{2\pi\varepsilon r}\mathbf{a}_r$$

For a sheet charge of density ρ_s C/m^2 in the x-y plane:

$$\mathbf{E}_s = \frac{\rho_s}{2\varepsilon}\mathbf{a}_z, z > 0$$

Gauss' law states that the integral of the electric flux density $\mathbf{D} = \varepsilon\mathbf{E}$ over a closed surface is equal to the charge enclosed or

$$Q_{encl} = \oiint_{Sv} \varepsilon\mathbf{E} \cdot d\mathbf{S}$$

The force on a point charge Q in an electric field with intensity $\mathbf{E}$ is $\mathbf{F} = Q\mathbf{E}$.

The work done by an external agent in moving a charge Q in an electric field from point p_1 to point p_2 is

$$W = -Q \int_{p_1}^{p_2} \mathbf{E} \cdot d\mathbf{l}$$

The energy stored W_E in an electric field $\mathbf{E}$ is

$$W_E = (1/2) \iiint_V \varepsilon |\mathbf{E}|^2 \, dv$$

Voltage

The potential difference V between two points is the work per unit charge required to move the charge between the points.

For two parallel plates with potential difference V, separated by distance d, the strength of the E field between the plates is

$$E = \frac{V}{d}$$

directed from the + plate to the – plate.

Current

Electric current $i(t)$ through a surface is defined as the rate of charge transport through that surface or

$$i(t) = dq(t)/dt, \text{ which is a function of time } t$$

since $q(t)$ denotes instantaneous charge.

A constant current $i(t)$ is written as I, and the vector current density in amperes/m^2 is defined as $\mathbf{J}$.

Magnetic Fields

For a current carrying wire on the z-axis

$$\mathbf{H} = \frac{\mathbf{B}}{\mu} = \frac{I\mathbf{a}_\phi}{2\pi r}, \text{ where}$$

$\mathbf{H}$ = the magnetic field strength (amperes/meter),

$\mathbf{B}$ = the magnetic flux density (tesla),

$\mathbf{a}_\phi$ = the unit vector in positive ϕ direction in cylindrical coordinates,

I = the current, and

μ = the permeability of the medium.

For air: $\mu = \mu_o = 4\pi \times 10^{-7}$ H/m

Force on a current carrying conductor in a uniform magnetic field is

$$\mathbf{F} = I\mathbf{L} \times \mathbf{B}, \text{ where}$$

$\mathbf{L}$ = the length vector of a conductor.

The energy stored W_H in a magnetic field $\mathbf{H}$ is

$$W_H = (1/2) \iiint_V \mu |\mathbf{H}|^2 \, dv$$

Induced Voltage

Faraday's Law; For a coil of N turns enclosing flux ϕ:

$$v = -N \, d\phi/dt, \text{ where}$$

v = the induced voltage, and

ϕ = the flux (webers) enclosed by the N conductor turns, and

ϕ = $\int_S \mathbf{B} \cdot d\mathbf{S}$

Resistivity

For a conductor of length L, electrical resistivity ρ, and area A, the resistance is

$$R = \frac{\rho L}{A}$$

For metallic conductors, the resistivity and resistance vary linearly with changes in temperature according to the following relationships:

$$\rho = \rho_o [1 + \alpha (T - T_o)], \text{ and}$$

$$R = R_o [1 + \alpha (T - T_o)], \text{ where}$$

ρ_o is resistivity at T_o, R_o is the resistance at T_o, and

α is the temperature coefficient.

Ohm's Law: $V = IR$; $v(t) = i(t) R$

Resistors in Series and Parallel

For series connections, the current in all resistors is the same and the equivalent resistance for n resistors in series is

$$R_T = R_1 + R_2 + \ldots + R_n$$

For parallel connections of resistors, the voltage drop across each resistor is the same and the resistance for n resistors in parallel is

$$R_T = 1/(1/R_1 + 1/R_2 + \ldots + 1/R_n)$$

For two resistors R_1 and R_2 in parallel

$$R_T = \frac{R_1 R_2}{R_1 + R_2}$$

Power in a Resistive Element

$$P = VI = \frac{V^2}{R} = I^2 R$$

Kirchhoff's Laws

Kirchhoff's voltage law for a closed path is expressed by

$$\Sigma\, V_{\text{rises}} = \Sigma\, V_{\text{drops}}$$

Kirchhoff's current law for a closed surface is

$$\Sigma\, I_{\text{in}} = \Sigma\, I_{\text{out}}$$

SOURCE EQUIVALENTS

For an arbitrary circuit

The Thévenin equivalent is

$$R_{eq} = \frac{V_{oc}}{I_{sc}}$$

The open circuit voltage V_{oc} is $V_a - V_b$, and the short circuit current is I_{sc} from a to b.

The Norton equivalent circuit is

where I_{sc} and R_{eq} are defined above.

A load resistor R_L connected across terminals a and b will draw maximum power when $R_L = R_{eq.}$

CAPACITORS AND INDUCTORS

The charge $q_C(t)$ and voltage $v_C(t)$ relationship for a capacitor C in farads is

$$C = q_C(t)/v_C(t) \qquad \text{or} \qquad q_C(t) = Cv_C(t)$$

A parallel plate capacitor of area A with plates separated a distance d by an insulator with a permittivity ε has a capacitance

$$C = \frac{\varepsilon A}{d}$$

The current-voltage relationships for a capacitor are

$$v_C(t) = v_C(0) + \frac{1}{C}\int_0^t i_C(\tau)d\tau$$

and

$$i_C(t) = C\,(dv_C/dt)$$

The energy stored in a capacitor is expressed in joules and given by

$$\text{Energy} = Cv_C^2/2 = q_C^2/2C = q_C v_C/2$$

The inductance L of a coil is

$$L = N\phi/i_L$$

and using Faraday's law, the voltage-current relations for an inductor are

$$v_L(t) = L\,(di_L/dt)$$

$$i_L(t) = i_L(0) + \frac{1}{L}\int_0^t v_L(\tau)d\tau, \text{ where}$$

v_L = inductor voltage,

L = inductance (henrys), and

i = current (amperes).

The energy stored in an inductor is expressed in joules and given by

$$\text{Energy} = Li_L^2/2$$

Capacitors and Inductors in Parallel and Series

Capacitors in Parallel

$$C_{eq} = C_1 + C_2 + \ldots + C_n$$

Capacitors in Series

$$C_{eq} = \frac{1}{1/C_1 + 1/C_2 + \ldots + 1/C_n}$$

Inductors in Parallel

$$L_{eq} = \frac{1}{1/L_1 + 1/L_2 + \ldots + 1/L_n}$$

Inductors in Series

$$L_{eq} = L_1 + L_2 + \ldots + L_n$$

RC AND RL TRANSIENTS

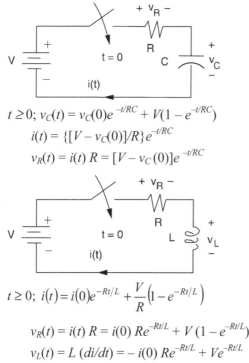

$t \geq 0;\ v_C(t) = v_C(0)e^{-t/RC} + V(1 - e^{-t/RC})$

$i(t) = \{[V - v_C(0)]/R\}e^{-t/RC}$

$v_R(t) = i(t)\,R = [V - v_C(0)]e^{-t/RC}$

$t \geq 0;\ i(t) = i(0)e^{-Rt/L} + \dfrac{V}{R}(1 - e^{-Rt/L})$

$v_R(t) = i(t)\,R = i(0)\,Re^{-Rt/L} + V(1 - e^{-Rt/L})$

$v_L(t) = L\,(di/dt) = -i(0)\,Re^{-Rt/L} + Ve^{-Rt/L}$

where $v(0)$ and $i(0)$ denote the initial conditions and the parameters RC and L/R are termed the respective circuit time constants.

OPERATIONAL AMPLIFIERS

$v_o = A(v_1 - v_2)$

where

A is large ($> 10^4$), and

$v_1 - v_2$ is small enough so as not to saturate the amplifier.

For the ideal operational amplifier, assume that the input currents are zero and that the gain A is infinite so when operating linearly $v_2 - v_1 = 0$.

For the two-source configuration with an ideal operational amplifier,

$v_o = -\dfrac{R_2}{R_1}v_a + \left(1 + \dfrac{R_2}{R_1}\right)v_b$

If $v_a = 0$, we have a non-inverting amplifier with

$v_o = \left(1 + \dfrac{R_2}{R_1}\right)v_b$

If $v_b = 0$, we have an inverting amplifier with

$v_o = -\dfrac{R_2}{R_1}v_a$

AC CIRCUITS

For a sinusoidal voltage or current of frequency f (Hz) and period T (seconds),

$f = 1/T = \omega/(2\pi)$, where

$\omega = $ the angular frequency in radians/s.

Average Value

For a periodic waveform (either voltage or current) with period T,

$$X_{\text{ave}} = (1/T)\int_0^T x(t)\,dt$$

The average value of a full-wave rectified sine wave is

$$X_{\text{ave}} = (2X_{\max})/\pi$$

and half this for a half-wave rectification, where

$X_{\max} = $ the peak amplitude of the waveform.

Effective or RMS Values

For a periodic waveform with period T, the rms or effective value is

$$X_{\text{rms}} = \left[(1/T)\int_0^T x^2(t)\,dt\right]^{1/2}$$

For a sinusoidal waveform and full-wave rectified sine wave,

$$X_{\text{rms}} = X_{\max}/\sqrt{2}$$

For a half-wave rectified sine wave,

$$X_{\text{rms}} = X_{\max}/2$$

Sine-Cosine Relations

$\cos(\omega t) = \sin(\omega t + \pi/2) = -\sin(\omega t - \pi/2)$

$\sin(\omega t) = \cos(\omega t - \pi/2) = -\cos(\omega t + \pi/2)$

Phasor Transforms of Sinusoids

$P[V_{\max}\cos(\omega t + \phi)] = V_{\text{rms}} \angle \phi = \mathbf{V}$

$P[I_{\max}\cos(\omega t + \theta)] = I_{\text{rms}} \angle \theta = \mathbf{I}$

For a circuit element, the impedance is defined as the ratio of phasor voltage to phasor current.

$$Z = \frac{V}{I}$$

For a Resistor,

$Z_R = R$

For a Capacitor,

$$Z_C = \frac{1}{j\omega C} = jX_C$$

For an Inductor,

$Z_L = j\omega L = jX_L$, where

X_C and X_L are the capacitive and inductive reactances respectively defined as

$$X_C = -\frac{1}{\omega C} \quad \text{and} \quad X_L = \omega L$$

Impedances in series combine additively while those in parallel combine according to the reciprocal rule just as in the case of resistors.

Complex Power

Real power P (watts) is defined by

$$P = (\tfrac{1}{2})V_{max}I_{max} \cos \theta$$
$$= V_{rms}I_{rms} \cos \theta$$

where θ is the angle measured from V to I. If I leads (lags) V, then the power factor ($p.f.$),

$$p.f. = \cos \theta$$

is said to be a leading (lagging) $p.f.$

Reactive power Q (vars) is defined by

$$Q = (\tfrac{1}{2})V_{max}I_{max} \sin \theta$$
$$= V_{rms}I_{rms} \sin \theta$$

Complex power S (volt-amperes) is defined by

$$S = VI^* = P + jQ,$$

where I^* is the complex conjugate of the phasor current.

For resistors, $\theta = 0$, so the real power is

$$P = V_{rms}I_{rms} = V_{rms}^2/R = I_{rms}^2 R$$

RESONANCE

The radian resonant frequency for both parallel and series resonance situations is

$$\omega_o = \frac{1}{\sqrt{LC}} = 2\pi f_o \ (\text{rad/s})$$

Series Resonance

$$\omega_o L = \frac{1}{\omega_o C}$$

$Z = R$ at resonance.

$$Q = \frac{\omega_o L}{R} = \frac{1}{\omega_o CR}$$

$$BW = \omega_o/Q \ (\text{rad/s})$$

Parallel Resonance

$$\omega_o L = \frac{1}{\omega_o C} \quad \text{and}$$

$Z = R$ at resonance.

$$Q = \omega_o RC = \frac{R}{\omega_o L}$$

$$BW = \omega_o/Q \ (\text{rad/s})$$

TRANSFORMERS

Turns Ratio

$$a = N_1/N_2$$

$$a = \left|\frac{V_p}{V_s}\right| = \left|\frac{I_s}{I_p}\right|$$

The impedance seen at the input is

$$Z_P = a^2 Z_S$$

ALGEBRA OF COMPLEX NUMBERS

Complex numbers may be designated in rectangular form or polar form. In rectangular form, a complex number is written in terms of its real and imaginary components.

$$z = a + jb, \text{ where}$$

a = the real component,

b = the imaginary component, and

j = $\sqrt{-1}$

In polar form

$$z = c \angle \theta, \text{ where}$$

c = $\sqrt{a^2 + b^2}$,

θ = $\tan^{-1}(b/a)$,

a = $c \cos \theta$, and

b = $c \sin \theta$.

Complex numbers are added and subtracted in rectangular form. If

$$z_1 = a_1 + jb_1 \quad = c_1 (\cos \theta_1 + j\sin \theta_1)$$
$$= c_1 \angle \theta_1 \text{ and}$$
$$z_2 = a_2 + jb_2 \quad = c_2 (\cos \theta_2 + j\sin \theta_2)$$
$$= c_2 \angle \theta_2, \text{ then}$$
$$z_1 + z_2 \quad = (a_1 + a_2) + j (b_1 + b_2) \text{ and}$$
$$z_1 - z_2 \quad = (a_1 - a_2) + j (b_1 - b_2)$$

While complex numbers can be multiplied or divided in rectangular form, it is more convenient to perform these operations in polar form.

$$z_1 \times z_2 \quad = (c_1 \times c_2) \angle \theta_1 + \theta_2$$
$$z_1/z_2 \quad = (c_1/c_2) \angle \theta_1 - \theta_2$$

The complex conjugate of a complex number $z_1 = (a_1 + jb_1)$ is defined as $z_1^* = (a_1 - jb_1)$. The product of a complex number and its complex conjugate is $z_1 z_1^* = a_1^2 + b_1^2$.

COMPUTERS, MEASUREMENT, AND CONTROLS

COMPUTER KNOWLEDGE

Examinees are expected to possess a level of computer expertise required to perform in a typical undergraduate environment. Thus only generic problems that do not require a knowledge of a specific language or computer type will be required. Examinees are expected to be familiar with flow charts, pseudo code, and spread sheets (Lotus, Quattro-Pro, Excel, etc.).

INSTRUMENTATION

General Considerations

In making any measurement, the response of the total measurement system, including the behavior of the sensors and any signal processors, is best addressed using the methods of control systems. Response time and the effect of the sensor on the parameter being measured may affect accuracy of a measurement. Moreover, many transducers exhibit some sensitivity to phenomena other than the primary parameter being measured. All of these considerations affect accuracy, stability, noise sensitivity, and precision of any measurement. In the case of digital measurement systems, the limit of resolution corresponds to one bit.

Examples of Types of Sensors

Fluid-based sensors such as manometers, orifice and venturi flow meters, and pitot tubes are discussed in the **FLUID MECHANICS** section.

Resistance-based sensors include resistance temperature detectors (RTDs), which are metal resistors, and thermistors, which are semiconductors. Both have electrical resistivities that are temperature dependent.

Electrical-resistance strain gages are metallic or semi-conducting foils whose resistance changes with dimensional change (strain). They are widely used in load cells. The gage is attached to the surface whose strain is to be measured. The gage factor (G.F.) of these devices is defined by

$$\text{G.F.} = \frac{\Delta R/R}{\Delta L/L} = \frac{\Delta R/R}{\varepsilon}, \quad \text{where}$$

R = electrical resistance,

L = the length of the gage section, and

ε = the normal strain sensed by the gage.

Strain gages sense normal strain along their principal axis. They do not respond to shear strain. Therefore, multiple gages must be used along with Mohr's circle techniques to determine the complete plane strain state.

Resistance-based sensors are generally used in a bridge circuit that detects small changes in resistance. The output of a bridge circuit with only one variable resistor (quarter bridge configuration) is given by

$$V_{\text{out}} = V_{\text{input}} \times [\Delta R/(4R)]$$

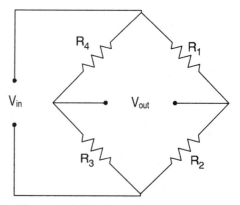

Half-bridge and full-bridge configurations use two or four variable resistors, respectively. A full-bridge strain gage circuit gives a voltage output of

$$V_{\text{out}} = V_{\text{input}} \times \text{G.F.} \times (\varepsilon_1 - \varepsilon_2 + \varepsilon_3 - \varepsilon_4)/4$$

Half- or full-strain gage bridge configurations can be developed that are sensitive to only some types of loading (axial, bending, shear) while being insensitive to others.

Piezoelectric sensors produce a voltage in response to a mechanical load. These transducers are widely used as force or pressure transducers. With the addition of an inertial mass, they are used as accelerometers.

Thermocouples are junctions of dissimilar metals which produce a voltage whose magnitude is temperature dependent.

Capacitance-based transducers are used as position sensors. The capacitance of two flat plates depends on their separation or on the area of overlap.

Inductance-based transducers or differential transformers also function as displacement transducers. The inductive coupling between a primary and secondary coil depends on the position of a soft magnetic core. This is the basis for the Linear Variable Differential Transformer (LVDT).

MEASUREMENT UNCERTAINTY

Suppose that a calculated result R depends on measurements whose values are $x_1 \pm w_1$, $x_2 \pm w_2$, $x_3 \pm w_3$, etc., where $R = f(x_1, x_2, x_3, \ldots x_n)$, x_i is the measured value, and w_i is the uncertainty in that value. The uncertainty in R, w_R, can be estimated using the Kline-McClintock equation:

$$w_R = \sqrt{\left(w_1 \frac{\partial f}{\partial x_1}\right)^2 + \left(w_2 \frac{\partial f}{\partial x_2}\right)^2 + \ldots + \left(w_n \frac{\partial f}{\partial x_n}\right)^2}$$

CONTROL SYSTEMS

The linear time-invariant transfer function model represented by the block diagram

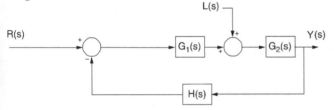

can be expressed as the ratio of two polynomials in the form

$$\frac{Y(s)}{X(s)} = G(s) = \frac{N(s)}{D(s)} = K \frac{\prod\limits_{m=1}^{M}(s - z_m)}{\prod\limits_{n=1}^{N}(s - p_n)}$$

where the M zeros, z_m, and the N poles, p_n, are the roots of the numerator polynomial, $N(s)$, and the denominator polynomial, $D(s)$, respectively.

One classical negative feedback control system model block diagram is

where $G_1(s)$ is a controller or compensator, $G_2(s)$ represents a plant model, and $H(s)$ represents the measurement dynamics. $Y(s)$ represents the controlled variable, $R(s)$ represents the reference input, and $L(s)$ represents a load disturbance. $Y(s)$ is related to $R(s)$ and $L(s)$ by

$$Y(s) = \frac{G_1(s)G_2(s)}{1 + G_1(s)G_2(s)H(s)}R(s)$$

$$+ \frac{G_2(s)}{1 + G_1(s)G_2(s)H(s)}L(s)$$

$G_1(s)\ G_2(s)\ H(s)$ is the open-loop transfer function. The closed-loop characteristic equation is

$$1 + G_1(s)\ G_2(s)\ H(s) = 0$$

System performance studies normally include:

1. Steady-state analysis using constant inputs is based on the Final Value Theorem. If all poles of a $G(s)$ function have negative real parts, then

$$\text{Steady State Gain} = \lim_{s \to 0} G(s)$$

Note that $G(s)$ could refer to either an open-loop or a closed-loop transfer function.

For the unity feedback control system model

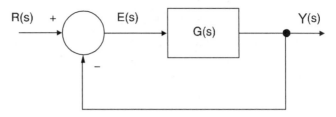

with the open-loop transfer function defined by

$$G(s) = \frac{K_B}{s^T} \times \frac{\prod\limits_{m=1}^{M}(1 + s/\omega_m)}{\prod\limits_{n=1}^{N}(1 + s/\omega_n)}$$

The following steady-state error analysis table can be constructed where T denotes the type of system; i.e., type 0, type 1, etc.

Steady-State Error $e_{ss}(t)$			
Input Type	$T = 0$	$T = 1$	$T = 2$
Unit Step	$1/(K_B + 1)$	0	0
Ramp	∞	$1/K_B$	0
Acceleration	∞	∞	$1/K_B$

2. Frequency response evaluations to determine dynamic performance and stability. For example, relative stability can be quantified in terms of

   a. Gain margin (GM) which is the additional gain required to produce instability in the unity gain feedback control system. If at $\omega = \omega_{180}$,

      $$\angle\ G(j\omega_{180}) = -180°; \text{ then}$$

      $$\text{GM} = -20\log_{10}(\,|\,G(j\omega_{180})\,|\,)$$

   b. Phase margin (PM) which is the additional phase required to produce instability. Thus,

      $$\text{PM} = 180° + \angle\ G(j\omega_{0dB})$$

      where ω_{0dB} is the ω that satisfies $|\,G(j\omega)\,| = 1$.

3. Transient responses are obtained by using Laplace Transforms or computer solutions with numerical integration.

Common Compensator/Controller forms are

PID Controller $G_C(s) = K\left(1 + \dfrac{1}{T_I s} + T_D s\right)$

Lag or Lead Compensator $G_C(s) = K\left(\dfrac{1 + sT_1}{1 + sT_2}\right)$

depending on the ratio of T_1/T_2.

Routh Test

For the characteristic equation

$$a_n s^n + a_{n-1} s^{n-1} + a_{n-2} s^{n-2} + \ldots + a_0 = 0$$

the coefficients are arranged into the first two rows of an array. Additional rows are computed. The array and coefficient computations are defined by:

a_n	a_{n-2}	a_{n-4}	$\ldots$	$\ldots$	$\ldots$
a_{n-1}	a_{n-3}	a_{n-5}	$\ldots$	$\ldots$	$\ldots$
b_1	b_2	b_3	$\ldots$	$\ldots$	$\ldots$
c_1	c_2	c_3	$\ldots$	$\ldots$	$\ldots$

where

$$b_1 = \frac{a_{n-1}a_{n-2} - a_n a_{n-3}}{a_{n-1}} \qquad c_1 = \frac{a_{n-3}b_1 - a_{n-1}b_2}{b_1}$$

$$b_2 = \frac{a_{n-1}a_{n-4} - a_n a_{n-5}}{a_{n-1}} \qquad c_2 = \frac{a_{n-5}b_1 - a_{n-1}b_3}{b_1}$$

$$\ldots$$

The necessary and sufficient conditions for all the roots of the equation to have negative real parts is that all the elements in the first column be of the same sign and nonzero.

Second-Order Control-System Models

One standard second-order control-system model is

$$\frac{Y(s)}{R(s)} = \frac{K\omega_n^2}{s^2 + 2\zeta\omega_n s + \omega_n^2}, \text{ where}$$

K = steady state gain,

ζ = the damping ratio,

ω_n = the undamped natural ($\zeta = 0$) frequency,

$\omega_d = \omega_n\sqrt{1 - \zeta^2}$, the damped natural frequency,

and

$\omega_p = \omega_n\sqrt{1 - 2\zeta^2}$, the damped resonant frequency.

If the damping ratio ζ is less than unity, the system is said to be underdamped; if ζ is equal to unity, it is said to be critically damped; and if ζ is greater than unity, the system is said to be overdamped.

For a unit step input to a normalized underdamped second-order control system, the time required to reach a peak value t_p and the value of that peak M_p are given by

$$t_p = \pi \Big/ \left(\omega_n\sqrt{1 - \zeta^2} \right)$$

$$M_p = 1 + e^{-\pi\zeta/\sqrt{1-\zeta^2}}$$

For an underdamped second-order system, the logarithmic decrement is

$$\delta = \frac{1}{m}\ln\left(\frac{x_k}{x_{k+m}}\right) = \frac{2\pi\zeta}{\sqrt{1-\zeta^2}}$$

where x_k and x_{k+m} are the amplitudes of oscillation at cycles k and $k + m$, respectively. The period of oscillation τ is related to ω_d by

$$\omega_d \tau = 2\pi$$

The time required for the output of a second-order system to settle to within 2% of its final value is defined to be

$$T_s = \frac{4}{\zeta\omega_n}$$

State-Variable Control-System Models

One common state-variable model for dynamic systems has the form

$$\dot{\mathbf{x}}(t) = \mathbf{A}\mathbf{x}(t) + \mathbf{B}\mathbf{u}(t) \qquad \text{(state equation)}$$

$$\mathbf{y}(t) = \mathbf{C}\mathbf{x}(t) + \mathbf{D}\mathbf{u}(t) \qquad \text{(output equation)}$$

where

$\mathbf{x}(t) =$ N by 1 state vector (N state variables),

$\mathbf{u}(t) =$ R by 1 input vector (R inputs),

$\mathbf{y}(t) =$ M by 1 output vector (M outputs),

$\mathbf{A}$ = system matrix,

$\mathbf{B}$ = input distribution matrix,

$\mathbf{C}$ = output matrix, and

$\mathbf{D}$ = feed-through matrix.

The orders of the matrices are defined via variable definitions.

State-variable models automatically handle multiple inputs and multiple outputs. Furthermore, state-variable models can be formulated for open-loop system components or the complete closed-loop system.

The Laplace transform of the time-invariant state equation is

$$s\mathbf{X}(s) - \mathbf{x}(0) = \mathbf{A}\mathbf{X}(s) + \mathbf{B}\mathbf{U}(s)$$

from which

$$\mathbf{X}(s) = \mathbf{\Phi}(s)\,\mathbf{x}(0) + \mathbf{\Phi}(s)\,\mathbf{B}\mathbf{U}(s)$$

where the Laplace transform of the state transition matrix is

$$\mathbf{\Phi}(s) = [s\mathbf{I} - \mathbf{A}]^{-1}.$$

The state-transition matrix

$$\mathbf{\Phi}(t) = L^{-1}\{\mathbf{\Phi}(s)\}$$

(also defined as $e^{\mathbf{A}t}$) can be used to write

$$\mathbf{x}(t) = \mathbf{\Phi}(t)\,\mathbf{x}(0) + \int_0^t \mathbf{\Phi}(t - \tau)\,\mathbf{B}\mathbf{u}(\tau)\,d\tau$$

The output can be obtained with the output equation; e.g., the Laplace transform output is

$$\mathbf{Y}(s) = \{\mathbf{C}\mathbf{\Phi}(s)\,\mathbf{B} + \mathbf{D}\}\mathbf{U}(s) + \mathbf{C}\mathbf{\Phi}(s)\,\mathbf{x}(0)$$

The latter term represents the output(s) due to initial conditions whereas the former term represents the output(s) due to the $\mathbf{U}(s)$ inputs and gives rise to transfer function definitions.

ENGINEERING ECONOMICS

Factor Name	Converts	Symbol	Formula
Single Payment Compound Amount	to F given P	$(F/P, i\%, n)$	$(1+i)^n$
Single Payment Present Worth	to P given F	$(P/F, i\%, n)$	$(1+i)^{-n}$
Uniform Series Sinking Fund	to A given F	$(A/F, i\%, n)$	$\dfrac{i}{(1+i)^n - 1}$
Capital Recovery	to A given P	$(A/P, i\%, n)$	$\dfrac{i(1+i)^n}{(1+i)^n - 1}$
Uniform Series Compound Amount	to F given A	$(F/A, i\%, n)$	$\dfrac{(1+i)^n - 1}{i}$
Uniform Series Present Worth	to P given A	$(P/A, i\%, n)$	$\dfrac{(1+i)^n - 1}{i(1+i)^n}$
Uniform Gradient Present Worth	to P given G	$(P/G, i\%, n)$	$\dfrac{(1+i)^n - 1}{i^2(1+i)^n} - \dfrac{n}{i(1+i)^n}$
Uniform Gradient † Future Worth	to F given G	$(F/G, i\%, n)$	$\dfrac{(1+i)^n - 1}{i^2} - \dfrac{n}{i}$
Uniform Gradient Uniform Series	to A given G	$(A/G, i\%, n)$	$\dfrac{1}{i} - \dfrac{n}{(1+i)^n - 1}$

NOMENCLATURE AND DEFINITIONS

A.......... Uniform amount per interest period
B.......... Benefit
BV....... Book Value
C.......... Cost
d.......... Combined interest rate per interest period
D_j........ Depreciation in year j
F.......... Future worth, value, or amount
f........... General inflation rate per interest period
G......... Uniform gradient amount per interest period
i........... Interest rate per interest period
i_e.......... Annual effective interest rate
m......... Number of compounding periods per year
n.......... Number of compounding periods; or the expected life of an asset
P.......... Present worth, value, or amount
r........... Nominal annual interest rate
S_n........ Expected salvage value in year n

Subscripts

j........... at time j
n.......... at time n
†.......... $F/G = (F/A - n)/i = (F/A) \times (A/G)$

NON-ANNUAL COMPOUNDING

$$i_e = \left(1 + \frac{r}{m}\right)^m - 1$$

Discount Factors for <u>Continuous Compounding</u>

(n is the number of years)

$(F/P, r\%, n) = e^{rn}$

$(P/F, r\%, n) = e^{-rn}$

$(A/F, r\%, n) = \dfrac{e^r - 1}{e^{rn} - 1}$

$(F/A, r\%, n) = \dfrac{e^{rn} - 1}{e^r - 1}$

$(A/P, r\%, n) = \dfrac{e^r - 1}{1 - e^{-rn}}$

$(P/A, r\%, n) = \dfrac{1 - e^{-rn}}{e^r - 1}$

BOOK VALUE

$$BV = \text{initial cost} - \Sigma D_j$$

DEPRECIATION

Straight Line
$$D_j = \frac{C - S_n}{n}$$

Accelerated Cost Recovery System (ACRS)

$D_j = (\text{factor}) \, C$

A table of modified factors is provided below.

CAPITALIZED COSTS

Capitalized costs are present worth values using an assumed perpetual period of time.

$$\text{Capitalized Costs} = P = \frac{A}{i}$$

BONDS

Bond Value equals the present worth of the payments the purchaser (or holder of the bond) receives during the life of the bond at some interest rate i.

Bond Yield equals the computed interest rate of the bond value when compared with the bond cost.

RATE-OF-RETURN

The minimum acceptable rate-of-return is that interest rate that one is willing to accept, or the rate one desires to earn on investments. The rate-of-return on an investment is the interest rate that makes the benefits and costs equal.

BREAK-EVEN ANALYSIS

By altering the value of any one of the variables in a situation, holding all of the other values constant, it is possible to find a value for that variable that makes the two alternatives equally economical. This value is the break-even point.

Break-even analysis is used to describe the percentage of capacity of operation for a manufacturing plant at which income will just cover expenses.

The payback period is the period of time required for the profit or other benefits of an investment to equal the cost of the investment.

INFLATION

To account for inflation, the dollars are deflated by the general inflation rate per interest period f, and then they are shifted over the time scale using the interest rate per interest period i. Use a combined interest rate per interest period d for computing present worth values P and Net P. The formula for d is

$$d = i + f + (i \times f)$$

BENEFIT-COST ANALYSIS

In a benefit-cost analysis, the benefits B of a project should exceed the estimated costs C.

$$B - C \geq 0, \text{ or } \quad B/C \geq 1$$

MODIFIED ACRS FACTORS				
	Recovery Period (Years)			
	3	5	7	10
Year	Recovery Rate (Percent)			
1	33.3	20.0	14.3	10.0
2	44.5	32.0	24.5	18.0
3	14.8	19.2	17.5	14.4
4	7.4	11.5	12.5	11.5
5		11.5	8.9	9.2
6		5.8	8.9	7.4
7			8.9	6.6
8			4.5	6.6
9				6.5
10				6.5
11				3.3

Factor Table - $i = 0.50\%$

n	P/F	P/A	P/G	F/P	F/A	A/P	A/F	A/G
1	0.9950	0.9950	0.0000	1.0050	1.0000	1.0050	1.0000	0.0000
2	0.9901	1.9851	0.9901	1.0100	2.0050	0.5038	0.4988	0.4988
3	0.9851	2.9702	2.9604	1.0151	3.0150	0.3367	0.3317	0.9967
4	0.9802	3.9505	5.9011	1.0202	4.0301	0.2531	0.2481	1.4938
5	0.9754	4.9259	9.8026	1.0253	5.0503	0.2030	0.1980	1.9900
6	0.9705	5.8964	14.6552	1.0304	6.0755	0.1696	0.1646	2.4855
7	0.9657	6.8621	20.4493	1.0355	7.1059	0.1457	0.1407	2.9801
8	0.9609	7.8230	27.1755	1.0407	8.1414	0.1278	0.1228	3.4738
9	0.9561	8.7791	34.8244	1.0459	9.1821	0.1139	0.1089	3.9668
10	0.9513	9.7304	43.3865	1.0511	10.2280	0.1028	0.0978	4.4589
11	0.9466	10.6770	52.8526	1.0564	11.2792	0.0937	0.0887	4.9501
12	0.9419	11.6189	63.2136	1.0617	12.3356	0.0861	0.0811	5.4406
13	0.9372	12.5562	74.4602	1.0670	13.3972	0.0796	0.0746	5.9302
14	0.9326	13.4887	86.5835	1.0723	14.4642	0.0741	0.0691	6.4190
15	0.9279	14.4166	99.5743	1.0777	15.5365	0.0694	0.0644	6.9069
16	0.9233	15.3399	113.4238	1.0831	16.6142	0.0652	0.0602	7.3940
17	0.9187	16.2586	128.1231	1.0885	17.6973	0.0615	0.0565	7.8803
18	0.9141	17.1728	143.6634	1.0939	18.7858	0.0582	0.0532	8.3658
19	0.9096	18.0824	160.0360	1.0994	19.8797	0.0553	0.0503	8.8504
20	0.9051	18.9874	177.2322	1.1049	20.9791	0.0527	0.0477	9.3342
21	0.9006	19.8880	195.2434	1.1104	22.0840	0.0503	0.0453	9.8172
22	0.8961	20.7841	214.0611	1.1160	23.1944	0.0481	0.0431	10.2993
23	0.8916	21.6757	233.6768	1.1216	24.3104	0.0461	0.0411	10.7806
24	0.8872	22.5629	254.0820	1.1272	25.4320	0.0443	0.0393	11.2611
25	0.8828	23.4456	275.2686	1.1328	26.5591	0.0427	0.0377	11.7407
30	0.8610	27.7941	392.6324	1.1614	32.2800	0.0360	0.0310	14.1265
40	0.8191	36.1722	681.3347	1.2208	44.1588	0.0276	0.0226	18.8359
50	0.7793	44.1428	1,035.6966	1.2832	56.6452	0.0227	0.0177	23.4624
60	0.7414	51.7256	1,448.6458	1.3489	69.7700	0.0193	0.0143	28.0064
100	0.6073	78.5426	3,562.7934	1.6467	129.3337	0.0127	0.0077	45.3613

Factor Table - $i = 1.00\%$

n	P/F	P/A	P/G	F/P	F/A	A/P	A/F	A/G
1	0.9901	0.9901	0.0000	1.0100	1.0000	1.0100	1.0000	0.0000
2	0.9803	1.9704	0.9803	1.0201	2.0100	0.5075	0.4975	0.4975
3	0.9706	2.9410	2.9215	1.0303	3.0301	0.3400	0.3300	0.9934
4	0.9610	3.9020	5.8044	1.0406	4.0604	0.2563	0.2463	1.4876
5	0.9515	4.8534	9.6103	1.0510	5.1010	0.2060	0.1960	1.9801
6	0.9420	5.7955	14.3205	1.0615	6.1520	0.1725	0.1625	2.4710
7	0.9327	6.7282	19.9168	1.0721	7.2135	0.1486	0.1386	2.9602
8	0.9235	7.6517	26.3812	1.0829	8.2857	0.1307	0.1207	3.4478
9	0.9143	8.5650	33.6959	1.0937	9.3685	0.1167	0.1067	3.9337
10	0.9053	9.4713	41.8435	1.1046	10.4622	0.1056	0.0956	4.4179
11	0.8963	10.3676	50.8067	1.1157	11.5668	0.0965	0.0865	4.9005
12	0.8874	11.2551	60.5687	1.1268	12.6825	0.0888	0.0788	5.3815
13	0.8787	12.1337	71.1126	1.1381	13.8093	0.0824	0.0724	5.8607
14	0.8700	13.0037	82.4221	1.1495	14.9474	0.0769	0.0669	6.3384
15	0.8613	13.8651	94.4810	1.1610	16.0969	0.0721	0.0621	6.8143
16	0.8528	14.7179	107.2734	1.1726	17.2579	0.0679	0.0579	7.2886
17	0.8444	15.5623	120.7834	1.1843	18.4304	0.0643	0.0543	7.7613
18	0.8360	16.3983	134.9957	1.1961	19.6147	0.0610	0.0510	8.2323
19	0.8277	17.2260	149.8950	1.2081	20.8109	0.0581	0.0481	8.7017
20	0.8195	18.0456	165.4664	1.2202	22.0190	0.0554	0.0454	9.1694
21	0.8114	18.8570	181.6950	1.2324	23.2392	0.0530	0.0430	9.6354
22	0.8034	19.6604	198.5663	1.2447	24.4716	0.0509	0.0409	10.0998
23	0.7954	20.4558	216.0660	1.2572	25.7163	0.0489	0.0389	10.5626
24	0.7876	21.2434	234.1800	1.2697	26.9735	0.0471	0.0371	11.0237
25	0.7798	22.0232	252.8945	1.2824	28.2432	0.0454	0.0354	11.4831
30	0.7419	25.8077	355.0021	1.3478	34.7849	0.0387	0.0277	13.7557
40	0.6717	32.8347	596.8561	1.4889	48.8864	0.0305	0.0205	18.1776
50	0.6080	39.1961	879.4176	1.6446	64.4632	0.0255	0.0155	22.4363
60	0.5504	44.9550	1,192.8061	1.8167	81.6697	0.0222	0.0122	26.5333
100	0.3697	63.0289	2,605.7758	2.7048	170.4814	0.0159	0.0059	41.3426

Factor Table - $i = 1.50\%$

n	P/F	P/A	P/G	F/P	F/A	A/P	A/F	A/G
1	0.9852	0.9852	0.0000	1.0150	1.0000	1.0150	1.0000	0.0000
2	0.9707	1.9559	0.9707	1.0302	2.0150	0.5113	0.4963	0.4963
3	0.9563	2.9122	2.8833	1.0457	3.0452	0.3434	0.3284	0.9901
4	0.9422	3.8544	5.7098	1.0614	4.0909	0.2594	0.2444	1.4814
5	0.9283	4.7826	9.4229	1.0773	5.1523	0.2091	0.1941	1.9702
6	0.9145	5.6972	13.9956	1.0934	6.2296	0.1755	0.1605	2.4566
7	0.9010	6.5982	19.4018	1.1098	7.3230	0.1516	0.1366	2.9405
8	0.8877	7.4859	26.6157	1.1265	8.4328	0.1336	0.1186	3.4219
9	0.8746	8.3605	32.6125	1.1434	9.5593	0.1196	0.1046	3.9008
10	0.8617	9.2222	40.3675	1.1605	10.7027	0.1084	0.0934	4.3772
11	0.8489	10.0711	48.8568	1.1779	11.8633	0.0993	0.0843	4.8512
12	0.8364	10.9075	58.0571	1.1956	13.0412	0.0917	0.0767	5.3227
13	0.8240	11.7315	67.9454	1.2136	14.2368	0.0852	0.0702	5.7917
14	0.8118	12.5434	78.4994	1.2318	15.4504	0.0797	0.0647	6.2582
15	0.7999	13.3432	89.6974	1.2502	16.6821	0.0749	0.0599	6.7223
16	0.7880	14.1313	101.5178	1.2690	17.9324	0.0708	0.0558	7.1839
17	0.7764	14.9076	113.9400	1.2880	19.2014	0.0671	0.0521	7.6431
18	0.7649	15.6726	126.9435	1.3073	20.4894	0.0638	0.0488	8.0997
19	0.7536	16.4262	140.5084	1.3270	21.7967	0.0609	0.0459	8.5539
20	0.7425	17.1686	154.6154	1.3469	23.1237	0.0582	0.0432	9.0057
21	0.7315	17.9001	169.2453	1.3671	24.4705	0.0559	0.0409	9.4550
22	0.7207	18.6208	184.3798	1.3876	25.8376	0.0537	0.0387	9.9018
23	0.7100	19.3309	200.0006	1.4084	27.2251	0.0517	0.0367	10.3462
24	0.6995	20.0304	216.0901	1.4295	28.6335	0.0499	0.0349	10.7881
25	0.6892	20.7196	232.6310	1.4509	30.0630	0.0483	0.0333	11.2276
30	0.6398	24.0158	321.5310	1.5631	37.5387	0.0416	0.0266	13.3883
40	0.5513	29.9158	524.3568	1.8140	54.2679	0.0334	0.0184	17.5277
50	0.4750	34.9997	749.9636	2.1052	73.6828	0.0286	0.0136	21.4277
60	0.4093	39.3803	988.1674	2.4432	96.2147	0.0254	0.0104	25.0930
100	0.2256	51.6247	1,937.4506	4.4320	228.8030	0.0194	0.0044	37.5295

Factor Table - $i = 2.00\%$

n	P/F	P/A	P/G	F/P	F/A	A/P	A/F	A/G
1	0.9804	0.9804	0.0000	1.0200	1.0000	1.0200	1.0000	0.0000
2	0.9612	1.9416	0.9612	1.0404	2.0200	0.5150	0.4950	0.4950
3	0.9423	2.8839	2.8458	1.0612	3.0604	0.3468	0.3268	0.9868
4	0.9238	3.8077	5.6173	1.0824	4.1216	0.2626	0.2426	1.4752
5	0.9057	4.7135	9.2403	1.1041	5.2040	0.2122	0.1922	1.9604
6	0.8880	5.6014	13.6801	1.1262	6.3081	0.1785	0.1585	2.4423
7	0.8706	6.4720	18.9035	1.1487	7.4343	0.1545	0.1345	2.9208
8	0.8535	7.3255	24.8779	1.1717	8.5830	0.1365	0.1165	3.3961
9	0.8368	8.1622	31.5720	1.1951	9.7546	0.1225	0.1025	3.8681
10	0.8203	8.9826	38.9551	1.2190	10.9497	0.1113	0.0913	4.3367
11	0.8043	9.7868	46.9977	1.2434	12.1687	0.1022	0.0822	4.8021
12	0.7885	10.5753	55.6712	1.2682	13.4121	0.0946	0.0746	5.2642
13	0.7730	11.3484	64.9475	1.2936	14.6803	0.0881	0.0681	5.7231
14	0.7579	12.1062	74.7999	1.3195	15.9739	0.0826	0.0626	6.1786
15	0.7430	12.8493	85.2021	1.3459	17.2934	0.0778	0.0578	6.6309
16	0.7284	13.5777	96.1288	1.3728	18.6393	0.0737	0.0537	7.0799
17	0.7142	14.2919	107.5554	1.4002	20.0121	0.0700	0.0500	7.5256
18	0.7002	14.9920	119.4581	1.4282	21.4123	0.0667	0.0467	7.9681
19	0.6864	15.6785	131.8139	1.4568	22.8406	0.0638	0.0438	8.4073
20	0.6730	16.3514	144.6003	1.4859	24.2974	0.0612	0.0412	8.8433
21	0.6598	17.0112	157.7959	1.5157	25.7833	0.0588	0.0388	9.2760
22	0.6468	17.6580	171.3795	1.5460	27.2990	0.0566	0.0366	9.7055
23	0.6342	18.2922	185.3309	1.5769	28.8450	0.0547	0.0347	10.1317
24	0.6217	18.9139	199.6305	1.6084	30.4219	0.0529	0.0329	10.5547
25	0.6095	19.5235	214.2592	1.6406	32.0303	0.0512	0.0312	10.9745
30	0.5521	22.3965	291.7164	1.8114	40.5681	0.0446	0.0246	13.0251
40	0.4529	27.3555	461.9931	2.2080	60.4020	0.0366	0.0166	16.8885
50	0.3715	31.4236	642.3606	2.6916	84.5794	0.0318	0.0118	20.4420
60	0.3048	34.7609	823.6975	3.2810	114.0515	0.0288	0.0088	23.6961
100	0.1380	43.0984	1,464.7527	7.2446	312.2323	0.0232	0.0032	33.9863

Factor Table - i = 4.00%

n	P/F	P/A	P/G	F/P	F/A	A/P	A/F	A/G
1	0.9615	0.9615	0.0000	1.0400	1.0000	1.0400	1.0000	0.0000
2	0.9246	1.8861	0.9246	1.0816	2.0400	0.5302	0.4902	0.4902
3	0.8890	2.7751	2.7025	1.1249	3.1216	0.3603	0.3203	0.9739
4	0.8548	3.6299	5.2670	1.1699	4.2465	0.2755	0.2355	1.4510
5	0.8219	4.4518	8.5547	1.2167	5.4163	0.2246	0.1846	1.9216
6	0.7903	5.2421	12.5062	1.2653	6.6330	0.1908	0.1508	2.3857
7	0.7599	6.0021	17.0657	1.3159	7.8983	0.1666	0.1266	2.8433
8	0.7307	6.7327	22.1806	1.3686	9.2142	0.1485	0.1085	3.2944
9	0.7026	7.4353	27.8013	1.4233	10.5828	0.1345	0.0945	3.7391
10	0.6756	8.1109	33.8814	1.4802	12.0061	0.1233	0.0833	4.1773
11	0.6496	8.7605	40.3772	1.5395	13.4864	0.1141	0.0741	4.6090
12	0.6246	9.3851	47.2477	1.6010	15.0258	0.1066	0.0666	5.0343
13	0.6006	9.9856	54.4546	1.6651	16.6268	0.1001	0.0601	5.4533
14	0.5775	10.5631	61.9618	1.7317	18.2919	0.0947	0.0547	5.8659
15	0.5553	11.1184	69.7355	1.8009	20.0236	0.0899	0.0499	6.2721
16	0.5339	11.6523	77.7441	1.8730	21.8245	0.0858	0.0458	6.6720
17	0.5134	12.1657	85.9581	1.9479	23.6975	0.0822	0.0422	7.0656
18	0.4936	12.6593	94.3498	2.0258	25.6454	0.0790	0.0390	7.4530
19	0.4746	13.1339	102.8933	2.1068	27.6712	0.0761	0.0361	7.8342
20	0.4564	13.5903	111.5647	2.1911	29.7781	0.0736	0.0336	8.2091
21	0.4388	14.0292	120.3414	2.2788	31.9692	0.0713	0.0313	8.5779
22	0.4220	14.4511	129.2024	2.3699	34.2480	0.0692	0.0292	8.9407
23	0.4057	14.8568	138.1284	2.4647	36.6179	0.0673	0.0273	9.2973
24	0.3901	15.2470	147.1012	2.5633	39.0826	0.0656	0.0256	9.6479
25	0.3751	15.6221	156.1040	2.6658	41.6459	0.0640	0.0240	9.9925
30	0.3083	17.2920	201.0618	3.2434	56.0849	0.0578	0.0178	11.6274
40	0.2083	19.7928	286.5303	4.8010	95.0255	0.0505	0.0105	14.4765
50	0.1407	21.4822	361.1638	7.1067	152.6671	0.0466	0.0066	16.8122
60	0.0951	22.6235	422.9966	10.5196	237.9907	0.0442	0.0042	18.6972
100	0.0198	24.5050	563.1249	50.5049	1,237.6237	0.0408	0.0008	22.9800

Factor Table - i = 6.00%

n	P/F	P/A	P/G	F/P	F/A	A/P	A/F	A/G
1	0.9434	0.9434	0.0000	1.0600	1.0000	1.0600	1.0000	0.0000
2	0.8900	1.8334	0.8900	1.1236	2.0600	0.5454	0.4854	0.4854
3	0.8396	2.6730	2.5692	1.1910	3.1836	0.3741	0.3141	0.9612
4	0.7921	3.4651	4.9455	1.2625	4.3746	0.2886	0.2286	1.4272
5	0.7473	4.2124	7.9345	1.3382	5.6371	0.2374	0.1774	1.8836
6	0.7050	4.9173	11.4594	1.4185	6.9753	0.2034	0.1434	2.3304
7	0.6651	5.5824	15.4497	1.5036	8.3938	0.1791	0.1191	2.7676
8	0.6274	6.2098	19.8416	1.5938	9.8975	0.1610	0.1010	3.1952
9	0.5919	6.8017	24.5768	1.6895	11.4913	0.1470	0.0870	3.6133
10	0.5584	7.3601	29.6023	1.7908	13.1808	0.1359	0.0759	4.0220
11	0.5268	7.8869	34.8702	1.8983	14.9716	0.1268	0.0668	4.4213
12	0.4970	8.3838	40.3369	2.0122	16.8699	0.1193	0.0593	4.8113
13	0.4688	8.8527	45.9629	2.1329	18.8821	0.1130	0.0530	5.1920
14	0.4423	9.2950	51.7128	2.2609	21.0151	0.1076	0.0476	5.5635
15	0.4173	9.7122	57.5546	2.3966	23.2760	0.1030	0.0430	5.9260
16	0.3936	10.1059	63.4592	2.5404	25.6725	0.0990	0.0390	6.2794
17	0.3714	10.4773	69.4011	2.6928	28.2129	0.0954	0.0354	6.6240
18	0.3505	10.8276	75.3569	2.8543	30.9057	0.0924	0.0324	6.9597
19	0.3305	11.1581	81.3062	3.0256	33.7600	0.0896	0.0296	7.2867
20	0.3118	11.4699	87.2304	3.2071	36.7856	0.0872	0.0272	7.6051
21	0.2942	11.7641	93.1136	3.3996	39.9927	0.0850	0.0250	7.9151
22	0.2775	12.0416	98.9412	3.6035	43.3923	0.0830	0.0230	8.2166
23	0.2618	12.3034	104.7007	3.8197	46.9958	0.0813	0.0213	8.5099
24	0.2470	12.5504	110.3812	4.0489	50.8156	0.0797	0.0197	8.7951
25	0.2330	12.7834	115.9732	4.2919	54.8645	0.0782	0.0182	9.0722
30	0.1741	13.7648	142.3588	5.7435	79.0582	0.0726	0.0126	10.3422
40	0.0972	15.0463	185.9568	10.2857	154.7620	0.0665	0.0065	12.3590
50	0.0543	15.7619	217.4574	18.4202	290.3359	0.0634	0.0034	13.7964
60	0.0303	16.1614	239.0428	32.9877	533.1282	0.0619	0.0019	14.7909
100	0.0029	16.6175	272.0471	339.3021	5,638.3681	0.0602	0.0002	16.3711

Factor Table - $i = 8.00\%$

n	P/F	P/A	P/G	F/P	F/A	A/P	A/F	A/G
1	0.9259	0.9259	0.0000	1.0800	1.0000	1.0800	1.0000	0.0000
2	0.8573	1.7833	0.8573	1.1664	2.0800	0.5608	0.4808	0.4808
3	0.7938	2.5771	2.4450	1.2597	3.2464	0.3880	0.3080	0.9487
4	0.7350	3.3121	4.6501	1.3605	4.5061	0.3019	0.2219	1.4040
5	0.6806	3.9927	7.3724	1.4693	5.8666	0.2505	0.1705	1.8465
6	0.6302	4.6229	10.5233	1.5869	7.3359	0.2163	0.1363	2.2763
7	0.5835	5.2064	14.0242	1.7138	8.9228	0.1921	0.1121	2.6937
8	0.5403	5.7466	17.8061	1.8509	10.6366	0.1740	0.0940	3.0985
9	0.5002	6.2469	21.8081	1.9990	12.4876	0.1601	0.0801	3.4910
10	0.4632	6.7101	25.9768	2.1589	14.4866	0.1490	0.0690	3.8713
11	0.4289	7.1390	30.2657	2.3316	16.6455	0.1401	0.0601	4.2395
12	0.3971	7.5361	34.6339	2.5182	18.9771	0.1327	0.0527	4.5957
13	0.3677	7.9038	39.0463	2.7196	21.4953	0.1265	0.0465	4.9402
14	0.3405	8.2442	43.4723	2.9372	24.2149	0.1213	0.0413	5.2731
15	0.3152	8.5595	47.8857	3.1722	27.1521	0.1168	0.0368	5.5945
16	0.2919	8.8514	52.2640	3.4259	30.3243	0.1130	0.0330	5.9046
17	0.2703	9.1216	56.5883	3.7000	33.7502	0.1096	0.0296	6.2037
18	0.2502	9.3719	60.8426	3.9960	37.4502	0.1067	0.0267	6.4920
19	0.2317	9.6036	65.0134	4.3157	41.4463	0.1041	0.0241	6.7697
20	0.2145	9.8181	69.0898	4.6610	45.7620	0.1019	0.0219	7.0369
21	0.1987	10.0168	73.0629	5.0338	50.4229	0.0998	0.0198	7.2940
22	0.1839	10.2007	76.9257	5.4365	55.4568	0.0980	0.0180	7.5412
23	0.1703	10.3711	80.6726	5.8715	60.8933	0.0964	0.0164	7.7786
24	0.1577	10.5288	84.2997	6.3412	66.7648	0.0950	0.0150	8.0066
25	0.1460	10.6748	87.8041	6.8485	73.1059	0.0937	0.0137	8.2254
30	0.0994	11.2578	103.4558	10.0627	113.2832	0.0888	0.0088	9.1897
40	0.0460	11.9246	126.0422	21.7245	259.0565	0.0839	0.0039	10.5699
50	0.0213	12.2335	139.5928	46.9016	573.7702	0.0817	0.0017	11.4107
60	0.0099	12.3766	147.3000	101.2571	1,253.2133	0.0808	0.0008	11.9015
100	0.0005	12.4943	155.6107	2,199.7613	27,484.5157	0.0800		12.4545

Factor Table - $i = 10.00\%$

n	P/F	P/A	P/G	F/P	F/A	A/P	A/F	A/G
1	0.9091	0.9091	0.0000	1.1000	1.0000	1.1000	1.0000	0.0000
2	0.8264	1.7355	0.8264	1.2100	2.1000	0.5762	0.4762	0.4762
3	0.7513	2.4869	2.3291	1.3310	3.3100	0.4021	0.3021	0.9366
4	0.6830	3.1699	4.3781	1.4641	4.6410	0.3155	0.2155	1.3812
5	0.6209	3.7908	6.8618	1.6105	6.1051	0.2638	0.1638	1.8101
6	0.5645	4.3553	9.6842	1.7716	7.7156	0.2296	0.1296	2.2236
7	0.5132	4.8684	12.7631	1.9487	9.4872	0.2054	0.1054	2.6216
8	0.4665	5.3349	16.0287	2.1436	11.4359	0.1874	0.0874	3.0045
9	0.4241	5.7590	19.4215	2.3579	13.5735	0.1736	0.0736	3.3724
10	0.3855	6.1446	22.8913	2.5937	15.9374	0.1627	0.0627	3.7255
11	0.3505	6.4951	26.3962	2.8531	18.5312	0.1540	0.0540	4.0641
12	0.3186	6.8137	29.9012	3.1384	21.3843	0.1468	0.0468	4.3884
13	0.2897	7.1034	33.3772	3.4523	24.5227	0.1408	0.0408	4.6988
14	0.2633	7.3667	36.8005	3.7975	27.9750	0.1357	0.0357	4.9955
15	0.2394	7.6061	40.1520	4.1772	31.7725	0.1315	0.0315	5.2789
16	0.2176	7.8237	43.4164	4.5950	35.9497	0.1278	0.0278	5.5493
17	0.1978	8.0216	46.5819	5.5045	40.5447	0.1247	0.0247	5.8071
18	0.1799	8.2014	49.6395	5.5599	45.5992	0.1219	0.0219	6.0526
19	0.1635	8.3649	52.5827	6.1159	51.1591	0.1195	0.0195	6.2861
20	0.1486	8.5136	55.4069	6.7275	57.2750	0.1175	0.0175	6.5081
21	0.1351	8.6487	58.1095	7.4002	64.0025	0.1156	0.0156	6.7189
22	0.1228	8.7715	60.6893	8.1403	71.4027	0.1140	0.0140	6.9189
23	0.1117	8.8832	63.1462	8.9543	79.5430	0.1126	0.0126	7.1085
24	0.1015	8.9847	65.4813	9.8497	88.4973	0.1113	0.0113	7.2881
25	0.0923	9.0770	67.6964	10.8347	98.3471	0.1102	0.0102	7.4580
30	0.0573	9.4269	77.0766	17.4494	164.4940	0.1061	0.0061	8.1762
40	0.0221	9.7791	88.9525	45.2593	442.5926	0.1023	0.0023	9.0962
50	0.0085	9.9148	94.8889	117.3909	1,163.9085	0.1009	0.0009	9.5704
60	0.0033	9.9672	97.7010	304.4816	3,034.8164	0.1003	0.0003	9.8023
100	0.0001	9.9993	99.9202	13,780.6123	137,796.1234	0.1000		9.9927

Factor Table - $i = 12.00\%$

n	P/F	P/A	P/G	F/P	F/A	A/P	A/F	A/G
1	0.8929	0.8929	0.0000	1.1200	1.0000	1.1200	1.0000	0.0000
2	0.7972	1.6901	0.7972	1.2544	2.1200	0.5917	0.4717	0.4717
3	0.7118	2.4018	2.2208	1.4049	3.3744	0.4163	0.2963	0.9246
4	0.6355	3.0373	4.1273	1.5735	4.7793	0.3292	0.2092	1.3589
5	0.5674	3.6048	6.3970	1.7623	6.3528	0.2774	0.1574	1.7746
6	0.5066	4.1114	8.9302	1.9738	8.1152	0.2432	0.1232	2.1720
7	0.4523	4.5638	11.6443	2.2107	10.0890	0.2191	0.0991	2.5515
8	0.4039	4.9676	14.4714	2.4760	12.2997	0.2013	0.0813	2.9131
9	0.3606	5.3282	17.3563	2.7731	14.7757	0.1877	0.0677	3.2574
10	0.3220	5.6502	20.2541	3.1058	17.5487	0.1770	0.0570	3.5847
11	0.2875	5.9377	23.1288	3.4785	20.6546	0.1684	0.0484	3.8953
12	0.2567	6.1944	25.9523	3.8960	24.1331	0.1614	0.0414	4.1897
13	0.2292	6.4235	28.7024	4.3635	28.0291	0.1557	0.0357	4.4683
14	0.2046	6.6282	31.3624	4.8871	32.3926	0.1509	0.0309	4.7317
15	0.1827	6.8109	33.9202	5.4736	37.2797	0.1468	0.0268	4.9803
16	0.1631	6.9740	36.3670	6.1304	42.7533	0.1434	0.0234	5.2147
17	0.1456	7.1196	38.6973	6.8660	48.8837	0.1405	0.0205	5.4353
18	0.1300	7.2497	40.9080	7.6900	55.7497	0.1379	0.0179	5.6427
19	0.1161	7.3658	42.9979	8.6128	63.4397	0.1358	0.0158	5.8375
20	0.1037	7.4694	44.9676	9.6463	72.0524	0.1339	0.0139	6.0202
21	0.0926	7.5620	46.8188	10.8038	81.6987	0.1322	0.0122	6.1913
22	0.0826	7.6446	48.5543	12.1003	92.5026	0.1308	0.0108	6.3514
23	0.0738	7.7184	50.1776	13.5523	104.6029	0.1296	0.0096	6.5010
24	0.0659	7.7843	51.6929	15.1786	118.1552	0.1285	0.0085	6.6406
25	0.0588	7.8431	53.1046	17.0001	133.3339	0.1275	0.0075	6.7708
30	0.0334	8.0552	58.7821	29.9599	241.3327	0.1241	0.0041	7.2974
40	0.0107	8.2438	65.1159	93.0510	767.0914	0.1213	0.0013	7.8988
50	0.0035	8.3045	67.7624	289.0022	2,400.0182	0.1204	0.0004	8.1597
60	0.0011	8.3240	68.8100	897.5969	7,471.6411	0.1201	0.0001	8.2664
100		8.3332	69.4336	83,522.2657	696,010.5477	0.1200		8.3321

Factor Table - $i = 18.00\%$

n	P/F	P/A	P/G	F/P	F/A	A/P	A/F	A/G
1	0.8475	0.8475	0.0000	1.1800	1.0000	1.1800	1.0000	0.0000
2	0.7182	1.5656	0.7182	1.3924	2.1800	0.6387	0.4587	0.4587
3	0.6086	2.1743	1.9354	1.6430	3.5724	0.4599	0.2799	0.8902
4	0.5158	2.6901	3.4828	1.9388	5.2154	0.3717	0.1917	1.2947
5	0.4371	3.1272	5.2312	2.2878	7.1542	0.3198	0.1398	1.6728
6	0.3704	3.4976	7.0834	2.6996	9.4423	0.2859	0.1059	2.0252
7	0.3139	3.8115	8.9670	3.1855	12.1415	0.2624	0.0824	2.3526
8	0.2660	4.0776	10.8292	3.7589	15.3270	0.2452	0.0652	2.6558
9	0.2255	4.3030	12.6329	4.4355	19.0859	0.2324	0.0524	2.9358
10	0.1911	4.4941	14.3525	5.2338	23.5213	0.2225	0.0425	3.1936
11	0.1619	4.6560	15.9716	6.1759	28.7551	0.2148	0.0348	3.4303
12	0.1372	4.7932	17.4811	7.2876	34.9311	0.2086	0.0286	3.6470
13	0.1163	4.9095	18.8765	8.5994	42.2187	0.2037	0.0237	3.8449
14	0.0985	5.0081	20.1576	10.1472	50.8180	0.1997	0.0197	4.0250
15	0.0835	5.0916	21.3269	11.9737	60.9653	0.1964	0.0164	4.1887
16	0.0708	5.1624	22.3885	14.1290	72.9390	0.1937	0.0137	4.3369
17	0.0600	5.2223	23.3482	16.6722	87.0680	0.1915	0.0115	4.4708
18	0.0508	5.2732	24.2123	19.6731	103.7403	0.1896	0.0096	4.5916
19	0.0431	5.3162	24.9877	23.2144	123.4135	0.1881	0.0081	4.7003
20	0.0365	5.3527	25.6813	27.3930	146.6280	0.1868	0.0068	4.7978
21	0.0309	5.3837	26.3000	32.3238	174.0210	0.1857	0.0057	4.8851
22	0.0262	5.4099	26.8506	38.1421	206.3448	0.1848	0.0048	4.9632
23	0.0222	5.4321	27.3394	45.0076	244.4868	0.1841	0.0041	5.0329
24	0.0188	5.4509	27.7725	53.1090	289.4944	0.1835	0.0035	5.0950
25	0.0159	5.4669	28.1555	62.6686	342.6035	0.1829	0.0029	5.1502
30	0.0070	5.5168	29.4864	143.3706	790.9480	0.1813	0.0013	5.3448
40	0.0013	5.5482	30.5269	750.3783	4,163.2130	0.1802	0.0002	5.5022
50	0.0003	5.5541	30.7856	3,927.3569	21,813.0937	0.1800		5.5428
60	0.0001	5.5553	30.8465	20,555.1400	114,189.6665	0.1800		5.5526
100		5.5556	30.8642	15,424,131.91	85,689,616.17	0.1800		5.5555

ETHICS

Engineering is considered to be a "profession" rather than an "occupation" because of several important characteristics shared with other recognized learned professions, law, medicine, and theology: special knowledge, special privileges, and special responsibilities. Professions are based on a large knowledge base requiring extensive training. Professional skills are important to the well-being of society. Professions are self-regulating, in that they control the training and evaluation processes that admit new persons to the field. Professionals have autonomy in the workplace; they are expected to utilize their independent judgment in carrying out their professional responsibilities. Finally, professions are regulated by ethical standards.[1]

The expertise possessed by engineers is vitally important to public welfare. In order to serve the public effectively, engineers must maintain a high level of technical competence. However, a high level of technical expertise without adherence to ethical guidelines is as much a threat to public welfare as is professional incompetence. Therefore, engineers must also be guided by ethical principles.

The ethical principles governing the engineering profession are embodied in codes of ethics. Such codes have been adopted by state boards of registration, professional engineering societies, and even by some private industries. An example of one such code is the NCEES Rules of Professional Conduct, found in Section 240 of *Model Rules* and presented here. As part of his/her responsibility to the public, an engineer is responsible for knowing and abiding by the code. Additional rules of conduct are also included in *Model Rules*.

The three major sections of the model rules address (1) Licensee's Obligation to Society, (2) Licensee's Obligation to Employers and Clients, and (3) Licensee's Obligation to Other Licensees. The principles amplified in these sections are important guides to appropriate behavior of professional engineers.

Application of the code in many situations is not controversial. However, there may be situations in which applying the code may raise more difficult issues. In particular, there may be circumstances in which terminology in the code is not clearly defined, or in which two sections of the code may be in conflict. For example, what constitutes "valuable consideration" or "adequate" knowledge may be interpreted differently by qualified professionals. These types of questions are called <u>conceptual issues</u>, in which definitions of terms may be in dispute. In other situations, <u>factual issues</u> may also affect ethical dilemmas. Many decisions regarding engineering design may be based upon interpretation of disputed or incomplete information. In addition, <u>tradeoffs</u> revolving around competing issues of risk *vs.* benefit, or safety *vs.* economics may require judgments that are not fully addressed simply by application of the code.

No code can give immediate and mechanical answers to all ethical and professional problems that an engineer may face. Creative problem solving is often called for in ethics, just as it is in other areas of engineering.

Model Rules, Section 240.15, Rules of Professional Conduct

I. LICENSEE'S OBLIGATION TO SOCIETY

a. Licensees, in the performance of their services for clients, employers, and customers, shall be cognizant that their first and foremost responsibility is to the public welfare.

b. Licensees shall approve and seal only those design documents and surveys that conform to accepted engineering and land surveying standards and safeguard the life, health, property, and welfare of the public.

c. Licensees shall notify their employer or client and such other authority as may be appropriate when their professional judgment is overruled under circumstances where the life, health, property, or welfare of the public is endangered.

d. Licensees shall be objective and truthful in professional reports, statements, or testimony. They shall include all relevant and pertinent information in such reports, statements, or testimony.

e. Licensees shall express a professional opinion publicly only when it is founded upon an adequate knowledge of the facts and a competent evaluation of the subject matter.

f. Licensees shall issue no statements, criticisms, or arguments on technical matters which are inspired or paid for by interested parties, unless they explicitly identify the interested parties on whose behalf they are speaking and reveal any interest they have in the matters.

g. Licensees shall not permit the use of their name or firm name by, nor associate in the business ventures with, any person or firm which is engaging in fraudulent or dishonest business or professional practices.

h. Licensees having knowledge of possible violations of any of these rules of professional conduct shall provide the board with the information and assistance necessary to make the final determination of such violation.

[1] Harris, C.E., M.S. Pritchard, & M.J. Rabins, *Engineering Ethics: Concepts and Cases*, Copyright © 1995 by Wadsworth Publishing Company, pages 27–28

II. LICENSEE'S OBLIGATION TO EMPLOYER AND CLIENTS

a. Licensees shall undertake assignments only when qualified by education or experience in the specific technical fields of engineering or land surveying involved.

b. Licensees shall not affix their signatures or seals to any plans or documents dealing with subject matter in which they lack competence, nor to any such plan or document not prepared under their direct control and personal supervision.

c. Licensees may accept assignments for coordination of an entire project, provided that each design segment is signed and sealed by the licensee responsible for preparation of that design segment.

d. Licensees shall not reveal facts, data, or information obtained in a professional capacity without the prior consent of the client or employer except as authorized or required by law.

e. Licensees shall not solicit or accept financial or other valuable consideration, directly or indirectly, from contractors, their agents, or other parties in connection with work for employers or clients.

f. Licensees shall make full prior disclosures to their employers or clients of potential conflicts of interest or other circumstances which could influence or appear to influence their judgment or the quality of their service.

g. Licensees shall not accept compensation, financial or otherwise, from more than one party for services pertaining to the same project, unless the circumstances are fully disclosed and agreed to by all interested parties.

h. Licensees shall not solicit or accept a professional contract from a governmental body on which a principal or officer of their organization serves as a member. Conversely, licensees serving as members, advisors, or employees of a government body or department, who are the principals or employees of a private concern, shall not participate in decisions with respect to professional services offered or provided by said concern to the governmental body which they serve.

III. LICENSEE'S OBLIGATION TO OTHER LICENSEES

a. Licensees shall not falsify or permit misrepresentation of their, or their associates', academic or professional qualifications. They shall not mis-represent or exaggerate their degree of responsibility in prior assignments nor the complexity of said assignments. Presentations incident to the solicitation of employment or business shall not misrepresent pertinent facts concerning employers, employees, associates, joint ventures, or past accomplishments.

b. Licensees shall not offer, give, solicit, or receive, either directly or indirectly, any commission, or gift, or other valuable consideration in order to secure work, and shall not make any political contribution with the intent to influence the award of a contract by public authority.

c. Licensees shall not attempt to injure, maliciously or falsely, directly or indirectly, the professional reputation, prospects, practice, or employment of other licensees, nor indiscriminately criticize other licensees' work.

CHEMICAL ENGINEERING

For additional information concerning heat transfer and fluid mechanics, refer to the **HEAT TRANSFER, THERMODYNAMICS,** or **FLUID MECHANICS** sections.

CHEMICAL THERMODYNAMICS

Vapor-Liquid Equilibrium

For a multi-component mixture at equilibrium

$$\hat{f}_i^V = \hat{f}_i^L \text{, where}$$

$\hat{f}_i^V = $ fugacity of component i in the vapor phase, and

$\hat{f}_i^L = $ fugacity of component i in the liquid phase.

Fugacities of component i in a mixture are commonly calculated in the following ways:

For a liquid $\quad \hat{f}_i^L = x_i \gamma_i f_i^L$, where

$x_i = $ mole fraction of component i,

$\gamma_i = $ activity coefficient of component i, and

$f_i^L = $ fugacity of pure liquid component i.

For a vapor $\quad \hat{f}_i^V = y_i \hat{\Phi}_i P$, where

$y_i = $ mole fraction of component i in the vapor,

$\hat{\Phi}_i = $ fugacity coefficient of component i in the vapor, and

$P = $ system pressure.

The activity coefficient γ_i is a correction for liquid phase non-ideality. Many models have been proposed for γ_i such as the Van Laar model:

$$\ln\gamma_1 = A_{12}\left(1 + \frac{A_{12}x_1}{A_{21}x_2}\right)^{-2}$$

$$\ln\gamma_2 = A_{21}\left(1 + \frac{A_{21}x_2}{A_{12}x_1}\right)^{-2} \quad \text{, where}$$

$\gamma_1 = $ activity coefficient of component 1 in a two-component system,

$\gamma_2 = $ activity coefficient of component 2 in a two-component system, and

$A_{12}, A_{21} = $ constants, typically fitted from experimental data.

The pure component fugacity is calculated as:

$$f_i^L = \Phi_i^{sat} P_i^{sat} \exp\{v_i^L (P - P_i^{sat})/(RT)\}, \text{ where}$$

$\Phi_i^{sat} = $ fugacity coefficient of pure saturated i,

$P_i^{sat} = $ saturation pressure of pure i,

$v_i^L = $ specific volume of pure liquid i, and

$R = $ Ideal Gas Law Constant.

Often at system pressures close to atmospheric:

$$f_i^L \cong P_i^{sat}$$

The fugacity coefficient $\hat{\Phi}_i$ for component i in the vapor is calculated from an equation of state (e.g., Virial). Sometimes it is approximated by a pure component value from a correlation. Often at pressures close to atmospheric, $\hat{\Phi}_i = 1$. The fugacity coefficient is a correction for vapor phase non-ideality.

For sparingly soluble gases the liquid phase is sometimes represented as

$$\hat{f}_i^L = x_i k_i$$

where k_i is a constant set by experiment (Henry's constant). Sometimes other concentration units are used besides mole fraction with a corresponding change in k_i.

Reactive Systems

Conversion: moles reacted/moles fed

Extent: For each species in a reaction, the mole balance may be written:

$$\text{moles}_{i,out} = \text{moles}_{i,in} + v_i\xi \text{ where}$$

ξ is the **extent**

v_i is the stoichiometric coefficient of the ith species, sign of which is negative for reactants and positive for products.

Limiting reactant: reactant that would be consumed first if reaction proceeded to completion. Other reactants are **excess reactants**.

Selectivity: moles of desired product formed/moles of undesired product formed.

Yield: moles of desired product formed/moles that would have been formed if there were no side reactions and limiting reactant had reacted completely.

Chemical Reaction Equilibrium

For reaction

$$aA + bB \rightleftharpoons cC + dD$$

$$\Delta G^\circ = -RT \ln K_a$$

$$K_a = \frac{(\hat{a}_C^c)(\hat{a}_D^d)}{(\hat{a}_A^a)(\hat{a}_B^b)} = \prod_i (\hat{a}_i)^{v_i} \text{ , where}$$

$\hat{a}_i = $ activity of component i $= \dfrac{\hat{f}_i}{f_i^o}$

$f_i^o = $ fugacity of pure i in its standard state

$v_i = $ stoichiometric coefficient of component i

$\Delta G^\circ = $ standard Gibbs energy change of reaction

$K_a = $ chemical equilibrium constant

For mixtures of ideal gases:

f_i^o = unit pressure, often 1 bar

$$\hat{f}_i = y_i P = p_i$$

where p_i = partial pressure of component i.

Then $K_a = K_p = \dfrac{\left(p_C^c\right)\left(p_D^d\right)}{\left(p_A^a\right)\left(p_B^b\right)} = P^{c+d-a-b}\dfrac{\left(y_C^c\right)\left(y_D^d\right)}{\left(y_A^a\right)\left(y_B^b\right)}$

For solids $\hat{a}_i = 1$

For liquids $\hat{a}_i = x_i\gamma_i$

The effect of temperature on the equilibrium constant is

$$\frac{d\ln K}{dT} = \frac{\Delta H^o}{RT^2}$$

where ΔH^o = standard enthalpy change of reaction.

HEATS OF REACTION

For a chemical reaction the associated energy can be defined in terms of heats of formation of the individual species $\left(\Delta\hat{H}_f^{\,o}\right)$ at the standard state

$$\left(\Delta\hat{H}_r^o\right) = \sum_{products} \nu_i\left(\Delta\hat{H}_f^o\right)_i - \sum_{reactants} \nu_i\left(\Delta\hat{H}_f^o\right)_i$$

The standard state is 25°C and 1 bar.

The heat of formation is defined as the enthalpy change associated with the formation of a compound from its atomic species as they normally occur in nature (i.e., $O_{2(g)}$, $H_{2(g)}$, $C_{(solid)}$, etc.)

The heat of reaction for a combustion process using oxygen is also known as the heat of combustion. The principal products are $CO_{2(g)}$ and $H_2O_{(e)}$.

CHEMICAL REACTION ENGINEERING

A chemical reaction may be expressed by the general equation

$$a\mathrm{A} + b\mathrm{B} \leftrightarrow c\mathrm{C} + d\mathrm{D}.$$

The rate of reaction of any component is defined as the moles of that component formed per unit time per unit volume.

$$-r_A = -\frac{1}{V}\frac{dN_A}{dt} \qquad \text{[negative because A disappears]}$$

$$-r_A = \frac{-dC_A}{dt} \qquad \text{if V is constant}$$

The rate of reaction is frequently expressed by

$$-r_A = kf_r\left(C_A, C_B, ...\right), \text{ where}$$

k = reaction rate constant and

C_I = concentration of component I.

The Arrhenius equation gives the dependence of k on temperature

$$k = Ae^{-E_a/\overline{R}T}, \text{ where}$$

A = pre-exponential or frequency factor,

E_a = activation energy (J/mol, cal/mol),

T = temperature (K), and

$\overline{R}$ = gas law constant = 8.314 J/(mol·K).

In the conversion of A, the fractional conversion X_A, is defined as the moles of A reacted per mole of A fed.

$$X_A = (C_{Ao} - C_A)/C_{Ao} \qquad \text{if V is constant}$$

Reaction Order

If $-r_A = kC_A^x C_B^y$

the reaction is x order with respect to reactant A and y order with respect to reactant B. The overall order is

$$n = x + y$$

BATCH REACTOR, CONSTANT T AND V

Zero-Order Reaction

$$-r_A = kC_A^o = k\,(1)$$
$$-dC_A/dt = k \qquad \text{or}$$
$$C_A = C_{Ao}\,e^{-kt}$$
$$dX_A/dt = k/C_{Ao} \qquad \text{or}$$
$$C_{Ao}X_A = kt$$

First-Order Reaction

$$-r_A = kC_A$$
$$-dC_A/dt = kC_A \qquad \text{or}$$
$$\ln(C_A/C_{Ao}) = -kt$$
$$dX_A/dt = k\,(1-X_A) \qquad \text{or}$$
$$\ln(1-X_A) = -kt$$

Second-Order Reaction

$$-r_A = kC_A^2$$
$$-dC_A/dt = kC_A^2 \qquad \text{or}$$
$$1/C_A - 1/C_{Ao} = kt$$
$$dX_A/dt = kC_{Ao}\,(1-X_A)^2 \qquad \text{or}$$
$$X_A/[C_{Ao}\,(1-X_A)] = kt$$

Batch Reactor, General

For a well-mixed, constant-volume, batch reactor

$$-r_A = dC_A/dt$$
$$t = -C_{Ao}\int_o^{X_A} dX_A/(-r_A)$$

If the volume of the reacting mass varies with the conversion according to

$$V = V_{X_A=0}(1 + \varepsilon_A X_A)$$

$$\varepsilon_A = \frac{V_{X_A=1} - V_{X_A=0}}{V_{X_A=0}}$$

then

$$t = -C_{Ao} \int_o^{X_A} dX_A / [(1 + \varepsilon_A X_A)(-r_A)]$$

FLOW REACTORS, STEADY STATE

Space-time τ is defined as the reactor volume divided by the inlet volumetric feed rate. Space-velocity SV is the reciprocal of space-time, $SV = 1/\tau$.

Plug-Flow Reactor (PFR)

$$\tau = \frac{C_{Ao} V_{PFR}}{F_{Ao}} = C_{Ao} \int_o^{X_A} \frac{dX_A}{(-r_A)}, \text{ where}$$

F_{Ao} = moles of A fed per unit time.

Continuous Stirred Tank Reactor (CSTR)

For a constant volume, well-mixed, CSTR

$$\frac{\tau}{C_{Ao}} = \frac{V_{CSTR}}{F_{Ao}} = \frac{X_A}{-r_A}, \text{ where}$$

$-r_A$ is evaluated at exit stream conditions.

Continuous Stirred Tank Reactors in Series

With a first-order reaction $A \rightarrow R$, no change in volume.

$$\tau_{N\text{-reactors}} = N\tau_{\text{individual}}$$

$$= \frac{N}{k}\left[\left(\frac{C_{Ao}}{C_{AN}}\right)^{1/N} - 1\right], \text{ where}$$

N = number of CSTRs (equal volume) in series, and

C_{AN} = concentration of A leaving the Nth CSTR.

DISTILLATION

Flash (or equilibrium) Distillation

Component material balance:

$$Fz_F = yV + xL$$

Overall material balance:

$$F = V + L$$

Differential (Simple or Rayleigh) Distillation

$$\ln\left(\frac{W}{W_o}\right) = \int_{x_o}^{x} \frac{dx}{y - x}$$

When the relative volatility α is constant,

$$y = \alpha x / [1 + (\alpha - 1) x]$$

can be substituted to give

$$\ln\left(\frac{W}{W_o}\right) = \frac{1}{(\alpha - 1)} \ln\left[\frac{x(1 - x_o)}{x_o(1 - x)}\right] + \ln\left[\frac{1 - x_o}{1 - x}\right]$$

For binary system following Raoult's Law

$$\alpha = (y/x)_a / (y/x)_b = p_a / p_b, \text{ where}$$

p_i = partial pressure of component i.

Continuous Distillation (binary system)

Constant molal overflow is assumed (trays counted downward)

Overall Material Balances

Total Material:

$$F = D + B$$

Component A:

$$Fz_F = Dx_D + Bx_B$$

Operating Lines

Rectifying Section

Total Material:

$$V_{n+1} = L_n + D$$

Component A:

$$V_{n+1}y_{n+1} = L_n x_n + Dx_D$$

$$y_{n+1} = [L_n/(L_n + D)] x_n + Dx_D/(L_n + D)$$

Stripping Section

Total Material:

$$L_m = V_{m+1} + B$$

Component A:

$$L_m x_m = V_{m+1}y_{m+1} + Bx_B$$

$$y_{m+1} = [L_m/(L_m - B)] x_m - Bx_B/(L_m - B)$$

Reflux Ratio

Ratio of reflux to overhead product

$$R_D = L/D = (V - D)/D$$

Minimum reflux ratio is defined as that value which results in an infinite number of contact stages. For a binary system the equation of the operating line is

$$y = \frac{R_{min}}{R_{min} + 1} x + \frac{x_D}{R_{min} + 1}$$

Feed Condition Line

$$\text{slope} = q/(q - 1), \text{ where}$$

$$q = \frac{\text{heat to convert one mol of feed to saturated vapor}}{\text{molar heat of vaporization}}$$

Murphree Plate Efficiency

$$E_{ME} = (y_n - y_{n+1})/(y^*_n - y_{n+1}), \text{ where}$$

y = concentration of vapor above plate n,

y_{n+1} = concentration of vapor entering from plate below n, and

y^*_n = concentration of vapor in equilibrium with liquid leaving plate n.

A similar expression can be written for the stripping section by replacing n with m.

Definitions:

α = relative volatility,

B = molar bottoms-product rate,

D = molar overhead-product rate,

F = molar feed rate,

L = molar liquid downflow rate,

R_D = ratio of reflux to overhead product,

V = molar vapor upflow rate,

W = weight in still pot,

x = mole fraction of the more volatile component in the liquid phase, and

y = mole fraction of the more volatile component in the vapor phase.

Subscripts

B = bottoms product,

D = overhead product,

F = feed,

m = any plate in stripping section of column,

$m+1$ = plate below plate m,

n = any plate in rectifying section of column,

$n+1$ = plate below plate n, and

o = original charge in still pot.

MASS TRANSFER

Diffusion

<u>Molecular Diffusion</u>

Gas: $\dfrac{N_A}{A} = \dfrac{p_A}{P}\left(\dfrac{N_A}{A} + \dfrac{N_B}{A}\right) - \dfrac{D_m}{RT}\dfrac{\partial p_A}{\partial z}$

Liquid: $\dfrac{N_A}{A} = x_A\left(\dfrac{N_A}{A} + \dfrac{N_B}{A}\right) - CD_m\dfrac{\partial x_A}{\partial z}$

in which $(p_B)_{lm}$ is the log mean of p_{B2} and p_{B1},

<u>Unidirectional Diffusion of a Gas A Through a Second Stagnant Gas B ($N_b = 0$)</u>

$$\dfrac{N_A}{A} = \dfrac{D_m P}{\overline{R}T(p_B)_{lm}} \times \dfrac{(p_{A2} - p_{A1})}{z_2 - z_1}$$

in which $(p_B)_{lm}$ is the log mean of p_{B2} and p_{B1},

N_I = diffusive flow of component I through area A, in z direction, and

D_m = mass diffusivity.

EQUIMOLAR COUNTER-DIFFUSION (GASES)

($N_B = -N_A$)

$$N_A/A = D_m/(\overline{R}T) \times [(p_{A1} - p_{A2})/(z_2 - z_1)]$$

Unsteady State Diffusion in a Gas

$$\partial p_A/\partial t = D_m (\partial^2 p_A/\partial z^2)$$

CONVECTION

Two-Film Theory (for Equimolar Counter-Diffusion)

$$\begin{aligned} N_A/A &= k'_G (p_{AG} - p_{Ai}) \\ &= k'_L (C_{Ai} - C_{AL}) \\ &= K'_G (p_{AG} - p_A^*) \\ &= K'_L (C_A^* - C_{AL}) \end{aligned}$$

where p_A^* is partial pressure in equilibrium with C_{AL}, and

C_A^* = concentration in equilibrium with p_{AG}.

Overall Coefficients

$$1/K'_G = 1/k'_G + H/k'_L$$

$$1/K'_L = 1/Hk'_G + 1/k'_L$$

Dimensionless Group Equation (Sherwood)

For the turbulent flow inside a tube the Sherwood number

$\left(\dfrac{k_m D}{D_m}\right)$ is given by: $\left(\dfrac{k_m D}{D_m}\right) = 0.023 \left(\dfrac{D\upsilon\rho}{\mu}\right)^{0.8} \left(\dfrac{\mu}{\rho D_m}\right)^{1/3}$

where,

D = inside diameter,

D_m = diffusion coefficient,

V = average velocity in the tube,

ρ = fluid density, and

μ = fluid viscosity.

CHEMICAL PROCESS SAFETY

Threshold Limit Value (TLV)

TLV is the lowest dose (ppm by volume in the atmosphere) the body is able to detoxify without any detectable effects. Examples are:

Compound	TLV
Ammonia	25
Chlorine	0.5
Ethyl Chloride	1,000
Ethyl Ether	400

Flammability

LFL = lower flammability limit (volume % in air)

UFL = upper flammability limit (volume % in air)

A vapor-air mixture will only ignite and burn over the range of compositions between LFL and UFL. Examples are:

Compound	LFL	UFL
Ethyl alcohol	3.3	19
Ethyl ether	1.9	36.0
Ethylene	2.7	36.0
Methane	5	15
Propane	2.1	9.5

Concentrations of Vaporized Liquids

Vaporization Rate (Q_m, mass/time) from a Liquid Surface

$$Q_m = [MKA_S P^{sat}/(R_g T_L)]$$

M = molecular weight of volatile substance

K = mass transfer coefficient

A_S = area of liquid surface

P^{sat} = saturation vapor pressure of the pure liquid at T_L

R_g = ideal gas constant

T_L = absolute temperature of the liquid

Mass Flow Rate of Liquid from a Hole in the Wall of a Process Unit

$$Q_m = A_H C_o (2\rho g_c P_g)^{\frac{1}{2}}$$

A_H = area of hole

C_o = discharge coefficient

ρ = density of the liquid

g_c = gravitational constant

P_g = gauge pressure within the process unit

Concentration (C_{ppm}) of Vaporized Liquid in Ventilated Space

$$C_{ppm} = [Q_m R_g T \times 10^6/(k Q_V P M)]$$

T = absolute ambient temperature

k = nonideal mixing factor

Q_V = ventilation rate

P = absolute ambient pressure

Concentration in the Atmosphere

See "Atmospheric Dispersion Modeling" under **AIR POLLUTION** in the **ENVIRONMENTAL ENGINEERING** section.

Sweep-Through Concentration Change in a Vessel

$$Q_V t = V \ln[(C_1 - C_o)/(C_2 - C_o)]$$

Q_V = volumetric flow rate

t = time

V = vessel volume

C_o = inlet concentration

C_1 = initial concentration

C_2 = final concentration

CIVIL ENGINEERING

GEOTECHNICAL

Definitions

c = cohesion

c_c = coefficient of curvature or gradation

   = $(D_{30})^2/[(D_{60})(D_{10})]$, where

D_{10}, D_{30}, D_{60} = particle diameter corresponding to 10%, 30%, and 60% finer on grain-size curve.

c_u = uniformity coefficient = D_{60}/D_{10}

e = void ratio = V_v/V_s, where

V_v = volume of voids, and

V_s = volume of the solids.

K = coefficient of permeability = hydraulic conductivity

   = $Q/(iA)$ (from Darcy's equation), where

Q = discharge rate

i = hydraulic gradient = dH/dx,

H = hydraulic head,

A = cross-sectional area.

q_u = unconfined compressive strength = $2c$

w = water content (%) = $(W_w/W_s) \times 100$, where

W_w = weight of water, and

W_s = weight of solids.

C_c = compression index = $\Delta e/\Delta \log p$

   = $(e_1 - e_2)/(\log p_2 - \log p_1)$, where

e_1 and e_2 = void ratio, and

p_1 and p_2 = pressure.

D_r = relative density (%)

   = $[(e_{max} - e)/(e_{max} - e_{min})] \times 100$

   = $[(1/\gamma_{min} - 1/\gamma_d)/(1/\gamma_{min} - 1/\gamma_{max})] \times 100$, where

e_{max} and e_{min} = maximum and minimum void ratio, and

γ_{max} and γ_{min} = maximum and minimum unit dry weight.

G_s = specific gravity = $W_s/(V_s\gamma_w)$, where

γ_w = unit weight of water (62.4 lb/ft^3 or 1,000 kg/m^3).

ΔH = settlement = $H[C_c/(1 + e_i)] \log[(p_i + \Delta p)/p_i]$

   = $H\Delta e/(1 + e_i)$, where

H = thickness of soil layer

Δe = change in void ratio, and

p = pressure.

PI = plasticity index = $LL - PL$, where

LL = liquid limit, and

PL = plasticity limit.

S = degree of saturation (%) = $(V_w/V_v) \times 100$, where

V_w = volume of water,

V_v = volume of voids.

Q = $KH(N_f/N_d)$ (for flow nets, Q per unit width), where

K = coefficient permeability,

H = total hydraulic head (potential),

N_f = number of flow tubes, and

N_d = number of potential drops.

γ = total unit weight of soil = W/V

γ_d = dry unit weight of soil = W_s/V

   = $G\gamma_w/(1 + e) = \gamma/(1 + w)$, where

Gw = Se

γ_s = unit weight of solid = W_s/V_s

n = porosity = $V_v/V = e/(1 + e)$

τ = general shear strength = $c + \sigma\tan\phi$, where

ϕ = angle of internal friction,

σ = normal stress = P/A,

P = force, and

A = area.

K_a = coefficient of active earth pressure

   = $\tan^2(45 - \phi/2)$

K_p = coefficient of passive earth pressure

   = $\tan^2(45 + \phi/2)$

P_a = active resultant force = $0.5\gamma H^2 K_a$, where

H = height of wall.

q_{ult} = bearing capacity equation

   = $cN_c + \gamma D_f N_q + 0.5\gamma B N_\gamma$, where

N_c, N_q, and N_γ = bearing capacity factors

B = width of strip footing, and

D_f = depth of footing below surface.

FS = factor of safety (slope stability)

   = $\dfrac{cL + W\cos\alpha\,\tan\phi}{W\sin\alpha}$, where

L = length of slip plane,

α = slope of slip plane,

ϕ = angle of friction, and

W = total weight of soil above slip plane.

C_v = coefficient of consolidation = TH^2/t, where

T = time factor,

t = consolidation time.

H_{dr} = length of drainage path

n = number of drainage layers

C_c = compression index for normally consolidated clay

   = $0.009(LL - 10)$

σ' = effective stress = $\sigma - u$, where

σ = normal stress, and

u = pore water pressure.

UNIFIED SOIL CLASSIFICATION SYSTEM (ASTM D-2487)

Major Divisions			Group Symbols		Typical Names	Laboratory Classification Criteria	
Coarse-grained soils (More than half of material is larger than No. 200 sieve size)	Gravels (More than half of coarse fraction is larger than No. 4 sieve size)	Clean gravels (Little or no fines)	GW		Well-graded gravels, gravel-sand mixtures, little or no fines	$c_u = \dfrac{D_{60}}{D_{10}}$ greater than 4; $c_c = \dfrac{(D_{30})^2}{D_{10} \times D_{60}}$ between 1 and 3	Determine percentages of sand and gravel from grain-size curve. Depending on percentage of fines (fraction smaller than No. 200 sieve size), coarse-grained soils are classified as follows: Less than 5 percent: GW, GP, SW, SP — More than 12 percent: GM, GC, SM, SC — 5 to 12 percent: Borderline cases requiring dual symbols[b]
			GP		Poorly-graded gravels, gravel-sand mixtures, little or no fines	Not meeting all gradation requirements for GW	
		Gravels with fines (Appreciable amount of fines)	GM[a]	d / u	Silty gravels, gravel-sand-silt mixtures	Atterberg limits below "A" line or PI less than 4 — Above "A" line with PI between 4 and 7 are borderline cases requiring use of dual symbols	
			GC		Clayey gravels, gravel-sand-clay mixtures	Atterberg limits above "A" line with PI greater than 7	
	Sands (More than half of coarse fraction is smaller than No. 4 sieve size)	Clean sands (Little or no fines)	SW		Well-graded sands, gravelly sands, little or no fines	$c_u = \dfrac{D_{60}}{D_{10}}$ greater than 6; $c_c = \dfrac{(D_{30})^2}{D_{10} \times D_{60}}$ between 1 and 3	
			SP		Poorly graded sand, gravelly sands, little or no fines	Not meeting all gradation requirements for SW	
		Sands with fines (Appreciable amount of fines)	SM[a]	d / u	Silty sands, sand-silt mixtures	Atterberg limits below "A" line or PI less than 4 — Limits plotting in hatched zone with PI between 4 and 7 are borderline cases requiring use of dual symbols	
			SC		Clayey sands, sand-clay mixtures	Atterberg limits above "A" line with PI greater than 7	
Fine-grained soils (More than half material is smaller than No. 200 sieve)	Silts and clays (Liquid limit less than 50)		ML		Inorganic silts and very fine sands, rock flour, silty or clayey fine sands, or clayey silts with slight plasticity		
			CL		Inorganic clays of low to medium plasticity, gravelly clays, sandy clays, silty clays, lean clays		
			OL		Organic silts and organic silty clays of low plasticity		
	Silts and clays (Liquid limit greater than 50)		MH		Inorganic silts, micaceous or diatomaceous fine sandy or silty soils, elastic silts		
			CH		Inorganic clays of high plasticity, fat clays		
			OH		Organic clays of medium to high plasticity, organic silts		
	Highly organic soils		Pt		Peat and other highly organic soils		

PLASTICITY CHART

[a] Division of GM and SM groups into subdivisions of d and u are for roads and airfields only. Subdivision is based on Atterberg limits; suffix d used when LL is 28 or less and the PI is 6 or less; the suffix u used when LL is greater than 28.

[b] Borderline classification, used for soils possessing characteristics of two groups, are designated by combinations of group symbols. For example GW-GC, well-graded gravel-sand mixture with clay binder.

STRUCTURAL ANALYSIS

Influence Lines

An influence diagram shows the variation of a function (reaction, shear, bending moment) as a single unit load moves across the structure. An influence line is used to (1) determine the position of load where a maximum quantity will occur and (2) determine the maximum value of the quantity.

Deflection of Trusses

Principle of virtual work as applied to trusses

$\Delta = \Sigma f_Q \delta L$

Δ = deflection at point of interest

f_Q = member force due to virtual unit load applied at the point of interest

δL = change in member length

   = $\alpha L(\Delta T)$ for temperature

   = $F_p L/AE$ for external load

α = coefficient of thermal expansion

L = member length

Fp = member force due to external load

A = cross-sectional area of member

E = modulus of elasticity

ΔT = $T–T_O$; T = final temperature, and T_O = initial temperature

Deflection of Frames

The principle of virtual work as applied to frames:

$$\Delta = \Sigma \left\{ \int_O^L \frac{mM}{EI} dx \right\}$$

m = bending moment as a funtion of x due to virtual unit load applied at the point of interest

M = bending moment as a function of x due to external loads

BEAM FIXED-END MOMENT FORMULAS

$$FEM_{AB} = \frac{Pab^2}{L^2}$$

$$FEM_{BA} = \frac{Pa^2b}{L^2}$$

$$FEM_{AB} = \frac{w_oL^2}{12}$$

$$FEM_{BA} = \frac{w_oL^2}{12}$$

$$FEM_{AB} = \frac{w_oL^2}{30}$$

$$FEM_{BA} = \frac{w_oL^2}{20}$$

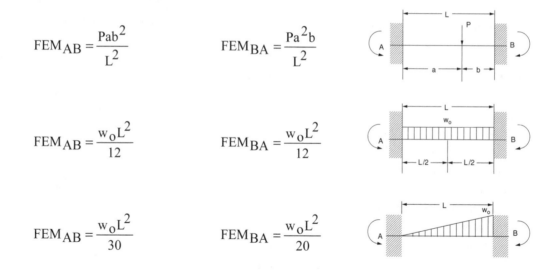

Live Load Reduction

The live load applied to a structure member can be reduced as the loaded area supported by the member is increased. A typical reduction model (as used in ASCE 7 and in building codes) for a column supporting two or more floors is:

$$L_{reduced} = L_{nominal} \left(0.25 + \frac{15}{\sqrt{k_{LL} A_T}} \right) \ge 0.4\, L_{nominal}$$

Columns: $k_{LL} = 4$

Beams: $k_{LL} = 2$

where $L_{nominal}$ is the nominal live load (as given in a load standard or building code), A_T is the floor tributary area(s) supported by the member, and k_{LL} is the ratio of the area of influence to the tributary area.

REINFORCED CONCRETE DESIGN   ACI 318-02

US Customary units

Definitions

a = depth of equivalent rectangular stress block, in

A_g = gross area of column, in^2

A_s = area of tension reinforcement, in^2

A_s' = area of compression reinforcement, in^2

A_{st} = total area of longitudinal reinforcement, in^2

A_v = area of shear reinforcment within a distance s, in

b = width of compression face of member, in

b_e = effective compression flange width, in

b_w = web width, in

β_1 = ratio of depth of rectangular stress block, a, to depth to neutral axis, c

= $0.85 \geq 0.85 - 0.05\left(\dfrac{f_c' - 4{,}000}{1{,}000}\right) \geq 0.65$

c = distance from extreme compression fiber to neutral axis, in

d = distance from extreme compression fiber to centroid of nonprestressed tension reinforcement, in

d_t = distance from extreme tension fiber to extreme tension steel, in

E_c = modulus of elasticity = $33\, w_c^{1.5}\sqrt{f_c'}$, psi

ε_t = net tensile strain in extreme tension steel at nominal strength

f_c' = compressive strength of concrete, psi

f_y = yield strength of steel reinforcement, psi

h_f = T-beam flange thickness, in

M_c = factored column moment, including slenderness effect, in-lb

M_n = nominal moment strength at section, in-lb

ϕM_n = design moment strength at section, in-lb

M_u = factored moment at section, in-lb

P_n = nominal axial load strength at given eccentricity, lb

ϕP_n = design axial load strength at given eccentricity, lb

P_u = factored axial force at section, lb

ρ_g = ratio of total reinforcement area to cross-sectional area of column = A_{st}/A_g

s = spacing of shear ties measured along longitudinal axis of member, in

V_c = nominal shear strength provided by concrete, lb

V_n = nominal shear strength at section, lb

ϕV_n = design shear strength at section, lb

V_s = nominal shear strength provided by reinforcement, lb

V_u = factored shear force at section, lb

ASTM STANDARD REINFORCING BARS

BAR SIZE	DIAMETER, IN	AREA, IN^2	WEIGHT, LB/FT
#3	0.375	0.11	0.376
#4	0.500	0.20	0.668
#5	0.625	0.31	1.043
#6	0.750	0.44	1.502
#7	0.875	0.60	2.044
#8	1.000	0.79	2.670
#9	1.128	1.00	3.400
#10	1.270	1.27	4.303
#11	1.410	1.56	5.313
#14	1.693	2.25	7.650
#18	2.257	4.00	13.60

LOAD FACTORS FOR REQUIRED STRENGTH

$U = 1.4\,D$

$U = 1.2\,D + 1.6\,L$

SELECTED ACI MOMENT COEFFICIENTS

Approximate moments in continuous beams of three or more spans, provided:

1. Span lengths approximately equal   (length of longer adjacent span within 20% of shorter)

2. Uniformly distributed load

3. Live load not more than three times dead load

$M_u = coefficient * w_u * L_n^{\,2}$

w_u = factored load per unit beam length

L_n = clear span for positive moment; average adjacent clear spans for negative moment

Column

Spandrel beam

Unrestrained end

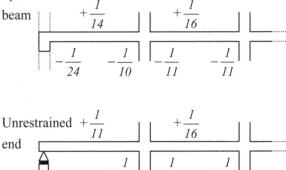

End span   **Interior span**

UNIFIED DESIGN PROVISIONS

Internal Forces and Strains

Net tensile strain: ε_t

Strain Conditions

$\varepsilon_t \geq 0.005$ | $0.005 > \varepsilon_t > 0.002$ | $\varepsilon_t \leq 0.002$

Tension-controlled section:
$c \leq 0.375\, d_t$

Transition section

Compression-controlled section:
$c \geq 0.6\, d_t$

Balanced Strain: $\varepsilon_t = \varepsilon_y$

$$\varepsilon_t = \varepsilon_y = \frac{f_y}{E_s} = 0.002$$

RESISTANCE FACTORS, ϕ

Tension-controlled sections ($\varepsilon_t \geq 0.005$): $\phi = 0.9$
Compression-controlled sections ($\varepsilon_t \leq 0.002$):
  Members with spiral reinforcement $\phi = 0.70$
  Members with tied reinforcement $\phi = 0.65$
Transition sections ($0.002 < \varepsilon_t < 0.005$):
  Members w/ spiral reinforcement $\phi = 0.57 + 67\varepsilon_t$
  Members w/ tied reinforcement $\phi = 0.48 + 83\varepsilon_t$
Shear and torsion $\phi = 0.75$
Bearing on concrete $\phi = 0.65$

BEAMS – FLEXURE: $\phi M_N \geq M_U$

For all beams

Net tensile strain: $a = \beta_1 c$

$$\varepsilon_t = \frac{0.003(d_t - c)}{c} = \frac{0.003(\beta_1 d_t - a)}{a}$$

Design moment strength: ϕM_n
  where: $\phi = 0.9\;[\varepsilon_t \geq 0.005]$
    $\phi = 0.48 + 83\varepsilon_t\;[0.004 \leq \varepsilon_t < 0.005]$
Reinforcement limits:

$A_{S,\,max}$ $\varepsilon_t = 0.004 @ M_n$

$$A_{S,\,min} = \text{larger} \begin{cases} \dfrac{3\sqrt{f_c'}\, b_w\, d}{f_y} & \text{or} & \dfrac{200 b_w\, d}{f_y} \end{cases}$$

$A_{s,\,min}$ limits need not be applied if
A_s (provided $\geq 1.33\, A_s$ (required)

Singly-reinforced beams

$$A_{s,\,max} = \frac{0.85 f_c' \beta_1 b}{f_y}\left(\frac{3 d_t}{7}\right)$$

$$a = \frac{A_s f_y}{0.85 f_c' b}$$

$$M_n = 0.85 f_c'\, a\, b\left(d - \frac{a}{2}\right) = A_s f_y\left(d - \frac{a}{2}\right)$$

Doubly-reinforced beams

Compression steel yields if:

$$A_s - A_s' \geq \frac{0.85\beta_1 f_c' d' b}{f_y}\left(\frac{87{,}000}{87{,}000 + f_y}\right)$$

If compression steel yields:

$$A_{s,\,max} = \frac{0.85 f_c' \beta_1 b}{f_y}\left(\frac{3 d_t}{7}\right) - A_s'$$

$$a = \frac{(A_s - A_s') f_y}{0.85 f_c' b}$$

$$M_n = f_y\left[(A_s - A_s')\left(d - \frac{a}{2}\right) + A_s'(d - d')\right]$$

If compression steel does not yield (*four steps*):

1. Solve for c:

$$c^2 + \left(\frac{(87{,}000 - 0.85 f_c')\, A_s' - A_s f_y}{0.85 f_c' \beta_1 b}\right)c - \frac{87{,}000\, A_s'\, d'}{0.85 f_c' \beta_1 b} = 0$$

BEAMS – FLEXURE: $\phi M_N \geq M_U$ (CONTINUED)

Doubly-reinforced beams (continued)

Compression steel does not yield (continued)

2. $f_s' = 87{,}000 \left(\dfrac{c - d'}{c} \right)$

3. $A_{s,max} = \dfrac{0.85 f_c' \beta_1 b}{f_y} \left(\dfrac{3 d_t}{7} \right) - A_s' \left(\dfrac{f_s'}{f_y} \right)$

4. $a = \dfrac{(A_s f_y - A_s' f_s')}{0.85 f_c' b}$

$M_n = f_s' \left[\left(\dfrac{A_s f_y}{f_s'} - A_s' \right) \left(d - \dfrac{a}{2} \right) + A_s' (d - d') \right]$

T-beams – tension reinforcement in stem

Effective flange width:

$$b_e = \underset{\text{smallest}}{} \begin{cases} 1/4 \bullet \text{span length} \\ b_w + 16 \bullet h_f \\ \text{beam centerline spacing} \end{cases}$$

Design moment strenth:

$a = \dfrac{A_s f_y}{0.85 f_c' b_e}$

If $a \leq h_f$:

$A_{s,max} = \dfrac{0.85 f_c' \beta_1 b_e}{f_y} \left(\dfrac{3 d_t}{7} \right)$

$M_n = 0.85 f_c' a b_e \left(d - \dfrac{a}{2} \right)$

If $a > h_f$:

$A_{s,max} = \dfrac{0.85 f_c' \beta_1 b_e}{f_y} \left(\dfrac{3 d_t}{7} \right) + \dfrac{0.85 f_c' (b_e - b_w) h_f}{f_y}$

$M_n = 0.85 f_c' \left[h_f (b_e - b_w) \left(d - \dfrac{h_f}{2} \right) \right.$

$\left. + a b_w \left(d - \dfrac{a}{2} \right) \right]$

BEAMS – SHEAR: $\phi V_N \geq V_u$

Beam width used in shear equations:

$$b_w = \begin{cases} b \ (\text{rectangular beams}) \\ b_w \ (\text{T–beams}) \end{cases}$$

Nominal shear strength:

$V_n = V_c + V_s$

$V_c = 2 b_w d \sqrt{f_c'}$

$V_s = \dfrac{A_v f_y d}{s}$ [may not exceed $8 b_w d \sqrt{f_c'}$]

Required and maximum-permitted stirrup spacing, s

$V_u \leq \dfrac{\phi V_c}{2}$: No stirrups required

$V_u > \dfrac{\phi V_c}{2}$: Use the following table (A_v given):

	$\dfrac{\phi V_c}{2} < V_u \leq \phi V_c$	$V_u > \phi V_c$
Required spacing	Smaller of: $s = \dfrac{A_v f_y}{50 b_w}$ $s = \dfrac{A_v f_y}{0.75 b_w \sqrt{f_c'}}$	$V_s = V_u - \phi V_c$: $s = \dfrac{\phi A_v f_y d}{V_s}$
Maximum permitted spacing	Smaller of: $s = \dfrac{d}{2}$ OR $s = 24''$	$V_s \leq 4 b_w d \sqrt{f_c'}$ Smaller of: $s = \dfrac{d}{2}$ OR $s = 24''$
		$V_s > 4 b_w d \sqrt{f_c'}$ Smaller of: $s = \dfrac{d}{4}$ $s = 12''$

SHORT COLUMNS:
Reinforcement limits:

$$\rho_g = \frac{A_{st}}{A_g}$$

$$0.01 \le \rho_g \le 0.08$$

Definition of a short column:

$$\frac{KL}{r} \le 34 - \frac{12M_1}{M_2}$$

where: $KL = L_{col}$ clear height of column
[assume $K = 1.0$]

$r = 0.288h$ rectangular column, h is side length perpendicular to buckling axis (*i.e.,* side length in the plane of buckling)

$r = 0.25h$ circular column, h = diameter

M_1 = smaller end moment
M_2 = larger end moment

$$\frac{M_1}{M_2} \Bigg\{$$

Concentrically-loaded short columns: $\phi P_n \ge P_u$

$$M_1 = M_2 = 0$$

$$\frac{KL}{r} \le 22$$

Design column strength, spiral columns: $\phi = 0.70$

$$\phi P_n = 0.85\phi [0.85 f_c' (A_g - A_{st}) + A_{st} f_y]$$

Design column strength, tied columns: $\phi = 0.65$

$$\phi P_n = 0.80\phi [0.85 f_c' (A_g - A_{st}) + A_{st} f_y]$$

Short columns with end moments:

$$M_u = M_2 \quad \text{or} \quad M_u = P_u e$$

Use *Load-moment strength interaction diagram* to:
1. Obtain ϕP_n at applied moment M_u
2. Obtain ϕP_n at eccentricity e
3. Select A_s for P_u, M_u

LONG COLUMNS − Braced (non-sway) frames
Definition of a long column:

$$\frac{KL}{r} > 34 - \frac{12M_1}{M_2}$$

Critical load:

$$P_c = \frac{\pi^2 EI}{(KL)^2} = \frac{\pi^2 EI}{(L_{col})^2}$$

where: $EI = 0.25 E_c I_g$

Concentrically-loaded long columns:

$e_{min} = (0.6 + 0.03h)$ minimum eccentricity
$M_1 = M_2 = P_u e_{min}$ (positive curvature)

$$\frac{KL}{r} > 22$$

$$M_c = \frac{M_2}{1 - \dfrac{P_u}{0.75P_c}}$$

Use *Load-moment strength interaction diagram*
to design/analyze column for P_u, M_u

Long columns with end moments:

M_1 = smaller end moment
M_2 = larger end moment

$\dfrac{M_1}{M_2}$ positive if M_1, M_2 produce **single** curvature

$$C_m = 0.6 + \frac{0.4 M_1}{M_2} \ge 0.4$$

$$M_c = \frac{C_m M_2}{1 - \dfrac{P_u}{0.75P_c}} \ge M_2$$

Use *Load-moment strength interaction diagram*
to design/analyze column for P_u, M_u

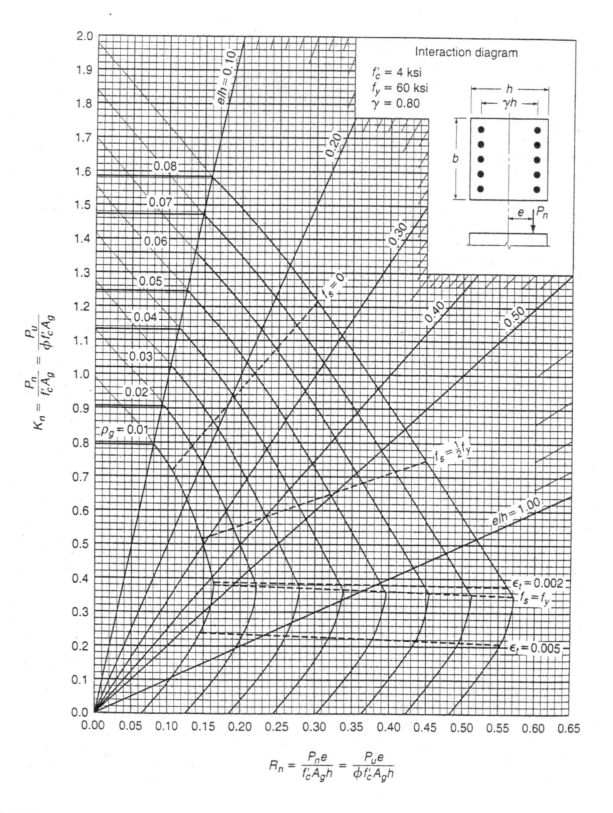

GRAPH A.11

Column strength interaction diagram for rectangular section with bars on end faces and $\gamma = 0.80$ (for instructional use only).

Design of Concrete Structures, 13th Edition (2004), Nilson, Darwin, Dolan

McGraw-Hill ISBN 0-07-248305-9 GRAPH A.11, Page 762

Used by permission

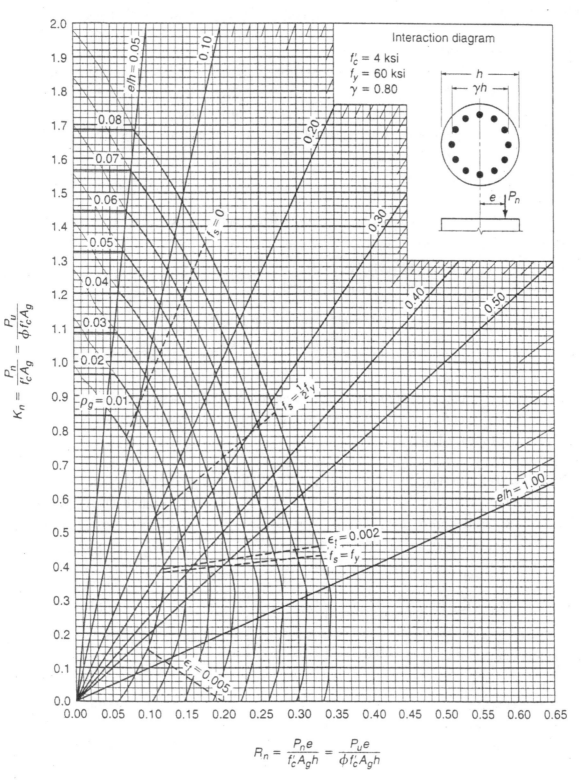

GRAPH A.15

Column strength interaction diagram for circular section $\gamma = 0.80$ (for instructional use only).

Design of Concrete Structures, 13th Edition (2004), Nilson, Darwin, Dolan

McGraw-Hill ISBN 0-07-248305-9 GRAPH A.15, Page 766

Used by permission

STEEL STRUCTURES

References: AISC LRFD Manual, 3rd Edition

AISC ASD Manual, 9th Edition

LOAD COMBINATIONS (LRFD)

Floor systems: $1.4D$

$1.2D + 1.6L$

Roof systems: $1.2D + 1.6(L_r \text{ or } S \text{ or } R) + 0.8W$

$1.2D + 0.5(L_r \text{ or } S \text{ or } R) + 1.3W$

$0.9D \pm 1.3W$

where: D = dead load due to the weight of the structure and permanent features

L = live load due to occupancy and moveable equipment

L_r = roof live load

S = snow load

R = load due to initial rainwater (excluding ponding) or ice

W = wind load

TENSION MEMBERS: flat plates, angles (bolted or welded)

Gross area: $A_g = b_g\, t$ (use tabulated value for angles)

Net area: $A_n = (b_g - \Sigma D_h + \dfrac{s^2}{4g})\, t$ across critical chain of holes

where: b_g = gross width

t = thickness

s = longitudinal center-to-center spacing (pitch) of two consecutive holes

g = transverse center-to-center spacing (gage) between fastener gage lines

D_h = bolt-hole diameter

Effective area (bolted members):

$A_e = UA_n$ $\begin{cases} U = 1.0 \text{ (flat bars)} \\ U = 0.85 \text{ (angles with} \geq 3 \text{ bolts in line)} \\ U = 0.75 \text{ (angles with 2 bolts in line)} \end{cases}$

Effective area (welded members):

$A_e = UA_g$ $\begin{cases} U = 1.0 \text{ (flat bars, } L \geq 2w) \\ U = 0.87 \text{ (flat bars, } 2w > L \geq 1.5w) \\ U = 0.75 \text{ (flat bars, } 1.5w > L \geq w) \\ U = 0.85 \text{ (angles)} \end{cases}$

LRFD

Yielding: $\phi T_n = \phi_y A_g F_y = 0.9\, A_g F_y$

Fracture: $\phi T_n = \phi_f A_e F_u = 0.75\, A_e F_u$

Block shear rupture (bolted tension members):

A_{gt} = gross tension area

A_{gv} = gross shear area

A_{nt} = net tension area

A_{nv} = net shear area

When $F_u A_{nt} \geq 0.6\, F_u A_{nv}$:

$\phi R_n = \underset{\text{smaller}}{} \begin{cases} 0.75\, [0.6\, F_y A_{gv} + F_u A_{nt}] \\ 0.75\, [0.6\, F_u A_{nv} + F_u A_{nt}] \end{cases}$

When $F_u A_{nt} < 0.6\, F_u A_{nv}$:

$\phi R_n = \underset{\text{smaller}}{} \begin{cases} 0.75\, [0.6\, F_u A_{nv} + F_y A_{gt}] \\ 0.75\, [0.6\, F_u A_{nv} + F_u A_{nt}] \end{cases}$

ASD

Yielding: $T_a = A_g F_t = A_g (0.6\, F_y)$

Fracture: $T_a = A_e F_t = A_e (0.5\, F_u)$

Block shear rupture (bolted tension members):

$T_a = (0.30\, F_u)\, A_{nv} + (0.5\, F_u)\, A_{nt}$

A_{nt} = net tension area

A_{nv} = net shear area

BEAMS: homogeneous beams, flexure about x-axis

Flexure – local buckling:

No local buckling if section is **compact**: $\dfrac{b_f}{2t_f} \leq \dfrac{65}{\sqrt{F_y}}$ **and** $\dfrac{h}{t_w} \leq \dfrac{640}{\sqrt{F_y}}$

where: For **rolled** sections, use tabulated values of $\dfrac{b_f}{2t_f}$ and $\dfrac{h}{t_w}$

For **built-up** sections, h is clear distance between flanges

For $F_y \leq 50$ ksi, all **rolled shapes** except W6 × 19 are compact.

Flexure – lateral-torsional buckling: L_b = unbraced length

LRFD–compact rolled shapes

$\left. \begin{aligned} L_p &= \frac{300\, r_y}{\sqrt{F_y}} \\[2em] L_r &= \frac{r_y X_1}{F_L}\sqrt{1 + \sqrt{1 + X_2 F_L^2}} \end{aligned} \right\}$ Z_x Table

where: $F_L = F_y - 10$ ksi

$\left. \begin{aligned} X_1 &= \frac{\pi}{S_x}\sqrt{\frac{EGJA}{2}} \\[1.5em] X_2 &= 4\,\frac{C_w}{I_y}\left(\frac{S_x}{GJ}\right)^2 \end{aligned} \right\}$ W-Shapes Dimensions and Properties Table

$\phi \;=\; 0.90$

$\left. \begin{aligned} \phi M_p &= \phi\, F_y Z_x \\ \phi M_r &= \phi\, F_L S_x \end{aligned} \right\}$ Z_x Table

$C_b = \dfrac{12.5\, M_{\max}}{2.5\, M_{\max} + 3\, M_A + 4\, M_B + 3\, M_C}$

$L_b \leq L_p$: $\phi M_n = \phi M_p$

$L_p < L_b \leq L_r$:

$\phi M_n = C_b \left[\phi M_p - (\phi M_p - \phi M_r)\left(\dfrac{L_b - L_p}{L_r - L_p}\right) \right]$

$\qquad = C_b \left[\phi M_p - BF\,(L_b - L_p) \right] \leq \phi M_p$

See Z_x *Table for BF*

$L_b > L_r$:

$\phi M_n = \dfrac{\phi C_b S_x X_1 \sqrt{2}}{L_b / r_y}\sqrt{1 + \dfrac{X_1^2 X_2}{2\left(L_b / r_y\right)^2}} \leq \phi M_p$

See *Beam Design Moments* curve

ASD–compact rolled shapes

$L_c = \dfrac{76\, b_f}{\sqrt{F_y}}$ *or* $\dfrac{20{,}000}{(d / A_f)\, F_y}$ use smaller

$C_b = 1.75 + 1.05(M_1/M_2) + 0.3(M_1/M_2)^2 \leq 2.3$

$\qquad M_1$ is smaller end moment

$\qquad M_1/M_2$ is positive for reverse curvature

$M_a = S\, F_b$

$L_b \leq L_c$: $F_b = 0.66\, F_y$

$L_b > L_c$:

$F_b = \left[\dfrac{2}{3} - \dfrac{F_y\,(L_b/r_T)^2}{1{,}530{,}000\,C_b} \right] \leq 0.6\, F_y \qquad$ (F1-6)

$F_b = \dfrac{170{,}000\, C_b}{(L_b/r_T)^2} \leq 0.6\, F_y \qquad$ (F1-7)

$F_b = \dfrac{12{,}000\, C_b}{L_b d / A_f} \leq 0.6\, F_y \qquad$ (F1-8)

For: $\sqrt{\dfrac{102{,}000\, C_b}{F_y}} < \dfrac{L_b}{r_T} \leq \sqrt{\dfrac{510{,}000\, C_b}{F_y}}$:

$\qquad$ Use larger of (F1-6) and (F1-8)

For: $\dfrac{L_b}{r_T} > \sqrt{\dfrac{510{,}000\, C_b}{F_y}}$:

$\qquad$ Use larger of (F1-7) and (F1-8)

See *Allowable Moments in Beams* curve

Shear – unstiffened beams

LRFD – E = 29,000 ksi

$\phi = 0.90 \qquad A_w = d\,t_w$

$\dfrac{h}{t_w} \le \dfrac{417}{\sqrt{F_y}} \qquad \phi V_n = \phi\,(0.6\,F_y)\,A_w$

$\dfrac{417}{\sqrt{F_y}} < \dfrac{h}{t_w} \le \dfrac{523}{\sqrt{F_y}}$

$\phi V_n = \phi\,(0.6\,F_y)\,A_w \left[\dfrac{417}{(h/t_w)\sqrt{F_y}} \right]$

$\dfrac{523}{\sqrt{F_y}} < \dfrac{h}{t_w} \le 260$

$\phi V_n = \phi\,(0.6\,F_y)\,A_w \left[\dfrac{218{,}000}{(h/t_w)^2\,F_y} \right]$

ASD

For $\dfrac{h}{t_w} \le \dfrac{380}{\sqrt{F_y}}:\quad F_v = 0.40\,F_y$

For $\dfrac{h}{t_w} > \dfrac{380}{\sqrt{F_y}}:\quad F_v = \dfrac{F_y}{2.89}(C_v) \le 0.4\,F_y$

where for unstiffened beams:

$k_v = 5.34$

$C_v = \dfrac{190}{h/t_w}\sqrt{\dfrac{k_v}{F_y}} = \dfrac{439}{(h/t_w)\sqrt{F_y}}$

COLUMNS

Column effective length *KL*:

AISC Table C-C2.1 (**LRFD** and **ASD**)– *Effective Length Factors (K) for Columns*

AISC Figure C-C2.2 (**LRFD** and **ASD**)– *Alignment Chart for Effective Length of Columns in Frames*

Column capacities:

LRFD

Column slenderness parameter:

$\lambda_c = \left(\dfrac{KL}{r} \right)_{max} \left(\dfrac{1}{\pi}\sqrt{\dfrac{F_y}{E}} \right)$

Nominal capacity of axially loaded columns (doubly symmetric section, no local buckling):

$\phi = 0.85$

$\lambda_c \le 1.5: \qquad \phi F_{cr} = \phi\left(0.658^{\lambda_c^2} \right) F_y$

$\lambda_c > 1.5: \qquad \phi F_{cr} = \phi\left[\dfrac{0.877}{\lambda_c^2} \right] F_y$

See *Table 3-50: Design Stress for Compression Members (F$_y$ = 50 ksi, ϕ = 0.85)*

ASD

Column slenderness parameter:

$C_c = \sqrt{\dfrac{2\pi^2 E}{F_y}}$

Allowable stress for axially loaded columns (doubly symmetric section, no local buckling):

When $\left(\dfrac{KL}{r} \right)_{max} \le C_c$

$F_a = \dfrac{\left[1 - \dfrac{(KL/r)^2}{2C_c^{\,2}} \right] F_y}{\dfrac{5}{3} + \dfrac{3(KL/r)}{8C_c} - \dfrac{(KL/r)^3}{8C_c^{\,3}}}$

When $\left(\dfrac{KL}{r} \right)_{max} > C_c: \quad F_a = \dfrac{12\pi^2 E}{23(KL/r)^2}$

See *Table C-50: Allowable Stress for Compression Members (F$_y$ = 50 ksi)*

BEAM-COLUMNS: Sidesway prevented, x-axis bending, transverse loading between supports (no moments at ends), ends unrestrained against rotation in the plane of bending

<table>
<tr><td align="center">LRFD</td><td align="center">ASD</td></tr>
<tr><td>

$\dfrac{P_u}{\phi P_n} \geq 0.2:$ $\dfrac{P_u}{\phi P_n} + \dfrac{8}{9}\dfrac{M_u}{\phi M_n} \leq 1.0$

$\dfrac{P_u}{\phi P_n} < 0.2:$ $\dfrac{P_u}{2\phi P_n} + \dfrac{M_u}{\phi M_n} \leq 1.0$

where:

$M_u = B_1 M_{nt}$

$B_1 = \dfrac{C_m}{1 - \dfrac{P_u}{P_{ex}}} \geq 1.0$

$C_m = 1.0$ for conditions stated above

$P_{ex} = \left(\dfrac{\pi^2 E I_x}{(KL_x)^2} \right)$ x-axis bending

</td><td>

$\dfrac{f_a}{F_a} > 0.15:$ $\dfrac{f_a}{F_a} + \dfrac{C_m f_b}{\left(1 - \dfrac{f_a}{F_e'}\right)F_b} \leq 1.0$

$\dfrac{f_a}{F_a} \leq 0.15:$ $\dfrac{f_a}{F_a} + \dfrac{f_b}{F_b} \leq 1.0$

where:

$C_m = 1.0$ for conditions stated above

$F_e' = \dfrac{12\pi^2 E}{23(KL_x/r_x)^2}$ x-axis bending

</td></tr>
</table>

BOLTED CONNECTIONS: A325 bolts d_b = nominal bolt diameter A_b = nominal bolt area

s = spacing between centers of bolt holes in direction of force

L_e = distance between center of bolt hole and edge of member in direction of force

t = member thickness

D_h = bolt hole diameter = $d_b + {}^1/_{16}"$ [standard holes]

Bolt tension and shear strengths:

<table>
<tr><td colspan="4" align="center">LRFD</td></tr>
<tr><td colspan="4">

Design strength (kips / bolt):

    Tension: $\phi R_t = \phi F_t A_b$

    Shear: $\phi R_v = \phi F_v A_b$

Design resistance to slip at factored loads

    (kips / bolt): ϕR_n

</td></tr>
<tr><td rowspan="2">Bolt strength</td><td colspan="3" align="center">Bolt size</td></tr>
<tr><td align="center">3/4"</td><td align="center">7/8"</td><td align="center">1"</td></tr>
<tr><td align="center">ϕR_t</td><td align="center">29.8</td><td align="center">40.6</td><td align="center">53.0</td></tr>
<tr><td align="center">ϕR_v (A325-N)</td><td align="center">15.9</td><td align="center">21.6</td><td align="center">28.3</td></tr>
<tr><td align="center">ϕR_n (A325-SC)</td><td align="center">10.4</td><td align="center">14.5</td><td align="center">19.0</td></tr>
<tr><td colspan="4">ϕR_v and ϕR_n values are single shear</td></tr>
</table>

<table>
<tr><td colspan="4" align="center">ASD</td></tr>
<tr><td colspan="4">

Design strength (kips / bolt):

    Tension: $R_t = F_t A_b$

    Shear: $R_v = F_v A_b$

Design resistance to slip at service loads

    (kips / bolt): R_v

</td></tr>
<tr><td rowspan="2">Bolt strength</td><td colspan="3" align="center">Bolt size</td></tr>
<tr><td align="center">3/4"</td><td align="center">7/8"</td><td align="center">1"</td></tr>
<tr><td align="center">R_t</td><td align="center">19.4</td><td align="center">26.5</td><td align="center">34.6</td></tr>
<tr><td align="center">R_v (A325-N)</td><td align="center">9.3</td><td align="center">12.6</td><td align="center">16.5</td></tr>
<tr><td align="center">R_v (A325-SC)</td><td align="center">6.63</td><td align="center">9.02</td><td align="center">11.8</td></tr>
<tr><td colspan="4">R_v values are single shear</td></tr>
</table>

Bearing strength

LRFD

Design strength (kips/bolt/inch thickness):

$$\phi r_n = \phi \, 1.2 \, L_c \, F_u \leq \phi \, 2.4 \, d_b \, F_u$$

$$\phi = 0.75$$

L_c = clear distance between edge of hole and edge of adjacent hole, or edge of member, in direction of force

$$L_c = s - D_h$$

$$L_c = L_e - \frac{D_h}{2}$$

Design bearing strength (kips/bolt/inch thickness) for various bolt spacings, s, and end distances, L_e:

Bearing strength ϕr_n (k/bolt/in	Bolt size		
	3/4"	7/8"	1"
s = $2\,^2/_3$ d_b (minimum permitted)			
F_u = 58 ksi	62.0	72.9	83.7
F_u = 65 ksi	69.5	81.7	93.8
s = 3"			
F_u = 58 ksi	78.3	91.3	101
F_u = 65 ksi	87.7	102	113
L_e = 1 1/4"			
F_u = 58 ksi	44.0	40.8	37.5
F_u = 65 ksi	49.4	45.7	42.0
L_e = 2"			
F_u = 58 ksi	78.3	79.9	76.7
F_u = 65 ksi	87.7	89.6	85.9

The bearing resistance of the connection shall be taken as the sum of the bearing resistances of the individual bolts.

ASD

Design strength (kips/bolt/inch thickness):

When $s \geq 3\,d_b$ and $L_e \geq 1.5\,d_b$

$$r_b = 1.2\,F_u\,d_b$$

When $L_e < 1.5\,d_b$: $r_b = \dfrac{L_e\,F_u}{2}$

When $s < 3\,d_b$:

$$r_b = \frac{\left(s - \dfrac{d_b}{2}\right)F_u}{2} \leq 1.2\,F_u\,d_b$$

Design bearing strength (kips/bolt/inch thickness) for various bolt spacings, s, and end distances, L_e:

Bearing strength r_b(k/bolt/in)	Bolt size		
	3/4"	7/8"	1"
s ≥ 3 d_b and L_e ≥ 1.5 d_b			
F_u = 58 ksi	52.2	60.9	69.6
F_u = 65 ksi	58.5	68.3	78.0
s = 2 2/3 d_b (minimum permitted)			
F_u = 58 ksi	47.1	55.0	62.8
F_u = 65 ksi	52.8	61.6	70.4
L_e = 1 1/4"			
F_u = 58 ksi	36.3 [all bolt sizes]		
F_u = 65 ksi	40.6 [all bolt sizes]		

106

Table 1-1: W-Shapes Dimensions and Properties

From: AISC LRFD Manual, 3rd Edition, except as noted.

Shape	Area A in.^{2}	Depth d in.	Web t_w in.	Flange b_f in.	Flange t_f in.	Compact section $b_f/2t_f$	Compact section h/t_w	X_1 ksi	X_2 x10^6 1/ksi	r_T ** in.	d/A_f ** 1/in.	Axis X-X I in.^{4}	Axis X-X S in.^{3}	Axis X-X r in.	Axis X-X Z in.^{3}	Axis Y-Y I in.^{4}	Axis Y-Y r in.
W24 × 103	30.3	24.5	0.55	9.00	0.98	4.59	39.2	2390	5310	2.33	2.78	3000	245	9.96	280	119	1.99
W24 × 94	27.7	24.3	0.52	9.07	0.88	5.18	41.9	2180	7800	2.33	3.06	2700	222	9.87	254	109	1.98
W24 × 84	24.7	24.1	0.47	9.02	0.77	5.86	45.9	1950	12200	2.31	3.47	2370	196	9.79	224	94.4	1.95
W24 × 76	22.4	23.9	0.44	8.99	0.68	6.61	49.0	1760	18600	2.29	3.91	2100	176	9.69	200	82.5	1.92
W24 × 68	20.1	23.7	0.42	8.97	0.59	7.66	52.0	1590	29000	2.26	4.52	1830	154	9.55	177	70.4	1.87
W24 × 62	18.3	23.7	0.43	7.04	0.59	5.97	49.7	1730	23800	1.71	5.72	1560	132	9.24	154	34.5	1.37
W24 × 55	16.3	23.6	0.40	7.01	0.51	6.94	54.1	1570	36500	1.68	6.66	1360	115	9.13	135	29.1	1.34
W21 × 93	27.3	21.6	0.58	8.42	0.93	4.53	32.3	2680	3460	2.17	2.76	2070	192	8.70	221	92.9	1.84
W21 × 83	24.3	21.4	0.52	8.36	0.84	5.00	36.4	2400	5250	2.15	3.07	1830	171	8.67	196	81.4	1.83
W21 × 73	21.5	21.2	0.46	8.30	0.74	5.60	41.2	2140	8380	2.13	3.46	1600	151	8.64	172	70.6	1.81
W21 × 68	20.0	21.1	0.43	8.27	0.69	6.04	43.6	2000	10900	2.12	3.73	1480	140	8.60	160	64.7	1.80
W21 × 62	18.3	21.0	0.40	8.24	0.62	6.70	46.9	1820	15900	2.10	4.14	1330	127	8.54	144	57.5	1.77
* W21 × 55	16.2	20.8	0.38	8.22	0.52	7.87	50.0	1630	25800	---	---	1140	110	8.40	126	48.4	1.73
* W21 × 48	14.1	20.6	0.35	8.14	0.43	9.47	53.6	1450	43600	---	---	959	93.0	8.24	107	38.7	1.66
W21 × 57	16.7	21.1	0.41	6.56	0.65	5.04	46.3	1960	13100	1.64	4.94	1170	111	8.36	129	30.6	1.35
W21 × 50	14.7	20.8	0.38	6.53	0.54	6.10	49.4	1730	22600	1.60	5.96	984	94.5	8.18	110	24.9	1.30
W21 × 44	13.0	20.7	0.35	6.50	0.45	7.22	53.6	1550	36600	1.57	7.06	843	81.6	8.06	95.4	20.7	1.26

* LRFD Manual only   ** AISC ASD Manual, 9th Edition

Table 1-1: W-Shapes Dimensions and Properties (continued)

Shape	Area A	Depth d	Web t_w	Flange b_f	Flange t_f	Compact section $b_f/2t_f$	Compact section h/t_w	X_1 ksi	X_2 x 10^6 1/ksi	r_T ** in.	d/A_f ** 1/in.	Axis X-X I in.^{4}	Axis X-X S in.^{3}	Axis X-X r in.	Axis X-X Z in.^{3}	Axis Y-Y I in.^{4}	Axis Y-Y r in.
	in.^{2}	in.	in.	in.	in.												
W18 × 86	25.3	18.4	0.48	11.1	0.77	7.20	33.4	2460	4060	2.97	2.15	1530	166	7.77	186	175	2.63
W18 × 76	22.3	18.2	0.43	11.0	0.68	8.11	37.8	2180	6520	2.95	2.43	1330	146	7.73	163	152	2.61
W18 × 71	20.8	18.5	0.50	7.64	0.81	4.71	32.4	2690	3290	1.98	2.99	1170	127	7.50	146	60.3	1.70
W18 × 65	19.1	18.4	0.45	7.59	0.75	5.06	35.7	2470	4540	1.97	3.22	1070	117	7.49	133	54.8	1.69
W18 × 60	17.6	18.2	0.42	7.56	0.70	5.44	38.7	2290	6080	1.96	3.47	984	108	7.47	123	50.1	1.68
W18 × 55	16.2	18.1	0.39	7.53	0.63	5.98	41.1	2110	8540	1.95	3.82	890	98.3	7.41	112	44.9	1.67
W18 × 50	14.7	18.0	0.36	7.50	0.57	6.57	45.2	1920	12400	1.94	4.21	800	88.9	7.38	101	40.1	1.65
W18 × 46	13.5	18.1	0.36	6.06	0.61	5.01	44.6	2060	10100	1.54	4.93	712	78.8	7.25	90.7	22.5	1.29
W18 × 40	11.8	17.9	0.32	6.02	0.53	5.73	50.9	1810	17200	1.52	5.67	612	68.4	7.21	78.4	19.1	1.27
W18 × 35	10.3	17.7	0.30	6.00	0.43	7.06	53.5	1590	30800	1.49	6.94	510	57.6	7.04	66.5	15.3	1.22
W16 × 89	26.4	16.8	0.53	10.4	0.88	5.92	25.9	3160	1460	2.79	1.85	1310	157	7.05	177	163	2.48
W16 × 77	22.9	16.5	0.46	10.3	0.76	6.77	29.9	2770	2460	2.77	2.11	1120	136	7.00	152	138	2.46
W16 × 67	20.0	16.3	0.40	10.2	0.67	7.70	34.4	2440	4040	2.75	2.40	970	119	6.97	132	119	2.44
W16 × 57	16.8	16.4	0.43	7.12	0.72	4.98	33.0	2650	3400	1.86	3.23	758	92.2	6.72	105	43.1	1.60
W16 × 50	14.7	16.3	0.38	7.07	0.63	5.61	37.4	2340	5530	1.84	3.65	659	81.0	6.68	92.0	37.2	1.59
W16 × 45	13.3	16.1	0.35	7.04	0.57	6.23	41.1	2120	8280	1.83	4.06	586	72.7	6.65	82.3	32.8	1.57
W16 × 40	11.8	16.0	0.31	7.00	0.51	6.93	46.5	1890	12700	1.82	4.53	518	64.7	6.63	73.0	28.9	1.57
W16 × 36	10.6	15.9	0.30	6.99	0.43	8.12	48.1	1700	20400	1.79	5.28	448	56.5	6.51	64.0	24.5	1.52
W16 × 31	9.1	15.9	0.28	5.53	0.44	6.28	51.6	1740	19900	1.39	6.53	375	47.2	6.41	54.0	12.4	1.17
W16 × 26	7.7	15.7	0.25	5.50	0.35	7.97	56.8	1480	40300	1.36	8.27	301	38.4	6.26	44.2	9.59	1.12
W14 × 120	35.3	14.5	0.59	14.7	0.94	7.80	19.3	3830	601	4.04	1.05	1380	190	6.24	212	495	3.74
W14 × 109	32.0	14.3	0.53	14.6	0.86	8.49	21.7	3490	853	4.02	1.14	1240	173	6.22	192	447	3.73
W14 × 99	29.1	14.2	0.49	14.6	0.78	9.34	23.5	3190	1220	4.00	1.25	1110	157	6.17	173	402	3.71
W14 × 90	26.5	14.0	0.44	14.5	0.71	10.2	25.9	2900	1750	3.99	1.36	999	143	6.14	157	362	3.70
W14 × 82	24.0	14.3	0.51	10.1	0.86	5.92	22.4	3590	849	2.74	1.65	881	123	6.05	139	148	2.48
W14 × 74	21.8	14.2	0.45	10.1	0.79	6.41	25.4	3280	1200	2.72	1.79	795	112	6.04	126	134	2.48
W14 × 68	20.0	14.0	0.42	10.0	0.72	6.97	27.5	3020	1660	2.71	1.94	722	103	6.01	115	121	2.46
W14 × 61	17.9	13.9	0.38	9.99	0.65	7.75	30.4	2720	2470	2.70	2.15	640	92.1	5.98	102	107	2.45
W14 × 53	15.6	13.9	0.37	8.06	0.66	6.11	30.9	2830	2250	2.15	2.62	541	77.8	5.89	87.1	57.7	1.92
W14 × 48	14.1	13.8	0.34	8.03	0.60	6.75	33.6	2580	3250	2.13	2.89	484	70.2	5.85	78.4	51.4	1.91
W12 × 106	31.2	12.9	0.61	12.2	0.99	6.17	15.9	4660	285	3.36	1.07	933	145	5.47	164	301	3.11
W12 × 96	28.2	12.7	0.55	12.2	0.90	6.76	17.7	4250	407	3.34	1.16	833	131	5.44	147	270	3.09
W12 × 87	25.6	12.5	0.52	12.1	0.81	7.48	18.9	3880	586	3.32	1.28	740	118	5.38	132	241	3.07
W12 × 79	23.2	12.4	0.47	12.1	0.74	8.22	20.7	3530	839	3.31	1.39	662	107	5.34	119	216	3.05
W12 × 72	21.1	12.3	0.43	12.0	0.67	8.99	22.6	3230	1180	3.29	1.52	597	97.4	5.31	108	195	3.04
W12 × 65	19.1	12.1	0.39	12.0	0.61	9.92	24.9	2940	1720	3.28	1.67	533	87.9	5.28	96.8	174	3.02
W12 × 58	17.0	12.2	0.36	10.0	0.64	7.82	27.0	3070	1470	2.72	1.90	475	78.0	5.28	86.4	107	2.51
W12 × 53	15.6	12.1	0.35	9.99	0.58	8.69	28.1	2820	2100	2.71	2.10	425	70.6	5.23	77.9	95.8	2.48
W12 × 50	14.6	12.2	0.37	8.08	0.64	6.31	26.8	3120	1500	2.17	2.36	391	64.2	5.18	71.9	56.3	1.96
W12 × 45	13.1	12.1	0.34	8.05	0.58	7.00	29.6	2820	2210	2.15	2.61	348	57.7	5.15	64.2	50.0	1.95
W12 × 40	11.7	11.9	0.30	8.01	0.52	7.77	33.6	2530	3360	2.14	2.90	307	51.5	5.13	57.0	44.1	1.94

** AISC ASD Manual, 9th Edition

Shape	X-X AXIS							
	Z_x	I_x	$\phi_b M_p$	$\phi_b M_r$	L_p	L_r	BF	$\phi_v V_n$
	in.^{3}	in.^{4}	kip-ft	kip-ft	ft	ft	kips	kips
W 24 × 55	**135**	**1360**	**506**	**345**	**4.73**	**12.9**	**19.8**	**252**
W 18 × 65	133	1070	499	351	5.97	17.1	13.3	224
W 12 × 87	132	740	495	354	10.8	38.4	5.13	174
W 16 × 67	131	963	491	354	8.65	23.8	9.04	174
W 10 × 100	130	623	488	336	9.36	50.8	3.66	204
W 21 × 57	129	1170	484	333	4.77	13.2	17.8	231
W 21 × 55	**126**	**1140**	**473**	**330**	**6.11**	**16.1**	**14.3**	**211**
W 14 × 74	126	796	473	336	8.76	27.9	7.12	173
W 18 × 60	123	984	461	324	5.93	16.6	12.9	204
W 12 × 79	119	662	446	321	10.8	35.7	5.03	157
W 14 × 68	115	722	431	309	8.69	26.4	6.91	157
W 10 × 88	113	534	424	296	9.29	45.1	3.58	176
W 18 × 55	**112**	**890**	**420**	**295**	**5.90**	**16.1**	**12.2**	**191**
W 21 × 50	**111**	**989**	**416**	**285**	**4.59**	**12.5**	**16.5**	**213**
W 12 × 72	108	597	405	292	10.7	33.6	4.93	143
W 21 × 48	**107**	**959**	**401**	**279**	**6.09**	**15.4**	**13.2**	**195**
W 16 × 57	105	758	394	277	5.65	16.6	10.7	190
W 14 × 61	102	640	383	277	8.65	25.0	6.50	141
W 18 × 50	101	800	379	267	5.83	15.6	11.5	173
W 10 × 77	97.6	455	366	258	9.18	39.9	3.53	152
W 12 × 65	96.8	533	363	264	11.9	31.7	5.01	127
W 21 × 44	**95.8**	**847**	**359**	**246**	**4.45**	**12.0**	**15.0**	**196**
W 16 × 50	92.0	659	345	243	5.62	15.7	10.1	167
W 18 × 46	90.7	712	340	236	4.56	12.6	12.9	176
W 14 × 53	87.1	541	327	233	6.78	20.1	7.01	139
W 12 × 58	86.4	475	324	234	8.87	27.0	4.97	119
W 10 × 68	85.3	394	320	227	9.15	36.0	3.45	132
W 16 × 45	82.3	586	309	218	5.55	15.1	9.45	150
W 18 × 40	**78.4**	**612**	**294**	**205**	**4.49**	**12.0**	**11.7**	**152**
W 14 × 48	78.4	485	294	211	6.75	19.2	6.70	127
W 12 × 53	77.9	425	292	212	8.76	25.6	4.78	113
W 10 × 60	74.6	341	280	200	9.08	32.6	3.39	116
W 16 × 40	**73.0**	**518**	**274**	**194**	**5.55**	**14.7**	**8.71**	**132**
W 12 × 50	71.9	391	270	193	6.92	21.5	5.30	122
W 14 × 43	69.6	428	261	188	6.68	18.2	6.31	113
W 10 × 54	66.6	303	250	180	9.04	30.2	3.30	101
W 18 × 35	**66.5**	**510**	**249**	**173**	**4.31**	**11.5**	**10.7**	**143**
W 12 × 45	64.2	348	241	173	6.89	20.3	5.06	109
W 16 × 36	64.0	448	240	170	5.37	14.1	8.11	127
W 14 × 38	61.1	383	229	163	5.47	14.9	7.05	118
W 10 × 49	60.4	272	227	164	8.97	28.3	3.24	91.6
W 12 × 40	57.0	307	214	155	68.5	19.2	4.79	94.8
W 10 × 45	54.9	248	206	147	7.10	24.1	3.44	95.4
W 14 × 34	**54.2**	**337**	**203**	**145**	**5.40**	**14.3**	**6.58**	**108**

$F_y = 50$ ksi
$\phi_b = 0.9$
$\phi_v = 0.9$

Table 5-3
W-Shapes
Selection by Z_x

Z_x

Beam Design Moments (ϕ_b=0.9, C_b=1.0, F_y=50 ksi)

$\phi_b M_n$, Design Moment (2 kip-ft increments)

L_b, Unbraced Length (0.5 ft increments)

Table C – C.2.1. K VALUES FOR COLUMNS

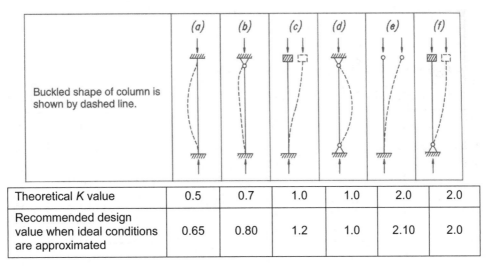

	(a)	(b)	(c)	(d)	(e)	(f)
Buckled shape of column is shown by dashed line.						
Theoretical K value	0.5	0.7	1.0	1.0	2.0	2.0
Recommended design value when ideal conditions are approximated	0.65	0.80	1.2	1.0	2.10	2.0

Figure C – C.2.2.

ALIGNMENT CHART FOR EFFECTIVE LENGTH OF COLUMNS IN CONTINUOUS FRAMES

The subscripts A and B refer to the joints at the two ends of the column section being considered. G is defined as

$$G = \frac{\Sigma\left(I_c/L_c\right)}{\Sigma\left(I_g/L_g\right)}$$

in which Σ indicates a summation of all members rigidly connected to that joint and lying on the plane in which buckling of the column is being considered. I_c is the moment of inertia and L_c the unsupported length of a column section, and I_g is the moment of inertia and L_g the unsupported length of a girder or other restraining member. I_c and I_g are taken about axes perpendicular to the plane of buckling being considered.

For column ends supported by but not rigidly connected to a footing or foundation, G is theoretically infinity, but, unless actually designed as a true friction-free pin, may be taken as "10" for practical designs. If the column end is rigidly attached to a properly designed footing, G may be taken as 1.0. Smaller values may be used if justified by analysis.

TABLE 3-50

Design Stress for Compression Members of 50 ksi Specified Yield Stress Steel, $\phi_c = 0.85$

$\dfrac{Kl}{r}$	$\phi_c F_{cr}$ ksi	$\dfrac{Kl}{r}$	$\phi_c F_{cr}$ ksi	$\dfrac{Kl}{r}$	$\phi_c F_{cr}$ ksi	$\dfrac{Kl}{r}$	$\phi_c F_{cr}$ ksi	$\dfrac{Kl}{r}$	$\phi_c F_{cr}$ ksi
1	42.5	41	37.6	81	26.3	121	14.6	161	8.23
2	42.5	42	37.4	82	26.0	122	14.3	162	8.13
3	42.5	43	37.1	83	25.7	123	14.1	163	8.03
4	42.5	44	36.9	84	25.4	124	13.9	164	7.93
5	42.4	45	36.7	85	25.1	125	13.7	165	7.84
6	42.4	46	36.4	86	24.8	126	13.4	166	7.74
7	42.4	47	36.2	87	24.4	127	13.2	167	7.65
8	42.3	48	35.9	88	24.1	128	13.0	168	7.56
9	42.3	49	35.7	89	23.8	129	12.8	169	7.47
10	42.2	50	35.4	90	23.5	130	12.6	170	7.38
11	42.1	51	35.1	91	23.2	131	12.4	171	7.30
12	42.1	52	34.9	92	22.9	132	12.3	172	7.21
13	42.0	53	34.6	93	22.6	133	12.1	173	7.13
14	41.9	54	34.3	94	22.3	134	11.9	174	7.05
15	41.8	55	34.1	95	22.0	135	11.7	175	6.97
16	41.7	56	33.8	96	21.7	136	11.5	176	6.89
17	41.6	57	33.5	97	21.4	137	11.4	177	6.81
18	41.5	58	33.2	98	21.1	138	11.2	178	6.73
19	41.4	59	33.0	99	20.8	139	11.0	179	6.66
20	41.3	60	32.7	100	20.5	140	10.9	180	6.59
21	41.2	61	32.4	101	20.2	141	10.7	181	6.51
22	41.0	62	32.1	102	19.9	142	10.6	182	6.44
23	40.9	63	31.8	103	19.6	143	10.4	183	6.37
24	40.8	64	31.5	104	19.3	144	10.3	184	6.30
25	40.6	65	31.2	105	19.0	145	10.2	185	6.23
26	40.5	66	30.9	106	18.7	146	10.0	186	6.17
27	40.3	67	30.6	107	18.4	147	9.87	187	6.10
28	40.1	68	30.3	108	18.1	148	9.74	188	6.04
29	40.0	69	30.0	109	17.8	149	9.61	189	5.97
30	39.8	70	29.7	110	17.6	150	9.48	190	5.91
31	39.6	71	29.4	111	17.3	151	9.36	191	5.85
32	39.4	72	29.1	112	17.0	152	9.23	192	5.79
33	39.3	73	28.8	113	16.7	153	9.11	193	5.73
34	39.1	74	28.5	114	16.4	154	9.00	194	5.67
35	38.9	75	28.2	115	16.1	155	8.88	195	5.61
36	38.7	76	27.9	116	15.9	156	8.77	196	5.55
37	38.5	77	27.6	117	15.6	157	8.66	197	5.50
38	38.2	78	27.2	118	15.3	158	8.55	198	5.44
39	38.0	79	26.9	119	15.1	159	8.44	199	5.39
40	37.8	80	26.6	120	14.8	160	8.33	200	5.33

ALLOWABLE STRESS DESIGN SELECTION TABLE
For shapes used as beams
S_x

F_y = 50 ksi			S_x	SHAPE	F_y = 36 ksi		
L_c	L_u	M_R			L_c	L_u	M_R
Ft	Ft	Kip-ft	In.^{3}		Ft	Ft	Kip-ft
5.0	**6.3**	**314**	**114**	**W 24 X 55**	**7.0**	**7.5**	**226**
9.0	18.6	308	112	W 14 x 74	10.6	25.9	222
5.9	6.7	305	111	W 21 x 57	6.9	9.4	220
6.8	9.6	297	108	W 18 x 60	8.0	13.3	214
10.8	24.0	294	107	W 12 x 79	12.8	33.3	212
9.0	17.2	283	103	W 14 x 68	10.6	23.9	204
6.7	**8.7**	**270**	**98.3**	**W 18 X 55**	**7.9**	**12.1**	**195**
10.8	21.9	268	97.4	W 12 x 72	12.7	30.5	193
5.6	**6.0**	**260**	**94.5**	**W 21 X 50**	**6.9**	**7.8**	**187**
6.4	10.3	254	92.2	W 16 x 57	7.5	14.3	183
9.0	15.5	254	92.2	W 14 x 61	10.6	21.5	183
6.7	**7.9**	**244**	**88.9**	**W 18 X 50**	**7.9**	**11.0**	**176**
10.7	20.0	238	87.9	W 12 x 65	12.7	27.7	174
4.7	**5.9**	**224**	**81.6**	**W 21 X 44**	**6.6**	**7.0**	**162**
6.3	9.1	223	81.0	W 16 x 50	7.5	12.7	160
5.4	6.8	217	78.8	W 18 x 46	6.4	9.4	156
9.0	17.5	215	78.0	W 12 x 58	10.6	24.4	154
7.2	12.7	214	77.8	W 14 x 53	8.5	17.7	154
6.3	8.2	200	72.7	W 16 x 45	7.4	11.4	144
9.0	15.9	194	70.6	W 12 x 53	10.6	22.0	140
7.2	11.5	193	70.3	W 14 x 48	8.5	16.0	139
5.4	**5.9**	**188**	**68.4**	**W 18 X 40**	**6.3**	**8.2**	**135**
9.0	22.4	183	66.7	W 10 x 60	10.6	31.1	132
6.3	**7.4**	**178**	**64.7**	**W 16 X 40**	**7.4**	**10.2**	**128**
7.2	14.1	178	64.7	W 12 x 50	8.5	19.6	128
7.2	10.4	172	62.7	W 14 x 43	8.4	14.4	124
9.0	20.3	165	60.0	W 10 x 54	10.6	28.2	119
7.2	12.8	160	58.1	W 12 x 45	8.5	17.7	115
4.8	**5.6**	**158**	**57.6**	**W 18 X 35**	**6.3**	**6.7**	**114**
6.3	6.7	115	56.5	W 16 x 36	7.4	8.8	112
6.1	8.3	150	54.6	W 14 x 38	7.1	11.5	108
9.0	18.7	150	54.6	W 10 x 49	10.6	26.0	108
7.2	11.5	143	51.9	W 12 x 40	8.4	16.0	103
7.2	16.4	135	49.1	W 10 x 45	8.5	22.8	97
6.0	**7.3**	**134**	**48.6**	**W 14 X 34**	**7.1**	**10.2**	**96**
4.9	**5.2**	**130**	**47.2**	**W 16 X 31**	**5.8**	**7.1**	**93**
5.9	9.1	125	45.6	W 12 x 35	6.9	12.6	90
7.2	14.2	116	42.1	W 10 x 39	8.4	19.8	83
6.0	**6.5**	**116**	**42.0**	**W 14 X 30**	**7.1**	**8.7**	**83**
5.8	**7.8**	**106**	**38.6**	**W 12 X 30**	**6.9**	**10.8**	**76**
4.0	**5.1**	**106**	**38.4**	**W 16 x 26**	**5.6**	**6.0**	**76**

ALLOWABLE MOMENTS IN BEAMS $(C_b=1, F_y=50$ ksi$)$

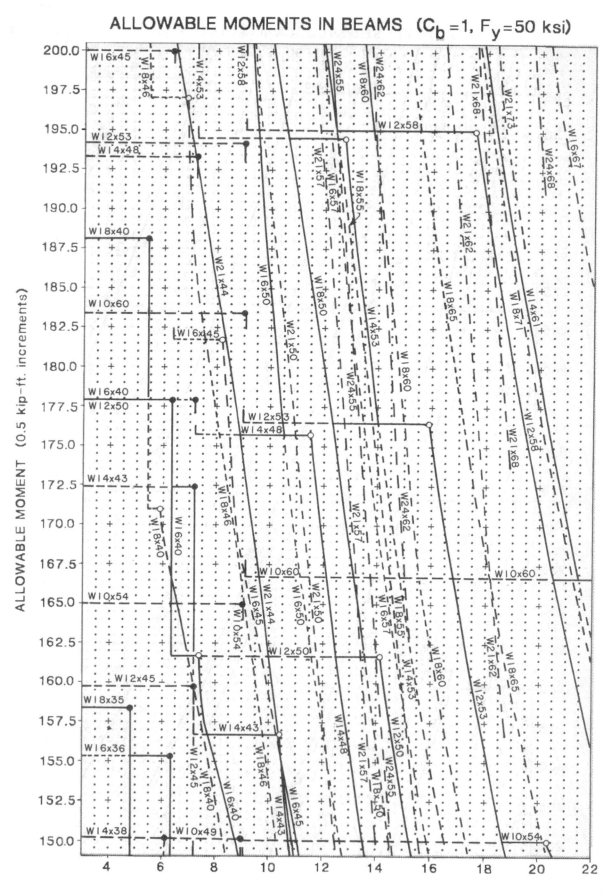

ASD Table C–50. Allowable Stress
for Compression Members of 50-ksi Specified Yield Stress Steel[a,b]

$\frac{Kl}{r}$	F_a (ksi)	$\frac{Kl}{r}$	F_a (ksi)	$\frac{Kl}{r}$	F_a (ksi)	$\frac{Kl}{r}$	F_a (ksi)	$\frac{Kl}{r}$	F_a (ksi)
1	29.94	41	25.69	81	18.81	121	10.20	161	5.76
2	29.87	42	25.55	82	18.61	122	10.03	162	5.69
3	29.80	43	25.40	83	18.41	123	9.87	163	5.62
4	29.73	44	25.26	84	18.20	124	9.71	164	5.55
5	29.66	45	25.11	85	17.99	125	9.56	165	5.49
6	29.58	46	24.96	86	17.79	126	9.41	166	5.42
7	29.50	47	24.81	87	17.58	127	9.26	167	5.35
8	29.42	48	24.66	88	17.37	128	9.11	168	5.29
9	29.34	49	24.51	89	17.15	129	8.97	169	5.23
10	29.26	50	24.35	90	16.94	130	8.84	170	5.17
11	29.17	51	24.19	91	16.72	131	8.70	171	5.11
12	29.08	52	24.04	92	16.50	132	8.57	172	5.05
13	28.99	53	23.88	93	16.29	133	8.44	173	4.99
14	28.90	54	23.72	94	16.06	134	8.32	174	4.93
15	28.80	55	23.55	95	15.84	135	8.19	175	4.88
16	28.71	56	23.39	96	15.62	136	8.07	176	4.82
17	28.61	57	23.22	97	15.39	137	7.96	177	4.77
18	28.51	58	23.06	98	15.17	138	7.84	178	4.71
19	28.40	59	22.89	99	14.94	139	7.73	179	4.66
20	28.30	60	22.72	100	14.71	140	7.62	180	4.61
21	28.19	61	22.55	101	14.47	141	7.51	181	4.56
22	28.08	62	22.37	102	14.24	142	7.41	182	4.51
23	27.97	63	22.20	103	14.00	143	7.30	183	4.46
24	27.86	64	22.02	104	13.77	144	7.20	184	4.41
25	27.75	65	21.85	105	13.53	145	7.10	185	4.36
26	27.63	66	21.67	106	13.29	146	7.01	186	4.32
27	27.52	67	21.49	107	13.04	147	6.91	187	4.27
28	27.40	68	21.31	108	12.80	148	6.82	188	4.23
29	27.28	69	21.12	109	12.57	149	6.73	189	4.18
30	27.15	70	20.94	110	12.34	150	6.64	190	4.14
31	27.03	71	20.75	111	12.12	151	6.55	191	4.09
32	26.90	72	20.56	112	11.90	152	6.46	192	4.05
33	26.77	73	20.38	113	11.69	153	6.38	193	4.01
34	26.64	74	20.10	114	11.49	154	6.30	194	3.97
35	26.51	75	19.99	115	11.29	155	6.22	195	3.93
36	26.38	76	19.80	116	11.10	156	6.14	196	3.89
37	26.25	77	19.61	117	10.91	157	6.06	197	3.85
38	26.11	78	19.41	118	10.72	158	5.98	198	3.81
39	25.97	79	19.21	119	10.55	159	5.91	199	3.77
40	25.83	80	19.01	120	10.37	160	5.83	200	3.73

[a] When element width-to-thickness ratio exceeds noncompact section limits of Sect. B5.1, see Appendix B5.

[b] Values also applicable for steel of any yield stress ≥ 39 ksi.

Note: C_c = 107.0

ENVIRONMENTAL ENGINEERING

For information about environmental engineering refer to the **ENVIRONMENTAL ENGINEERING** section.

HYDROLOGY

NRCS (SCS) Rainfall-Runoff

$$Q = \frac{(P-0.2S)^2}{P+0.8S},$$

$$S = \frac{1,000}{CN} - 10,$$

$$CN = \frac{1,000}{S+10},$$

P = precipitation (inches),

S = maximum basin retention (inches),

Q = runoff (inches), and

CN = curve number.

Rational Formula

$$Q = CIA, \text{ where}$$

A = watershed area (acres),

C = runoff coefficient,

I = rainfall intensity (in/hr), and

Q = peak discharge (cfs).

DARCY'S EQUATION

$$Q = -KA(dh/dx), \text{ where}$$

Q = Discharge rate (ft³/s or m³/s),

K = Hydraulic conductivity (ft/s or m/s),

h = Hydraulic head (ft or m), and

A = Cross-sectional area of flow (ft² or m²).

q = $-K(dh/dx)$

q = specific discharge or Darcy velocity

v = q/n = $-K/n(dh/dx)$

v = average seepage velocity

n = effective porosity

Unit hydrograph: The direct runoff hydrograph that would result from one unit of effective rainfall occurring uniformly in space and time over a unit period of time.

Transmissivity, T, is the product of hydraulic conductivity and thickness, b, of the aquifer (L^2T^{-1}).

Storativity or storage coefficient, S, of an aquifer is the volume of water taken into or released from storage per unit surface area per unit change in potentiometric (piezometric) head.

SEWAGE FLOW RATIO CURVES

CurveA$_2$: $\frac{5}{P^{0.167}}$

CurveB: $\frac{14}{4+\sqrt{P}}+1$

CurveG: $\frac{18+\sqrt{P}}{4+\sqrt{P}}$

HYDRAULIC-ELEMENTS GRAPH FOR CIRCULAR SEWERS

Values of: $\dfrac{f}{f_f}$ and $\dfrac{n}{n_f}$

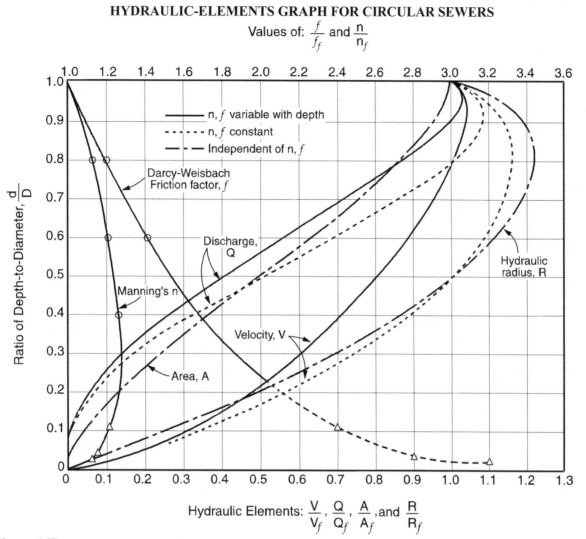

Hydraulic Elements: $\dfrac{V}{V_f}$, $\dfrac{Q}{Q_f}$, $\dfrac{A}{A_f}$, and $\dfrac{R}{R_f}$

Open-Channel Flow

Specific Energy

$$E = \alpha \frac{V^2}{2g} + y = \frac{\alpha Q^2}{2gA^2} + y \text{, where}$$

E = specific energy,

Q = discharge,

V = velocity,

y = depth of flow,

A = cross-sectional area of flow, and

α = kinetic energy correction factor, usually 1.0.

Critical Depth = that depth in a channel at minimum specific energy

$$\frac{Q^2}{g} = \frac{A^3}{T}$$

where Q and A are as defined above,

g = acceleration due to gravity, and

T = width of the water surface.

For rectangular channels

$$y_c = \left(\frac{q^2}{g} \right)^{1/3} \text{, where}$$

y_c = critical depth,

q = unit discharge = Q/B,

B = channel width, and

g = acceleration due to gravity.

Froude Number = ratio of inertial forces to gravity forces

$$F = \frac{V}{\sqrt{gy_h}} \text{, where}$$

V = velocity, and

y_h = hydraulic depth = A/T

Specific Energy Diagram

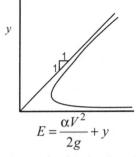

$$E = \frac{\alpha V^2}{2g} + y$$

Alternate depths: depths with the same specific energy.

Uniform flow: a flow condition where depth and velocity do not change along a channel.

Manning's Equation

$$Q = \frac{K}{n} AR^{2/3} S^{1/2}$$

Q = discharge (m³/s or ft³/s),

K = 1.486 for USCS units, 1.0 for SI units,

A = cross-sectional area of flow (m² or ft²),

R = hydraulic radius = A/P (m or ft),

P = wetted perimeter (m or ft),

S = slope of hydraulic surface (m/m or ft/ft), and

n = Manning's roughness coefficient.

Normal depth – the uniform flow depth

$$AR^{2/3} = \frac{Qn}{KS^{1/2}}$$

Weir Formulas

Fully submerged with no side restrictions
$$Q = CLH^{3/2}$$
V-Notch
$$Q = CH^{5/2}, \text{ where}$$

Q = discharge (cfs or m³/s),

C = 3.33 for submerged rectangular weir (USCS units),

C = 1.84 for submerged rectangular weir (SI units),

C = 2.54 for 90° V-notch weir (USCS units),

C = 1.40 for 90° V-notch weir (SI units),

L = weir length (ft or m), and

H = head (depth of discharge over weir) ft or m.

Hazen-Williams Equation

$$V = k_1 CR^{0.63} S^{0.54}, \text{ where}$$

C = roughness coefficient,

k_1 = 0.849 for SI units, and

k_1 = 1.318 for USCS units,

R = hydraulic radius (ft or m),

S = slope of energy gradeline,

  = h_f/L (ft/ft or m/m), and

V = velocity (ft/s or m/s).

Values of Hazen-Williams Coefficient C

Pipe Material	C
Concrete (regardless of age)	130
Cast iron:	
New	130
5 yr old	120
20 yr old	100
Welded steel, new	120
Wood stave (regardless of age)	120
Vitrified clay	110
Riveted steel, new	110
Brick sewers	100
Asbestos-cement	140
Plastic	150

For additional fluids information, see the **FLUID MECHANICS** section.

TRANSPORTATION

Stopping Sight Distance

U.S. Customary Units Equation

$$S = \frac{V^2}{30[(a/32.2) \pm G]} + 1.47Vt$$

Metric Equation:

$$S = \frac{V^2}{254[(a/9.81) \pm G]} + 0.278Vt,$$

where (as appropriate):

S = stopping sight distance (ft or m),

G = percent grade divided by 100,

V = design speed (mph or km/h),

a = deceleration rate (ft/s² or m/s²),

  = 11.2 ft/s² = 3.4 m/s² and

t = driver reaction time (s).

Sight Distance Related to Curve Length

a. Crest Vertical Curve (general equations):

$$L = \frac{AS^2}{200\left(\sqrt{h_1} + \sqrt{h_2}\right)^2} \quad \text{for } S \le L$$

$$L = 2S - \frac{200\left(\sqrt{h_1} + \sqrt{h_2}\right)^2}{A} \quad \text{for } S > L$$

where

L = length of vertical curve (ft or m),

A = algebraic difference in grades (%),

S = sight distance for stopping or passing, (ft or m),

h_1 = height of drivers' eyes above the roadway surface (ft or m), and

h_2 = height of object above the roadway surface (ft or m).

U.S. Customary Units:

When $h_1 = 3.50$ ft and $h_2 = 2.0$ ft,

$$L = \frac{AS^2}{2{,}158} \qquad \text{for } S \le L$$

$$L = 2S - \frac{2{,}158}{A} \qquad \text{for } S > L$$

Metric Units:

When $h_1 = 1{,}080$ mm and $h_2 = 600$ mm,

$$L = \frac{AS^2}{658} \qquad \text{for } S \le L$$

$$L = 2S - \frac{658}{A} \qquad \text{for } S > L$$

b. Sag Vertical Curve (based on standard headlight criteria):

U.S. Customary Units

$$L = \frac{AS^2}{400 + 3.5\,S} \qquad \text{for } S \le L$$

$$L = 2S - \frac{400 + 3.5\,A}{A} \qquad \text{for } S > L$$

Metric Units

$$L = \frac{AS^2}{120 + 3.5\,S} \qquad \text{for } S \le L$$

$$L = 2S - \frac{120 + 3.5\,A}{A} \qquad \text{for } S > L$$

c. Sag Vertical Curve (based on adequate sight distance under an overhead structure to see an object beyond a sag vertical curve)

$$L = \frac{AS^2}{800}\left(C - \frac{h_1 + h_2}{2}\right)^{-1} \qquad \text{for } S \le L$$

$$L = 2S - \frac{800}{A}\left(C - \frac{h_1 + h_2}{2}\right) \qquad \text{for } S > L$$

where

C = vertical clearance for overhead structure (underpass) located within 200 ft (60 m) of the midpoint of the curve (ft or m).

d. Sag Vertical Curve (based on riding comfort):

U.S. Customary Units

$$L = \frac{AV^2}{46.5},$$

Metric Units

$$L = \frac{AV^2}{395},$$

where (as appropriate):

L = length of vertical curve (ft or m),
V = design speed (mph or km/hr), and
A = algebraic difference in grades (%)

e. Horizontal curve (to see around obstruction):

$$M = R\left[1 - \cos\left(\frac{28.65\,S}{R}\right)\right]$$

where

R = radius (ft or m)
M = middle ordinate (ft or m),
S = stopping sight distance (ft or m).

Superelevation of Horizontal Curves

a. Highways:

U.S. Customary Units:

$$\frac{e}{100} + f = \frac{V^2}{15R}$$

Metric Units:

$$\frac{e}{100} + f = \frac{V^2}{127R}$$

where (as appropriate):

e = superelevation (%),
f = side-friction factor,
V = vehicle speed (mph or km/hr), and
R = radius of curve (ft or m).

b. Railroads:

$$E = \frac{Gv^2}{gR}$$

where

E = equilibrium elevation of outer rail (in.),
G = effective gage (center-to-center of rails) (in.),
v = train speed (ft/s),
g = acceleration of gravity (ft/s^2), and
R = radius of curve (ft).

Spiral Transitions to Horizontal Curves

a. Highways:

U.S. Customary Units:

$$L_s = \frac{3.15V^3}{RC}$$

Metric Units:

$$L_s = \frac{0.0214V^3}{RC}$$

119

where (as appropriate):

L_s = length of spiral (ft or m),

V = design speed (mph or km/hr),

R = curve radius (ft or m),

C = rate of increase of lateral acceleration $(ft/s^3$ or $m/s^3) = 1\ ft/s^3 = 0.3m/s^3$

b. Railroads:

$$L_s = 62E$$

$$E = 0.0007V^2D$$

where

L_s = length of spiral (ft),

E = equilibrium elevation of outer rail (in.),

V = speed (mph),

D = degree of curve.

Modified Davis Equation – Railroads

$$R = 0.6 + 20/W + 0.01V + KV^2/(WN)$$

where

K = air resistance coefficient,

N = number of axles,

R = level tangent resistance [lb/(ton of car weight)],

V = train or car speed (mph), and

W = average load per axle (tons).

Standard values of K

K = 0.0935, containers on flat car,

K = 0.16, trucks or trailers on flat car, and

K = 0.07, all other standard rail units.

Railroad curve resistance is 0.8 lb per ton of car weight per degree of curvature.

$$TE = 375\ (HP)\ e/V,\ \text{where}$$

e = efficiency of diesel-electric drive system (0.82 to 0.93),

HP = rated horsepower of a diesel-electric locomotive unit,

TE = tractive effort (lb force of a locomotive unit), and

V = locomotive speed (mph).

AREA Vertical Curve Criteria for Track Profile

Maximum Rate of Change of Gradient in Percent Grade per Station		
Line Rating	In Sags	On Crests
High-speed Main Line Tracks	0.05	0.10
Secondary or Branch Line Tracks	0.10	0.20

Transportation Models

Optimization models and methods, including queueing theory, can be found in the **INDUSTRIAL ENGINEERING** section.

Traffic Flow Relationships ($q = kv$)

AIRPORT LAYOUT AND DESIGN

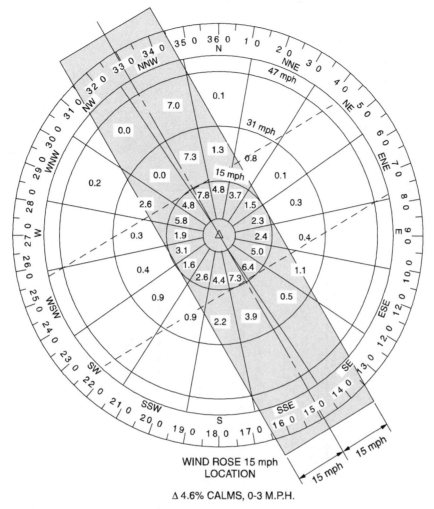

WIND ROSE 15 mph
LOCATION

△ 4.6% CALMS, 0-3 M.P.H.

1. Cross-wind component of 12 mph maximum for aircraft of 12,500 lb or less weight and 15 mph maximum for aircraft weighing more than 12,500 lb.

2. Cross-wind components maximum shall not be exceeded more than 5% of the time at an airport having a single runway.

3. A cross-wind runway is to be provided if a single runway does not provide 95% wind coverage with less than the maximum cross-wind component.

LONGITUDINAL GRADE DESIGN CRITERIA FOR RUNWAYS

Item	Transport Airports	Utility Airports
Maximum longitudinal grade (percent)	1.5	2.0
Maximum grade change such as A or B (percent)	1.5	2.0
Maximum grade, first and last quarter of runway (percent)	0.8	------
Minimum distance (D, feet) between PI's for vertical curves	$1,000 (A + B)^a$	$250 (A + B)^a$
Minimum length of vertical curve (L, feet) per 1 percent grade change	1,000	300
[a] Use absolute values of A and B (percent).		

121

AUTOMOBILE PAVEMENT DESIGN

AASHTO Structural Number Equation

$SN = a_1D_1 + a_2D_2 + \ldots + a_nD_n$, where

SN = structural number for the pavement

a_i = layer coefficient and D_i = thickness of layer (inches).

Gross Axle Load		Load Equivalency Factors		Gross Axle Load		Load Equivalency Factors	
kN	lb	Single Axles	Tandem Axles	kN	lb	Single Axles	Tandem Axles
4.45	1,000	0.00002		187.0	42,000	25.64	2.51
8.9	2,000	0.00018		195.7	44,000	31.00	3.00
17.8	4,000	0.00209		200.0	45,000	34.00	3.27
22.25	5,000	0.00500		204.5	46,000	37.24	3.55
26.7	**6,000**	**0.01043**		**213.5**	**48,000**	**44.50**	**4.17**
35.6	8,000	0.0343		222.4	50,000	52.88	4.86
44.5	10,000	0.0877	0.00688	231.3	52,000		5.63
53.4	12,000	0.189	0.0144	240.2	54,000		6.47
62.3	14,000	0.360	0.0270	244.6	55,000		6.93
66.7	**15,000**	**0.478**	**0.0360**	**249.0**	**56,000**		**7.41**
71.2	16,000	0.623	0.0472	258.0	58,000		8.45
80.0	18,000	1.000	0.0773	267.0	60,000		9.59
89.0	20,000	1.51	0.1206	275.8	62,000		10.84
97.8	22,000	2.18	0.180	284.5	64,000		12.22
106.8	**24,000**	**3.03**	**0.260**	**289.0**	**65,000**		**12.96**
111.2	25,000	3.53	0.308	293.5	66,000		13.73
115.6	26,000	4.09	0.364	302.5	68,000		15.38
124.5	28,000	5.39	0.495	311.5	70,000		17.19
133.5	30,000	6.97	0.658	320.0	72,000		19.16
142.3	**32,000**	**8.88**	**0.857**	**329.0**	**74,000**		**21.32**
151.2	34,000	11.18	1.095	333.5	75,000		22.47
155.7	35,000	12.50	1.23	338.0	76,000		23.66
160.0	36,000	13.93	1.38	347.0	78,000		26.22
169.0	38,000	17.20	1.70	356.0	80,000		28.99
178.0	**40,000**	**21.08**	**2.08**				

Note: kN converted to lb are within 0.1 percent of lb shown.

EARTHWORK FORMULAS

Distance between A_1 and $A_2 = L$

Average End Area Formula, $V = L(A_1 + A_2)/2$,

Prismoidal Formula, $V = L (A_1 + 4A_m + A_2)/6$, where A_m = area of mid-section

Pyramid or Cone, $V = h$ (Area of Base)/3,

AREA FORMULAS

Area by Coordinates: Area = $[X_A (Y_B - Y_N) + X_B (Y_C - Y_A) + X_C (Y_D - Y_B) + \ldots + X_N (Y_A - Y_{N-1})] / 2$,

Trapezoidal Rule: Area = $w\left(\dfrac{h_1 + h_n}{2} + h_2 + h_3 + h_4 + \ldots + h_{n-1}\right)$ w = common interval,

Simpson's 1/3 Rule: Area = $w\left[h_1 + 2\left(\displaystyle\sum_{k=3,5,\ldots}^{n-2} h_k\right) + 4\left(\displaystyle\sum_{k=2,4,\ldots}^{n-1} h_k\right) + h_n\right]\bigg/3$ n must be odd number of measurements,

        w = common interval

CONSTRUCTION

Construction project scheduling and analysis questions may be based on either activity-on-node method or on activity-on-arrow method.

CPM PRECEDENCE RELATIONSHIPS (ACTIVITY ON NODE)

Start-to-start: start of B
depends on the start of A

Finish-to-finish: finish of B
depends on the finish of A

Finish-to-start: start of B
depends on the finish of A

VERTICAL CURVE FORMULAS

VERTICAL CURVE FORMULAS
NOT TO SCALE

L = Length of Curve (horizontal)

PVC = Point of Vertical Curvature

PVI = Point of Vertical Intersection

PVT = Point of Vertical Tangency

g_1 = Grade of Back Tangent

x = Horizontal Distance from PVC
(or point of tangency) to Point on Curve

g_2 = Grade of Forward Tangent

a = Parabola Constant

y = Tangent Offset

E = Tangent Offset at PVI

r = Rate of Change of Grade

x_m = Horizontal Distance to Min/Max Elevation on Curve $= -\dfrac{g_1}{2a} = \dfrac{g_1 L}{g_1 - g_2}$

Tangent Elevation $\quad=\quad Y_{PVC} + g_1 x \qquad$ and $\qquad = Y_{PVI} + g_2(x - L/2)$

Curve Elevation $\qquad=\quad Y_{PVC} + g_1 x + ax^2 = Y_{PVC} + g_1 x + [(g_2 - g_1)/(2L)]x^2$

$$y = ax^2; \qquad\qquad a = \frac{g_2 - g_1}{2L};$$

$$E = a\left(\frac{L}{2}\right)^2; \qquad\qquad r = \frac{g_2 - g_1}{L}$$

HORIZONTAL CURVE FORMULAS

D $\quad=\quad$ Degree of Curve, Arc Definition

P.C. $\;=\;$ Point of Curve (also called B.C.)

P.T. $\;=\;$ Point of Tangent (also called E.C.)

P.I. $\;=\;$ Point of Intersection

I $\qquad=\quad$ Intersection Angle (also called Δ)

Angle between two tangents

L $\qquad=\quad$ Length of Curve,

from P.C. to P.T.

T $\qquad=\quad$ Tangent Distance

E $\qquad=\quad$ External Distance

R $\qquad=\quad$ Radius

L.C. $\;=\;$ Length of Long Chord

M $\qquad=\quad$ Length of Middle Ordinate

c $\qquad=\quad$ Length of Sub-Chord

d $\qquad=\quad$ Angle of Sub-Chord

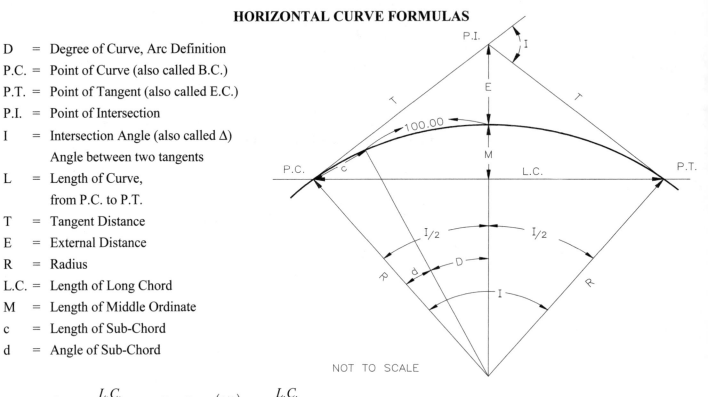

NOT TO SCALE

$$R = \frac{L.C.}{2\,\sin(I/2)}; \quad T = R\tan(I/2) = \frac{L.C.}{2\cos(I/2)}$$

$$R = \frac{5729.58}{D}; \qquad L = RI\frac{\pi}{180} = \frac{I}{D}100$$

$$M = R\left[1 - \cos(I/2)\right]$$

$$\frac{R}{E+R} = \cos(I/2); \quad \frac{R-M}{R} = \cos(I/2)$$

$$c = 2R\sin(d/2);$$

$$E = R\left[\frac{1}{\cos(I/2)} - 1\right]$$

Deflection angle per 100 feet of arc length equals $\dfrac{D}{2}$

LATITUDES AND DEPARTURES

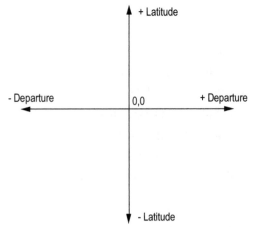

ENVIRONMENTAL ENGINEERING

PLANNING

Population Projection Equations

Linear Projection = Algebraic Projection

$$P_T = P_0 + k\Delta t, \text{ where}$$

P_T = population at time T,

P_0 = population at time zero (fitting parameter),

k = growth rate (fitting parameter), and

Δt = elapsed time in years relative to time zero.

Log Growth = Exponential Growth = Geometric Growth

$$P_T = P_0 e^{k\Delta t}$$

$$\ln P_T = \ln P_0 + k\Delta t, \text{ where}$$

P_T = population at time T,

P_0 = population at time zero (fitting parameter),

k = growth rate (fitting parameter), and

Δt = elapsed time in years relative to time zero.

WATER

For information about fluids, refer to the **CIVIL ENGINEERING** and **FLUID MECHANICS** sections.

For information about hydrology and geohydrology, refer to the **CIVIL ENGINEERING** section.

Stream Modeling: Streeter Phelps

$$D = \frac{k_d S_o}{k_a - k_d}\left[\exp(-k_d t) - \exp(-k_a t)\right] + D_o \exp(-k_a t)$$

$$t_c = \frac{1}{k_a - k_d}\ln\left[\frac{k_a}{k_d}\left(1 - D_o \frac{(k_a - k_d)}{k_d S_o}\right)\right]$$

$$D = DO_{sat} - DO, \text{ where}$$

D = dissolved oxygen deficit (mg/L),

k_d = deoxygenation rate constant, base e (days^{-1}),

t = time (days),

k_a = reaeration rate, base e (days^{-1}),

S_o = initial BOD ultimate in mixing zone (mg/L),

D_o = initial dissolved oxygen deficit in mixing zone (mg/L),

t_c = time which corresponds with minimum dissolved oxygen (days),

DO_{sat} = saturated dissolved oxygen concentration (mg/L), and

DO = dissolved oxygen concentration (mg/L).

WATER AND WASTEWATER TECHNOLOGIES

For information about reactor design (batch, plug flow, and complete mix), refer to the **CHEMICAL ENGINEERING** section.

Approach velocity = horizontal velocity = Q/A_x,

Hydraulic loading rate = Q/A, and

Hydraulic residence time = $V/Q = \theta$.

where

Q = flow rate,

A_x = cross-sectional area,

A = surface area, plan view, and

V = tank volume.

Lime-Soda Softening Equations

50 mg/L as $CaCO_3$ equivalent = 1 meq/L

1. Carbon dioxide removal
$$CO_2 + Ca(OH)_2 \rightarrow CaCO_3(s) + H_2O$$

2. Calcium carbonate hardness removal
$$Ca(HCO_3)_2 + Ca(OH)_2 \rightarrow 2CaCO_3(s) + 2H_2O$$

3. Calcium non-carbonate hardness removal
$$CaSO_4 + Na_2CO_3 \rightarrow CaCO_3(s) + 2Na^+ + SO_4^{-2}$$

4. Magnesium carbonate hardness removal
$$Mg(HCO_3)_2 + 2Ca(OH)_2 \rightarrow 2CaCO_3(s) + Mg(OH)_2(s) + 2H_2O$$

5. Magnesium non-carbonate hardness removal
$$MgSO_4 + Ca(OH)_2 + Na_2CO_3 \rightarrow CaCO_3(s) + Mg(OH)_2(s) + 2Na^+ + SO_4^{2-}$$

6. Destruction of excess alkalinity
$$2HCO_3^- + Ca(OH)_2 \rightarrow CaCO_3(s) + CO_3^{2-} + 2H_2O$$

7. Recarbonation
$$Ca^{2+} + 2OH^- + CO_2 \rightarrow CaCO_3(s) + H_2O$$

Equivalent Weights	Molecular Weight	*n* # Equiv mole	Equivalent Weight
CO_3^{2-}	60.008	2	30.004
CO_2	44.009	2	22.004
$Ca(OH)_2$	74.092	2	37.046
$CaCO_3$	100.086	2	50.043
$Ca(HCO_3)_2$	**162.110**	**2**	**81.055**
$CaSO_4$	136.104	2	68.070
Ca^{2+}	40.078	2	20.039
H^+	1.008	1	1.008
HCO_3^-	61.016	1	61.016
$Mg(HCO_3)_2$	**146.337**	**2**	**73.168**
$Mg(OH)_2$	58.319	2	29.159
$MgSO_4$	120.367	2	60.184
Mg^{2+}	24.305	2	12.152
Na^+	22.990	1	22.990
Na_2CO_3	**105.988**	**2**	**52.994**
OH^-	17.007	1	17.007
SO_4^{2-}	96.062	2	48.031

Rapid Mix and Flocculator Design

$$G = \sqrt{\frac{P}{\mu V}} = \sqrt{\frac{\gamma H_L}{t\,\mu}}$$

$$Gt = 10^4 - 10^5$$

where

G = mixing intensity = root mean square velocity gradient,

P = power,

V = volume,

μ = bulk viscosity,

γ = specific weight of water,

H_L = head loss in mixing zone, and

t = time in mixing zone.

Reel and Paddle

$$P_{\text{BOARD}} = \frac{C_D A_P \rho_f v_p^3}{2}, \text{ where}$$

C_D = drag coefficient = 1.8 for flat blade with a L:W > 20:1,

A_p = area of blade (m^2) perpendicular to the direction of travel through the water,

ρ_f = density of H_2O (kg/m^3),

v_p = relative velocity of paddle (m/sec), and

v = $v_{\text{actual}} \cdot$ slip coefficient.

slip coefficient = 0.5 – 0.75.

Turbulent Flow Impeller Mixer

$$P = K_T (n)^3 (D_i)^5 \rho_f, \text{ where}$$

K_T = impeller constant (see table),

n = rotational speed (rev/sec), and

D_i = impeller diameter (m).

Values of the Impeller Constant K_T
(Assume Turbulent Flow)

Type of Impeller	K_T
Propeller, pitch of 1, 3 blades	0.32
Propeller, pitch of 2, 3 blades	1.00
Turbine, 6 flat blades, vaned disc	6.30
Turbine, 6 curved blades	4.80
Fan turbine, 6 blades at 45°	1.65
Shrouded turbine, 6 curved blades	1.08
Shrouded turbine, with stator, no baffles	1.12

Note: Constant assumes baffled tanks having four baffles at the tank wall with a width equal to 10% of the tank diameter.
Source: J. H. Rushton, "Mixing of Liquids in Chemical Processing," *Industrial & Engineering Chemistry*, v. 44, no. 12, p. 2931, 1952.

Settling Equations

General Spherical

$$v_t = \sqrt{\frac{4/3\,g(\rho_p - \rho_f)d}{C_D \rho_f}}$$

$$C_D = \frac{24}{Re} \quad (\text{Laminar; } Re \le 1.0)$$

$$= \frac{24}{Re} + \frac{3}{(Re)^{1/2}} + 0.34 \quad (\text{Transitional})$$

$$= 0.4 (\text{Turbulent; } Re \ge 10^4)$$

$$Re = \text{Reynolds number} = \frac{v_t \rho d}{\mu}, \text{ where}$$

g = gravitational constant,

ρ_p and ρ_f = density of particle and fluid respectively,

d = diameter of sphere,

C_D = spherical drag coefficient,

μ = bulk viscosity of liquid = absolute viscosity, and

v_t = terminal settling velocity.

Stokes' Law

$$v_t = \frac{g(\rho_p - \rho_f)d^2}{18\mu}$$

Filtration Equations

Effective size = d_{10}

Uniformity coefficient = d_{60}/d_{10}

d_x = diameter of particle class for which $x\%$ of sample is less than (units meters or feet).

Head Loss Through Clean Bed

Rose Equation

Monosized Media   Multisized Media

$$h_f = \frac{1.067(V_s)^2 L C_D}{g\eta^4 d} \qquad h_f = \frac{1.067(V_s)^2 L}{g\eta^4} \sum \frac{C_{D_{ij}} x_{ij}}{d_{ij}}$$

Carmen-Kozeny Equation

Monosized Media   Multisized Media

$$h_f = \frac{f'L(1-\eta)V_s^2}{\eta^3 g d_p} \qquad h_f = \frac{L(1-\eta)V_s^2}{\eta^3 g} \sum \frac{f'_{ij} x_{ij}}{d_{ij}}$$

$$f' = \text{friction factor} = 150\left(\frac{1-\eta}{Re}\right) + 1.75, \text{ where}$$

h_f = head loss through the cleaner bed (m of H_2O),

L = depth of filter media (m),

η = porosity of bed = void volume/total volume,

V_s = filtration rate = empty bed approach velocity = Q/A_{plan} (m/s), and

g = gravitational acceleration (m/s^2).

$$Re = \text{Reynolds number} = \frac{V_s \rho d}{\mu}$$

d_{ij}, d_p, d = diameter of filter media particles; arithmetic average of adjacent screen openings (m); i = filter media (sand, anthracite, garnet); j = filter media particle size,

x_{ij} = mass fraction of media retained between adjacent sieves,

f'_{ij} = friction factors for each media fraction, and

C_D = drag coefficient as defined in settling velocity equations.

Bed Expansion

Monosized

$$L_{fb} = \frac{L_o(1-\eta_o)}{1 - \left(\dfrac{V_B}{V_t}\right)^{0.22}}$$

Multisized

$$L_{fb} = L_o(1-\eta_o)\sum \frac{x_{ij}}{1 - \left(\dfrac{V_B}{V_{t,i,j}}\right)^{0.22}}$$

$$\eta_{fb} = \left(\frac{V_B}{V_t}\right)^{0.22}, \text{ where}$$

L_{fb} = depth of fluidized filter media (m),

V_B = backwash velocity (m/s), Q/A_{plan},

V_t = terminal setting velocity, and

η_{fb} = porosity of fluidized bed.

L_o = initial bed depth

η_o = initial bed porosity

Clarifier

Overflow rate	= v_o	= $Q/A_{surface}$
Weir overflow rate	= WOR	= $Q/\text{Weir Length}$
Horizontal velocity	= v_h	= $Q/A_{cross\text{-}section} = Q/A_x$
Hydraulic residence time	= Vol/Q	

Typical Primary Clarifier Efficiency Percent Removal

	Overflow rates			
	1,200 (gpd/ft^2) 48.9 (m/d)	1,000 (gpd/ft^2) 40.7 (m/d)	800 (gpd/ft^2) 32.6 (m/d)	600 (gpd/ft^2) 24.4 (m/d)
Suspended Solids	54%	58%	64%	68%
BOD$_5$	30%	32%	34%	36%

Design Data for Clarifiers for Activated-Sludge Systems

Type of Treatment	Overflow rate, m^3/m^2·d		Loading kg/m^2·h		Depth (m)
	Average	Peak	Average	Peak	
Settling following air-activated sludge (excluding extended aeration)	16–32	40–48	3.0–6.0	9.0	3.5–5
Settling following extended aeration	8–16	24–32	1.0–5.0	7.0	3.5–5

Source: Adapted from Metcalf & Eddy, Inc. [5–36]

Design Criteria for Sedimentation Basins

Type of Basin	Overflow Rate (gpd/ft^2)	Hydraulic Residence Time (hr)
Water Treatment		
Presedimentation	300–500	3–4
Clarification following coagulation and flocculation		
1. Alum coagulation	350–550	4–8
2. Ferric coagulation	550–700	4–8
3. Upflow clarifiers		
a. Ground water	1,500–2,200	1
b. Surface water	1,000–1,500	4
Clarification following lime-soda softening		
1. Conventional	550–1,000	2–4
2. Upflow clarifiers		
a. Ground water	1,000–2,500	1
b. Surface water	1,000–1,800	4
Wastewater Treatment		
Primary clarifiers	600–1,200	2
Fixed film reactors		
1. Intermediate and final clarifiers	400–800	2
Activated sludge	800–1,200	2
Chemical precipitation	800–1,200	2

Weir Loadings

1. Water Treatment—weir overflow rates should not exceed 20,000 gpd/ft

2. Wastewater Treatment

   a. Flow ≤ 1 MGD: weir overflow rates should not exceed 10,000 gpd/ft

   b. Flow > 1 MGD: weir overflow rates should not exceed 15,000 gpd/ft

Horizontal Velocities

1. Water Treatment—horizontal velocities should not exceed 0.5 fpm

2. Wastewater Treatment—no specific requirements (use the same criteria as for water)

Dimensions

1. Rectangular tanks

   a. Length:Width ratio = 3:1 to 5:1

   b. Basin width is determined by the scraper width (or multiples of the scraper width)

   c. Bottom slope is set at 1%

   d. Minimum depth is 10 ft

2. Circular Tanks

   a. Diameters up to 200 ft

   b. Diameters must match the dimensions of the sludge scraping mechanism

   c. Bottom slope is less than 8%

   d. Minimum depth is 10 ft

Length:Width Ratio

Clarifier	3:1 to 5:1
Filter bay	1.2:1 to 1.5:1
Chlorine contact chamber	20:1 to 50:1

Activated Carbon Adsorption

Freundlich Isotherm

$$\frac{x}{m} = X = KC_e^{1/n}, \text{ where}$$

x = mass of solute adsorbed,

m = mass of adsorbent,

X = mass ratio of the solid phase—that is, the mass of adsorbed solute per mass of adsorbent,

C_e = equilibrium concentration of solute, mass/volume, and

K, n = experimental constants.

Linearized Form

$$ln\frac{x}{m} = 1/n \, ln\, C_e + ln\, K$$

For linear isotherm, n = 1

Langmuir Isotherm

$$\frac{x}{m} = X = \frac{aKC_e}{1 + KC_e}, \text{ where}$$

a = mass of adsorbed solute required to saturate completely a unit mass of adsorbent, and

K = experimental constant.

Linearized Form

$$\frac{m}{x} = \frac{1}{a} + \frac{1}{aK}\frac{1}{C_e}$$

Depth of Sorption Zone

$$Z_s = Z\left[\frac{V_Z}{V_T - 0.5V_Z}\right], \text{ where}$$

V_Z = $V_T - V_B$

Z_S = depth of sorption zone,

Z = total carbon depth,

V_T = total volume treated at exhaustion ($C = 0.95\, C_o$),

V_B = total volume at breakthrough ($C = C_\alpha = 0.05\, C_o$), and

C_o = concentration of contaminant in influent.

Reverse Osmosis

Osmotic Pressure of Solutions of Electrolytes

$$\pi = \phi v \frac{n}{V} RT, \text{ where}$$

π = osmotic pressure,

ϕ = osmotic coefficient,

v = number of ions formed from one molecule of electrolyte,

n = number of moles of electrolyte,

V = volume of solvent,

R = universal gas constant, and

T = absolute pressure.

A CONTINUOUS-FLOW
REVERSE OSMOSIS UNIT

Water Flux

$$J_w = W_p \times (\Delta P - \Delta \pi), \text{ where}$$

J_w = water flux through the membrane [gmol/(cm$^2\cdot$ s)],

W_p = coefficient of water permeation, a characteristic of the particular membrane [gmol/(cm$^2 \cdot$ s $\cdot$ atm)],

ΔP = pressure differential across membrane = $P_{in} - P_{out}$ (atm), and

$\Delta \pi$ = osmotic pressure differential across membrane $\pi_{in} - \pi_{out}$ (atm).

Salt Flux through the Membrane

$$J_s = (D_s K_s / \Delta Z)(C_{in} - C_{out}), \text{ where}$$

J_s = salt flux through the membrane [gmol/(cm$^2 \cdot$s)],

D_s = diffusivity of the solute in the membrane (cm^2/s),

K_s = solute distribution coefficient (dimensionless),

C = concentration (gmol/cm^3),

ΔZ = membrane thickness (cm), and

$$J_s = K_p \times (C_{in} - C_{out})$$

K_p = membrane solute mass transfer coefficient = $\dfrac{D_s K_s}{\Delta Z}$ (L/t, cm/s).

Ultrafiltration

$$J_w = \frac{\varepsilon r^2 \int \Delta P}{8 \mu \delta}, \text{ where}$$

ε = membrane porosity,

r = membrane pore size,

ΔP = net transmembrane pressure,

μ = viscosity,

δ = membrane thickness, and

J_w = volumetric flux (m/s).

Electrodialysis

In n Cells, the Required Current Is:

$$I = (FQN/n) \times (E_1 / E_2), \text{ where}$$

I = current (amperes),

F = Faraday's constant = 96,487 C/g-equivalent,

Q = flow rate (L/s),

N = normality of solution (g-equivalent/L),

n = number of cells between electrodes,

E_1 = removal efficiency (fraction), and

E_2 = current efficiency (fraction).

Voltage

$$E = IR, \text{ where}$$

E = voltage requirement (volts), and

R = resistance through the unit (ohms).

Required Power

$$P = I^2 R \text{ (watts)}$$

Air Stripping

$$A_{out} = H'C_{in}$$

$$Q_w[C_{in}] = Q_A [H'C_{in}]$$

$$Q_w = Q_A[H']$$

$$H'(Q_A / Q_W) = 1$$

where

A_{out} = concentration in the effluent air,

H = Henry's Law constant,

H' = H/RT = dimensionless Henry's Law constant,

T = temperature in units consistent with R

R = universal gas constant,

Q_W = water flow rate (m^3/s),

Q_A = air flow rate (m^3/s),

A = concentration of contaminant in air (kmol/m^3), and

C = concentration of contaminants in water (kmol/m^3).

Stripper Packing Height = Z

$$Z = \text{HTU} \times \text{NTU}$$

$$\text{NTU} = \left(\frac{R}{R-1}\right) ln\left(\frac{(C_{in}/C_{out})(R-1)+1}{R}\right)$$

NTU = number of transfer units

where

R = stripping factor $H'(Q_A / Q_W)$,

C_{in} = concentration in the effluent water (kmol/m^3), and

C_{out} = concentration in the effluent water (kmol/m^3).

$$\text{HTU} = \text{Height of Transfer Units} = \frac{L}{M_W K_L a},$$

where

L = liquid molar loading rate [kmol/(s · m^2)],

M_W = molar density of water (55.6 kmol/m^3) = 3.47 lbmol/ft^3, and

$K_L a$ = overall transfer rate constant (s^{-1}).

Environmental Microbiology

BOD Exertion

$$y_t = L(1 - e^{-kt})$$

where

k = reaction rate constant (base e, days^{-1}),

L = ultimate BOD (mg/L),

t = time (days), and

y_t = the amount of BOD exerted at time t (mg/L).

Monod Kinetics

$$\mu = \mu_{max}\frac{S}{K_s + S}, \text{ where}$$

μ = specific growth rate (time^{-1}),

μ_{max} = maximum specific growth rate (time^{-1}),

S = concentration of substrate in solution (mass/unit volume), and

K_s = half-velocity constant = half-saturation constant (i.e., substrate concentration at which the specific growth rate is one-half μ_{max}) (mass/unit volume).

Half-Life of a Biologically Degraded Contaminant Assuming First-Order Rate Constant

$$k = \frac{0.693}{t_{1/2}}, \text{ where}$$

$t_{1/2}$ = half-life (days).

Activated Sludge

$$X_A = \frac{\theta_c Y(S_o - S_e)}{\theta(1 + k_d \theta_c)}, \text{ where}$$

X_A = biomass concentration in aeration tank (MLSS or MLVSS kg/m^3);

S_o = influent BOD or COD concentration (kg/m^3);

S_e = effluent BOD or COD concentration (kg/m^3);

k_d = microbial death ratio; kinetic constant; day^{-1}; typical range 0.1–0.01, typical domestic wastewater value = 0.05 day^{-1};

Y = yield coefficient Kg biomass/Kg BOD consumed; range 0.4–1.2; and

θ = hydraulic residence time = V / Q

θ_c = Solids residence time = $\dfrac{V_A X_A}{Q_w X_w + Q_e X_e}$

V_s = Sludge volume/day: $Q_s = \dfrac{M(100)}{\rho_s(\% \, solids)}$

Solids loading rate = $Q X/A$

For activated sludge secondary clarifier $Q = Q_o + Q_R$

Organic loading rate (volumetric) = $Q_o S_o / V$

Organic loading rate (F:M) = $Q_o S_o / (V_A X_A)$

Organic loading rate (surface area) = $Q_o S_o / A_M$

$$\text{SVI} = \frac{\text{Sludge volume after settling(mL/L)} * 1{,}000}{\text{MLSS(mg/L)}}$$

Steady State Mass Balance for Secondary Clarifier:

$$(Q_o + Q_R)X_A = Q_e X_e + Q_R X_w + Q_w X_w$$

A = surface area of unit,

A_M = surface area of media in fixed-film reactor,

A_x = cross-sectional area of channel,

M = sludge production rate (dry weight basis),

Q_o = flow rate, influent

Q_e = effluent flow rate,

Q_w = waste sludge flow rate,

ρ_s = wet sludge density,

R = recycle ratio = Q_R/Q_o

Q_R = recycle flow rate = $Q_o R$,

X_e = effluent suspended solids concentration,

X_w = waste sludge suspended solids concentration,

V = tank volume,

V_A = aeration basin volume,

Q = flow rate.

DESIGN AND OPERATIONAL PARAMETERS FOR ACTIVATED-SLUDGE
TREATMENT OF MUNICIPAL WASTEWATER

Type of Process	Mean cell residence time (θ_c, d)	Food-to-mass ratio (kg BOD$_5$/kg MLSS)	Volumetric loading (V_L kg BOD$_5$/m^3)	Hydraulic residence time in aeration basin (θ, h)	Mixed liquor suspended solids (MLSS, mg/L)	Recycle ratio (Q_r/Q)	Flow regime*	BOD$_5$ removal efficiency (%)	Air supplied (m^3/kg BOD$_5$)
Tapered aeration	5–15	0.2–0.4	0.3–0.6	4–8	1,500–3,000	0.25–0.5	PF	85–95	45–90
Conventional	4–15	0.2–0.4	0.3–0.6	4–8	1,500–3,000	0.25–0.5	PF	85–95	45–90
Step aeration	4–15	0.2–0.4	0.6–1.0	3–5	2,000–3,500	0.25–0.75	PF	85–95	45–90
Completely mixed	4–15	0.2–0.4	0.8–2.0	3–5	3,000–6,000	0.25–1.0	CM	85–95	45–90
Contact stabilization	4–15	0.2–0.6	1.0–1.2			0.25–1.0			45–90
Contact basin				0.5–1.0	1,000–3,000		PF	80–90	
Stabilization basin				4–6	4,000–10,000		PF		
High-rate aeration	4–15	0.4–1.5	1.6–16	0.5–2.0	4,000–10,000	1.0–5.0	CM	75–90	25–45
Pure oxygen	8–20	0.2–1.0	1.6–4	1–3	6,000–8,000	0.25–0.5	CM	85–95	
Extended aeration	20–30	0.05–0.15	0.16–0.40	18–24	3,000–6,000	0.75–1.50	CM	75–90	90–125

Source: Adapted from Metcalf & Eddy, Inc. [5-36] and Steele and McGhee [5-50].
*PF = plug flow, CM = completely mixed.

Facultative Pond

BOD Loading

Mass (lb/day) = Flow (MGD) × Concentration (mg/L)
$$\times\ 8.34(\text{lb/MGal})/(\text{mg/L})$$

Total System ≤ 35 pounds BOD$_5$/acre/day

Minimum = 3 ponds

Depth = 3–8 ft

Minimum t = 90–120 days

Biotower

Fixed-Film Equation without Recycle

$$\frac{S_e}{S_o} = e^{-kD/q^n}$$

Fixed-Film Equation with Recycle

$$\frac{S_e}{S_a} = \frac{e^{-kD/q^n}}{(1+R) - R\left(e^{-kD/q^n}\right)}$$

$$S_a = \frac{S_o + RS_e}{1+R}, \text{ where}$$

S_e = effluent BOD$_5$ (mg/L),

S_o = influent BOD$_5$ (mg/L),

D = depth of biotower media (m),

q = hydraulic loading (m^3/m^2/min),

= $(Q_o + RQ_o)/A_{plan}$ (with recycle),

k = treatability constant; functions of wastewater and medium (min^{-1}); range 0.01–0.1; for municipal wastewater and modular plastic media 0.06 min^{-1} @ 20°C,

k_T = $k_{2o}(1.035)^{T-20}$,

n = coefficient relating to media characteristics; modular plastic, n = 0.5,

R = recycle ratio = Q_o / Q_R, and

Q_R = recycle flow rate.

Anaerobic Digester

Design parameters for anaerobic digesters

Parameter	Standard-rate	High-rate
Solids residence time, d	30–90	10–20
Volatile solids loading, kg/m^3/d	0.5–1.6	1.6–6.4
Digested solids concentration, %	4–6	4–6
Volatile solids reduction, %	35–50	45–55
Gas production (m^3/kg VSS added)	0.5–0.55	0.6–0.65
Methane content, %	65	65

Source: Adapted from Metcalf & Eddy, Inc. [5-36]

Standard Rate

$$\text{Reactor Volume} = \frac{V_1 + V_2}{2}t_r + V_2 t_s$$

High Rate
First stage
$$\text{Reactor Volume} = V_1 t_r$$

Second Stage
$$\text{Reactor Volume} = \frac{V_1 + V_2}{2}t_t + V_2 t_s, \text{ where}$$

V_1 = raw sludge input (volume/day),

V_2 = digested sludge accumulation (volume/day),

t_r = time to react in a high-rate digester = time to react and thicken in a standard-rate digester,

t_t = time to thicken in a high-rate digester, and

t_s = storage time.

Aerobic Digestion

Tank Volume

$$V = \frac{Q_i(X_i + FS_i)}{X_d(K_d P_v + 1/\theta_c)}, \text{ where}$$

V = volume of aerobic digester (ft^3),

Q_i = influent average flowrate to digester (ft^3/d),

X_i = influent suspended solids (mg/L),

F = fraction of the influent BOD_5 consisting of raw primary sludge (expressed as a decimal),

S_i = influent BOD_5 (mg/L),

X_d = digester suspended solids (mg/L),

K_d = reaction-rate constant (d^{-1}),

P_v = volatile fraction of digester suspended solids (expressed as a decimal), and

θ_c = solids residence time (sludge age) (d).

AIR POLLUTION

For information on Ideal Gas Law equations refer to the **THERMODYNAMICS** Section.

Atmospheric Dispersion Modeling (Gaussian)

σ_y and σ_z as a function of downwind distance and stability class, see following figures.

$$C = \frac{Q}{2\pi u \sigma_y \sigma_z} \exp\left(-\frac{1}{2}\frac{y^2}{\sigma_y^2}\right)\left[\exp\left(-\frac{1}{2}\frac{(z-H)^2}{\sigma_z^2}\right) + \exp\left(-\frac{1}{2}\frac{(z+H)^2}{\sigma_z^2}\right)\right]$$

where

C = steady-state concentration at a point (x, y, z) ($\mu g/m^3$),

Q = emissions rate ($\mu g/s$),

σ_y = horizontal dispersion parameter (m),

σ_z = vertical dispersion parameter (m),

u = average wind speed at stack height (m/s),

y = horizontal distance from plume centerline (m),

z = vertical distance from ground level (m),

H = effective stack height (m) = h + Δh

where h = physical stack height

Δh = plume rise, and

x = downwind distance along plume centerline (m).

Concentration downwind from elevated source

$$C_{(max)} = \frac{Q}{\pi u \sigma_y \sigma_z} \exp\left(-\frac{1}{2}\frac{(H^2)}{\sigma_z^2}\right)$$

where variables as previous except

$C_{(max)}$ = maximum ground-level concentration.

$\sigma_z = \dfrac{H}{\sqrt{2}}$ for neutral atmospheric conditions

Atmospheric Stability Under Various Conditions

Surface Wind Speed[a] (m/s)	Day Solar Insolation			Night Cloudiness[e]	
	Strong[b]	Moderate[c]	Slight[d]	Cloudy (≥4/8)	Clear (≤3/8)
<2	A	A–B[f]	B	E	F
2–3	A–B	B	C	E	F
3–5	B	B–C	C	D	E
5–6	C	C–D	D	D	D
>6	C	D	D	D	D

Notes:

a. Surface wind speed is measured at 10 m above the ground.

b. Corresponds to clear summer day with sun higher than 60° above the horizon.

c. Corresponds to a summer day with a few broken clouds, or a clear day with sun 35-60° above the horizon.

d. Corresponds to a fall afternoon, or a cloudy summer day, or clear summer day with the sun 15-35°.

e. Cloudiness is defined as the fraction of sky covered by the clouds.

f. For A–B, B–C, or C–D conditions, average the values obtained for each.

* A = Very unstable   D = Neutral
B = Moderately unstable   E = Slightly stable
C = Slightly unstable   F = Stable

Regardless of wind speed, Class D should be assumed for overcast conditions, day or night.

SOURCE: Turner, 1970.

VERTICAL STANDARD DEVIATIONS OF A PLUME

HORIZONTAL STANDARD DEVIATIONS OF A PLUME

A - EXTREMELY UNSTABLE
B - MODERATELY UNSTABLE
C   SLIGHTLY UNSTABLE
D - NEUTRAL
E - SLIGHTLY STABLE
F - MODERATELY STABLE

$$\left(\frac{Cu}{Q}\right) \text{ max, m}^{-2}$$

NOTE: Effective stack height shown on curves numerically.

SOURCE: Turner, D. B., "Workbook of Atmospheric Dispersion Estimates," Washington, DC, U.S. Environmental Protection Agency, 1970.

$$\left(\frac{Cu}{Q}\right) \text{ max} = e^{[a + b\,lnH + c\,(lnH)^2 + d(lnH)^3]}$$

H = effective stack height, stack height + plume rise, m

Values of Curve-Fit Constants for Estimating $(Cu/Q)_{max}$ from H as a Function of Atmospheric Stability

Stability	Constants			
	a	b	c	d
A	−1.0563	−2.7153	0.1261	0
B	−1.8060	−2.1912	0.0389	0
C	−1.9748	−1.9980	0	0
D	−2.5302	−1.5610	−0.0934	0
E	−1.4496	−2.5910	0.2181	−0.0343
F	−1.0488	−3.2252	0.4977	−0.0765

Adapted from Ranchoux, 1976.

Incineration

$$DRE = \frac{W_{in} - W_{out}}{W_{in}} \times 100\%, \text{ where}$$

DRE = destruction and removal efficiency (%),

W_{in} = mass feed rate of a particular POHC (kg/h or lb/h), and

W_{out} = mass emission rate of the same POHC (kg/h or lb/h).

$$CE = \frac{CO_2}{CO_2 + CO} \times 100\%, \text{ where}$$

CO_2 = volume concentration (dry) of CO_2 (parts per million, volume, ppmv),

CO = volume concentration (dry) of CO (ppmv),

CE = combustion efficiency, and

POHC = principal organic hazardous contaminant.

Cyclone

AIR POLLUTION CONTROL

CYCLONE DIMENSIONS

PLAN VIEW

ELEVATION VIEW

Cyclone Ratio of Dimensions to Body Diameter

Dimension		High Efficiency	Conventional	High Throughput
Inlet height	H	0.44	0.50	0.80
Inlet width	W	0.21	0.25	0.35
Body length	L_b	1.40	1.75	1.70
Cone length	L_c	2.50	2.00	2.00
Vortex finder length	S	0.50	0.60	0.85
Gas exit diameter	D_e	0.40	0.50	0.75
Dust outlet diameter	D_d	0.40	0.40	0.40

Cyclone Effective Number of Turns Approximation

$$N_e = \frac{1}{H}\left[L_b + \frac{L_c}{2}\right], \text{ where}$$

N_e = number of effective turns gas makes in cyclone,
H = inlet height of cyclone (m),
L_b = length of body cyclone (m), and
L_c = length of cone of cyclone (m).

Cyclone 50% Collection Efficiency for Particle Diameter

$$d_{pc} = \left[\frac{9\mu W}{2\pi N_e v_i (\rho_p - \rho_g)}\right]^{0.5}, \text{ where}$$

d_{pc} = diameter of particle that is collected with 50% efficiency (m),
μ = viscosity of gas (kg/m-s),
W = inlet width of cyclone (m),
N_e = number of effective turns gas makes in cyclone,
v_i = inlet velocity into cyclone (m/s),
ρ_p = density of particle (kg/m^3), and
ρ_g = density of gas (kg/m^3).

Cyclone Collection Efficiency

Cyclone Collection (Particle Removal) Efficiency

$$\eta = \frac{1}{1 + (d_{pc}/d_p)^2}, \text{ where}$$

d_{pc} = diameter of particle collected with 50% efficiency,
d_p = diameter of particle of interest, and
η = fractional particle collection efficiency.

Bag House

Air-to-Cloth Ratio for Baghouses

Dust	Shaker/Woven Reverse Air/Woven (m^3/min/m^2)	Pulse Jet/Felt (m^3/min/m^2)
alumina	0.8	2.4
asbestos	0.9	3.0
bauxite	0.8	2.4
carbon black	0.5	1.5
coal	0.8	2.4
cocoa	0.8	3.7
clay	0.8	2.7
cement	0.6	2.4
cosmetics	0.5	3.0
enamel frit	0.8	2.7
feeds, grain	1.1	4.3
feldspar	0.7	2.7
fertilizer	0.9	2.4
flour	0.9	3.7
fly ash	0.8	1.5
graphite	0.6	1.5
gypsum	0.6	3.0
iron ore	0.9	3.4
iron oxide	0.8	2.1
iron sulfate	0.6	1.8
lead oxide	0.6	1.8
leather dust	1.1	3.7
lime	0.8	3.0
limestone	0.8	2.4
mica	0.8	2.7
paint pigments	0.8	2.1
paper	1.1	3.0
plastics	0.8	2.1
quartz	0.9	2.7
rock dust	0.9	2.7
sand	0.8	3.0
sawdust (wood)	1.1	3.7
silica	0.8	2.1
slate	1.1	3.7
soap detergents	0.6	1.5
spices	0.8	3.0
starch	0.9	2.4
sugar	0.6	2.1
talc	0.8	3.0
tobacco	1.1	4.0
zinc oxide	0.6	1.5

U.S. EPA OAQPS Control Cost Manual. 4th ed., EPA 450/3-90-006 (NTIS PB 90-169954). January 1990

Electrostatic Precipitator Efficiency

Deutsch-Anderson equation:

$\eta = 1 - e^{(-WA/Q)}$, where

η = fractional collection efficiency,

W = terminal drift velocity,

A = total collection area, and

Q = volumetric gas flow rate.

Note that any consistent set of units can be used for W, A, and Q (for example, ft/min, ft^2, and ft^3/min).

NOISE POLLUTION

$SPL (dB) = 10 \log_{10} \left(P^2 / P_o^2 \right)$

$SPL_{total} = 10 \log_{10} \Sigma\, 10^{SPL/10}$

Point Source Attenuation

$\Delta SPL (dB) = 10 \log_{10} (r_1/r_2)^2$

Line Source Attenuation

$\Delta SPL (dB) = 10 \log_{10} (r_1/r_2)$

where

SPL (dB) = sound pressure level, measured in decibels

P = sound pressure (Pa)

P_0 = reference sound pressure (2×10^{-5} Pa)

SPL_{total} = sum of multiple sources

Δ SPL (dB) = change in sound pressure level with distance

r_1 = distance from source to receptor at point 1

r_2 = distance from source to receptor at point 2

RADIATION HALF-LIFE

$N = N_o e^{-0.693\, t/\tau}$, where

N_o = original number of atoms,

N = final number of atoms,

t = time, and

τ = half-life.

Flux at distance 2 = (Flux at distance 1) $(r_1/r_2)^2$

EFFECTIVE HALF-LIFE

Effective half-life, τ_e, is the combined radioactive and biological half-life.

$$\frac{1}{\tau_e} = \frac{1}{\tau_r} + \frac{1}{\tau_b}$$

where

τ_r = radioactive half-life

τ_b = biological half-life

RISK ASSESSMENT

Risk is a product of toxicity and exposure.

Risk assessment process

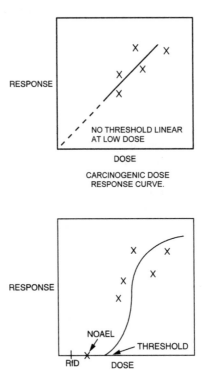

CARCINOGENIC DOSE RESPONSE CURVE.

Dose is expressed as the mass intake of the chemical normalized to the body weight of the exposed individual and the time period of exposure.

NOAEL = No Observable Adverse Effect Level. The dose below which there are no harmful effects.

CSF = Cancer Slope Factor. Determined from the dose-response curve for carcinogenic materials.

Exposure and Intake Rates

Soil Ingestion Rate
100 mg/day (>6 years old)
200 mg/day (children 1 to 6 years old)

Exposure Duration
30 years at one residence (adult)
6 years (child)

Body Mass
70 kg (adult)
10 kg (child)

Averaging Period
non-carcinogens, actual exposure duration
carcinogens, 70 years

Water Consumption Rate
2.0 L/day (adult)
1.0 L/day (child)

Inhalation Rate

0.83 m³/hr (adult)

0.46 m³/hr (child)

Exposure assessment calculates the actual or potential dose that an exposed individual receives and delineates the affected population by identifying possible exposure paths.

$$\text{Daily Dose (mg/kg-day)} = \frac{(C)(I)(EF)(ED)(AF)}{(AT)(BW)}, \text{ where}$$

C = concentration (mass/volume),

I = intake rate (volume/time),

EF = exposure frequency (time/time),

ED = exposure duration (time),

AF = absorption factor (mass/mass),

AT = averaging time (time),

BW = body weight (mass), and

$LADD$ = lifetime average daily dose (daily dose, in mg/kg-day, over an assumed 70-year lifetime).

Risk

Risk characterization estimates the probability of adverse incidence occurring under conditions identified during exposure assessment.

For carcinogens the added risk of cancer is calculated as follows:

Risk = dose × toxicity = daily dose × CSF

Reference Dose

For noncarcinogens, a hazard index (HI) is calculated as follows:

HI = chronic daily intake/RfD

Reference dose (RfD) is determined from the Noncarcinogenic Dose-Response Curve Using NOAEL

RfD = NOAEL/a safety factor

SAMPLING AND MONITORING

For information about Student t-Distribution, Standard Deviation, and Confidence Intervals, refer to the **MATHEMATICS** section.

FATE AND TRANSPORT

Partition Coefficients

Octanol-Water Partition Coefficient

The ratio of a chemical's concentration in the octanol phase to its concentration in the aqueous phase of a two-phase octanol-water system.

$K_{ow} = C_o / C_w$, where

C_o = concentration of chemical in octanol phase (mg/L or μg/L) and

C_w = concentration of chemical in aqueous phase (mg/L or μg/L).

Soil-Water Partition Coefficient $K_{sw} = K_\rho$

$K_{sw} = X/C$, where

X = concentration of chemical in soil (ppb or μg/kg) and

C = concentration of chemical in water (ppb or μg/kg).

Organic Carbon Partition Coefficient K_{oc}

$K_{oc} = C_{soil} / C_{water}$, where

C_{soil} = concentration of chemical in organic carbon component of soil (μg adsorbed/kg organic C, or ppb), and

C_{water} = concentration of chemical in water (ppb or μg/kg)

$K_{sw} = K_{oc} f_{oc}$, where

f_{oc} = fraction of organic carbon in the soil (dimensionless).

Bioconcentration Factor BCF

The amount of a chemical to accumulate in aquatic organisms.

$BCF = C_{org} /C$, where

C_{org} = equilibrium concentration in organism (mg/kg or ppm), and

C = concentration in water (ppm).

Retardation Factor R

$R = 1 + (\rho/\eta)K_d$, where

ρ = bulk density,

η = porosity, and

K_d = distribution coefficient.

LANDFILL

Gas Flux

$$N_A = \frac{D\eta^{4/3}\left(C_{A_{atm}} - C_{A_{fill}}\right)}{L}, \text{ where}$$

N_A = gas flux of compound A, g/cm² · s(lb · mol/ft² · d),

$C_{A_{atm}}$ = concentration of compound A at the surface of the landfill cover, g/cm³ (lb · mol/ft³),

$C_{A_{fill}}$ = concentration of compound A at the bottom of the landfill cover, g/cm³ (lb · mol/ft³), and

L = depth of the landfill cover, cm (ft).

Typical values for the coefficient of diffusion for methane and carbon dioxide are 0.20 cm²/s (18.6 ft²/d) and 0.13 cm²/s (12.1 ft²/d), respectively.

D = diffusion coefficient, cm²/s (ft²/d),

η_{gas} = gas-filled porosity, cm³/cm³ (ft³/ft³), and

η = total porosity, cm³/cm³ (ft³/ft³)

138

Break-Through Time for Leachate to Penetrate a Clay Liner

$$t = \frac{d^2\eta}{K(d+h)}, \text{ where}$$

t = breakthrough time (yr),

d = thickness of clay liner (ft),

η = effective porosity,

K = coefficient of permeability (ft/yr), and

h = hydraulic head (ft).

Typical effective porosity values for clays with a coefficient of permeability in the range of 10^{-6} to 10^{-8} cm/s vary from 0.1 to 0.3.

Soil Landfill Cover Water Balance

$$\Delta S_{LC} = P - R - ET - PER_{sw}, \text{ where}$$

ΔS_{LC} = change in the amount of water held in storage in a unit volume of landfill cover (in.),

P = amount of precipitation per unit area (in.),

R = amount of runoff per unit area (in.),

ET = amount of water lost through evapotranspiration per unit area (in.), and

PER_{sw} = amount of water percolating through the unit area of landfill cover into compacted solid waste (in.).

Effect of Overburden Pressure

$$SW_p = SW_i + \frac{p}{a+bp}$$

where

SW_p = specific weight of the waste material at pressure p (lb/yd^3) (typical 1,750 to 2,150),

SW_i = initial compacted specific weight of waste (lb/yd^3) (typical 1,000),

p = overburden pressure (lb/in^2),

a = empirical constant (yd^3/lb)(lb/in^2), and

b = empirical constant (yd^3/lb).

Data Quality Objectives (DQO) for Sampling Soils and Solids

Investigation Type	Confidence Level $(1-\alpha)$ (%)	Power $(1-\beta)$ (%)	Minimum Detectable Relative Difference (%)
Preliminary site investigation	70–80	90–95	10–30
Emergency clean-up	80–90	90–95	10–20
Planned removal and remedial response operations	90–95	90–95	10–20

EPA Document "EPA/600/8–89/046" *Soil Sampling Quality Assurance User's Guide*, Chapter 7.

Confidence level: $1-$ (Probability of a Type I Error) $= 1 - \alpha$ = size probability of not making a Type I error

Power $= 1-$ (Probability of a Type II error) $= 1 - \beta$ = probability of not making a Type II error.

$CV = (100 * s)/\bar{x}$

CV = coefficient of variation

s = standard deviation of sample

$\bar{x}$ = sample average

Minimum Detectable Relative Difference = Relative increase over background $[100 \, (\mu_s - \mu_B)/ \, \mu_B]$ to be detectable with a probability $(1-\beta)$

Number of samples required in a one-sided one-sample t-test to achieve a minimum detectable relative difference at confidence level (1–α) and power of (1–β)

Coefficient of Variation (%)	Power (%)	Confidence Level (%)	Minimum Detectable Relative Difference (%)				
			5	10	20	30	40
15	95	99	145	39	12	7	5
		95	99	26	8	5	3
		90	78	21	6	3	3
		80	57	15	4	2	2
	90	99	120	32	11	6	5
		95	79	21	7	4	3
		90	60	16	5	3	2
		80	41	11	3	2	1
	80	99	94	26	9	6	5
		95	58	16	5	3	3
		90	42	11	4	2	2
		80	26	7	2	2	1
25	95	99	397	102	28	14	9
		95	272	69	19	9	6
		90	216	55	15	7	5
		80	155	40	11	5	3
	90	99	329	85	24	12	8
		95	272	70	19	9	6
		90	166	42	12	6	4
		80	114	29	8	4	3
	80	99	254	66	19	10	7
		95	156	41	12	6	4
		90	114	30	8	4	3
		80	72	19	5	3	2
35	95	99	775	196	42	25	15
		95	532	134	35	17	10
		90	421	106	28	13	8
		80	304	77	20	9	6
	90	99	641	163	43	21	13
		95	421	107	28	14	8
		90	323	82	21	10	6
		80	222	56	15	7	4
	80	99	495	126	34	17	11
		95	305	78	21	10	7
		90	222	57	15	7	5
		80	140	36	10	5	3

HAZARDOUS WASTE COMPATIBILITY CHART

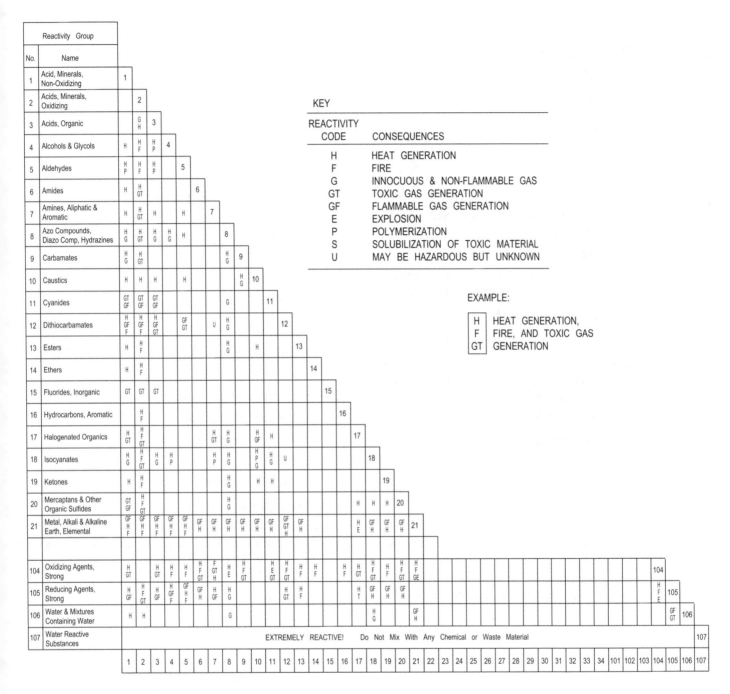

ELECTRICAL AND COMPUTER ENGINEERING

ELECTROMAGNETIC DYNAMIC FIELDS

The integral and point form of Maxwell's equations are

$$\oint \mathbf{E} \cdot d\mathbf{l} = -\iint_S (\partial \mathbf{B}/\partial t) \cdot d\mathbf{S}$$

$$\oint \mathbf{H} \cdot d\mathbf{l} = I_{enc} + \iint_S (\partial \mathbf{D}/\partial t) \cdot d\mathbf{S}$$

$$\oiint_{S_V} \mathbf{D} \cdot d\mathbf{S} = \iiint_V \rho \, dv$$

$$\oiint_{S_V} \mathbf{B} \cdot d\mathbf{S} = 0$$

$$\nabla \times \mathbf{E} = -\partial \mathbf{B}/\partial t$$

$$\nabla \times \mathbf{H} = \mathbf{J} + \partial \mathbf{D}/\partial t$$

$$\nabla \cdot \mathbf{D} = \rho$$

$$\nabla \cdot \mathbf{B} = 0$$

The sinusoidal wave equation in $\mathbf{E}$ for an isotropic homogeneous medium is given by

$$\nabla^2 \mathbf{E} = -\omega^2 \mu \varepsilon \mathbf{E}$$

The *EM* energy flow of a volume V enclosed by the surface S_V can be expressed in terms of the Poynting's Theorem

$$-\oiint_{S_V} (\mathbf{E} \times \mathbf{H}) \cdot d\mathbf{S} = \iiint_V \mathbf{J} \cdot \mathbf{E} \, dv$$

$$+ \partial/\partial t \{\iiint_V (\varepsilon E^2/2 + \mu H^2/2) \, dv\}$$

where the left-side term represents the energy flow per unit time or power flow into the volume V, whereas the $\mathbf{J} \cdot \mathbf{E}$ represents the loss in V and the last term represents the rate of change of the energy stored in the $\mathbf{E}$ and $\mathbf{H}$ fields.

LOSSLESS TRANSMISSION LINES

The wavelength, λ, of a sinusoidal signal is defined as the distance the signal will travel in one period.

$$\lambda = \frac{U}{f}$$

where U is the velocity of propagation and f is the frequency of the sinusoid.

The characteristic impedance, Z_o, of a transmission line is the input impedance of an infinite length of the line and is given by

$$Z_0 = \sqrt{L/C}$$

where L and C are the per unit length inductance and capacitance of the line.

The reflection coefficient at the load is defined as

$$\Gamma = \frac{Z_L - Z_0}{Z_L + Z_0}$$

and the standing wave ratio SWR is

$$SWR = \frac{1 + |\Gamma|}{1 - |\Gamma|}$$

β = Propagation constant = $\dfrac{2\pi}{\lambda}$

For sinusoidal voltages and currents:

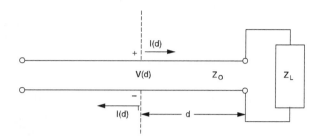

Voltage across the transmission line:

$$V(d) = V^+ e^{j\beta d} + V^- e^{-j\beta d}$$

Current along the transmission line:

$$I(d) = I^+ e^{j\beta d} + I^- e^{-j\beta d}$$

where $I^+ = V^+/Z_0$ and $I^- = -V^-/Z_0$

Input impedance at d

$$Z_{in}(d) = Z_0 \frac{Z_L + jZ_0 \tan(\beta d)}{Z_0 + jZ_L \tan(\beta d)}$$

AC MACHINES

The synchronous speed n_s for AC motors is given by

$$n_s = 120f/p, \text{ where}$$

f = the line voltage frequency in Hz and

p = the number of poles.

The slip for an induction motor is

$$\text{slip} = (n_s - n)/n_s, \text{ where}$$

n = the rotational speed (rpm).

DC MACHINES

The armature circuit of a DC machine is approximated by a series connection of the armature resistance R_a, the armature inductance L_a, and a dependent voltage source of value

$$V_a = K_a n\phi \quad \text{volts, where}$$

K_a = constant depending on the design,

n = is armature speed in rpm, and

ϕ = the magnetic flux generated by the field.

The field circuit is approximated by the field resistance R_f in series with the field inductance L_f. Neglecting saturation, the magnetic flux generated by the field current I_f is

$$\phi = K_f I_f \quad \text{webers}$$

The mechanical power generated by the armature is

$$P_m = V_a I_a \quad \text{watts}$$

where I_a is the armature current. The mechanical torque produced is

$$T_m = (60/2\pi)K_a \phi I_a \text{ newton-meters.}$$

BALANCED THREE-PHASE SYSTEMS

The three-phase line-phase relations are

$$I_L = \sqrt{3}I_p \quad \text{(for delta)}$$
$$V_L = \sqrt{3}V_p \quad \text{(for wye)}$$

where subscripts L/p denote line/phase respectively. Three-phase complex power is defined by

$$S = P + jQ$$

$$S = \sqrt{3}V_L I_L (\cos\theta_p + j\sin\theta_p), \text{ where}$$

S = total complex volt-amperes,

P = real power (watts),

Q = reactive power (VARs), and

θ_p = power factor angle of each phase.

CONVOLUTION

Continuous-time convolution:

$$V(t) = x(t) * y(t) = \int_{-\infty}^{\infty} x(\tau)y(t-\tau)d\tau$$

Discrete-time convolution:

$$V[n] = x[n] * y[n] = \sum_{k=-\infty}^{\infty} x[k]y[n-k]$$

DIGITAL SIGNAL PROCESSING

A discrete-time, linear, time-invariant (DTLTI) system with a single input $x[n]$ and a single output $y[n]$ can be described by a linear difference equation with constant coefficients of the form

$$y[n] + \sum_{i=1}^{k} b_i y[n-i] = \sum_{i=0}^{l} a_i x[n-i]$$

If all initial conditions are zero, taking a z-transform yields a transfer function

$$H(z) = \frac{Y(z)}{X(z)} = \frac{\sum_{i=0}^{l} a_i z^{k-i}}{z^k + \sum_{i=1}^{k} b_i z^{k-i}}$$

Two common discrete inputs are the unit-step function $u[n]$ and the unit impulse function $\delta[n]$, where

$$u[n] = \begin{cases} 0 & n < 0 \\ 1 & n \ge 0 \end{cases} \quad \text{and} \quad \delta[n] = \begin{cases} 1 & n = 0 \\ 0 & n \ne 0 \end{cases}$$

The impulse response $h[n]$ is the response of a discrete-time system to $x[n] = \delta[n]$.

A finite impulse response (FIR) filter is one in which the impulse response $h[n]$ is limited to a finite number of points:

$$h[n] = \sum_{i=0}^{k} a_i \delta[n-i]$$

The corresponding transfer function is given by

$$H(z) = \sum_{i=0}^{k} a_i z^{-i}$$

where k is the order of the filter.

An infinite impulse response (IIR) filter is one in which the impulse response $h[n]$ has an infinite number of points:

$$h[n] = \sum_{i=0}^{\infty} a_i \delta[n-i]$$

COMMUNICATION THEORY CONCEPTS

Spectral characterization of communication signals can be represented by mathematical transform theory. An amplitude modulated (AM) signal form is

$$v(t) = A_c [1 + m(t)] \cos \omega_c t, \text{ where}$$

A_c = carrier signal amplitude.

If the modulation baseband signal $m(t)$ is of sinusoidal form with frequency ω_m or

$$m(t) = m\cos \omega_m t$$

then m is the index of modulation with $m > 1$ implying overmodulation. An angle modulated signal is given by

$$v(t) = A\cos [\omega_c t + \phi(t)]$$

where the angle modulation $\phi(t)$ is a function of the baseband signal. The angle modulation form

$$\phi(t) = k_p m(t)$$

is termed phase modulation since angle variations are proportional to the baseband signal $m_i(t)$. Alternately

$$\phi(t) = k_f \int_{-\infty}^{t} m(\tau)d\tau$$

is termed frequency modulation. Therefore, the instantaneous phase associated with $v(t)$ is defined by

$$\phi_i(t) = \omega_c t + k_f \int_{-\infty}^{t} m(\tau)d\tau$$

from which the instantaneous frequency is

$$\omega_i = \frac{d\phi_i(t)}{dt} = \omega_c + k_f m(t) = \omega_c + \Delta\omega(t)$$

where the frequency deviation is proportional to the baseband signal or

$$\Delta\omega(t) = k_f m(t)$$

These fundamental concepts form the basis of analog communication theory. Alternately, sampling theory, conversion, and PCM (Pulse Code Modulation) are fundamental concepts of digital communication.

FOURIER SERIES

Every periodic function $f(t)$ which has the period $T = 2\pi / \omega_0$ and has certain continuity conditions can be represented by a series plus a constant

$$f(t) = a_0 / 2 + \sum_{n=1}^{\infty} [a_n \cos(n\omega_0 t) + b_n \sin(n\omega_0 t)]$$

The above holds if $f(t)$ has a continuous derivative $f'(t)$ for all t. It should be noted that the various sinusoids present in the series are orthogonal on the interval 0 to T and as a result the coefficients are given by

$$a_n = (2/T)\int_0^T f(t)\cos(n\omega_0 T)dt \quad n = 0, 1, 2, \cdots$$

$$b_n = (2/T)\int_0^T f(t)\sin(n\omega_0 T)dt \quad n = 1, 2, \cdots$$

The constants a_n and b_n are the *Fourier coefficients* of $f(t)$ for the interval 0 to T and the corresponding series is called the *Fourier series of $f(t)$* over the same interval. The integrals have the same value when evaluated over any interval of length T.

If a Fourier series representing a periodic function is truncated after term $n = N$ the mean square value F_N^2 of the truncated series is given by the Parseval relation. This relation says that the mean-square value is the sum of the mean-square values of the Fourier components, or

$$F_N^2 = (a_0/2)^2 + (1/2)\sum_{n=1}^N \left(a_n^2 + b_n^2\right)$$

and the RMS value is then defined to be the square root of this quantity or F_N.

Three useful and common Fourier series forms are defined in terms of the following graphs (with $\omega_o = 2\pi/T$).

Given:

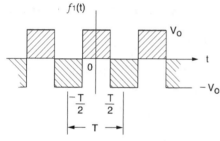

then

$$f_1(t) = \sum_{\substack{n=1 \\ (n\ \text{odd})}}^{\infty} (-1)^{(n-1)/2}(4V_o/n\pi)\cos(n\omega_o t)$$

Given:

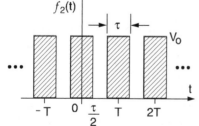

then

$$f_2(t) = \frac{V_o\tau}{T} + \frac{2V_o\tau}{T}\sum_{n=1}^{\infty}\frac{\sin(n\pi\tau/T)}{(n\pi\tau/T)}\cos(n\omega_o t)$$

$$f_2(t) = \frac{V_o\tau}{T}\sum_{n=-\infty}^{\infty}\frac{\sin(n\pi\tau/T)}{(n\pi\tau/T)}e^{jn\omega_o t}$$

Given:

$f_3(t) =$ "a train of impulses with weights

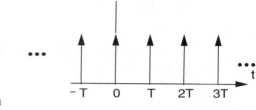

then

$$f_3(t) = \sum_{n=-\infty}^{\infty} A\delta(t - nT)$$

$$f_3(t) = (A/T) + (2A/T)\sum_{n=1}^{\infty}\cos(n\omega_o t)$$

$$f_3(t) = (A/T)\sum_{n=-\infty}^{\infty}e^{jn\omega_o t}$$

SOLID-STATE ELECTRONICS AND DEVICES

Conductivity of a semiconductor material:

$$\sigma = q\,(n\mu_n + p\mu_p), \text{ where}$$

$\mu_n \equiv$ electron mobility,

$\mu_p \equiv$ hole mobility,

$n \equiv$ electron concentration,

$p \equiv$ hole concentration, and

$q \equiv$ charge on an electron.

Doped material:

p-type material; $p_p \approx N_a$

n-type material; $n_n \approx N_d$

Carrier concentrations at equilibrium

$(p)(n) = n_i^2$, where

$n_i \equiv$ intrinsic concentration.

Built-in potential (contact potential) of a p-n junction:

$$V_0 = \frac{kT}{q}\ln\frac{N_a N_d}{n_i^2}$$

Thermal voltage

$$V_T = \frac{kT}{q}$$

$N_a =$ acceptor concentration,

$N_d =$ donor concentration,

$T =$ temperature (K), and

$k =$ Boltzmann's Constant $= 1.38\times 10^{-23}$ J /K

Capacitance of abrupt $p - n$ junction diode

$$C(V) = C_o/\sqrt{1 - V/V_{bi}} \text{ , where}$$

$C_o =$ junction capacitance at $V = 0$,

$V =$ potential of anode with respect to cathode, and

$V_{bi} =$ junction contact potential.

144

Resistance of a diffused layer is

$R = R_s\,(L/W)$, where

R_s = sheet resistance = ρ/d in ohms per square

ρ = resistivity,

d = thickness,

L = length of diffusion, and

W = width of diffusion.

TABULATED CHARACTERISTICS FOR:

Diodes

Bipolar Junction Transistor (BJT)

N-Channel JFET and MOSFET

Enhancement MOSFETs

are on the following pages.

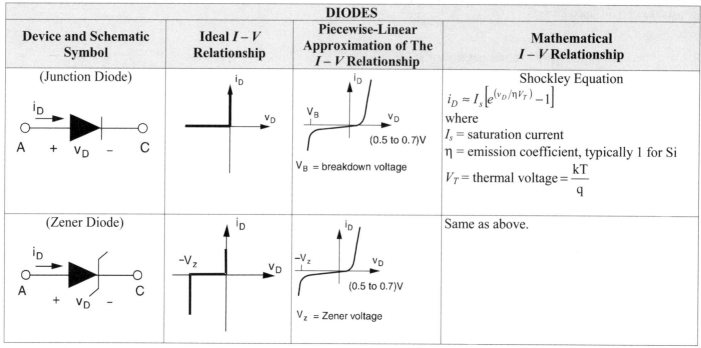

DIODES

Device and Schematic Symbol	Ideal $I-V$ Relationship	Piecewise-Linear Approximation of The $I-V$ Relationship	Mathematical $I-V$ Relationship
(Junction Diode)		V_B $(0.5$ to $0.7)$V V_B = breakdown voltage	Shockley Equation $$i_D \approx I_s\left[e^{(v_D/\eta V_T)}-1\right]$$ where I_s = saturation current η = emission coefficient, typically 1 for Si V_T = thermal voltage $= \dfrac{kT}{q}$
(Zener Diode)	$-V_z$	$-V_z$ $(0.5$ to $0.7)$V V_z = Zener voltage	Same as above.

NPN Bipolar Junction Transistor (BJT)

Schematic Symbol	Mathematical Relationships	Large-Signal (DC) Equivalent Circuit	Low-Frequency Small-Signal (AC) Equivalent Circuit
NPN - Transistor	$i_E = i_B + i_C$ $i_C = \beta i_B$ $i_C = \alpha i_E$ $\alpha = \beta/(\beta + 1)$ $i_C \approx I_S e^{(V_{BE}/V_T)}$ I_S = emitter saturation current V_T = thermal voltage Note: These relationships are valid in the active mode of operation.	Active Region: base emitter junction forward biased; base collector junction reverse biased Saturation Region: both junctions forward biased	Low Frequency: $g_m \approx I_{CQ}/V_T$ $r_\pi \approx \beta/g_m,$ $r_o = \left[\dfrac{\partial v_{CE}}{\partial i_c}\right]_{Q_{point}} \approx \dfrac{V_A}{I_{CQ}}$ where I_{CQ} = dc collector current at the Q_{point} V_A = Early voltage
PNP - Transistor	Same as for NPN with current directions and voltage polarities reversed.	Cutoff Region: both junctions reversed biased Same as NPN with current directions and voltage polarities reversed	Same as for NPN.

	N-Channel Junction Field Effect Transistors (JFETs) and Depletion MOSFETs (Low and Medium Frequency)		
Schematic Symbol	**Mathematical Relationships**		**Small-Signal (AC) Equivalent Circuit**

N-CHANNEL JFET

P-CHANNEL JFET

N-CHANNEL DEPLETION MOSFET (NMOS)

SIMPLIFIED SYMBOL

<u>Cutoff Region</u>: $v_{GS} < V_p$
$i_D = 0$

<u>Triode Region</u>: $v_{GS} > V_p$ and $v_{GD} > V_p$
$i_D = (I_{DSS}/V_p^2)[2v_{DS}(v_{GS} - V_p) - v_{DS}^2]$

<u>Saturation Region</u>: $v_{GS} > V_p$ and $v_{GD} < V_p$
$i_D = I_{DSS}(1 - v_{GS}/V_p)^2$
where
I_{DSS} = drain current with $v_{GS} = 0$ (in the saturation region)
     $= KV_p^2$,
K = conductivity factor, and
V_p = pinch-off voltage.

$g_m = \dfrac{2\sqrt{I_{DSS}I_D}}{|V_p|}$ in saturation region

where

$r_d = \left|\dfrac{\partial v_{ds}}{\partial i_d}\right|_{Q_{\text{point}}}$

P-Channel Depletion MOSFET (PMOS) 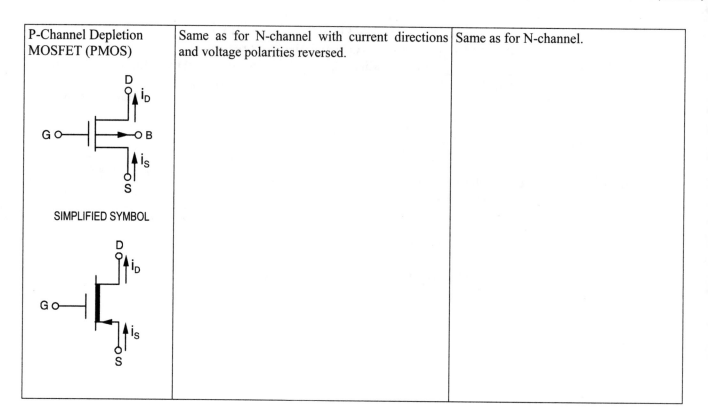 SIMPLIFIED SYMBOL	Same as for N-channel with current directions and voltage polarities reversed.	Same as for N-channel.

Enhancement MOSFET (Low and Medium Frequency)		
Schematic Symbol	**Mathematical Relationships**	**Small-Signal (AC) Equivalent Circuit**
N-CHANNEL ENHANCEMENT MOSFET (NMOS) SIMPLIFIED SYMBOL 	<u>Cutoff Region</u>: $v_{GS} < V_t$ $i_D = 0$ <u>Triode Region</u>: $v_{GS} > V_t$ and $v_{GD} > V_t$ $i_D = K[2v_{DS}(v_{GS} - V_t) - v_{DS}^2]$ <u>Saturation Region</u>: $v_{GS} > V_t$ and $v_{GD} < V_t$ $i_D = K(v_{GS} - V_t)^2$ where $K =$ conductivity factor $V_t =$ threshold voltage	$g_m = 2K(v_{GS} - V_t)$ in saturation region where $r_d = \left| \dfrac{\partial v_{ds}}{\partial i_d} \right|_{Q_{point}}$
P-CHANNEL ENHANCEMENT MOSFET (PMOS) SIMPLIFIED SYMBOL 	Same as for N-channel with current directions and voltage polarities reversed.	Same as for N-channel.

NUMBER SYSTEMS AND CODES

An unsigned number of base-r has a decimal equivalent D defined by

$$D = \sum_{k=0}^{n} a_k r^k + \sum_{i=1}^{m} a_i r^{-i}, \text{ where}$$

a_k = the $(k+1)$ digit to the left of the radix point and

a_i = the ith digit to the right of the radix point.

Binary Number System

In digital computers, the base-2, or binary, number system is normally used. Thus the decimal equivalent, D, of a binary number is given by

$$D = a_k 2^k + a_{k-1} 2^{k-1} + \ldots + a_0 + a_{-1} 2^{-1} + \ldots$$

Since this number system is so widely used in the design of digital systems, we use a short-hand notation for some powers of two:

$2^{10} = 1{,}024$ is abbreviated "K" or "kilo"

$2^{20} = 1{,}048{,}576$ is abbreviated "M" or "mega"

Signed numbers of base-r are often represented by the radix complement operation. If M is an N-digit value of base-r, the radix complement $R(M)$ is defined by

$$R(M) = r^N - M$$

The 2's complement of an N-bit binary integer can be written

$$\text{2's Complement } (M) = 2^N - M$$

This operation is equivalent to taking the 1's complement (inverting each bit of M) and adding one.

The following table contains equivalent codes for a four-bit binary value.

Binary Base-2	Decimal Base-10	Hexa-decimal Base-16	Octal Base-8	BCD Code	Gray Code
0000	0	0	0	0	0000
0001	1	1	1	1	0001
0010	2	2	2	2	0011
0011	3	3	3	3	0010
0100	4	4	4	4	0110
0101	5	5	5	5	0111
0110	6	6	6	6	0101
0111	7	7	7	7	0100
1000	8	8	10	8	1100
1001	9	9	11	9	1101
1010	10	A	12	---	1111
1011	11	B	13	---	1110
1100	12	C	14	---	1010
1101	13	D	15	---	1011
1110	14	E	16	---	1001
1111	15	F	17	---	1000

LOGIC OPERATIONS AND BOOLEAN ALGEBRA

Three basic logic operations are the "AND (·)," "OR (+)," and "Exclusive-OR $\oplus$" functions. The definition of each function, its logic symbol, and its Boolean expression are given in the following table.

Function			
Inputs			
$A\ B$	$C = A \cdot B$	$C = A + B$	$C = A \oplus B$
0 0	0	0	0
0 1	0	1	1
1 0	0	1	1
1 1	1	1	0

As commonly used, A AND B is often written AB or $A \cdot B$.

The not operator inverts the sense of a binary value

$(0 \rightarrow 1, 1 \rightarrow 0)$

NOT OPERATOR

Input	Output
A	$C = \bar{A}$
0	1
1	0

LOGIC SYMBOL

DeMorgan's Theorems

first theorem: $\overline{A + B} = \bar{A} \cdot \bar{B}$

second theorem: $\overline{A \cdot B} = \bar{A} + \bar{B}$

These theorems define the NAND gate and the NOR gate. Logic symbols for these gates are shown below.

NAND Gates: $\overline{A \cdot B} = \bar{A} + \bar{B}$

NOR Gates: $\overline{A + B} = \bar{A} \cdot \bar{B}$

150

FLIP-FLOPS

A flip-flop is a device whose output can be placed in one of two states, 0 or 1. The flip-flop output is synchronized with a clock (CLK) signal. Q_n represents the value of the flip-flop output before CLK is applied, and Q_{n+1} represents the output after CLK has been applied. Three basic flip-flops are described below.

SR	Q_{n+1}
00	Q_n no change
01	0
10	1
11	x invalid

JK	Q_{n+1}
00	Q_n no change
01	0
10	1
11	$\overline{Q_n}$ toggle

D	Q_{n+1}
0	0
1	1

Composite Flip-Flop State Transition						
Q_n	Q_{n+1}	S	R	J	K	D
0	0	0	x	0	x	0
0	1	1	0	1	x	1
1	0	0	1	x	1	0
1	1	x	0	x	0	1

Switching Function Terminology

Minterm, m_i – A product term which contains an occurrence of every variable in the function.

Maxterm, M_i – A sum term which contains an occurrence of every variable in the function.

Implicant – A Boolean algebra term, either in sum or product form, which contains one or more minterms or maxterms of a function.

Prime Implicant – An implicant which is not entirely contained in any other implicant.

Essential Prime Implicant – A prime implicant which contains a minterm or maxterm which is not contained in any other prime implicant.

A function can be described as a sum of minterms using the notation

$$F(ABCD) = \Sigma m(h, i, j, \ldots)$$
$$= m_h + m_i + m_j + \ldots$$

A function can be described as a product of maxterms using the notation

$$G(ABCD) = \Pi M(h, i, j, \ldots)$$
$$= M_h \cdot M_i \cdot M_j \ldots.$$

A function represented as a sum of minterms only is said to be in *canonical sum of products* (SOP) form. A function represented as a product of maxterms only is said to be in *canonical product of sums* (POS) form. A function in canonical SOP form is often represented as a *minterm list*, while a function in canonical POS form is often represented as a *maxterm list*.

A *Karnaugh Map* (K-Map) is a graphical technique used to represent a truth table. Each square in the K-Map represents one minterm, and the squares of the K-Map are arranged so that the adjacent squares differ by a change in exactly one variable. A four-variable K-Map with its corresponding minterms is shown below. K-Maps are used to simplify switching functions by visually identifying all essential prime implicants.

Four-variable Karnaugh Map

AB\CD	00	01	11	10
00	m_0	m_1	m_3	m_2
01	m_4	m_5	m_7	m_6
11	m_{12}	m_{13}	m_{15}	m_{14}
10	m_8	m_9	m_{11}	m_{10}

LINEAR PROGRAMMING

The general linear programming (LP) problem is:

$$\text{Maximize } Z = c_1 x_1 + c_2 x_2 + \ldots + c_n x_n$$

Subject to:

$$a_{11} x_1 + a_{12} x_2 + \ldots + a_{1n} x_n \leq b_1$$
$$a_{21} x_1 + a_{22} x_2 + \ldots + a_{2n} x_n \leq b_2$$
$$\ldots$$
$$\ldots$$
$$a_{m1} x_1 + a_{m2} x_2 + \ldots + a_{mn} x_n \leq b_m$$
$$x_1, \ldots, x_n \geq 0$$

An LP problem is frequently reformulated by inserting non-negative slack and surplus variables. Although these variables usually have zero costs (depending on the application), they can have non-zero cost coefficients in the objective function. A slack variable is used with a "less than" inequality and transforms it into an equality. For example, the inequality $5x_1 + 3x_2 + 2x_3 \leq 5$ could be changed to $5x_1 + 3x_2 + 2x_3 + s_1 = 5$ if s_1 were chosen as a slack variable. The inequality $3x_1 + x_2 - 4x_3 \geq 10$ might be transformed into $3x_1 + x_2 - 4x_3 - s_2 = 10$ by the addition of the surplus variable s_2. Computer printouts of the results of processing and LP usually include values for all slack and surplus variables, the dual prices, and the reduced cost for each variable.

Dual Linear Program

Associated with the above linear programming problem is another problem called the dual linear programming problem. If we take the previous problem and call it the primal problem, then in matrix form the primal and dual problems are respectively:

Primal	Dual
Maximize $Z = \mathbf{cx}$	Minimize $W = \mathbf{yb}$
Subject to: $\mathbf{Ax} \leq \mathbf{b}$	Subject to: $\mathbf{yA} \geq \mathbf{c}$
$\mathbf{x} \geq 0$	$\mathbf{y} \geq 0$

It is assumed that if A is a matrix of size $[m \times n]$, then $\mathbf{y}$ is an $[1 \times m]$ vector, $\mathbf{c}$ is an $[1 \times n]$ vector, $\mathbf{b}$ is an $[m \times 1]$ vector, and $\mathbf{x}$ is an $[n \times 1]$ vector.

STATISTICAL QUALITY CONTROL

Average and Range Charts

n	A_2	D_3	D_4
2	1.880	0	3.268
3	1.023	0	2.574
4	0.729	0	2.282
5	0.577	0	2.114
6	0.483	0	2.004
7	0.419	0.076	1.924
8	0.373	0.136	1.864
9	0.337	0.184	1.816
10	0.308	0.223	1.777

X_i = an individual observation
n = the sample size of a group
k = the number of groups
R = (range) the difference between the largest and smallest observations in a sample of size n.

$$\overline{X} = \frac{X_1 + X_2 + \ldots + X_n}{n}$$

$$\overline{\overline{X}} = \frac{\overline{X}_1 + \overline{X}_2 + \ldots + \overline{X}_k}{k}$$

$$\overline{R} = \frac{R_1 + R_2 + \ldots + R_k}{k}$$

The R Chart formulas are:

$$CL_R = \overline{R}$$
$$UCL_R = D_4 \overline{R}$$
$$LCL_R = D_3 \overline{R}$$

The $\overline{X}$ Chart formulas are:

$$CL_X = \overline{\overline{X}}$$
$$UCL_X = \overline{\overline{X}} + A_2 \overline{R}$$
$$LCL_X = \overline{\overline{X}} - A_2 \overline{R}$$

Standard Deviation Charts

n	A_3	B_3	B_4
2	2.659	0	3.267
3	1.954	0	2.568
4	1.628	0	2.266
5	1.427	0	2.089
6	1.287	0.030	1.970
7	1.182	0.119	1.882
8	1.099	0.185	1.815
9	1.032	0.239	1.761
10	0.975	0.284	1.716

$$UCL_X = \overline{\overline{X}} + A_3 \overline{S}$$
$$CL_X = \overline{\overline{X}}$$
$$LCL_X = \overline{\overline{X}} - A_3 \overline{S}$$
$$UCL_S = B_4 \overline{S}$$
$$CL_S = \overline{S}$$
$$LCL_S = B_3 \overline{S}$$

Approximations

The following table and equations may be used to generate initial approximations of the items indicated.

n	c_4	d_2	d_3
2	0.7979	1.128	0.853
3	0.8862	1.693	0.888
4	0.9213	2.059	0.880
5	0.9400	2.326	0.864
6	0.9515	2.534	0.848
7	0.9594	2.704	0.833
8	0.9650	2.847	0.820
9	0.9693	2.970	0.808
10	0.9727	3.078	0.797

$$\hat{\sigma} = \overline{R}/d_2$$

$$\hat{\sigma} = \overline{S}/c_4$$

$$\sigma_R = d_3\hat{\sigma}$$

$$\sigma_s = \hat{\sigma}\sqrt{1 - c_4^2}, \text{ where}$$

$\hat{\sigma}$ = an estimate of σ,

σ_R = an estimate of the standard deviation of the ranges of the samples, and

σ_S = an estimate of the standard deviation of the standard deviations of the samples.

Tests for Out of Control

1. A single point falls outside the (three sigma) control limits.

2. Two out of three successive points fall on the same side of and more than two sigma units from the center line.

3. Four out of five successive points fall on the same side of and more than one sigma unit from the center line.

4. Eight successive points fall on the same side of the center line.

QUEUEING MODELS

Definitions

P_n = probability of n units in system,

L = expected number of units in the system,

L_q = expected number of units in the queue,

W = expected waiting time in system,

W_q = expected waiting time in queue,

λ = mean arrival rate (constant),

$\tilde{\lambda}$ = effective arrival rate,

μ = mean service rate (constant),

ρ = server utilization factor, and

s = number of servers.

Kendall notation for describing a queueing system:
$A / B / s / M$

A = the arrival process,

B = the service time distribution,

s = the number of servers, and

M = the total number of customers including those in service.

Fundamental Relationships

$$L = \lambda W$$

$$L_q = \lambda W_q$$

$$W = W_q + 1/\mu$$

$$\rho = \lambda/(s\mu)$$

Single Server Models ($s = 1$)

Poisson Input—Exponential Service Time: $M = \infty$

$$P_0 = 1 - \lambda/\mu = 1 - \rho$$

$$P_n = (1 - \rho)\rho^n = P_0\rho^n$$

$$L = \rho/(1 - \rho) = \lambda/(\mu - \lambda)$$

$$L_q = \lambda^2/[\mu\,(\mu - \lambda)]$$

$$W = 1/[\mu\,(1 - \rho)] = 1/(\mu - \lambda)$$

$$W_q = W - 1/\mu = \lambda/[\mu\,(\mu - \lambda)]$$

Finite queue: $M < \infty$

$$\tilde{\lambda} = \lambda(1 - P_n)$$

$$P_0 = (1 - \rho)/(1 - \rho^{M+1})$$

$$P_n = [(1 - \rho)/(1 - \rho^{M+1})]\rho^n$$

$$L = \rho/(1 - \rho) - (M + 1)\rho^{M+1}/(1 - \rho^{M+1})$$

$$L_q = L - (1 - P_0)$$

Poisson Input—Arbitrary Service Time

Variance σ^2 is known. For constant service time, $\sigma^2 = 0$.

$$P_0 = 1 - \rho$$

$$L_q = (\lambda^2\sigma^2 + \rho^2)/[2\,(1 - \rho)]$$

$$L = \rho + L_q$$

$$W_q = L_q / \lambda$$

$$W = W_q + 1/\mu$$

Poisson Input—Erlang Service Times, $\sigma^2 = 1/(k\mu^2)$

$$L_q = [(1 + k)/(2k)][(\lambda^2)/(\mu\,(\mu - \lambda))]$$

$$= [\lambda^2/(k\mu^2) + \rho^2]/[2(1 - \rho)]$$

$$W_q = [(1 + k)/(2k)]\{\lambda/[\mu\,(\mu - \lambda)]\}$$

$$W = W_q + 1/\mu$$

Multiple Server Model ($s > 1$)

Poisson Input—Exponential Service Times

$$P_0 = \left\{ \sum_{n=0}^{s-1} \frac{\left(\frac{\lambda}{\mu}\right)^n}{n!} + \frac{\left(\frac{\lambda}{\mu}\right)^s}{s!}\left[\frac{1}{1 - \frac{\lambda}{s\mu}}\right] \right\}^{-1}$$

$$= 1 \bigg/ \left[\sum_{n=0}^{s-1} \frac{(s\rho)^n}{n!} + \frac{(s\rho)^s}{s!(1 - \rho)} \right]$$

$$L_q = \frac{P_0\left(\frac{\lambda}{\mu}\right)^s \rho}{s!(1 - \rho)^2}$$

$$= \frac{P_0 s^s \rho^{s+1}}{s!(1 - \rho)^2}$$

$$P_n = P_0 (\lambda/\mu)^n/n! \qquad 0 \le n \le s$$

$$P_n = P_0 (\lambda/\mu)^n/(s!\, s^{n-s}) \quad n \ge s$$

$$W_q = L_q/\lambda$$

$$W = W_q + 1/\mu$$

$$L = L_q + \lambda/\mu$$

Calculations for P_0 and L_q can be time consuming; however, the following table gives formulas for 1, 2, and 3 servers.

s	P_0	L_q
1	$1 - \rho$	$\rho^2/(1 - \rho)$
2	$(1 - \rho)/(1 + \rho)$	$2\rho^3/(1 - \rho^2)$
3	$\dfrac{2(1-\rho)}{2 + 4\rho + 3\rho^2}$	$\dfrac{9\rho^4}{2 + 2\rho - \rho^2 - 3\rho^3}$

SIMULATION

1. Random Variate Generation

The linear congruential method of generating pseudo-random numbers U_i between 0 and 1 is obtained using $Z_n = (aZ_n+C) \ (\text{mod } m)$ where a, C, m, and Z_o are given non-negative integers and where $U_i = Z_i/m$. Two integers are equal (mod m) if their remainders are the same when divided by m.

2. Inverse Transform Method

If X is a continuous random variable with cumulative distribution function $F(x)$, and U_i is a uniform random number between 0 and 1, then the value of X_i corresponding to U_i can be calculated by solving $U_i = F(X_i)$ for X_i. The solution obtained is $X_i = F^{-1}(U_i)$, where F^{-1} is the inverse function of F.

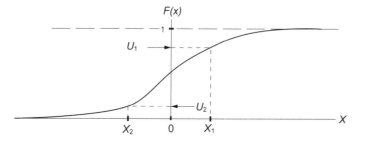

Inverse Transform Method for Continuous Random Variables

FORECASTING

Moving Average

$$\hat{d}_t = \frac{\sum\limits_{i=1}^{n} d_{t-i}}{n}, \text{ where}$$

$\hat{d}_t$ = forecasted demand for period t,

d_{t-i} = actual demand for ith period preceding t, and

n = number of time periods to include in the moving average.

Exponentially Weighted Moving Average

$$\hat{d}_t = \alpha d_{t-1} + (1 - \alpha)\,\hat{d}_{t-1}, \text{ where}$$

$\hat{d}_t$ = forecasted demand for t, and

α = smoothing constant, $0 \le \alpha \le 1$

LINEAR REGRESSION

Least Squares

$$y = \hat{a} + \hat{b}x, \text{ where}$$

y-intercept: $\hat{a} = \bar{y} - \hat{b}\bar{x}$,

and slope: $\hat{b} = SS_{xy}/SS_{xx}$,

$$S_{xy} = \sum_{i=1}^{n} x_i y_i - (1/n)\left(\sum_{i=1}^{n} x_i\right)\left(\sum_{i=1}^{n} y_i\right),$$

$$S_{xx} = \sum_{i=1}^{n} x_i^2 - (1/n)\left(\sum_{i=1}^{n} x_i\right)^2,$$

n = sample size,

$$\bar{y} = (1/n)\left(\sum_{i=1}^{n} y_i\right), \text{ and}$$

$$\bar{x} = (1/n)\left(\sum_{i=1}^{n} x_i\right).$$

Standard Error of Estimate

$$S_e^2 = \frac{S_{xx}S_{yy} - S_{xy}^2}{S_{xx}(n-2)} = MSE, \text{ where}$$

$$S_{yy} = \sum_{i=1}^{n} y_i^2 - (1/n)\left(\sum_{i=1}^{n} y_i\right)^2$$

Confidence Interval for a

$$\hat{a} \pm t_{\alpha/2, n-2}\sqrt{\left(\frac{1}{n} + \frac{\bar{x}^2}{S_{xx}}\right)MSE}$$

Confidence Interval for b

$$\hat{b} \pm t_{\alpha/2, n-2}\sqrt{\frac{MSE}{S_{xx}}}$$

Sample Correlation Coefficient

$$r = \frac{S_{xy}}{\sqrt{S_{xx}S_{yy}}}$$

2^n FACTORIAL EXPERIMENTS

Factors: $X_1, X_2, \ldots, X_n$

Levels of each factor: 1, 2 (sometimes these levels are represented by the symbols – and +, respectively)

r = number of observations for each experimental condition (treatment),

E_i = estimate of the effect of factor X_i, $i = 1, 2, \ldots, n$,

E_{ij} = estimate of the effect of the interaction between factors X_i and X_j,

$\overline{Y}_{ik}$ = average response value for all $r2^{n-1}$ observations having X_i set at level k, $k = 1, 2$, and

$\overline{Y}_{ij}^{km}$ = average response value for all $r2^{n-2}$ observations having X_i set at level k, $k = 1, 2$, and X_j set at level m, $m = 1, 2$.

$$E_i = \overline{Y}_{i2} - \overline{Y}_{i1}$$

$$E_{ij} = \frac{\left(\overline{Y}_{ij}^{22} - \overline{Y}_{ij}^{21}\right) - \left(\overline{Y}_{ij}^{12} - \overline{Y}_{ij}^{11}\right)}{2}$$

ONE-WAY ANALYSIS OF VARIANCE (ANOVA)

Given independent random samples of size n_i from k populations, then:

$$\sum_{i=1}^{k}\sum_{j=1}^{n_i}\left(x_{ij} - \overline{x}\right)^2$$

$$= \sum_{i=1}^{k}\sum_{j=1}^{n_i}\left(x_{ij} - \overline{x}\right)^2 + \sum_{i=1}^{k}n_i\left(\overline{x}_i - \overline{x}\right)^2 \quad \text{or}$$

$$SS_{\text{Total}} = SS_{\text{Error}} + SS_{\text{Treatments}}$$

Let T be the grand total of all $N = \Sigma_i n_i$ observations and T_i be the total of the n_i observations of the ith sample. See the One-Way ANOVA table on page 159.

$$C = T^2/N$$

$$SS_{\text{Total}} = \sum_{i=1}^{k}\sum_{j=1}^{n_i}x_{ij}^2 - C$$

$$SS_{\text{Treatments}} = \sum_{i=1}^{k}\left(T_i^2/n_i\right) - C$$

$$SS_{\text{Error}} = SS_{\text{Total}} - SS_{\text{Treatments}}$$

RANDOMIZED BLOCK DESIGN

The experimental material is divided into n randomized blocks. One observation is taken at random for every treatment within the same block. The total number of observations is $N = nk$. The total value of these observations is equal to T. The total value of observations for treatment i is T_i. The total value of observations in block j is B_j.

$$C = T^2/N$$

$$SS_{\text{Total}} = \sum_{i=1}^{k}\sum_{j=1}^{n}x_{ij}^2 - C$$

$$SS_{\text{Blocks}} = \sum_{j=1}^{n}\left(B_j^2/k\right) - C$$

$$SS_{\text{Treatments}} = \sum_{i=1}^{k}\left(T_i^2/n\right) - C$$

$$SS_{\text{Error}} = SS_{\text{Total}} - SS_{\text{Blocks}} - SS_{\text{Treatments}}$$

See Two-Way ANOVA table on page 159.

ANALYSIS OF VARIANCE FOR 2^n FACTORIAL DESIGNS

Main Effects

Let E be the estimate of the effect of a given factor, let L be the orthogonal contrast belonging to this effect. It can be proved that

$$E = \frac{L}{2^{n-1}}$$

$$L = \sum_{c=1}^{m}a_{(c)}\overline{Y}_{(c)}$$

$$SS_L = \frac{rL^2}{2^n}, \text{ where}$$

m = number of experimental conditions ($m = 2^n$ for n factors),

$a_{(c)}$ = -1 if the factor is set at its low level (level 1) in experimental condition c,

$a_{(c)}$ = $+1$ if the factor is set at its high level (level 2) in experimental condition c,

r = number of replications for each experimental condition

$\overline{Y}_{(c)}$ = average response value for experimental condition c, and

SS_L = sum of squares associated with the factor.

Interaction Effects

Consider any group of two or more factors.

$a_{(c)} = +1$ if there is an even number (or zero) of factors in the group set at the low level (level 1) in experimental condition $c = 1, 2, \ldots, m$

$a_{(c)} = -1$ if there is an odd number of factors in the group set at the low level (level 1) in experimental condition $c = 1, 2 \ldots, m$

It can be proved that the interaction effect E for the factors in the group and the corresponding sum of squares SS_L can be determined as follows:

$$E = \frac{L}{2^{n-1}}$$

$$L = \sum_{c=1}^{m} a_{(c)} \overline{Y}_{(c)}$$

$$SS_L = \frac{rL^2}{2^n}$$

Sum of Squares of Random Error

The sum of the squares due to the random error can be computed as

$$SS_{\text{error}} = SS_{\text{total}} - \Sigma_i SS_i - \Sigma_i \Sigma_j SS_{ij} - \ldots - SS_{12\ldots n}$$

where SS_i is the sum of squares due to factor X_i, SS_{ij} is the sum of squares due to the interaction of factors X_i and X_j, and so on. The total sum of squares is equal to

$$SS_{total} = \sum_{c=1}^{m} \sum_{k=1}^{r} Y_{ck}^2 - \frac{T^2}{N}$$

where Y_{ck}, is the kth observation taken for the cth experimental condition, $m = 2^n$, T is the grand total of all observations, and $N = r2^n$.

RELIABILITY

If P_i is the probability that component i is functioning, a reliability function $R(P_1, P_2, .., P_n)$ represents the probability that a system consisting of n components will work.

For n independent components connected in series,

$$R(P_1, P_2, \ldots P_n) = \prod_{i=1}^{n} P_i$$

For n independent components connected in parallel,

$$R(P_1, P_2, \ldots Pn) = 1 - \prod_{i=1}^{n} (1 - P_i)$$

LEARNING CURVES

The time to do the repetition N of a task is given by

$$T_N = KN^s, \text{ where}$$

K = constant, and

s = ln (learning rate, as a decimal)/ln 2.

If N units are to be produced, the average time per unit is given by

$$T_{\text{avg}} = \frac{K}{N(1+s)} \left[(N + 0.5)^{(1+s)} - 0.5^{(1+s)} \right]$$

INVENTORY MODELS

For instantaneous replenishment (with constant demand rate, known holding and ordering costs, and an infinite stockout cost), the economic order quantity is given by

$$EOQ = \sqrt{\frac{2AD}{h}}, \text{ where}$$

A = cost to place one order,

D = number of units used per year, and

h = holding cost per unit per year.

Under the same conditions as above with a finite replenishment rate, the economic manufacturing quantity is given by

$$EMQ = \sqrt{\frac{2AD}{h(1 - D/R)}}, \text{ where}$$

R = the replenishment rate.

ERGONOMICS

NIOSH Formula

Recommended Weight Limit (U.S. Customary Units)

$= 51(10/H)(1 - 0.0075|V - 30|)(0.82 + 1.8/D)(1 - 0.0032A)$

where

H = horizontal distance of the hand from the midpoint of the line joining the inner ankle bones to a point projected on the floor directly below the load center,

V = vertical distance of the hands from the floor,

D = vertical travel distance of the hands between the origin and destination of the lift, and

A = asymmetric angle, in degrees.

The NIOSH formula as stated here assumes that (1) lifting frequency is no greater than one lift every 5 minutes; (2) the person can get a good grip on the object being lifted.

Biomechanics of the Human Body

Basic Equations

$$H_x + F_x = 0$$
$$H_y + F_y = 0$$
$$H_z + F_z = 0$$
$$T_{Hxz} + T_{Fxz} = 0$$
$$T_{Hyz} + T_{Fyz} = 0$$
$$T_{Hxy} + T_{Fxy} = 0$$

The coefficient of friction μ and the angle α at which the floor is inclined determine the equations at the foot.

$$F_x = \mu F_z$$

With the slope angle α

$$F_x = \mu F_z \cos \alpha$$

Of course, when motion must be considered, dynamic conditions come into play according to Newton's Second Law. Force transmitted with the hands is counteracted at the foot. Further, the body must also react with internal forces at all points between the hand and the foot.

PERMISSIBLE NOISE EXPOSURES *

Duration per day, hours	Sound level, dBA
8	90
6	92
4	95
3	97
2	100
1 1/2	102
1	105
1/2	110
1/4 or less	115

* Exposure to impulsive or impact noise should not exceed 140 dB peak sound pressure level.

FACILITY PLANNING

Equipment Requirements

P_{ij} = desired production rate for product i on machine j, measured in pieces per production period,

T_{ij} = production time for product i on machine j, measured in hours per piece,

C_{ij} = number of hours in the production period available for the production of product i on machine j,

M_j = number of machines of type j required per production period, and

n = number of products.

Therefore, M_j can be expressed as

$$M_j = \sum_{i=1}^{n} \frac{P_{ij}T_{ij}}{C_{ij}}$$

People Requirements

$$A_j = \sum_{i=1}^{n} \frac{P_{ij}T_{ij}}{C_{ij}}, \text{ where}$$

A_j = number of crews required for assembly operation j,

P_{ij} = desired production rate for product i and assembly operation j (pieces per day),

T_{ij} = standard time to perform operation j on product i (minutes per piece),

C_{ij} = number of minutes available per day for assembly operation j on product i, and

n = number of products.

Standard Time Determination

$$ST = NT \times AF$$

where

NT = normal time, and

AF = allowance factor.

<u>Case 1</u>: Allowances are based on the *job time*.

$$AF_{\text{job}} = 1 + A_{\text{job}}$$

A_{job} = allowance fraction (percentage) based on *job time*.

<u>Case 2</u>: Allowances are based on *workday*.

$$AF_{\text{time}} = 1/(1 - A_{\text{day}})$$

A_{day} = allowance fraction (percentage) based on *workday*.

Plant Location

The following is one formulation of a discrete plant location problem.

Minimize

$$z = \sum_{i=1}^{m}\sum_{j=1}^{n} c_{ij}y_{ij} + \sum_{j=1}^{n} f_j x_j$$

subject to

$$\sum_{i=1}^{m} y_{ij} \le mx_j, \quad j = 1,\ldots,n$$

$$\sum_{j=1}^{n} y_{ij} = 1, \quad i = 1,\ldots,m$$

$$y_{ij} \ge 0, \text{ for all } i, j$$

$$x_j = (0, 1), \text{ for all } j, \text{ where}$$

m = number of customers,

n = number of possible plant sites,

y_{ij} = fraction or portion of the demand of customer i which is satisfied by a plant located at site j; $i = 1, \ldots, m; j = 1, \ldots, n$,

x_j = 1, if a plant is located at site j,

x_j = 0, otherwise,

c_{ij} = cost of supplying the entire demand of customer i from a plant located at site j, and

f_j = fixed cost resulting from locating a plant at site j.

Material Handling

Distances between two points (x_1, y_1) and (x_1, y_1) under different metrics:

Euclidean:

$$D = \sqrt{(x_1 - x_2)^2 + (y_1 - y_2)^2}$$

Rectilinear (or Manhattan):

$$D = |x_1 - x_2| + |y_1 - y_2|$$

Chebyshev (simultaneous x and y movement):

$$D = \max(|x_1 - x_2|, |y_1 - y_2|)$$

Line Balancing

$$N_{\min} = \left(OR \times \sum_i t_i \Big/ OT \right)$$

$$= \text{Theoretical minimum number of stations}$$

Idle Time/Station $= CT - ST$

Idle Time/Cycle $= \Sigma (CT - ST)$

$$\text{Percent Idle Time} = \frac{\text{Idle Time/Cycle}}{N_{\text{actual}} \times CT} \times 100, \text{ where}$$

$CT =$ cycle time (time between units),

$OT =$ operating time/period,

$OR =$ output rate/period,

$ST =$ station time (time to complete task at each station),

$t_i =$ individual task times, and

$N =$ number of stations.

Job Sequencing

Two Work Centers—Johnson's Rule

1. Select the job with the shortest time, from the list of jobs, and its time at each work center.
2. If the shortest job time is the time at the first work center, schedule it first, otherwise schedule it last. Break ties arbitrarily.
3. Eliminate that job from consideration.
4. Repeat 1, 2, and 3 until all jobs have been scheduled.

CRITICAL PATH METHOD (CPM)

$d_{ij} =$ duration of activity (i, j),

$CP =$ critical path (longest path),

$T =$ duration of project, and

$$T = \sum_{(i,j) \in CP} d_{ij}$$

PERT

$(a_{ij}, b_{ij}, c_{ij}) =$ (optimistic, most likely, pessimistic) durations for activity (i, j),

$\mu_{ij} =$ mean duration of activity (i, j),

$\sigma_{ij} =$ standard deviation of the duration of activity (i, j),

$\mu =$ project mean duration, and

$\sigma =$ standard deviation of project duration.

$$\mu_{ij} = \frac{a_{ij} + 4b_{ij} + c_{ij}}{6}$$

$$\sigma_{ij} = \frac{c_{ij} - a_{ij}}{6}$$

$$\mu = \sum_{(i,j) \in CP} \mu_{ij}$$

$$\sigma^2 = \sum_{(i,j) \in CP} \sigma_{ij}^2$$

MACHINING FORMULAS

Material Removal Rate Formulas

1. Drilling:

$$MRR = (\pi/4) D^2 f N, \text{ where}$$

$D =$ drill diameter,

$f =$ feed rate, and

$N =$ rpm of the drill.

$$\text{Power} = MRR \times \text{specific power}$$

2. Slab Milling:

Cutting speed is the peripheral speed of the cutter

$$V = \pi D N, \text{ where}$$

$D =$ cutter diameter, and

$N =$ cutter rpm.

Feed per tooth f is given by

$$f = v/(Nn), \text{ where}$$

$v =$ workpiece speed and

$n =$ number of teeth on the cutter.

$$t = (l + l_c)/v, \text{ where}$$

$t =$ cutting time,

$l =$ length of workpiece, and

$l_c =$ additional length of cutter's travel

$= \sqrt{Dd}$ (approximately).

If $l_c \ll l$

$$MRR = lwd/t, \text{ where}$$

$d =$ depth of cut,

$w =$ min (width of the cut, length of cutter), and cutting time $= t = l/v$.

3. Face Milling:

$$MRR = \text{width} \times \text{depth of cut} \times \text{workpiece speed}$$

$$\text{Cutting time} = \frac{(\text{workpiece length} + \text{tool clearance})}{\text{workpiece speed}}$$

$$= (l + 2l_c)/V$$

Feed (per tooth) $= V/(Nn)$

$l_c =$ tool travel necessary to completely clear the workpiece; usually $=$ tool diameter/2.

Taylor Tool Life Formula

$VT^n = C$, where

V = speed in surface feet per minute,

T = time before the tool reaches a certain percentage of possible wear, and

C, n = constants that depend on the material and on the tool.

Work Sampling Formulas

$$D = Z_{\alpha/2}\sqrt{\frac{p(1-p)}{n}} \quad \text{and} \quad R = Z_{\alpha/2}\sqrt{\frac{1-p}{pn}}, \text{ where}$$

p = proportion of observed time in an activity,

D = absolute error,

R = relative error $(R = D/p)$, and

n = sample size.

ONE-WAY ANOVA TABLE

Source of Variation	Degrees of Freedom	Sum of Squares	Mean Square	F
Between Treatments	$k-1$	$SS_{Treatments}$	$MST = \dfrac{SS_{Treatments}}{k-1}$	$\dfrac{MST}{MSE}$
Error	$N-k$	SS_{Error}	$MSE = \dfrac{SS_{Error}}{N-k}$	
Total	$N-1$	SS_{Total}		

TWO-WAY ANOVA TABLE

Source of Variation	Degrees of Freedom	Sum of Squares	Mean Square	F
Between Treatments	$k-1$	$SS_{Treatments}$	$MST = \dfrac{SS_{Treatments}}{k-1}$	$\dfrac{MST}{MSE}$
Between Blocks	$n-1$	SS_{Blocks}	$MSB = \dfrac{SS_{Blocks}}{n-1}$	$\dfrac{MSB}{MSE}$
Error	$(k-1)(n-1)$	SS_{Error}	$MSE = \dfrac{SS_{Error}}{(k-1)(n-1)}$	
Total	$N-1$	SS_{Total}		

PROBABILITY AND DENSITY FUNCTIONS: MEANS AND VARIANCES

Variable	Equation	Mean	Variance
Binomial Coefficient	$\binom{n}{x} = \dfrac{n!}{x!(n-x)!}$		
Binomial	$b(x;n,p) = \binom{n}{x} p^x (1-p)^{n-x}$	np	$np(1-p)$
Hyper Geometric	$h(x;n,r,N) = \binom{r}{x} \dfrac{\binom{N-r}{n-x}}{\binom{N}{n}}$	$\dfrac{nr}{N}$	$\dfrac{r(N-r)n(N-n)}{N^2(N-1)}$
Poisson	$f(x;\lambda) = \dfrac{\lambda^x e^{-\lambda}}{x!}$	λ	λ
Geometric	$g(x;p) = p\,(1-p)^{x-1}$	$1/p$	$(1-p)/p^2$
Negative Binomial	$f(y;r,p) = \binom{y+r-1}{r-1} p^r (1-p)^y$	r/p	$r\,(1-p)/p^2$
Multinomial	$f(x_1,\dots x_k) = \dfrac{n!}{x_1!,\dots,x_k!} p_1^{x_1} \cdots p_k^{x_k}$	np_i	$np_i\,(1-p_i)$
Uniform	$f(x) = 1/(b-a)$	$(a+b)/2$	$(b-a)^2/12$
Gamma	$f(x) = \dfrac{x^{\alpha-1} e^{-x/\beta}}{\beta^\alpha \Gamma(\alpha)};\quad \alpha > 0, \beta > 0$	$\alpha\beta$	$\alpha\beta^2$
Exponential	$f(x) = \dfrac{1}{\beta} e^{-x/\beta}$	β	β^2
Weibull	$f(x) = \dfrac{\alpha}{\beta} x^{\alpha-1} e^{-x^\alpha/\beta}$	$\beta^{1/\alpha} \Gamma[(\alpha+1)/\alpha]$	$\beta^{2/\alpha}\left[\Gamma\left(\dfrac{\alpha+1}{\alpha}\right) - \Gamma^2\left(\dfrac{\alpha+1}{\alpha}\right) \right]$
Normal	$f(x) = \dfrac{1}{\sigma\sqrt{2\pi}} e^{-\frac{1}{2}\left(\frac{x-\mu}{\sigma}\right)^2}$	μ	σ^2
Triangular	$f(x) = \begin{cases} \dfrac{2(x-a)}{(b-a)(m-a)} & \text{if } a \le x \le m \\ \dfrac{2(b-x)}{(b-a)(b-m)} & \text{if } m < x \le b \end{cases}$	$\dfrac{a+b+m}{3}$	$\dfrac{a^2+b^2+m^2-ab-am-bm}{18}$

Hypothesis Testing

Table *A*. Tests on means of normal distribution—variance known.

Hypothesis	Test Statistic	Criteria for Rejection
$H_0: \mu = \mu_0$ $H_1: \mu \neq \mu_0$		$\|Z_0\| > Z_{\alpha/2}$
$H_0: \mu = \mu_0$ $H_0: \mu < \mu_0$	$Z_0 = (\bar{y} - \mu_0)\left(\dfrac{\sigma}{n^{1/2}}\right)^{-1}$	$Z_0 < -Z_\alpha$
$H_0: \mu = \mu_0$ $H_1: \mu > \mu_0$		$Z_0 > Z_\alpha$
$H_0: \mu_1 - \mu_2 = \gamma$ $H_1: \mu_1 - \mu_2 \neq \gamma$		$\|Z_0\| > Z_{\alpha/2}$
$H_0: \mu_1 - \mu_2 = \gamma$ $H_1: \mu_1 - \mu_2 < \gamma$	$Z_0 = [(\bar{y}_1 - \bar{y}_2) - \gamma]\left(\dfrac{\sigma_1^2}{n_1} + \dfrac{\sigma_2^2}{n_2}\right)^{-1/2}$	$Z_0 < -Z_\alpha$
$H_0: \mu_1 - \mu_2 = \gamma$ $H_1: \mu_1 - \mu_2 > \gamma$		$Z_0 > Z_\alpha$

Table *B*. Tests on means of normal distribution—variance unknown.

Hypothesis	Test Statistic	Criteria for Rejection
$H_0: \mu = \mu_0$ $H_1: \mu \neq \mu_0$		$\|t_0\| > t_{\alpha/2,\, n-1}$
$H_0: \mu = \mu_0$ $H_1: \mu < \mu_0$	$t_0 = (\bar{y} - \mu_0)\left(\dfrac{S}{n^{1/2}}\right)^{-1}$	$t_0 < -t_{\alpha,\, n-1}$
$H_0: \mu = \mu_0$ $H_1: \mu > \mu_0$		$t_0 > t_{\alpha,\, n-1}$
$H_0: \mu_1 - \mu_2 = \gamma$ $H_1: \mu_1 - \mu_2 \neq \gamma$	$t_0 = (\bar{y}_1 - \bar{y}_2 - \gamma)\left[S_p\left(\dfrac{1}{n_1} + \dfrac{1}{n_2}\right)^{1/2}\right]^{-1}$ $v = n_1 + n_2 - 2$	$\|t_0\| > t_{\alpha/2,\, v}$
$H_0: \mu_1 - \mu_2 = \gamma$ $H_1: \mu_1 - \mu_2 < \gamma$	$t_0 = (\bar{y}_1 - \bar{y}_2 - \gamma)\left(\dfrac{S_1^2}{n_1} + \dfrac{S_2^2}{n_2}\right)^{-1/2}$	$t_0 < -t_{\alpha,\, v}$
$H_0: \mu_1 - \mu_2 = \gamma$ $H_1: \mu_1 - \mu_2 > \gamma$	$v = \left(\dfrac{S_1^2}{n_1} + \dfrac{S_2^2}{n_2}\right)^2 \left[\dfrac{\left(S_1^2 n_1^{-1}\right)^2}{n_1 - 1} + \dfrac{\left(S_2^2 n_2^{-1}\right)^2}{n_2 - 1}\right]^{-1}$	$t_0 > t_{\alpha,\, v}$

In Table B, $S_p^2 = [(n_1 - 1)S_1^2 + (n_2 - 1)S_2^2]/v$

Table *C*. Tests on variances of normal distribution with unknown mean.

Hypothesis	Test Statistic	Criteria for Rejection
H_0: $\sigma^2 = \sigma_0^2$ H_1: $\sigma^2 \neq \sigma_0^2$		$\chi_0^2 > \chi_{\alpha/2,n-1}^2$ or $\chi_0^2 < \chi_{1-\alpha/2,n-1}^2$
H_0: $\sigma^2 = \sigma_0^2$ H_1: $\sigma^2 < \sigma_0^2$	$\chi_0^2 = \dfrac{(n-1)S^2}{\sigma_0^2}$	$\chi_0^2 < \chi_{1-\alpha/2,\,n-1}^2$
H_0: $\sigma^2 = \sigma_0^2$ H_1: $\sigma^2 > \sigma_0^2$		$\chi_0^2 > \chi_{\alpha,\,n-1}^2$
H_0: $\sigma_1^2 = \sigma_2^2$ H_1: $\sigma_1^2 \neq \sigma_2^2$	$F_0 = \dfrac{S_1^2}{S_2^2}$	$F_0 > F_{\alpha/2,\,n_1-1,\,n_2-1}$ $F_0 < F_{1-\alpha/2,\,n_1-1,\,n_2-1}$
H_0: $\sigma_1^2 = \sigma_2^2$ H_1: $\sigma_1^2 < \sigma_2^2$	$F_0 = \dfrac{S_2^2}{S_1^2}$	$F_0 > F_{\alpha,\,n_2-1,\,n_1-1}$
H_0: $\sigma_1^2 = \sigma_2^2$ H_1: $\sigma_1^2 > \sigma_2^2$	$F_0 = \dfrac{S_1^2}{S_2^2}$	$F_0 > F_{\alpha,\,n_1-1,\,n_2-1}$

ANTHROPOMETRIC MEASUREMENTS

(AFTER SANDERS AND McCORMICK,
HUMAN FACTORS IN DESIGN, McGRAW HILL, 1987)

162

ERGONOMICS

US Civilian Body Dimensions, Female/Male, for Ages 20 to 60 Years (Centimeters)				
(See Anthropometric Measurements Figure)	Percentiles			
	5th	50th	95th	Std. Dev.
HEIGHTS				
Stature (height)	149.5 / 161.8	160.5 / 173.6	171.3 / 184.4	6.6 / 6.9
Eye height	138.3 / 151.1	148.9 / 162.4	159.3 / 172.7	6.4 / 6.6
Shoulder (acromion) height	121.1 / 132.3	131.1 / 142.8	141.9 / 152.4	6.1 / 6.1
Elbow height	93.6 / 100.0	101.2 / 109.9	108.8 / 119.0	4.6 / 5.8
Knuckle height	**64.3 / 69.8**	**70.2 / 75.4**	**75.9 / 80.4**	**3.5 / 3.2**
Height, sitting	78.6 / 84.2	85.0 / 90.6	90.7 / 96.7	3.5 / 3.7
Eye height, sitting	67.5 / 72.6	73.3 / 78.6	78.5 / 84.4	3.3 / 3.6
Shoulder height, sitting	49.2 / 52.7	55.7 / 59.4	61.7 / 65.8	3.8 / 4.0
Elbow rest height, sitting	18.1 / 19.0	23.3 / 24.3	28.1 / 29.4	2.9 / 3.0
Knee height, sitting	**45.2 / 49.3**	**49.8 / 54.3**	**54.5 / 59.3**	**2.7 / 2.9**
Popliteal height, sitting	35.5 / 39.2	39.8 / 44.2	44.3 / 48.8	2.6 / 2.8
Thigh clearance height	10.6 / 11.4	13.7 / 14.4	17.5 / 17.7	1.8 / 1.7
DEPTHS				
Chest depth	21.4 / 21.4	24.2 / 24.2	29.7 / 27.6	2.5 / 1.9
Elbow-fingertip distance	38.5 / 44.1	42.1 / 47.9	46.0 / 51.4	2.2 / 2.2
Buttock-knee distance, sitting	51.8 / 54.0	56.9 / 59.4	62.5 / 64.2	3.1 / 3.0
Buttock-popliteal distance, sitting	43.0 / 44.2	48.1 / 49.5	53.5 / 54.8	3.1 / 3.0
Forward reach, functional	64.0 / 76.3	71.0 / 82.5	79.0 / 88.3	4.5 / 5.0
BREADTHS				
Elbow-to-elbow breadth	31.5 / 35.0	38.4 / 41.7	49.1 / 50.6	5.4 / 4.6
Hip breadth, sitting	31.2 / 30.8	36.4 / 35.4	43.7 / 40.6	3.7 / 2.8
HEAD DIMENSIONS				
Head breadth	13.6 / 14.4	14.54 / 15.42	15.5 / 16.4	0.57 / 0.59
Head circumference	52.3 / 53.8	54.9 / 56.8	57.7 / 59.3	1.63 / 1.68
Interpupillary distance	5.1 / 5.5	5.83 / 6.20	6.5 / 6.8	0.4 / 0.39
HAND DIMENSIONS				
Hand length	16.4 / 17.6	17.95 / 19.05	19.8 / 20.6	1.04 / 0.93
Breadth, metacarpal	7.0 / 8.2	7.66 / 8.88	8.4 / 9.8	0.41 / 0.47
Circumference, metacarpal	16.9 / 19.9	18.36 / 21.55	19.9 / 23.5	0.89 / 1.09
Thickness, metacarpal III	2.5 / 2.4	2.77 / 2.76	3.1 / 3.1	0.18 / 0.21
Digit 1				
Breadth, interphalangeal	1.7 / 2.1	1.98 / 2.29	2.1 / 2.5	0.12 / 0.13
Crotch-tip length	4.7 / 5.1	5.36 / 5.88	6.1 / 6.6	0.44 / 0.45
Digit 2				
Breadth, distal joint	1.4 / 1.7	1.55 / 1.85	1.7 / 2.0	0.10 / 0.12
Crotch-tip length	6.1 / 6.8	6.88 / 7.52	7.8 / 8.2	0.52 / 0.46
Digit 3				
Breadth, distal joint	1.4 / 1.7	1.53 / 1.85	1.7 / 2.0	0.09 / 0.12
Crotch-tip length	7.0 / 7.8	7.77 / 8.53	8.7 / 9.5	0.51 / 0.51
Digit 4				
Breadth, distal joint	1.3 / 1.6	1.42 / 1.70	1.6 / 1.9	0.09 / 0.11
Crotch-tip length	6.5 / 7.4	7.29 / 7.99	8.2 / 8.9	0.53 / 0.47
Digit 5				
Breadth, distal joint	1.2 / 1.4	1.32 / 1.57	1.5 / 1.8	0.09/0.12
Crotch-tip length	4.8 / 5.4	5.44 / 6.08	6.2 / 6.99	0.44/0.47
FOOT DIMENSIONS				
Foot length	22.3 / 24.8	24.1 / 26.9	26.2 / 29.0	1.19 / 1.28
Foot breadth	8.1 / 9.0	8.84 / 9.79	9.7 / 10.7	0.50 / 0.53
Lateral malleolus height	5.8 / 6.2	6.78 / 7.03	7.8 / 8.0	0.59 / 0.54
Weight (kg)	46.2 / 56.2	61.1 / 74.0	89.9 / 97.1	13.8 / 12.6

ERGONOMICS—HEARING

The average shifts with age of the threshold of hearing for pure tones of persons with "normal" hearing, using a 25-year-old group as a reference group.

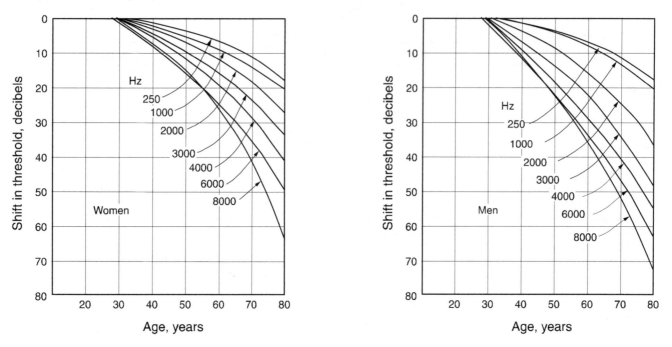

Equivalent sound-level contours used in determining the A-weighted sound level on the basis of an octave-band analysis. The curve at the point of the highest penetration of the noise spectrum reflects the A-weighted sound level.

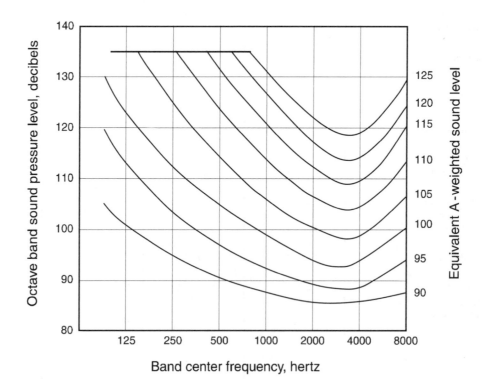

Estimated average trend curves for net hearing loss at 1,000, 2,000, and 4,000 Hz after continuous exposure to steady noise. Data are corrected for age, but not for temporary threshold shift. Dotted portions of curves represent extrapolation from available data.

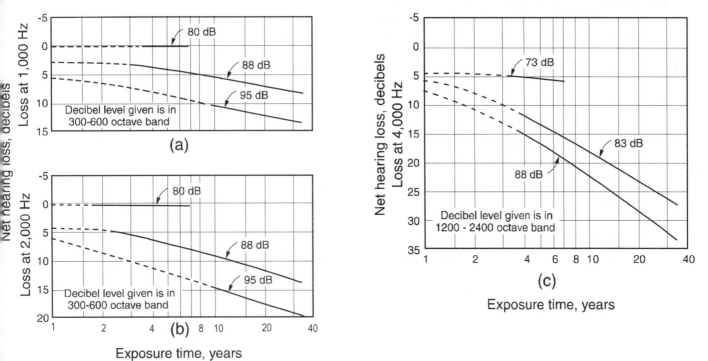

Tentative upper limit of effective temperature (ET) for unimpaired mental performance as related to exposure time; data are based on an analysis of 15 studies. Comparative curves of tolerable and marginal physiological limits are also given.

165

MECHANICAL ENGINEERING

Examinees should also review the material in sections titled **HEAT TRANSFER, THERMODYNAMICS, TRANSPORT PHENOMENA, FLUID MECHANICS,** and **COMPUTERS, MEASUREMENT, AND CONTROLS.**

REFRIGERATION AND HVAC
Two-Stage Cycle

The following equations are valid if the mass flows are the same in each stage.

$$\text{COP}_{\text{ref}} = \frac{\dot{Q}_{\text{in}}}{\dot{W}_{\text{in,1}} + \dot{W}_{\text{in,2}}} = \frac{h_5 - h_8}{h_2 - h_1 + h_6 - h_5}$$

$$\text{COP}_{\text{HP}} = \frac{\dot{Q}_{\text{out}}}{\dot{W}_{\text{in,1}} + \dot{W}_{\text{in,2}}} = \frac{h_2 - h_3}{h_2 - h_1 + h_6 - h_5}$$

Air Refrigeration Cycle

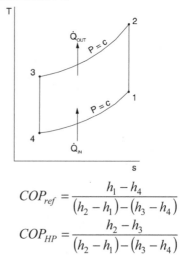

$$COP_{ref} = \frac{h_1 - h_4}{(h_2 - h_1) - (h_3 - h_4)}$$

$$COP_{HP} = \frac{h_2 - h_3}{(h_2 - h_1) - (h_3 - h_4)}$$

(see also **THERMODYNAMICS** section)

HVAC—Pure Heating and Cooling

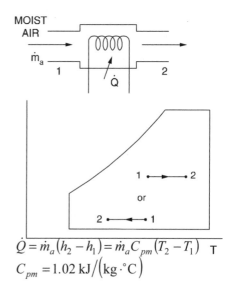

$$\dot{Q} = \dot{m}_a (h_2 - h_1) = \dot{m}_a C_{pm}(T_2 - T_1)$$
$$C_{pm} = 1.02 \text{ kJ}/(\text{kg} \cdot °\text{C})$$

Cooling and Dehumidification

166

Adiabatic Mixing

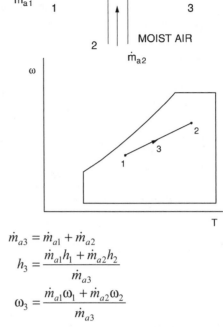

$$\dot{Q}_{out} = \dot{m}_a\left[(h_1 - h_2) - h_{f3}(\omega_1 - \omega_2)\right]$$
$$\dot{m}_w = \dot{m}_a(\omega_1 - \omega_2)$$

Heating and Humidification

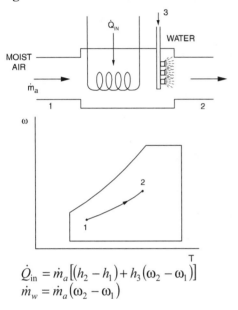

$$\dot{Q}_{in} = \dot{m}_a\left[(h_2 - h_1) + h_3(\omega_2 - \omega_1)\right]$$
$$\dot{m}_w = \dot{m}_a(\omega_2 - \omega_1)$$

$$\dot{m}_{a3} = \dot{m}_{a1} + \dot{m}_{a2}$$
$$h_3 = \frac{\dot{m}_{a1}h_1 + \dot{m}_{a2}h_2}{\dot{m}_{a3}}$$
$$\omega_3 = \frac{\dot{m}_{a1}\omega_1 + \dot{m}_{a2}\omega_2}{\dot{m}_{a3}}$$

distance $\overline{13} = \dfrac{\dot{m}_{a2}}{\dot{m}_{a3}} \times$ distance $\overline{12}$ measured on psychrometric chart

Heating Load
(see also **HEAT TRANSFER** section)

$$\dot{Q} = A(T_i - T_o)/R''$$
$$R'' = \frac{1}{h_1} + \frac{L_1}{k_1} + \frac{L_2}{k_2} + \frac{L_3}{k_3} + \frac{1}{h_2}, \text{ where}$$

$\dot{Q}$ = heat transfer rate,

A = wall surface area, and

R'' = thermal resistance.

Overall heat transfer coefficient = U

$$U = 1/R''$$
$$\dot{Q} = UA(T_i - T_o)$$

Adiabatic Humidification (evaporative cooling)

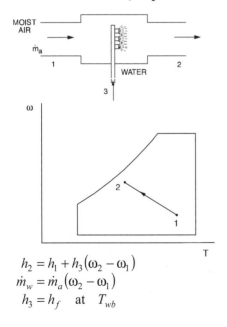

$$h_2 = h_1 + h_3(\omega_2 - \omega_1)$$
$$\dot{m}_w = \dot{m}_a(\omega_2 - \omega_1)$$
$$h_3 = h_f \text{ at } T_{wb}$$

Cooling Load

$$\dot{Q} = UA \, (\text{CLTD}), \text{ where}$$

CLTD = effective temperature difference.

CLTD depends on solar heating rate, wall or roof orientation, color, and time of day.

Infiltration

Air change method

$$\dot{Q} = \frac{\rho_a c_p V n_{AC}}{3,600} \left(T_i - T_o \right), \text{ where}$$

ρ_a = air density,

c_P = air specific heat,

V = room volume,

n_{AC} = number of air changes per hour,

T_i = indoor temperature, and

T_o = outdoor temperature.

Crack method

$$\dot{Q} = 1.2 CL \left(T_i - T_o \right)$$

where

C = coefficient, and

L = crack length.

FANS, PUMPS, AND COMPRESSORS

Scaling Laws

(see page 44 on Similitude)

$$\left(\frac{Q}{ND^3} \right)_2 = \left(\frac{Q}{ND^3} \right)_1$$

$$\left(\frac{\dot{m}}{\rho ND^3} \right)_2 = \left(\frac{\dot{m}}{\rho ND^3} \right)_1$$

$$\left(\frac{H}{N^2 D^2} \right)_2 = \left(\frac{H}{N^2 D^2} \right)_1$$

$$\left(\frac{P}{\rho N^2 D^2} \right)_2 = \left(\frac{P}{\rho N^2 D^2} \right)_1$$

$$\left(\frac{\dot{W}}{\rho N^3 D^5} \right)_2 = \left(\frac{\dot{W}}{\rho N^3 D^5} \right)_1$$

where

Q = volumetric flow rate,

$\dot{m}$ = mass flow rate,

H = head,

P = pressure rise,

$\dot{W}$ = power,

ρ = fluid density,

N = rotational speed, and

D = impeller diameter.

Subscripts 1 and 2 refer to different but similar machines or to different operating conditions of the same machine.

Fan Characteristics

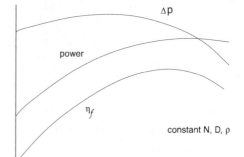

Typical Fan Curves
backward curved

$$\dot{W} = \frac{\Delta P Q}{\eta_f}, \text{ where}$$

$\dot{W}$ = fan power,

ΔP = pressure rise, and

η_f = fan efficiency.

Pump Characteristics

Net Positive Suction Head (*NPSH*)

$$NPSH = \frac{P_i}{\rho g} + \frac{V_i^2}{2g} - \frac{P_v}{\rho g}, \text{ where}$$

P_i = inlet pressure to pump,

V_i = velocity at inlet to pump, and

P_v = vapor pressure of fluid being pumped.

$$\dot{W} = \frac{\rho g H Q}{\eta}, \text{ where}$$

$\dot{W}$ = pump power,

η = pump efficiency, and

H = head increase.

Compressor Characteristics

where

$\dot{m}$ = mass flow rate and

P_e/P_i = exit to inlet pressure ratio.

$$\dot{W} = \dot{m}\left(h_e - h_i + \frac{V_e^2 - V_i^2}{2} \right)$$

$$= \dot{m}\left(c_p\left(T_e - T_i\right) + \frac{V_e^2 - V_i^2}{2} \right)$$

where

$\dot{W}$ = input power,

h_e, h_i = exit, inlet enthalpy,

V_e, V_i = exit, inlet velocity,

c_P = specific heat at constant pressure, and

T_e, T_i = exit, inlet temperature.

$$h_e = h_i + \frac{h_{es} - h_i}{\eta}$$

$$T_e = T_i + \frac{T_{es} - T_i}{\eta}, \text{ where}$$

h_{es} = exit enthalpy after isentropic compression,

T_{es} = exit temperature after isentropic compression, and

η = compression efficiency.

ENERGY CONVERSION AND POWER PLANTS
(see also **THERMODYNAMICS** section)

Internal Combustion Engines

OTTO CYCLE (see **THERMODYNAMICS** section)

Diesel Cycle

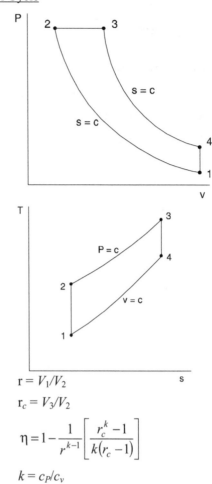

$r = V_1/V_2$

$r_c = V_3/V_2$

$$\eta = 1 - \frac{1}{r^{k-1}}\left[\frac{r_c^k - 1}{k\left(r_c - 1\right)} \right]$$

$k = c_P/c_v$

Brake Power

$$\dot{W}_b = 2\pi TN = 2\pi FRN, \text{ where}$$

$\dot{W}_b$ = brake power (W),

T = torque (N·m),

N = rotation speed (rev/s),

F = force at end of brake arm (N), and

R = length of brake arm (m).

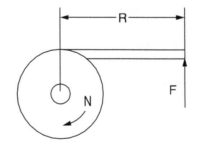

Indicated Power

$$\dot{W}_i = \dot{W}_b + \dot{W}_f, \text{ where}$$

$\dot{W}_i$ = indicated power (W), and

$\dot{W}_f$ = friction power (W).

169

Brake Thermal Efficiency

$$\eta_b = \frac{\dot{W}_b}{\dot{m}_f(HV)}, \text{ where}$$

η_b = brake thermal efficiency,

$\dot{m}_f$ = fuel consumption rate (kg/s), and

HV = heating value of fuel (J/kg).

Indicated Thermal Efficiency

$$\eta_i = \frac{\dot{W}_i}{\dot{m}_f(HV)}$$

Mechanical Efficiency

$$\eta_m = \frac{\dot{W}_b}{\dot{W}_i} = \frac{\eta_b}{\eta_i}$$

Displacement Volume

$$V_d = \frac{\pi B^2 S}{4}, \text{ m}^3 \text{ for each cylinder}$$

Total volume = $V_t = V_d + V_c$, m^3

V_c = clearance volume (m^3).

Compression Ratio

$$r_c = V_t/V_c$$

Mean Effective Pressure (MEP)

$$mep = \frac{\dot{W}n_s}{V_d n_c N}, \text{ where}$$

n_s = number of crank revolutions per power stroke,

n_c = number of cylinders, and

V_d = displacement volume per cylinder.

mep can be based on brake power (*bmep*), indicated power (*imep*), or friction power (*fmep*).

Volumetric Efficiency

$$\eta_v = \frac{2\dot{m}_a}{\rho_a V_d n_c N} \quad \text{(four-stroke cycles only)}$$

where

$\dot{m}_a$ = mass flow rate of air into engine (kg/s), and

ρ_a = density of air (kg/m^3).

Specific Fuel Consumption (SFC)

$$sfc = \frac{\dot{m}_f}{\dot{W}} = \frac{1}{\eta HV}, \quad \text{kg/J}$$

Use η_b and $\dot{W}_b$ for *bsfc* and η_i and $\dot{W}_i$ for *isfc*.

Gas Turbines

Brayton Cycle (Steady-Flow Cycle)

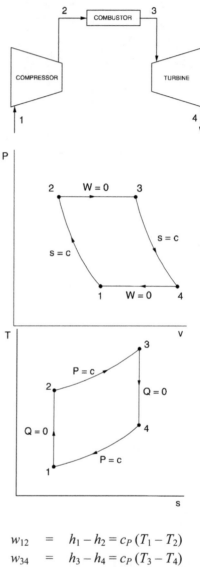

$$
\begin{aligned}
w_{12} &= h_1 - h_2 = c_P(T_1 - T_2) \\
w_{34} &= h_3 - h_4 = c_P(T_3 - T_4) \\
w_{net} &= w_{12} + w_{34} \\
q_{23} &= h_3 - h_2 = c_P(T_3 - T_2) \\
q_{41} &= h_1 - h_4 = c_P(T_1 - T_4) \\
q_{net} &= q_{23} + q_{41} \\
\eta &= w_{net}/q_{23}
\end{aligned}
$$

Brayton Cycle With Regeneration

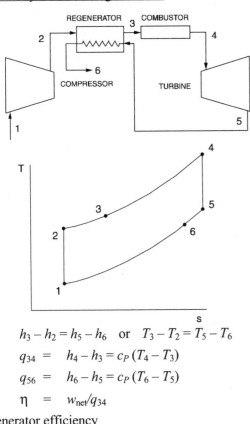

$$h_3 - h_2 = h_5 - h_6 \quad \text{or} \quad T_3 - T_2 = T_5 - T_6$$
$$q_{34} = h_4 - h_3 = c_P (T_4 - T_3)$$
$$q_{56} = h_6 - h_5 = c_P (T_6 - T_5)$$
$$\eta = w_{net}/q_{34}$$

Regenerator efficiency

$$\eta_{reg} = \frac{h_3 - h_2}{h_5 - h_2} = \frac{T_3 - T_2}{T_5 - T_2}$$
$$h_3 = h_2 + \eta_{reg} (h_5 - h_2)$$
or $\quad T_3 = T_2 + \eta_{reg} (T_5 - T_2)$

Steam Power Plants

Feedwater Heaters

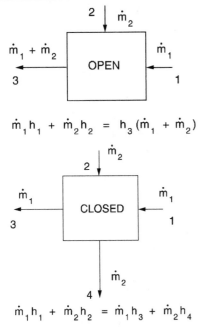

$$\dot{m}_1 h_1 + \dot{m}_2 h_2 = h_3 (\dot{m}_1 + \dot{m}_2)$$

$$\dot{m}_1 h_1 + \dot{m}_2 h_2 = \dot{m}_1 h_3 + \dot{m}_2 h_4$$

Steam Trap

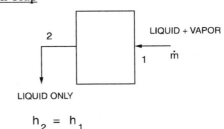

$$h_2 = h_1$$

Junction

$$\dot{m}_1 h_1 + \dot{m}_2 h_2 = h_3 (\dot{m}_1 + \dot{m}_2)$$

Pump

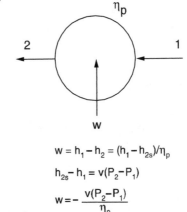

$$w = h_1 - h_2 = (h_1 - h_{2s})/\eta_p$$
$$h_{2s} - h_1 = v(P_2 - P_1)$$
$$w = -\frac{v(P_2 - P_1)}{\eta_p}$$

MACHINE DESIGN

Variable Loading Failure Theories

Modified Goodman Theory: The modified Goodman criterion states that a fatigue failure will occur whenever

$$\frac{\sigma_a}{S_e} + \frac{\sigma_m}{S_{ut}} \geq 1 \quad \text{or} \quad \frac{\sigma_{max}}{S_y} \geq 1, \quad \sigma_m \geq 0, \text{ where}$$

S_e = fatigue strength,
S_{ut} = ultimate strength,
S_y = yield strength,
σ_a = alternating stress, and
σ_m = mean stress.
$\sigma_{max} = \sigma_m + \sigma_a$

Soderberg Theory: The Soderberg theory states that a fatigue failure will occur whenever

$$\frac{\sigma_a}{S_e} + \frac{\sigma_m}{S_y} \geq 1, \quad \sigma_m \geq 0$$

Endurance Limit: When test data is unavailable, the endurance limit for steels may be estimated as

$$S'_e = \begin{Bmatrix} 0.5\, S_{ut}, & S_{ut} \le 1{,}400 \text{ MPa} \\ 700 \text{ MPa}, & S_{ut} > 1{,}400 \text{ MPa} \end{Bmatrix}$$

Endurance Limit Modifying Factors: Endurance limit modifying factors are used to account for the differences between the endurance limit as determined from a rotating beam test, S'_e, and that which would result in the real part, S_e.

$$S_e = k_a k_b k_c k_d k_e S'_e$$

where

Surface Factor, k_a: $k_a = aS_{ut}^b$

Surface Finish	Factor a		Exponent b
	kpsi	MPa	
Ground	1.34	1.58	−0.085
Machined or CD	2.70	4.51	−0.265
Hot rolled	14.4	57.7	−0.718
As forged	39.9	272.0	−0.995

Size Factor, k_b:

For bending and torsion:

$d \le 8$ mm; $\qquad\qquad k_b = 1$

$8 \text{ mm} \le d \le 250 \text{ mm};$ $\quad k_b = 1.189 d_{eff}^{-0.097}$

$d > 250$ mm; $\qquad\qquad 0.6 \le k_b \le 0.75$

For axial loading: $\qquad\quad k_b = 1$

Load Factor, k_c:

$k_c = 0.923$ $\qquad$ axial loading, $S_{ut} \le 1520$ MPa

$k_c = 1$ $\qquad\qquad$ axial loading, $S_{ut} > 1520$ MPa

$k_c = 1$ $\qquad\qquad$ bending

Temperature Factor, k_d:

for T $\le 450°$ C, $k_d = 1$

Miscellaneous Effects Factor, k_e: Used to account for strength reduction effects such as corrosion, plating, and residual stresses. In the absence of known effects, use $k_e = 1$.

Shafts and Axles

Static Loading: The maximum shear stress and the von Mises stress may be calculated in terms of the loads from

$$\tau_{max} = \frac{2}{\pi d^3}\left[(8M + Fd)^2 + (8T)^2\right]^{1/2},$$

$$\sigma' = \frac{4}{\pi d^3}\left[(8M + Fd)^2 + 48T^2\right]^{1/2}, \text{ where}$$

M = the bending moment,

F = the axial load,

T = the torque, and

d = the diameter.

Fatigue Loading: Using the maximum-shear-stress theory combined with the Soderberg line for fatigue, the diameter and safety factor are related by

$$\frac{\pi d^3}{32} = n\left[\left(\frac{M_m}{S_y} + \frac{K_f M_a}{S_e}\right)^2 + \left(\frac{T_m}{S_y} + \frac{K_{fs} T_a}{S_e}\right)^2\right]^{1/2}$$

where

d = diameter,

n = safety factor,

M_a = alternating moment,

M_m = mean moment,

T_a = alternating torque,

T_m = mean torque,

S_e = fatigue limit,

S_y = yield strength,

K_f = fatigue strength reduction factor, and

K_{fs} = fatigue strength reduction factor for shear.

Screws, Fasteners, and Connections

Square Thread Power Screws: The torque required to raise, T_R, or to lower, T_L, a load is given by

$$T_R = \frac{Fd_m}{2}\left(\frac{l + \pi\mu d_m}{\pi d_m - \mu l}\right) + \frac{F\mu_c d_c}{2},$$

$$T_L = \frac{Fd_m}{2}\left(\frac{\pi\mu d_m - l}{\pi d_m + \mu l}\right) + \frac{F\mu_c d_c}{2}, \text{ where}$$

d_c = mean collar diameter,

d_m = mean thread diameter,

l = lead,

F = load,

μ = coefficient of friction for thread, and

μ_c = coefficient of friction for collar.

The efficiency of a power screw may be expressed as

$$\eta = Fl/(2\pi T)$$

Threaded Fasteners: The load carried by a bolt in a threaded connection is given by

$$F_b = CP + F_i \qquad\qquad F_m < 0$$

while the load carried by the members is

$$F_m = (1 - C)P - F_i \qquad F_m < 0, \text{ where}$$

C = joint coefficient,

$\quad = k_b/(k_b + k_m)$

F_b = total bolt load,

F_i = bolt preload,

F_m = total material load,

P = externally applied load,

k_b = the effective stiffness of the bolt or fastener in the grip, and

k_m = the effective stiffness of the members in the grip.

Bolt stiffness may be calculated from

$$k_b = \frac{A_d A_t E}{A_d l_t + A_t l_d}, \text{ where}$$

A_d = major-diameter area,

A_t = tensile-stress area,

E = modulus of elasticity,

l_d = length of unthreaded shank, and

l_t = length of threaded shank contained within the grip.

If all members within the grip are of the same material, member stiffness may be obtained from

$$k_m = dEAe^{b(d/l)}, \text{ where}$$

d = bolt diameter,

E = modulus of elasticity of members, and

l = grip length.

Coefficient A and b are given in the table below for various joint member materials.

Material	A	b
Steel	0.78715	0.62873
Aluminum	0.79670	0.63816
Copper	0.79568	0.63553
Gray cast iron	0.77871	0.61616

The approximate tightening torque required for a given preload F_i and for a steel bolt in a steel member is given by $T = 0.2 F_i d$.

Threaded Fasteners—Design Factors: The bolt load factor is

$$n_b = (S_p A_t - F_i)/CP$$

The factor of safety guarding against joint separation is

$$n_s = F_i / [P (1 - C)]$$

Threaded Fasteners—Fatigue Loading: If the externally applied load varies between zero and P, the alternating stress is

$$\sigma_a = CP/(2A_t)$$

and the mean stress is

$$\sigma_m = \sigma_a + F_i / A_t$$

Bolted and Riveted Joints Loaded in Shear:

(a) FASTENER IN SHEAR

Failure by pure shear, (a)

$$\tau = F/A, \text{ where}$$

F = shear load, and

A = cross-sectional area of bolt or rivet.

(b) MEMBER RUPTURE

Failure by rupture, (b)

$$\sigma = F/A, \text{ where}$$

F = load and

A = net cross-sectional area of thinnest member.

(c) MEMBER OR FASTENER CRUSHING

Failure by crushing of rivet or member, (c)

$$\sigma = F/A, \text{ where}$$

F = load and

A = projected area of a single rivet.

(d) FASTENER GROUPS

Fastener groups in shear, (d)

The location of the centroid of a fastener group with respect to any convenient coordinate frame is:

$$\bar{x} = \frac{\sum\limits_{i=1}^{n} A_i x_i}{\sum\limits_{i=1}^{n} A_i}, \quad \bar{y} = \frac{\sum\limits_{i=1}^{n} A_i y_i}{\sum\limits_{i=1}^{n} A_i}, \text{ where}$$

n = total number of fasteners,

i = the index number of a particular fastener,

A_i = cross-sectional area of the ith fastener,

x_i = x-coordinate of the center of the ith fastener, and

y_i = y-coordinate of the center of the ith fastener.

The total shear force on a fastener is the **vector** sum of the force due to direct shear P and the force due to the moment M acting on the group at its centroid.

The magnitude of the direct shear force due to P is

$$\left| F_{1i} \right| = \frac{P}{n}.$$

This force acts in the same direction as P.

The magnitude of the shear force due to M is

$$\left| F_{2i} \right| = \frac{Mr_i}{\sum_{i=1}^{n} r_i^2}.$$

This force acts perpendicular to a line drawn from the group centroid to the center of a particular fastener. Its sense is such that its moment is in the same direction (CW or CCW) as M.

Mechanical Springs

Helical Linear Springs: The shear stress in a helical linear spring is

$$\tau = K_s \frac{8FD}{\pi d^3}, \text{ where}$$

d = wire diameter,

F = applied force,

D = mean spring diameter

K_s = $(2C + 1)/(2C)$, and

C = D/d.

The deflection and force are related by $F = kx$ where the spring rate (spring constant) k is given by

$$k = \frac{d^4 G}{8D^3 N}$$

where G is the shear modulus of elasticity and N is the number of active coils. See Table of Material Properties at the end of the **MECHANICS OF MATERIALS** section for values of G.

Spring Material: The minimum tensile strength of common spring steels may be determined from

$$S_{ut} = A/d^m$$

where S_{ut} is the tensile strength in MPa, d is the wire diameter in millimeters, and A and m are listed in the following table.

Material	ASTM	m	A
Music wire	A228	0.163	2060
Oil-tempered wire	A229	0.193	1610
Hard-drawn wire	A227	0.201	1510
Chrome vanadium	A232	0.155	1790
Chrome silicon	A401	0.091	1960

Maximum allowable torsional stress for static applications may be approximated as

$$S_{sy} = \tau = 0.45 S_{ut} \text{ cold-drawn carbon steel (A227, A228, A229)}$$

$$S_{sy} = \tau = 0.50 S_{ut} \text{ hardened and tempered carbon and low-alloy steels (A232, A401)}$$

Compression Spring Dimensions

Type of Spring Ends		
Term	**Plain**	**Plain and Ground**
End coils, N_e	0	1
Total coils, N_t	N	$N + 1$
Free length, L_0	$pN + d$	$p(N + 1)$
Solid length, L_s	$d(N_t + 1)$	dN_t
Pitch, p	$(L_0 - d)/N$	$L_0/(N + 1)$

Term	**Squared or Closed**	**Squared and Ground**
End coils, N_e	2	2
Total coils, N_t	$N + 2$	$N + 2$
Free length, L_0	$pN + 3d$	$pN + 2d$
Solid length, L_s	$d(N_t + 1)$	dN_t
Pitch, p	$(L_0 - 3d)/N$	$(L_0 - 2d)/N$

Helical Torsion Springs: The bending stress is given as

$$\sigma = K_i \left[32Fr/(\pi d^3) \right]$$

where F is the applied load and r is the radius from the center of the coil to the load.

K_i = correction factor

= $(4C^2 - C - 1)/[4C(C - 1)]$

C = D/d

The deflection θ and moment Fr are related by

$$Fr = k\theta$$

where the spring rate k is given by

$$k = \frac{d^4 E}{64DN}$$

where k has units of N·m/rad and θ is in radians.

Spring Material: The strength of the spring wire may be found as was done in the section on linear springs. The allowable stress σ is then given by

$$S_y = \sigma = 0.78 S_{ut} \text{ cold-drawn carbon steel (A227, A228, A229)}$$

$$S_y = \sigma = 0.87 S_{ut} \text{ hardened and tempered carbon and low-alloy steel (A232, A401)}$$

Ball/Roller Bearing Selection

The minimum required *basic load rating* (load for which 90% of the bearings from a given population will survive 1 million revolutions) is given by

$$C = PL^{\frac{1}{a}}, \text{ where}$$

C = minimum required basic load rating,

P = design radial load,

L = design life (in millions of revolutions), and

a = 3 for ball bearings, 10/3 for roller bearings.

When a ball bearing is subjected to both radial and axial loads, an equivalent radial load must be used in the equation above. The equivalent radial load is

$$P_{eq} = XVF_r + YF_a, \text{ where}$$

P_{eq} = equivalent radial load,

F_r = applied constant radial load, and

F_a = applied constant axial (thrust) load.

For radial contact, groove ball bearings:

$V = 1$ if inner ring rotating, 1.2 outer ring rotating,

If $F_a/(VF_r) > e$,

$$X = 0.56, \quad \text{and} \quad Y = 0.840 \left(\frac{F_a}{C_o}\right)^{-0.247}$$

$$\text{where} \quad e = 0.513 \left(\frac{F_a}{C_o}\right)^{0.236}, \quad \text{and}$$

C_o = basic static load rating, from bearing catalog.

If $F_a/(VF_r) \le e$, $X = 1$ and $Y = 0$.

Press/Shrink Fits

The interface pressure induced by a press/shrink fit is

$$p = \frac{0.5\delta}{\dfrac{r}{E_o}\left(\dfrac{r_o^2 + r^2}{r_o^2 - r^2} + v_o\right) + \dfrac{r}{E_i}\left(\dfrac{r^2 + r_i^2}{r^2 - r_i^2} + v_i\right)}$$

where the subscripts i and o stand for the inner and outer member, respectively, and

p = inside pressure on the outer member and outside pressure on the inner member,

δ = the diametral interference,

r = nominal interference radius,

r_i = inside radius of inner member,

r_o = outside radius of outer member,

E = Young's modulus of respective member, and

v = Poisson's ratio of respective member.

See the **MECHANICS OF MATERIALS** section on thick-wall cylinders for the stresses at the interface.

The maximum torque that can be transmitted by a press fit joint is approximately

$$T = 2\pi r^2 \mu p l,$$

where r and p are defined above,

T = torque capacity of the joint,

μ = coefficient of friction at the interface, and

l = length of hub engagement.

Intermediate- and Long-Length Columns

The slenderness ratio of a column is $S_r = l/k$, where l is the length of the column and k is the radius of gyration. The radius of gyration of a column cross-section is, $k = \sqrt{I/A}$

where I is the area moment of inertia and A is the cross-sectional area of the column. A column is considered to be intermediate if its slenderness ratio is less than or equal to $(S_r)_D$, where

$$(S_r)_D = \pi \sqrt{\frac{2E}{S_y}}, \quad \text{and}$$

E = Young's modulus of respective member, and

S_y = yield strength of the column material.

For intermediate columns, the critical load is

$$P_{cr} = A\left[S_y - \frac{1}{E}\left(\frac{S_y S_r}{2\pi}\right)^2\right], \text{ where}$$

P_{cr} = critical buckling load,

A = cross-sectional area of the column,

S_y = yield strength of the column material,

E = Young's modulus of respective member, and

S_r = slenderness ratio.

For long columns, the critical load is

$$P_{cr} = \frac{\pi^2 EA}{S_r^2}$$

where the variables are as defined above.

For both intermediate and long columns, the effective column length depends on the end conditions. The AISC recommended values for the effective lengths of columns are, for: rounded-rounded or pinned-pinned ends, $l_{eff} = l$; fixed-free, $l_{eff} = 2.1l$; fixed-pinned, $l_{eff} = 0.80l$; fixed-fixed, $l_{eff} = 0.65l$. The effective column length should be used when calculating the slenderness ratio.

Gearing

Gear Trains: *Velocity ratio*, m_v, is the ratio of the output velocity to the input velocity. Thus, $m_v = \omega_{out} / \omega_{in}$. For a two-gear train, $m_v = -N_{in}/N_{out}$ where N_{in} is the number of teeth on the input gear and N_{out} is the number of teeth on the output gear. The negative sign indicates that the output gear rotates in the opposite sense with respect to the input gear. In a *compound gear train*, at least one shaft carries more than one gear (rotating at the same speed). The velocity ratio for a compound train is:

$$m_v = \pm \frac{\text{product of number of teeth on driver gears}}{\text{product of number of teeth on driven gears}}$$

A *simple planetary gearset* has a sun gear, an arm that rotates about the sun gear axis, one or more gears (planets) that rotate about a point on the arm, and a ring (internal) gear that is concentric with the sun gear. The planet gear(s) mesh with the sun gear on one side and with the ring gear on the other. A planetary gearset has two independent inputs and one output (or two outputs and one input, as in a differential gearset).

Often, one of the inputs is zero, which is achieved by grounding either the sun or the ring gear. The velocities in a planetary set are related by

$$\frac{\omega_f - \omega_{arm}}{\omega_L - \omega_{arm}} = \pm m_v \text{, where}$$

ω_f = speed of the first gear in the train,

ω_L = speed of the last gear in the train, and

ω_{arm} = speed of the arm.

Neither the first nor the last gear can be one that has planetary motion. In determining m_v, it is helpful to invert the mechanism by grounding the arm and releasing any gears that are grounded.

Loading on Straight Spur Gears: The load, W, on straight spur gears is transmitted along a plane that, in edge view, is called the *line of action*. This line makes an angle with a tangent line to the pitch circle that is called the *pressure angle* ϕ. Thus, the contact force has two components: one in the tangential direction, W_t, and one in the radial direction, W_r. These components are related to the pressure angle by

$$W_r = W_t \tan(\phi).$$

Only the tangential component W_t transmits torque from one gear to another. Neglecting friction, the transmitted force may be found if either the transmitted torque or power is known:

$$W_t = \frac{2T}{d} = \frac{2T}{mN},$$

$$W_t = \frac{2H}{d\omega} = \frac{2H}{mN\omega} \text{, where}$$

W_t = transmitted force (newton),

T = torque on the gear (newton-mm),

d = pitch diameter of the gear (mm),

N = number of teeth on the gear,

m = gear module (mm) (same for both gears in mesh),

H = power (kW), and

ω = speed of gear (rad/sec).

Stresses in Spur Gears: Spur gears can fail in either bending (as a cantilever beam, near the root) or by surface fatigue due to contact stresses near the pitch circle. AGMA Standard 2001 gives equations for bending stress and surface stress. They are:

$$\sigma_b = \frac{W_t}{FmJ} \frac{K_a K_m}{K_v} K_s K_B K_I \text{, bending and}$$

$$\sigma_c = C_P \sqrt{\frac{W_t}{FId} \frac{C_a C_m}{C_v} C_s C_f} \text{, surface stress , where}$$

σ_b = bending stress,

σ_c = surface stress,

W_t = transmitted load,

F = face width,

m = module,

J = bending strength geometry factor,

K_a = application factor,

K_B = rim thickness factor,

K_I = idler factor,

K_m = load distribution factor,

K_s = size factor,

K_v = dynamic factor,

C_p = elastic coefficient,

I = surface geometry factor,

d = pitch diameter of gear being analyzed, and

C_f = surface finish factor.

C_a, C_m, C_s, and C_v are the same as K_a, K_m, K_s, and K_v, respectively.

INDEX

178

SCHOOL/INSTITUTION CODES

For Use on FE Morning Answer Sheet

State	Code	School
Alabama	**University of Alabama**	
	2101	Birmingham
	2102	Huntsville
	2103	Tuscaloosa
	Alabama A and M University	
	2104	(Engineering Technology)
	2105	(Engineering)
	2106	Auburn University
	2107	South Alabama, University of
	2108	Tuskegee University
Alaska	**University of Alaska**	
	6001	Anchorage
	6002	Fairbanks
Arizona	**Arizona State University**	
	2201	East (Engineering Technology)
	2202	(Engineering)
	2203	Arizona, University of
	2204	Devry Institute of Technology - Phoenix
	2205	Embry-Riddle Aeronautical University - Prescott
	2206	Northern Arizona University
Arkansas	**University of Arkansas**	
	4601	Fayetteville
	4602	Little Rock
	4603	Arkansas State University
	4604	Arkansas Tech University
	4605	John Brown University
California	**University of California**	
	5701	Berkeley
	5702	Davis
	5703	Irvine
	5704	Los Angeles
	5705	Riverside
	5706	San Diego
	5707	Santa Barbara
	5708	Santa Cruz
	5709	California Institute of Technology
	California Maritime Academy	
	5710	(Engineering Technology)
	5738	(Engineering)
	5711	California Polytechnic State University - San Luis Obispo
	California State Polytechnic University - Pomona	
	5712	(Engineering Technology)
	5713	(Engineering)
	California State University	
	5714	Chico
	5715	Fresno
	5716	Fullerton
	5717	Long Beach (Engineering Technology)
	5718	Long Beach (Engineering)
	5719	Los Angeles
	5720	Northridge
	5721	Sacramento (Engineering Technology)
	5722	Sacramento (Engineering)
	Devry Institute of Technology	
	5723	Fremont
	5724	Long Beach California
	5725	Pomona
	5726	Harvey Mudd College
	5727	Humboldt State University
	5728	Loyola Marymount University (California)
	5729	Naval Postgraduate School
	5730	Pacific, University of the
	5731	San Diego State University
	5732	San Diego, University of
	5733	San Francisco State University
	5734	San Jose State University
	5735	Santa Clara University
	5736	Southern California, University of
	5737	Stanford University

State	Code	School
Colorado	**University of Colorado**	
	6801	Boulder
	6802	Colorado Springs
	6803	Denver
	6804	Colorado School of Mines
	6805	Colorado State University
	Colorado Technical University	
	6806	(Engineering Technology)
	6807	(Engineering)
	6808	Denver, University of
	6809	Metropolitan State College of Denver
	University of Southern Colorado	
	6810	(Engineering Technology)
	6811	(Engineering)
	6812	US Air Force Academy
Connecticut	6901	Bridgeport, University of
	6902	Central Connecticut State University
	6903	Connecticut, University of
	6904	Fairfield University
	University of Hartford	
	6905	(Engineering Technology)
	6906	(Engineering)
	6907	New Haven, University of
	6908	Trinity College - Connecticut
	6909	US Coast Guard Academy
	6910	Yale University
Delaware	**University of Delaware**	
	2301	(Engineering Technology)
	2302	(Engineering)
District of Columbia	2401	Catholic University of America
	University of District of Columbia - Van Ness Campus	
	2402	(Engineering Technology)
	2403	(Engineering)
	2404	George Washington University
	2405	Howard University
Florida	**University of Central Florida**	
	5101	(Engineering Technology)
	5102	(Engineering)
	Embry-Riddle Aeronautical University - Daytona Beach	
	5103	(Engineering Technology)
	5104	(Engineering)
	5105	Florida A & M University (Engineering Technology)
	5106	Florida A & M / Florida State University (Engineering)
	5107	Florida Atlantic University
	5108	Florida Institute of Technology
	5109	Florida International University
	5110	Florida, University of
	5111	Miami, University of
	5112	North Florida, University of
	5113	South Florida, University of
Georgia	2501	Devry Institute of Technology – Decatur
	2502	Fort Valley State University
	2503	Georgia Institute of Technology
	2504	Georgia Southern University
	2505	Georgia, University of
	2506	Mercer University
	2507	Savannah State University
	2508	Southern Polytechnic State University
Hawaii	2601	Hawaii – Manoa, University of
Idaho	6101	Boise State University
	6102	Idaho State University
	6103	Idaho, University of

State	Code	School
Illinois	**Bradley University**	
	7001	(Engineering Technology)
	7002	(Engineering)
	Devry Institute of Technology	
	7003	Chicago
	7004	DuPage
	University of Illinois	
	7005	Chicago
	7006	Urbana Champaign
	7007	Illinois Institute of Technology
	7008	Northern Illinois University
	7009	Northwestern University
	7010	Olivet Nazarene University
	Southern Illinois University	
	7011	Carbondale (Engineering Technology)
	7012	Carbondale (Engineering)
	7013	Edwardsville
Indiana	6501	Ball State University
	6502	Evansville, University of
	6503	Indiana Institute of Technology
	Indiana University/Purdue University	
	6504	Fort Wayne (Engineering Technology)
	6505	Fort Wayne (Engineering)
	6506	Indianapolis (Engineering Technology)
	6507	Indianapolis (Engineering)
	6508	Notre Dame, University of
	Purdue University	
	6509	Calumet (Engineering Technology)
	6510	Calumet (Engineering)
	6511	Kokomo
	6512	North Central
	6513	West Lafayette (Engineering Technology)
	6514	West Lafayette (Engineering)
	6515	Rose Hulman Institute of Technology
	6516	Southern Indiana, University of
	6517	Tri-State University
	6518	Valparaiso University
Iowa	5201	Dordt College
	5202	Iowa State University
	5203	Iowa, University of
	5204	St. Ambrose College
Kansas	5301	Kansas State University
	5302	Kansas State University – Salina, College of Technology & Aviation (Engineering Technology)
	5303	Kansas, University of
	5304	Pittsburgh State University
	5305	Wichita State University
Kentucky	7101	Kentucky, University of
	7102	Louisville, University of
	Murray State University	
	7103	(Engineering Technology)
	7104	(Engineering)
	7105	Northern Kentucky University
	7106	Western Kentucky University
Louisiana	5410	Grambling State University
	5401	Louisiana at Lafayette, University of
	5402	Louisiana State University
	Louisiana Tech University	
	5403	(Engineering Technology)
	5404	(Engineering)
	McNeese State University	
	5411	(Engineering Technology)
	5405	(Engineering)
	5406	New Orleans, University of
	5407	Northwestern State University of Louisiana
	5408	Southern University and A & M College
	5409	Tulane University

State	Code	School
Maine	**University of Maine - Orono**	
	2701	(Engineering Technology)
	2702	(Engineering)
	Maine Maritime Academy - Castine	
	2703	(Engineering Technology)
	2704	(Engineering)
	2705	Southern Maine, University of
Maryland	**Capital College - Maryland**	
	4501	(Engineering Technology)
	4502	(Engineering)
	4503	Johns Hopkins University
	4504	Loyola College in Maryland
	University of Maryland	
	4505	Baltimore County
	4506	College Park
	4507	Morgan State University
	4508	US Naval Academy
Massachusetts	2801	Boston University
	2802	Harvard University
	University of Massachusetts	
	2803	Amherst
	2804	Dartmouth
	2805	Lowell, (Engineering Technology)
	2806	Lowell, (Engineering)
	2807	Massachusetts Institute of Technology
	2808	Merrimack College
	Northeastern University	
	2809	(Engineering Technology)
	2810	(Engineering)
	2811	Tufts University
	Wentworth Institute of Technology	
	2812	(Engineering Technology)
	2813	(Engineering)
	2814	Western New England College
	2815	Worcester Polytechnic Institute
Michigan	7201	Calvin College
	7202	Detroit Mercy, University of
	Ferris State University	
	7203	(Engineering Technology)
	7204	(Engineering)
	7205	Grand Valley State University
	7206	Hope College
	7207	Kettering University
	Lake Superior State University	
	7208	(Engineering Technology)
	7209	(Engineering)
	7210	Lawrence Technological University
	University of Michigan	
	7211	Ann Arbor
	7212	Dearborn
	7213	Michigan State University
	Michigan Technological University	
	7214	(Engineering Technology)
	7215	(Engineering)
	7216	Oakland University
	7217	Saginaw Valley State University
	Wayne State University	
	7218	(Engineering Technology)
	7219	(Engineering)
	Western Michigan University	
	7220	(Engineering Technology)
	7221	(Engineering)

SCHOOL/INSTITUTION CODES

For Use on FE Morning Answer Sheet

State	Code	School
Minnesota	**University of Minnesota**	
	5801	Duluth
	5802	Twin Cities
	Minnesota State University - Mankato	
	5803	(Engineering Technology)
	5804	(Engineering)
	5805	St. Cloud State University
	5806	St. Thomas, University of
	5807	Winona State University
Mississippi	2901	Mississippi State University
	2902	Mississippi, University of
	2903	Southern Mississippi, University of
Missouri	3001	Devry Institute of Technology - Kansas City
	University of Missouri	
	3002	Columbia
	3003	Kansas City
	3004	Rolla
	3005	St. Louis
	3006	Missouri Western State College
	3007	Parks College of Engineering and Aviation, St Louis University
	3008	Southeast Missouri State University
	3009	Washington University - St. Louis, MO
Montana	3101	Carroll College
	Montana State University - Bozeman	
	3102	(Engineering Technology)
	3103	(Engineering)
	3104	Montana State University - Northern
	3105	Montana Tech of the University of Montana - Butte
Nebraska	**University of Nebraska**	
	6301	Lincoln
	6302	Lincoln at Omaha
Nevada	**University of Nevada**	
	3201	Las Vegas
	3202	Reno
New Hampshire	3301	Dartmouth College
	University of New Hampshire	
	3302	(Engineering Technology)
	3303	(Engineering)
New Jersey	7301	Devry Institute of Technology - North Brunswick
	Fairleigh Dickinson University - Teaneck	
	7302	(Engineering Technology)
	7303	(Engineering)
	New Jersey Institute of Technology	
	7304	(Engineering Technology)
	7305	(Engineering)
	7306	New Jersey, College of
	7307	Princeton University
	7308	Rowan University
	7309	Rutgers University
	7310	Stevens Institute of Technology
New Mexico	4901	New Mexico Institute of Mining and Technology
	New Mexico State University	
	4902	(Engineering Technology)
	4903	(Engineering)
	4904	New Mexico, University of
New York	6701	Alfred University
	6702	Clarkson University
	6703	Columbia University
	6704	Cooper Union
	6705	Cornell University
	6706	CUNY, City College
	6707	CUNY, College of Staten Island
	6708	Devry Institute of Technology - Long Island City
	6709	Excelsior College

State	Code	School
New York	6710	Hofstra University
	6711	Manhattan College
	6712	New York City Technical College
	New York Institute of Technology	
	6713	Manhattan Center
	6714	Old Westbury (Engineering Technology)
	6715	Old Westbury (Engineering)
	6716	Polytechnic University Brooklyn, NY
	6717	Rensselaer Polytechnic Institute
	Rochester Institute of Tech	
	6718	(Engineering Technology)
	6719	(Engineering)
	6720	Rochester, University of
	SUNY	
	6721	Alfred (Alfred State College)
	6722	Binghamton
	6723	Buffalo (Engineering Technology)
	6724	Buffalo (Engineering)
	6725	College of Environmental Science & Forestry
	6726	Farmingdale
	6727	Institute of Technology at Utica/Rome
	6728	New Paltz
	6729	Stony Brook
	6730	Maritime College
	6731	Syracuse University
	6732	Union College
	6733	US Merchant Marine Academy
	6734	US Military Academy
	6735	Webb Institute
North Carolina	5901	Duke University
	University of North Carolina	
	5902	Chapel Hill
	5903	Charlotte (Engineering Technology)
	5904	Charlotte (Engineering)
	5905	North Carolina A and T University
	5906	North Carolina State University
	5907	Western Carolina University
North Dakota	4201	North Dakota State University
	4202	North Dakota, University of
Ohio	6401	Air Force Institute of Technology
	6402	Akron, Community and Technical College
	6403	Akron, University of
	6404	Case Western Reserve University
	6405	Cedarville University
	6406	Central State University
	6407	Cincinnati - OMI College of Applied Science, University of (Engineering Technology)
	6408	Cincinnati, University of (Engineering)
	Cleveland State University	
	6409	(Engineering Technology)
	6410	(Engineering)
	University of Dayton	
	6411	(Engineering Technology)
	6412	(Engineering)
	6413	Devry Institute of Technology - Columbus
	6414	Marietta College
	6415	Miami (OH) University
	6416	Ohio Northern University
	6417	Ohio State University
	6418	Ohio University
	University of Toledo	
	6419	(Engineering Technology)
	6420	(Engineering)
	6421	Wright State University

State	Code	School
Ohio	**Youngstown State University**	
(Cont'd)	6422	(Engineering Technology)
	6423	(Engineering)
Oklahoma	5501	Oklahoma Christian University of Science and Arts
	Oklahoma State University	
	5502	(Engineering Technology)
	5503	(Engineering)
	5504	Oklahoma, University of
	5505	Oral Roberts University
	5506	Southwestern Oklahoma State University
	5507	Tulsa, University of
Oregon	**Oregon Institute of Technology**	
	3401	(Engineering Technology)
	3402	(Engineering)
	3403	Oregon State University
	3404	Portland State University
	3405	Portland, University of
Pennsylvania	3501	Bucknell University
	3502	Carnegie-Mellon University
	3503	Drexel University
	3504	Gannon University
	3505	Geneva College
	3506	Grove City College
	3507	Lafayette College
	3508	Lehigh University
	3509	Messiah College
	Penn State University	
	3510	Altoona Campus
	3511	Behrend College (Engineering Technology)
	3512	Behrend College (Engineering)
	3513	Berks Campus, Berks-Lehigh Valley College
	3514	Capitol Campus
	3515	Harrisburg, The Capital College (Engineering Technology)
	3531	Harrisburg, The Capital College (Engineering)
	3516	Main Campus
	3517	Wilkes-Barre Campus Commonwealth College
	3518	Pennsylvania College of Technology
	3519	Pennsylvania, University of
	3520	Philadelphia University
	3521	Pittsburgh - Johnstown, University of
	3522	Pittsburgh, University of
	3523	Point Park College
	3524	Swarthmore College
	Temple University	
	3525	(Engineering Technology)
	3526	(Engineering)
	3527	Villanova University
	3528	Widener University
	3529	Wilkes University
	3530	York College of Pennsylvania
Puerto Rico	6201	Polytechnic University of Puerto Rico
	6202	University of Puerto Rico, Mayaguez
Rhode Island	5001	Brown University
	5002	New England Institute of Technology
	5003	Rhode Island, University of
	5004	Roger Williams University
South Carolina	3601	Citadel
	3602	Clemson University
	3603	South Carolina State University
	3604	South Carolina, University of
South Dakota	3701	South Dakota School of Mines and Technology
	3702	South Dakota State University

State	Code	School
Tennessee	3801	Christian Brothers University
	3802	East Tennessee State University
	University of Memphis	
	3803	(Engineering Technology)
	3804	(Engineering)
	3805	Middle Tennessee State University
	University of Tennessee	
	3806	Chattanooga
	3807	Knoxville
	3808	Martin
	3809	Tennessee State University
	3810	Tennessee Technological University
	3811	Vanderbilt University
Texas	3901	Baylor University
	3902	Devry Institute of Technology - Irving
	University of Houston	
	3903	Clear Lake (Engineering)
	3904	College of Technology (Engineering Technology)
	3905	Downtown (Engineering Technology)
	3906	Houston (Engineering)
	3907	Lamar University
	LeTourneau University	
	3908	(Engineering Technology)
	3909	(Engineering)
	3910	Midwestern State University
	3911	North Texas, University of
	Prairie View A and M University	
	3912	(Engineering Technology)
	3913	(Engineering)
	3914	Rice University
	3915	Southern Methodist University
	3916	St. Mary's University
	University of Texas	
	3917	Arlington
	3918	Austin
	3919	Dallas
	3920	El Paso
	3921	Pan American
	3922	San Antonio
	3932	Tyler
	Texas A and M University - College Station	
	3923	(Engineering Technology)
	3924	(Engineering)
	Texas A and M University	
	3925	Galveston
	3926	Kingsville
	3927	Texas Christian University
	3928	Texas Southern University
	Texas Tech University	
	3929	(Engineering Technology)
	3930	(Engineering)
	3931	Trinity University - Texas
Utah	**Brigham Young University**	
	4001	(Engineering Technology)
	4002	(Engineering)
	4003	Utah State University
	4004	Utah, University of
	4005	Weber State University
Vermont	4301	Norwich University
	4302	Vermont Technical College
	4303	Vermont, University of
Virginia	4101	Christopher Newport University
	4102	George Mason University
	4103	Hampton University
	Old Dominion University	
	4104	(Engineering Technology)
	4105	(Engineering)

SCHOOL/INSTITUTION CODES
For Use on FE Morning Answer Sheet

State	Code	School
Virginia (Cont'd)	4106	Virginia Commonwealth University
	4107	Virginia Military Institute
	4108	Virginia Polytechnic Institute
	4109	Virginia State University
	4110	Virginia, University of
Washington	5601	Central Washington University
	5602	Eastern Washington University
	5603	Gonzaga University
Henry Cogswell College		
	5604	(Engineering Technology)
	5605	(Engineering)
	5606	Seattle Pacific University
	5607	Seattle University
	5608	St. Martin's College
	5609	Walla Walla College
	5610	Washington State University
	5611	Washington, University of
	5612	Western Washington University
West Virginia	4401	Bluefield State College
	4402	Fairmont State College
	4403	West Virginia University
West Virginia University Institute of Technology		
	4404	(Engineering Technology)
	4405	(Engineering)
Wisconsin	6601	Marquette University
Milwaukee School of Engineering		
	6602	(Engineering Technology)
	6603	(Engineering)
University of Wisconsin		
	6604	Madison
	6605	Milwaukee
	6606	Platteville
	6607	Stout
Wyoming	7401	Wyoming, University of
Other	9001	Other (not listed)

Country	Code	School
Canada	8001	Alberta, University of
	8002	British Columbia, University of
	8003	Calgary, University of
	8004	Carleton University
	8005	Concordia University
	8006	Dalhousie University
	8007	Ecole De Technologie Superieure
	8008	Guelph, University of
	8009	Lakehead University
	8010	Laurentian University
	8011	Laval, University
	8012	Manitoba, University of
	8013	McGill University
	8014	McMaster University
	8015	Memorial University of Newfoundland
	8016	Moncton, Universite de
	8017	New Brunswick, University of
	8018	Ottawa, University of
	8019	Polytechnique, Ecole
	8020	Quebec A Chicoutimi, Universite du
	8021	Quebec A hull, Universite du
	8022	Quebec A Rimouski, Universite du
	8023	Quebec A Trois-Rivieres, Universite du
	8024	Quebec En Abitibi-temiscamingue, Universite du
	8025	Queen's University
	8026	Regina, University of
	8027	Royal Military College of Canada
	8028	Ryerson Polytechnical University
	8029	Saskatchewan, University of
	8030	Sherbrooke, Universite de
	8031	Simon Fraser University
	8032	Toronto, University of
	8033	Victoria, University of
	8034	Waterloo, University of
	8035	Western Ontario, University of
	8036	Windsor, University of
Other	9001	Other (not listed)